Sources of International Comparative Advantage

D0768203

Sources of International Comparative Advantage
Theory and Evidence

Edward E. Leamer

The MIT Press
Cambridge, Massachusetts
London, England

This book was set in Times New Roman by Asco Trade Typesetting Ltd., Hong Kong, and printed and bound by Halliday Lithograph in the United States of America

Library of Congress Cataloging in Publication Data

Leamer, Edward E.
  Sources of international comparative advantage.

  Bibliography: p.
  Includes index.
  1. Comparative advantage (Commerce).   2. International economic relations.
I. Title.
HF1412.L42 1984   382.1′042   83-19948
ISBN 0-262-12107-7

To my children: Abigail, Michael, and Stephanie

Contents

List of Figures

List of Tables

Preface

The micro half of international economics is surprisingly sparse in empirical work. It is difficult to name another substantive field in economics in which theorists make such great efforts to identify the unending stream of logical possibilities, and in which so little effort is made to attach empirical probabilities to their many models. Courses and books proudly use what seems to be a pejorative title, "pure theory," adopting "unstained" as the definition of "pure," rather than the alternative "mere."

This book is intended to be an empirical supplement to the traditional courses that offer mere theory. As is the case with all empirical exercises in econometrics, plenty of stains will be provided as well. Unlike many empirical researchers, I have gone to considerable effort to point out the stains that arise when the neat theories are translated into precise statements about a cluttered reality. I have tried to demonstrate what results are acceptably insensitive to the incredible assumptions that theoretical econometricians expect analyzers of data to make, and what results are not.

The scientific goal of this book is to leave the reader with a clear impression concerning the empirical validity of a central result of trade theory—the celebrated Heckscher-Ohlin theorem. This theorem, in its most general form, states that a country's trading relations with the rest of the world depend on its endowments of productive factors, usually identified in theory textbooks as land, labor, and capital. A second, but equally important, goal of this book is to describe succinctly and clearly the patterns of trade and the patterns of resource supplies of as many countries as the data permit. This will make the book a useful reference, whether or not it offers convincing evidence concerning the Heckscher-Ohlin theorem.

This book is not an exercise in pure empiricism. It is impossible to do any empirical work without some form of theoretical structure for selecting which variables to observe. But the use of a vague intuitive theory merely to select the variables to observe is not enough, since intuitively plausible empirical work can be completely inappropriate when viewed through the lens of a fully articulated theory. The two most frequent forms of empirical study in trade are excellent examples of this. Both the Leontief-type factor content studies and the cross-commodity regressions of net exports on factor intensities use intuition to generalize the 2-dimensional Heckscher-Ohlin theorem to a multifactor multicommodity reality.

Unfortunately, that intuition is incorrect, and the consequent empirical work is limited in value, as is argued in chapter 2.

The need for a fully articulated theoretical foundation for this study of trade data is met in chapter 1, which reviews the standard theory. Much of this chapter can be found in the standard texts, but some of it cannot; my empirical perspective forces the inclusion here, in the midst of a theoretical discussion, of various complications not often treated. This perspective is also useful since it forces one to limit or to eliminate empirically irrelevant theory. The need when doing empirical work for a fully defined mathematical model has dictated the adoption of the Heckscher-Ohlin-Vanek (HOV) model as the maintained hypothesis of the data analysis. A distinctive feature of chapter 1 is the algebraic development of trade theory as implied by the HOV model. For example, the Heckscher-Ohlin theorem is shown to be a consequence of the sign pattern of the inverse of a 2×2 positive matrix. My impression is that this chapter makes useful supplementary reading for students who have studied other approaches. I have also included in this chapter several tables of cross-national comparisons that indicate the extent to which such hypothesized relations as factor price equalization actually apply.

Chapter 2 is of a transitional character; it deals with what it means to test a theory when it is clear at the outset that the theory is not perfectly correct and when alternative theories are impossible to state precisely. The conclusion reached in this chapter is that it is possible to measure the accuracy of the theory but that the decision whether the theory is accurate "enough" must remain a matter of aesthetics and judgment. I have also provided a brief critical review of attempts in the literature to test the Heckscher-Ohlin theorem. These tests have all floundered for lack of an appropriate statement of the theorem applicable to a multifactor multigood reality.

Chapter 3 deals with the formation of trade aggregates. The number of traded commodities is much too large to allow analysis of each separately, and the first empirical step in this study will be to decide on some level of aggregation. The SITC grouping (Standard International Trade Classification, Revision 1) has 10 "1-digit" commodities, 69 "2-digit" commodities, and 182 "3-digit" commodities. At the 5-digit level one finds details such as "pineapples," "human hair," "cigarette paper," and "scissors." The lowest level of aggregation that is considered here is the 3-digit level. For ease of study and clarity of communication I wanted to work with 10–20 commodities. I was uncomfortable merely adopting the SITC 2-digit level since I suspected that the SITC scheme camouflaged major features of the more disaggregated data. I therefore formed my own aggregates from the 2-digit SITC data, and in one instance I checked the quality of these aggregates further by studying the 3-digit data. The 10 aggregates that I use are 2 primary products, 4 crops, and 4 manufactured goods.

Chapter 4 offers a view of the data that may prove more memorable than the econometric results presented subsequently. I have worked hard to devise tables and graphs that illustrate the salient features of the data. Included in this chapter are correlation matrices and boxplots. Also included in this chapter are discussions of trade dependence and resource abundance profiles, which may be found in appendix D. The trade dependence profiles illustrate the composition of net exports of the 10 trade aggregates relative to GNP. The resource abundance profiles illustrate the relative abundance of 11 different resources that are hypothesized to be the sources of comparative advantage. These profiles are provided for all countries in both 1958 and 1975. Some may argue that these displays are the most useful part of this book in that they provide a clear picture of the world's trading relations that is not available anywhere else.

Econometric methods are the subject of chapter 5. I am primarily a theoretical econometrician, and I have used this book as a showcase for some of my ideas. The basic theme of my theoretical work has been that a statistical analysis requires incredible assumptions and should be ignored unless the inferences are shown to be adequately insensitive to the choice of assumptions. Chapter 5 accordingly discusses the theory of sensitivity analyses that deal with gross errors, heteroscedasticity, chronic errors, and multicollinearity, all of which plague analyzers of cross-country data sets.

I have something of an ulterior motive for writing this book. I am a committed Bayesian, which means that I think it is silly to act as if human judgment had no effect on data analyses. On the contrary, any sensible, convincing analysis of economic data has economics as a major input. A Bayesian analysis has a formal procedure by which economic judgment can be introduced into the data analysis. It treats opinion as equivalent to a previous hypothetical data set. At a purely logical level the Bayesian theory is compelling, but when this method is actually applied, conjuring up all the features of the fictitious prior data set can become distinctly uncomfortable. This strikes me as the main reason why Bayesian methods are rarely used, though sheer ignorance plays a role as well. It is my hope that this book will serve as an example of a convincing, sensible data analysis using Bayesian methods and will encourage others also to use these methods. The uncomfortable feeling that necessarily attaches to the selection of the fictitious prior data set is combatted by a sensitivity analysis. The computer program SEARCH, which was used to do these calculations, is available on request.

Chapter 6 reports a statistical analysis of the relation between the 10 trade aggregates and 11 resource supplies. The Heckscher-Ohlin model has content only at an empirical level when one must select a list of measurable immobile resources and a functional relation between trade and these resources. The model that results is necessarily incredible because of limitations on both the list of resource variables and the family of functional forms. A judgment about the success of an empirical study of an approximation to a tautological theory is ultimately a matter of aesthetics. The general proposition that trade depends on resource endowments is not testable. At best one demonstrates that the data can be organized so that there appears to be a relation between trade and some function of a set of measured resources. If the list of resources is "brief" and "sensible," if the functional form is "plausible," and if the relation is "close," an empirical study will surprise and amuse.

I believe chapter 6 demonstrates that the main currents of international trade are well understood in terms of the abundance of a remarkably limited list of resources. In that sense the Heckscher-Ohlin theory comes out looking rather well. No real test of the theory is presented here because no alternative is fully articulated. Therefore you must judge the results as support for the theory if you are surprised by the quality of the explanation this abbreviated version of the theory offers and if you doubt that a fully articulated alternative could do as well or even add much to the understanding already achieved. The resulting image of the workings of the economy is admittedly cold and mechanical. Neither Henry Ford nor Vladimir Lenin plays a role. Nor does Thomas Edison, Karl Marx, Adam Smith, Queen Victoria, Christ, or Mohammed.... What distinguishes countries from one another is only their natural resources, work forces, and savings rates. But this mechanical explanation seems surprisingly complete, and the anomalies not explained by this limited list of resources do not elicit a feeling that Ford, Lenin, Edison, Marx, . . . have much impact on the structure of international trade.

Perhaps the most interesting finding is the reversed role from 1958 to 1975 of knowledge capital and physical capital as sources of comparative advantage in manufactured products. In 1958 the most highly skilled laborers contributed to comparative advantage in all four manufactured aggregates, but in 1975 these workers contributed positively to only the most skill intensive manufactured aggregate (chemicals). Conversely, in 1958 physical capital was a source of comparative advantage only in chemicals, but in 1975 it contributed positively to all four of the aggregates of manufactures. Another interesting finding is that coal production in 1958 was a source of comparative advantage in manufactured products, but that by 1975 this effect had reversed itself. Otherwise, the results are what you would expect: Unskilled labor and land are sources of comparative advantage in the agricultural products, and natural resources are sources of comparative advantage in the natural resource products.

In the last chapter of this book, chapter 7, the estimated model is used to study two counterfactual questions: (1) What change in trade would have occurred if the world's resources were rearranged? (2) What change in the functional distribution of income would have been induced by a change in tariff rates? The study of the first question allows us to identify the resources that were the most important determinants of trade. One finding is that physical capital and petroleum production in 1975 were the most critical resources, in the sense that trade could have been greatly reduced if they were reallocated. An explanation of this finding is that a large amount of international trade in 1975 amounted to the exchange of manufactured commodities for oil. In 1958, in contrast, trade is discovered to have been due principally to the uneven distribution internationally of the most highly skilled workers, other workers, and a type of land, in that order. Answers to the second counterfactual about the effect of tariffs on the functional distributional of income are based on Samuelson's reciprocity relations, which allow us to interpret the estimated derivative of outputs with respect to resource supplies as derivatives of factor returns with respect to product prices. These inferences are to be suspected for their indirectness, but they are amusing for their subtlety.

From my perspective there are several important shortcomings of this effort that I have been unable or unwilling to remedy. Most important,

I would have liked to have studied an alternative theory that explains trade in terms of scale economies, and I also would have liked to have used better measurements of the resources, especially physical and knowledge capital. Though it is beyond the scope of the present effort, a study of the dynamics of comparative advantage may well prove fruitful. In this book, cross-country comparisons of 1958 data and 1975 data are made separately, and no attempt is made to pool data across years.

Also from my perspective, this book makes three significant contributions. It provides a clear and complete statement of the theory of international comparative advantage and carefully links that theory to the empirical work. It provides illuminating data displays that will serve as a most convenient source of information about the international economy. And it presents a convincing data analysis using tools on the frontier of econometric theory in ways that are both understandable and sensible. Naturally, I hope the reader agrees.

Reading and understanding everything in this book will be a formidable task for most people. Chapters 3 and 4 and appendixes C and D, which summarize and display the data, are quite accessible; advanced undergraduates should find them readable. The economic theory presented in chapter 1 is perhaps a shade more mathematical than the more popular texts, but graduate students in economics ought to be able to handle the simple matrix expressions that appear there. The data analysis will perhaps cause the greatest problems, not because the procedure is truly complex, but only because it is unfamiliar. I have tried to deal with this by including a chapter on econometric methods that should be quite understandable to anyone who has had a course on the linear regression model.

It is not necessary to read the book in its entirety. The least mathematically sophisticated reader should find the trade dependence and resource abundance profiles in appendix D to be very informative summaries of the composition of trade and resource endowments. These displays are suggested by the Heckscher-Ohlin-Vanek model, and it would be wise for the reader to master at least the simplest 2×2 version of that model; this is described in section 1.2. The least sophisticated reader will also find the scatter plots in appendix C interesting, since they reveal in many cases a clear relation between trade composition and the resource endowments. Most of the rest of the book presupposes familiarity with simple matrix manipulations and introductory econometrics. It is suggested that the chapters be read in sequence, though much of the theoretical development in chapter 1 can be skimmed because it is not used directly in the data analysis.

Data collection and the analysis reported here have been supported by Ford Foundation grant 775-0692 and by Labor Department contract J9K80007. Work on the innovative econometric techniques used here has been funded by NSF grants SOC78-09479 and SES82-07532. Several UCLA graduate students have assisted on various phases of this project. The list includes Harry P. Bowen, Kenneth Tamor, Nancy Kane, Cary Knadler Morris, Eduardo Perez Mota, Jon Williams, and Robert Peterson. Harry Bowen and Sebastian Edwards made many useful comments on several of the chapters. Special thanks are offered to the anonymous referees, whose comments were especially useful.

General Notation

A $m \times n$ matrix of factor input requirements with elements A_{ij}
B $n \times n$ matrix of intermediate input requirements
C $n \times 1$ vector of consumption of final goods
F production function
f output per worker
f' first derivative of f
K capital
L labor
M land
k K/L
p $n \times 1$ vector of commodity prices
Q $n \times 1$ vector of production levels
s consumption share
T $n \times 1$ vector of net exports
X $n \times 1$ vector of final outputs
Y gross national product
V $m \times 1$ vector of factor endowments
w $m \times 1$ vector of factor prices

Subscripts

i factor; $i = 1, \ldots, m$
j commodity; $j = 1, \ldots, n$
c country; $c = 1, \ldots, p$
w   world

Sources of International Comparative Advantage

1 Theories of International Trade

This chapter offers a review of the standard Heckscher-Ohlin model of international trade that forms a basis for later empirical analysis of the sources of comparative advantage. The two fundamental hypotheses of this model are (1) there are factors of production that are immobile between countries, and (2) these factors are used in different combinations to produce different goods. A country will then possess a comparative advantage in good X if the country is relatively well endowed with factors that are used intensively in the production of X. Although a long list of restrictive assumptions is necessary to make this proposition a precisely defined mathematical truth, it nonetheless is hard to imagine a model in which the possession of immobile factors of production is not a source of comparative advantage. Moreover, with a broad definition of factors it becomes evident that the proposition that endowments are the source of comparative advantage is tautological. For example, the technological differences in the Ricardian model can be thought to arise from differing endowments of knowledge capital.

The way in which endowments confer comparative advantage is not tautological, however. In the simple traditional model with assumptions including constant returns to scale and equal numbers of factors and goods, trade is a linear function of the endowments. If the list of assumptions is altered, the relation between trade and endowments becomes nonlinear in ways that depend on the assumption that is altered. A linear relation between net exports and factor endowments serves as the working hypothesis for the empirical work subsequently presented. This choice is dictated by reasons of convenience and conceptual clarity, since, among the many convenient functional forms that could be used in the data analysis, only the linear form can be derived formally from a fully described general equilibrium model. An important purpose of this chapter is to alert the reader that there is a myriad of assumptions that could be made—and to discuss the kind of nonlinearities that might consequently be expected in the data set. Though overall the impression that is likely to be created is that the linear model is very fragile, it will be shown that linearity is preserved if there are nontraded goods, if there are more goods than factors, if consumption shares are income dependent, and even if there are certain kinds of transportation costs and tariff charges.

The traditional assumptions underlying the 2 × 2 textbook trade model are listed in section 1.1; the resulting theorems are derived in section 1.2; and the effects of departures from the assumptions are discussed in section 1.3. This chapter is meant to be a fairly complete statement of international trade theory as it relates to the determinants of the composition of trade and provided it seems useful in studying empirical data. Hypotheticals, such as "autarky prices," that have no observable counterparts are excluded from discussion, as are models that do not produce adequately clear descriptions of the relation between the composition of trade and its observable determinants.[1] The discussion in this chapter is detailed when a specific relation between trade and factors endowments can be derived, but the discussion is brief when the theory can provide only an impression. The subsequent empirical work rests primarily on the simplest model and its extension to high dimensions. It is therefore sufficient to read sections 1.1 and 1.2 and the part of section 1.3 dealing with dimensionality.

1.1 Assumptions

There are six classes of assumptions that are used to produce trade theory's sharpest results.

1. *Dimensionality*. The number of goods n and the number of productive factors m are equal to 2: $n = m = 2$.

2. *Mobility*. (a) Factors of production move costlessly between industries within a country, but are completely immobile between countries. (b) Commodities move internationally at zero cost of transport and there are no other impediments to trade.

3. *Competition*. Both commodity and factor markets clear competitively, in the sense that all agents act as if they could buy or sell unlimited quantities at the prevailing market prices.

4. *Technology*. The same technological knowledge about the production of goods is costlessly available to all countries. The production functions exhibit constant returns to scale and diminishing marginal products.

5. *Factor Endowment Similarity*. The variability of factor endowment ratios among countries is less than the variability of factor input intensities across industries. (A precise definition of "less variability" is given below.)

6. *Demand Similarity*. Individuals consume as if each were maximizing an identical homothetic utility function.

1.2 The Basic Trade Theorems

The core of general equilibrium trade theory consists of four theorems that describe the responsiveness of outputs and factor prices to changes in output prices and factor supplies and a fifth that identifies which commodities are exported and which are imported. The factor price equalization theorem deals with the responsiveness of factor prices to factor supplies, holding fixed output prices. The Stolper-Samuelson theorem describes the relation between factor prices and output prices, holding fixed factor supplies. The Rybczynski theorem links outputs to factor supplies, given output prices. And the Samuelson reciprocity relations describe the correspondence between the Stolper-Samuelson effects and the Rybczynski effects. The fifth theorem, the Heckscher-Ohlin theorem, identifies the structure of trade as a function of either (a) the difference between autarky (pretrade) prices and posttrade prices or (b) factor supplies. Since autarky prices are generally unobservable, this book will make use of only the quantity version of the Heckscher-Ohlin theorem.[2]

THE FACTOR PRICE EQUALIZATION THEOREM All countries have identical factor prices.

Proof Let the goods be labeled X_1 and X_2 and let the factors be labor (L) and capital (K). A *unit-value isoquant* for commodity X_1 is depicted in figure 1.1. This is the set of combinations of capital and labor minimally

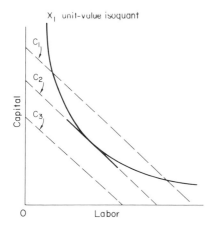

Figure 1.1
Unit-value isoquant and isocost lines.

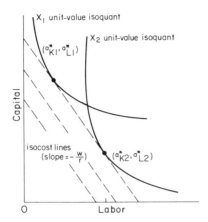

Figure 1.2
Equilibrium factor costs.

required to produce a unit value of output. Because commodity prices are assumed equalized by trade and because technologies are assumed identical, all countries have the same unit-value isoquant. The three straight lines labeled C_1, C_2, and C_3 in figure 1.1 are three hypothetical unit *isocost lines* defined as combinations of capital and labor that cost a unit value. A unit isocost line is defined algebraically as $1 = w_K K + w_L L$, where w_K and w_L are the rental rates for capital and labor services, respectively. Each isocost line has slope equal to $-w_L/w_K$, and from the fact that the three isocost lines in figure 1.1 are parallel we may infer that the ratio of w_L to w_K is the same in each case. Of these three unit isocost lines, only line C_2, which is tangent to the unit-value isoquant, is consistent with competitive equilibrium. If line C_1 were the unit-cost line, producers could hire a unit value of inputs and produce more than a unit value of output. In an attempt to exploit this profit opportunity by hiring inputs, producers would drive up the input costs, thereby shifting the unit-cost line downward, a process that continues until profit opportunities are exhausted, that is, until the unit-value isoquant and the unit-cost line are tangent. Likewise, if the isocost line were C_3, there would be no way for producers even to break even, and either factor costs would have to fall or the commodity would not be produced.

The unit-value isoquants for both commodities are depicted in the "Lerner diagram," figure 1.2 (Lerner, 1952). Only one unit-cost line is consistent with the production of both goods in equilibrium, since only

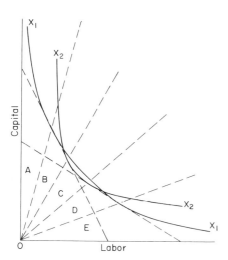

Figure 1.3
Factor intensity reversal.

one line is tangent to both unit-value isoquants. This line determines unique values for the factor rental rates w_K and w_L. Hence factor prices are equalized. Though this argument has referred to unit-value isoquants, the assumption of constant returns makes it apply to any level of output. ∎

This argument is deficient in one respect. There is no assurance that the unit-value isoquants admit only a single tangent isocost line. An example to the contrary is illustrated in figure 1.3, in which there is a high wage equilibrium with X_1 produced with a capital intensive technique and a low wage equilibrium with X_1 produced with a labor intensive technique. The commodities X_1 and X_2 are said in this case to exhibit a *factor intensity reversal*, since one of the commodities can be produced efficiently with capital/labor ratios either more or less than the capital/labor ratio of the other, depending on the relative factor returns.

When there is more than one possible equilibrium set of factor returns, the choice among them depends on the factor endowment of the country. The allocation of a given endowment of capital and labor between the industries is illustrated in figure 1.4, where the vector V_1 indicates the factors allocated to industry 1 and the vector V_2 indicates the factors allocated to industry 2. These two vectors must lie along the expansion paths of the two industries and they must sum to the endowment vector (K, L). If the endowment vector (K, L) lies outside the cone between the

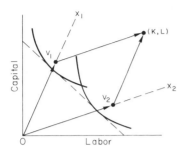

Figure 1.4
Allocation of factors between industries.

two expansion vectors, it is impossible to find two vectors along the expansion vectors that sum to the endowment vector, and consequently the factor prices associated with that cone are inconsistent with equilibrium. Return again to figure 1.3; this implies that the choice between the two factor price ratios depends on the endowment ratio. If the endowment is in a cone B with relative capital abundance, high wages are selected. If the endowment is in cone D with relative labor abundance, low wages are selected. If labor is even more abundant, and the endowment vector lies in region E, then the country specializes in X_1, and wages are still lower. Relative factor prices may then be found by placing an isocost line tangent to the X_1 isoquant at the endowment point.

The regions B and D in figure 1.3 are called *cones of diversification*. Countries with endowments in the same cone of diversification produce both goods using the same techniques and also have the same factor prices. Countries with endowments in different cones use different techniques and have different factor prices. Countries with endowments in none of the cones specialize in the production of one of the goods.

In order to ensure factor price equalization it is therefore necessary to invoke the following.

FACTOR ENDOWMENT SIMILARITY CONDITION   Given the equilibrium commodity prices and the consequent family of cones of diversification, all countries either have factor endowments in the same cone or identical factor endowment ratios.

The cones of diversification will be wider, the more dissimilar are the productive techniques, and this condition can be stated as above that endowments must be more similar than (equilibrium) input intensities.

It may be noted in passing that this demonstration has made use of assumptions 1–5 with the exception of the part of 2a describing the immobility of factors between countries. Because factor prices are equalized, the economic incentive for migration is eliminated, and international mobility of factors is immaterial, provided such mobility does not affect the assumption about factor endowment similarity. Assumption 6 is used only in the limited sense that the production side of the economy maximizes the value of output.

From the internationally determined prices of goods, we have been able to derive the factor prices and the factor input intensities (defined precisely below). These intensities are depicted in figure 1.2, where (a_{K1}^*, a_{L1}^*) and (a_{K2}^*, a_{L2}^*) are the amounts of capital and labor required to produce a unit value of X_1 and X_2, respectively. The input requirements a_{ij}^* per *unit value* of output can be transformed into input requirements a_{ij} per *unit* of output by multiplying by product prices: $a_{ij} = a_{ij}^* p_j$, where p_j is the product price. The input requirements a_{ij} are called *factor input intensities*, and can be collected into a *factor intensity matrix* symbolized by A.

The following definitions refer to relative factor intensities and relative factor abundance.

FACTOR INTENSITY DEFINITION   Commodity X_1 is said to be the relatively capital intensive commodity if

$$a_{K1}/a_{L1} > a_{K2}/a_{L2}.$$

FACTOR ABUNDANCE DEFINITION   A country endowed with capital K and labor L is said to be relatively abundant in capital if its share of the world's capital stock exceeds its share of the world's labor force:

$$K/K_w > L/L_w,$$

or equivalently if the country is more capital abundant than the world as a whole:

$$K/L > K_w/L_w,$$

where the w subscript refers to world totals. ∎

Having established factor price equalization, we may now demonstrate the Heckscher-Ohlin theorem.

THE HECKSCHER-OHLIN THEOREM   A country with balanced trade will export the commodity that uses intensively its relatively abundant factor and will import the commodity that uses intensively its relatively scarce factor.

Proof   Denoting the output levels by X_1 and X_2, we may set factor supply equal to factor demand to obtain

$$K = a_{K1}X_1 + a_{K2}X_2,$$

$$L = a_{L1}X_1 + a_{L2}X_2,$$

which is a system that can be solved for outputs as a function of the endowments. If V represents the vector of endowments (K, L) and X the vector of outputs (X_1, X_2), then these equations may be written in matrix form as $V = AX$, or inverted as

$$X = A^{-1}V, \tag{1.1}$$

where the inverse exists provided the relative input intensities are unequal: $a_{K1}/a_{L1} \neq a_{K2}/a_{L2}$. Because of the linearity of these equations (and the consequent unresponsiveness of total world outputs to factor migration), we can also write total world outputs X_w as a function of total world endowments V_w:

$$X_w = A^{-1}V_w.$$

Since the relative prices of goods are given in world markets and hence are the same for all countries, assumption 6 implies that each country consumes commodities in the same proportions, that is,

$$C = sX_w,$$

where s is the country's consumption share of world output and C is its consumption vector.

Trade balance requires that the value of production equal the value of consumption, that is, $p'X = p'C = sp'X_w$, where p is the price vector (p_1, p_2). Thus if trade is balanced, the consumption share is the ratio of own GNP to world GNP:

$$s = p'X/p'X_w. \tag{1.2}$$

The vector of *net exports* is the difference between production and consumption:

$$T = X - C$$

$$= A^{-1}V - sA^{-1}V_w \qquad (1.3)$$

$$= A^{-1}(V - sV_w),$$

which is A^{-1} times the vector of *excess factor supplies*:

$$V - sV_w = \begin{bmatrix} K - sK_w \\ L - sL_w \end{bmatrix}$$

$$= \begin{bmatrix} K_w\left(\dfrac{K}{K_w} - s\right) \\ L_w\left(\dfrac{L}{L_w} - s\right) \end{bmatrix}.$$

It will now be demonstrated that if the country in question is relatively capital abundant, $K/K_w > L/L_w$, then this excess factor supply vector has signs $(+, -)$. This follows from the fact that the consumption share is a weighted average of the capital share and the labor share

$$s = \frac{p'X}{p'X_w} = \frac{p'A^{-1}V}{p'A^{-1}V_w} = \frac{w'V}{w'V_w} = \frac{[w_K K_w(K/K_w) + w_L L_w(L/L_w)]}{w_K K_w + w_L L_w},$$

where w is the factor reward vector: $w = (A')^{-1}p$. Thus s must fall between K/K_w and L/L_w, and consequently $K/K_w > s$ is equivalent to $K/K_w > L/L_w$.

To determine the sign of the net export vector of a capital abundant country, we need to determine the effect of premultiplying a vector with signs $(+, -)$ by the inverse of the matrix A:

$$A^{-1} = \begin{bmatrix} a_{K1} & a_{K2} \\ a_{L1} & a_{L2} \end{bmatrix}^{-1} = \begin{bmatrix} a_{L2} & -a_{K2} \\ -a_{L1} & a_{K1} \end{bmatrix} / |A|,$$

where the determinant is

$$|A| = (a_{K1}a_{L2} - a_{L1}a_{K2}) = a_{L1}a_{L2}\left(\frac{a_{K1}}{a_{L1}} - \frac{a_{K2}}{a_{L2}}\right).$$

If X_1 is the capital intensive industry, then $|A| > 0$, and A^{-1} has the sign pattern

$$A^{-1} = \begin{bmatrix} + & - \\ - & + \end{bmatrix}.$$

If the country is abundant in capital, the vector of excess factor supplies has sign pattern $(+, -)$, and trade therefore has sign pattern

$$T = \begin{bmatrix} + & - \\ - & + \end{bmatrix} \begin{bmatrix} + \\ - \end{bmatrix} = \begin{bmatrix} + \\ - \end{bmatrix},$$

meaning the capital abundant country exports the capital intensive commodity X_1 and imports the labor intensive commodity X_2. All other cases of the Heckscher-Ohlin theorem follow similarly.[3] ■

The primary intent of this book is to study the linkages between trade and factor endowments, but for completeness I will briefly state the other basic trade theorems.

THE RYBCZYNSKI THEOREM   At constant commodity prices, an increase in the supply of a factor will lead to an increase in the output of the commodity that uses that factor intensively and a reduction in the output of the other commodity.

This follows directly from equation (1.1) and the sign patterns for A^{-1}. A somewhat more precise version of the theorem can be stated in terms of the percentage changes in outputs induced by percentage changes in inputs. From equation (1.1) we have

$$\hat{X}_1 = (dX_1)/X_1 = (a_{L2}dK - a_{K2}dL)/(a_{L2}K - a_{K2}L).$$

Thus

$$(a_{L2}K - a_{K2}L)\hat{X}_1 = a_{L2}K\hat{K} - a_{K2}L\hat{L},$$

$$a_{L2}K(\hat{X}_1 - \hat{K}) = a_{K2}L(\hat{X}_1 - \hat{L}),$$

or

$$(\hat{X}_1 - \hat{K}) = (\hat{X}_1 - \hat{L})(a_{K2}/a_{L2})/(K/L).$$

Thus if commodity one is the capital intensive commodity, $a_{K1}/a_{L1} > K/L > a_{K2}/a_{L2}$, we must have $|\hat{X}_1 - \hat{K}| < |\hat{X}_1 - \hat{L}|$, that is, X_1 must grow at a rate more similar to K than to L, and we must have $\text{sign}(\hat{X}_1 - \hat{K}) = \text{sign}(\hat{X}_1 - \hat{L})$. This implies that either $\hat{L} < \hat{K} < \hat{X}_1$ or $\hat{X}_1 < \hat{K} < \hat{L}$, which establishes.

JONES'S MAGNIFICATION RESULT   At constant commodity prices, $a_{K1}/a_{L1} > a_{K2}/a_{L2}$ and $\hat{K} > \hat{L}$ imply $\hat{X}_1 > \hat{K} > \hat{L} > \hat{X}_2$.

The next result links factor prices to commodity prices. This linkage is implied by the zero-profit conditions

$$A'w = p, \tag{1.4}$$

where p is the vector of prices (p_1, p_2) and w the vector of factor rewards. This condition asserts that the price of a commodity is equal to the cost of producing it. Differentiating this expression produces $A'(dw) = dp$, since $(dA')w = 0$ by cost minimization.[4] Writing this as

$$dw = (A')^{-1} dp, \tag{1.5}$$

and again referring to the sign pattern of the inverse of a 2×2 positive matrix, we obtain.

THE STOLPER SAMUELSON THEOREM   An increase in the price of the import good leads to an increase in the return to the scarce factor and a reduction in the return to the abundant factor.

Finally, by comparing (1.5) with (1.1) we obtain a result due to Samuelson (1953/1954):

THE RECIPROCITY RELATIONS

$$\partial X_j / \partial V_i = \partial w_i / \partial p_j, \qquad i = K, L, \quad j = 1, 2.$$

In words, the partial derivative of the supply of commodity j with respect to the total availability of factor i is equal to the partial derivative of the wage of factor i with respect to the price of commodity j. These reciprocity relations are used in chapter 7 to obtain indirect estimates of the effects of tariffs on factor returns from direct observation of the responsiveness of output to factor supplies.

1.3 The Effects of Departures from Assumptions

It takes neither great observational skills nor keen inquisitiveness to make one question the six assumptions and to make one wonder whether the results hold up if these assumptions are relaxed. A particularly troubling observation is the great international disparity in wage rates. For example, the agricultural wage rates reported in table 1.1 vary from a low of $.046 per hour in India to a high of $2.04 per hour in Denmark. Part of these differences might be explained by skill differences, but agricultural wages seem unlikely to include a reward for skills that is

Table 1.1
Agricultural wage rates ($/hour): 1972 or closest year data available

ARG	.31	JAP	.69
AUST	.97	KOR	.25
BLUX	1.30	MALA	.17
CAN	1.75	MAUR	.17
CHLE	.18	MEX	.22
CSTR	.22	NUZE	.86
CYP	.61	NOR	1.79
DEN	2.04	PHIL	.062
ELSAL	.63	PORT	.38
FIN	.96	SRIL	.078
FRA	.48	SPAIN	.38
GER	1.35	SWE	2.80
GANA	.18	TURK	.34
INDA	.046	UK	1.34
IRE	1.04	US	1.76
ISRL	.71	YUG	.49

Source: ILO, *Yearbook of Labor Statistics*, 1972.

sufficiently variable to account for the data in table 1.1. This observation encourages a search for assumptions that do not necessarily imply factor price equalization.

1.3.1 Dimensionality[5]

There surely are more than 2 commodities, and more than 2 factors as well. In an intertemporal model one might suppose that there are only 2 factors, labor and land, but these ought to be disaggregated along several quality dimensions. These primary factors can be combined to produce capital goods. But at a specific time, past savings decisions can be taken as given, and capital can be treated as a fixed input. At any instant there will be many types of capital that are relatively well suited to the production of particular commodities and that cannot be transformed into other kinds of capital. For example, human capital and machinery are not fungible except in the long run, and within a year, say, can be treated as separate factors of production. Identifying the particular categories of capital is a very delicate conceptual and empirical issue that interfaces with the mobility assumption. Automobile-stamping plants might be treated as a category of capital that is relatively suited to production of automobiles but not especially useful in the medium run to the production of textiles. For that matter, automobile workers have a certain amount of human capital invested in the auto industry because of special skills and mobility costs. An explanation of trade in terms of exceedingly fine measures of capital would be too close to a tautology to be very satisfying, but simple distinctions between human and physical capital are appealing. In any case, it is clear that there are more than 2 factors of production, and it is essential that the model be enlarged.

The Even Model, $n = m > 2$ The factor price equalization theorem holds in the even case regardless of the number of factors. Imagine the 3-dimensional picture analogous to figure 1.2. The three unit-value isoquants instead of being lines are surfaces—think of three bowls—and the isocost lines are planes instead of straight lines. Only one of these planes rests squarely on all three bowls; hence there is only one set of factor prices consistent with the production of all three goods. As in the 2-dimensional case, factor intensity reversals[6] can occur, but, regardless, for any set of commodity prices there will be a set of cones of diversification, and all countries in the same cone will have the same factor rewards.

The Heckscher-Ohlin theorem in one sense is dramatically altered, but in another sense is not altered at all by high dimensionality with $m = n$. The basic equations of the model, (1.1)–(1.3), which determine the output vector, the consumption share, and the trade vector, need not be altered. If factor prices are equalized, the factor intensity matrix A will be the same in each country, and equations (1.1)–(1.3) are an immediate consequence. However, the interpretation of these equations in the 2×2 case depends on properties of the inverse of a 2×2 positive matrix. Namely, the inverse of the factor intensity matrix A has one of two distinct sign patterns, depending on the ordering of the capital intensities of the 2 goods. Things become much more complex in higher dimensions.[7] Suppose the country is abundant in the first factor and scarce in the other two in the sense that the excess factor supply vector $V - sV_w$ has sign pattern $(+, -, -)$. You can then determine the sign of the first element of the trade vector $T = A^{-1}(V - sV_w)$ from knowledge of only the sign of A^{-1} in two cases:

$$\begin{bmatrix} + & - & - \\ \cdot & \cdot & \cdot \\ \cdot & \cdot & \cdot \end{bmatrix} \begin{bmatrix} + \\ - \\ - \end{bmatrix} = \begin{bmatrix} + \\ \cdot \\ \cdot \end{bmatrix},$$

$$\begin{bmatrix} - & + & + \\ \cdot & \cdot & \cdot \\ \cdot & \cdot & \cdot \end{bmatrix} \begin{bmatrix} + \\ - \\ - \end{bmatrix} = \begin{bmatrix} - \\ \cdot \\ \cdot \end{bmatrix}.$$

What are the circumstances in which the first row of A^{-1} has one of these two sign patterns? Consider the inverse of A with factors capital (K), labor (L), and land (M):

$$A = \begin{bmatrix} a_{K1} & a_{K2} & a_{K3} \\ a_{L1} & a_{L2} & a_{L3} \\ a_{M1} & a_{M2} & a_{M3} \end{bmatrix}.$$

To find the first row of A^{-1} we need to compute the cofactors

$$C_{11} = \det \begin{bmatrix} a_{L2} & a_{L3} \\ a_{M2} & a_{M3} \end{bmatrix} = a_{L2}a_{L3}\left(\frac{a_{M3}}{a_{L3}} - \frac{a_{M2}}{a_{L2}}\right),$$

$$C_{12} = -\det \begin{bmatrix} a_{K2} & a_{K3} \\ a_{M2} & a_{M3} \end{bmatrix} = a_{M2}a_{M3}\left(\frac{a_{K3}}{a_{M3}} - \frac{a_{K2}}{a_{M2}}\right),$$

$$C_{13} = \det \begin{bmatrix} a_{K2} & a_{K3} \\ a_{L2} & a_{L3} \end{bmatrix} = a_{L2}a_{L3}\left(\frac{a_{K2}}{a_{L2}} - \frac{a_{K3}}{a_{L3}}\right),$$

and the determinant of A:

$$|A| = a_{K1}C_{11} + a_{L1}C_{12} + a_{M1}C_{13}.$$

Then the relevant elements of $B = A^{-1}$ are

$$B_{11} = C_{11}/|A|,$$

$$B_{12} = C_{12}/|A|,$$

$$B_{13} = C_{13}/|A|.$$

The condition that we are seeking is that B_{11} has sign opposite of B_{12} and B_{13}. By inspection of the cofactors this places rather bizarre and complicated restrictions on the factor intensities in industries 2 and 3. If industry 2 is less land intensive than 3 (relative to labor), $C_{11} > 0$, then industry 2 must be more capital intensive (relative to land) than 3, but 2 must also be less capital intensive (relative to labor) than 3.

In higher dimensions it thus becomes impossible to state the Heckscher-Ohlin theorem in a useful way analogous to its statement in the 2-dimensional case. But who really cares? All this is saying is that there exists a simple algorithm for determining the sign of the trade vector T in the 2-dimensional case, but the algorithm becomes more complex in higher dimensions. The degree of complexity remains trivial for a computer given dimensions well above 3, even though 3 strains the human mind. What we might do to assist limited human beings is to rephrase the Heckscher-Ohlin theorem in a correct and informative way. To do this, note that the vector of factors required to produce the vector of outputs X is the vector AX. Thus

DEFINITION   The *factors embodied in net exports* form the vector AT, where A is the matrix of factor intensities and T is the vector of net exports.

The vector AT can have positive or negative elements, meaning that factor services (embodied in goods) can be either exported or imported. Then we can rewrite equation (1.3) as Vanek (1968) does,

$$AT = V - sV_{\mathrm{w}}, \tag{1.6}$$

meaning that the factors embodied in net exports equal the excess factor supplies. This set of equations serves as the foundation for the subsequent data analysis and are referred to as the *Heckscher-Ohlin-Vanek (HOV) equations*. In order to express these equations in the words of the Heckscher-Ohlin theorem, we need a definition of factor abundance applicable to the multidimensional case:

FACTOR ABUNDANCE DEFINITION   A country is said to be abundant in factor i if its share of the world's supply of the factor exceeds its consumption share ($V_i/V_{\mathrm{w}i} > s$).

Note that if trade is balanced, $B = 0$, then equation (1.6) implies that

$$s = p'X/p'X_{\mathrm{w}} = p'A^{-1}V/p'A^{-1}V_{\mathrm{w}} = w'V/w'V_{\mathrm{w}} = \sum w_i V_{\mathrm{w}i}(V_i/V_{\mathrm{w}i})/\sum w_i V_{\mathrm{w}i}.$$

In words, s is a weighted average of the abundance ratios $V_i/V_{\mathrm{w}i}$ with weights equal to world earnings $w_i V_{\mathrm{w}i}$. Thus the factor abundance definition compares the abundance ratio of a selected factor with an average of all abundance ratios. With this definition, we can interpret equation (1.6) as the

HECKSCHER-OHLIN-VANEK THEOREM   A country will export the services of abundant factors and import the services of scarce factors.

This way of reexpressing the Heckscher-Ohlin theorem properly emphasizes the point that it is factor services that are being exchanged through trade. Commodities serve only as a bundle within which factor services are wrapped.

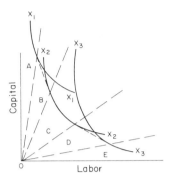

Figure 1.5
Unit-value isoquants, factor prices not equalized.

There is no simple algorithm in the $m = n > 2$ case for linking the signs of the trade vector to the signs of the excess factor supply vector. For the same reasons, the linkages of commodities to factors implied by the Stolper-Samuelson and the Rybczynski theorems become incomprehensibly complex. All three theorems depend on the sign pattern of the inverse of the factor intensity matrix, which in 2 dimensions is a function of rather straightforward qualitative information, namely, the sign of the determinant. In higher dimensions, the required qualitative information becomes so complex that it is just as convenient to condition these theorems on complete quantitative knowledge of the factor intensity matrix A. Namely, the derivatives of outputs with respect to endowments are collected in the matrix A^{-1}, and the derivatives of factor prices with respect to commodity prices are collected in the matrix A'^{-1}. Measuring A^{-1} is an important empirical task that can be done, as in Chipman (1977/1978), by regressing internal goods and factor prices on traded goods prices or, as in this work, by regressing outputs on factor supplies or trade on excess factor supplies.

More Goods Than Factors, $m < n$ If there are more goods than factors, there are new ways for the factor endowment similarity condition to be violated. Barring that possibility, the model remains basically the same as the $m = n > 2$ model. Consider, for example, the 3-good 2-factor case depicted in figure 1.5 with unit-value isoquants for goods X_1, X_2, X_3. This figure is similar to figure 1.3. As in that case, if the endowments of all countries are in the same cone of diversification, then all countries will have the same factor prices. Here, however, at least 1 of the 3 goods will

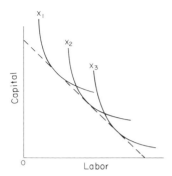

Figure 1.6
Unit-value isoquants, factor prices equalized.

then not be produced; for example, if the endowments are all in cone B, X_3 is not produced. The lack of supply of X_3 would then put upward pressure on the price of X_3. A rise in the price of X_3 shifts the unit-value isoquant in toward the origin until figure 1.6 occurs, at which point all three goods can be produced at nonnegative profit. What this means is that similarity in factor endowments will imply that commodity prices will adjust so that an equilibrium such as depicted in figure 1.6 occurs, with all countries having the same factor rewards and all using the same factor intensities A.

The matrix A is not square, however, and cannot be inverted. The set of equations $AX = V$ leaves X indeterminate. (X has n elements but there are only m equations, $m < n$.) Outputs, and consequently trade, have a degree of indeterminateness equal to $n - m$. As an illustration consider the 1-factor 2-good (Ricardian) model. All countries have straight line production possibilities curves with the same slopes. A country could attain its optimal consumption point with no trade by matching production and consumption. Alternatively, the production point can be anywhere on the production possibilities line, and the optimal consumption point can still be achieved by a suitable choice of trade. Although trade is indeterminate, the net flow of factor services is not. That is, equation (1.6) still holds. What is happening is that any given net export of factor services $V - sV_w$ can be achieved in many different bundles of net exports T.

A way to resolve the indeterminacy of trade and production is to hypothesize small international transportation costs that deter trade but are otherwise negligible. In the 1-factor Ricardian model, no trade would then occur. For the more general model suppose that it costs c_j to exchange commodity j internationally. If these costs are small enough that factor price equalization is imperceptibly altered, we can suppose that the economy minimizes transportation costs $\sum_j c_j |T_j|$ subject to the constraint $AT = V - sV_w$. Whatever the solution to this linear programming problem may be, it will have the property that it is a linear function of the excess factor supply vector $V - sV_w$.

More Factors Than Goods Results necessarily change more substantially if there are more factors than goods. Then it is impossible to derive the (internal) factor prices from the (external) commodity prices. This can be understood easily with reference to a model with 3 factors and 2 goods. A figure analogous to figure 1.2 is 3 dimensional, with each factor measured on a different axis. The unit-value isoquants are surfaces (bowls), and the isocost surface is a plane. In the 3×3 case, we have three bowls upon which to rest the plane. If there are only 2 goods, then there are only two bowls and the plane cannot be supported by these bowls alone. Thus there are many sets of factor prices that could support the production of both goods. Corresponding to each of these factor price planes there is a minimum cost combination of inputs. The factor exhaustion equation can be written as

$$\begin{bmatrix} V_1 \\ V_2 \\ V_3 \end{bmatrix} = \begin{bmatrix} a_{11} & a_{12} \\ a_{21} & a_{22} \\ a_{31} & a_{32} \end{bmatrix} \begin{bmatrix} X_1 \\ X_2 \end{bmatrix},$$

where the elements a_{ij} depend on the particular factor price plane. For most values of a_{ij} this system cannot be solved for (X_1, X_2). It is necessary to select factor prices such that the given endowment vector goes through the line connecting the two tangency points (a_{11}, a_{21}, a_{31}) and (a_{12}, a_{22}, a_{32}). Thus the factor matrix A will change in a complicated way as the endowment vector changes. The resulting relation between trade and endowments is highly complex.

1.3.2 Factor Endowment Similarity

If countries are sufficiently similar in their factor endowments, the factor price equalization theorem and a version of the Heckscher-Ohlin theorem hold provided the number of factors is less than or equal to the number of commodities. But if countries are sufficiently dissimilar, they may specialize production in different subsets of commodities, or they may use

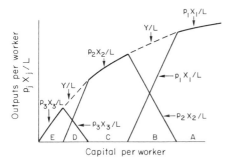

Figure 1.7
Outputs and GNP: 3 goods and 2 factors.

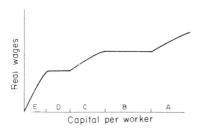

Figure 1.8
Wage rates: 3 goods and 2 factors.

different input combinations to produce the same commodity. If the first occurs, countries will be said to be *completely specialized*. If the second occurs, and if the country is not completely specialized, the technology is said to admit economically relevant *factor intensity reversals*. In either case, factor prices will not be equalized. If countries are completely specialized, the content of the Heckscher-Ohlin theorem is preserved, though the precise linear form is not. If factor intensity reversals occur, even the content of this theorem can be reversed.

Consider, for example, the model with 3 goods and 2 factors depicted in figure 1.5. Countries with endowment vectors located in cone *B* will specialize in the production of the relatively capital intensive commodities. Countries with less capital compared to labor, such that their endowment vectors are located in cone *D*, will have lower wage rates and will specialize in production of the two relatively labor intensive commodities. The outputs per man and the corresponding wage rates as a function of capital per man implied by figure 1.5 are depicted in figures 1.7 and 1.8.

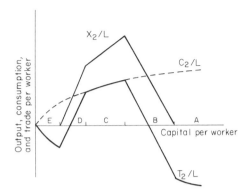

Figure 1.9
Output, consumption, and trade: 3 goods and 2 factors.

At very low capital/man endowment ratios, countries have low wage rates and specialize in X_3, the labor intensive commodity. As the capital per man increases, countries shift production progressively into more capital intensive industries, and wage rates correspondingly increase. In the cones of diversification B and D, the output per worker functions are linear in capital per worker, and the wage rates are insensitive to small changes in the endowments. In the regions of complete specialization, A, C, and E, countries produce only 1 good and have wage rates that increase with the capital abundance.[8]

It is apparent from figure 1.7 that the intellectual content of the Heckscher-Ohlin model is unaffected by this kind of dissimilarity in factor endowments. Countries with abundant capital will specialize in the capital intensive goods and will necessarily exchange these for the labor intensive goods. From an empirical standpoint, however, the relation between trade and endowments is not universally linear and rather unpleasant estimation problems arise. Take, for example, commodity X_2 and assume that half of GNP is spent on consuming X_2. Figure 1.9 depicts the output per man and consumption per man, assumed to be equal to half of GNP per man. Trade per man, the difference between output and consumption, is also shown. This is indeed a rather peculiarly shaped function, with X_2 exported by countries with intermediate capital abundance. We shall be alert to such nonlinearities when the data are examined.

Figure 1.7 can also be used to depict outputs if there are factor intensity reversals, except that X_3 is treated as the same product as X_1. As the

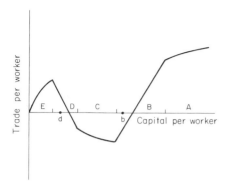

Figure 1.10
Trade per worker: factor intensity reversals.

capital per man endowment sweeps through the cones $A-E$ in figure 1.3, the output levels vary in the same way as they do as capital per man sweeps through the cones in figure 1.5. If, as before, we take consumption of $X_1 = X_3$ to be a fixed fraction of GNP, net exports per man become the function depicted in figure 1.10. If there are no factor intensity reversals, there will be one interval of capital abundance ratios K/L that imply exports of the commodity. The item is exported when the capital intensity of the commodity is similar to the capital abundance ratio of the country. If there are factor intensity reversals, the trade curve may wander back and forth across the horizontal axis many times, and there will be many intervals of K/L values for which the commodity is exported. Factor intensity reversals can, as a consequence, negate the Heckscher-Ohlin theorem. Consider a two-country world composed of country b in cone B and country d in cone D, depicted in figure 1.10, with b importing and d exporting X_1. As far as b is concerned, X_1 is the capital intensive good; an increase in k would increase net exports of X_1. But b, the capital abundant country, is importing the capital intensive good.

1.3.3 Mobility

The simple general equilibrium model uses an unlikely pair of extreme assumptions about the mobility of goods and factors. Goods can be moved anywhere without cost. Factors can move costlessly inside the boundaries of a country, but cannot climb over the high fences that are assumed to surround all countries. Both these mobility assumptions are studied in this section.

Table 1.2
Fraction of gross fixed capital formation financed from abroad[a]

Country	1960	1965	1970	1975	1977
United States	−.0261	−.0273	.0044	−.0486	.0999
Japan	−.0128	−.0375	−.0301	.0020	−.0528
Germany	−.1075	−.0025	−.0823	−.1389	−.1143
Korea	.8602	.4944	.4014	.3705	.0029
United Kingdom	.0955	.0446	−.0392	.1004	−.0045
France	−.0885	−.0355	−.0115	−.0319	.0230
Italy	.0882	−.0487	.0361	.0639	.0332
Canada	.0554	.0106	−.1299	.0617	.0014

Source: *International Financial Statistics*, selected monthly reports.
a. Trade deficit as a fraction of domestic investment.

International Factor Mobility   The international movement of capital and labor has for some countries in some time periods been quite substantial. For example, recent guest worker programs brought 30 million temporary workers to Europe. The Swiss labor force in 1970 was 33% foreign, a figure that fell to 18% by 1977 (Ruffin, 1982). Capital mobility also can be substantial, as is suggested by table 1.2, which indicates the share of domestic investment financed from foreign sources for several countries. Korea in the 1950s and 1960s was particularly dependent on foreign capital.

The international mobility of some factors may be so great that the assumption of free mobility is more accurate than the traditional one of mobility at infinite cost. A mobile factor should not properly be thought to be a source of comparative advantage. It will now be shown also that a mobile factor will not alter the basic structure of the model. Consider, for example, a 2-good model with 2 internationally immobile factors, labor (L) and land (M), and 1 internationally mobile factor, capital (K). The production functions can be written as

$$X_1 = F_1(L_1, M_1, K_1),$$

$$X_2 = F_2(L_2, M_2, K_2),$$

with each function exhibiting constant returns to scale. For any levels of L_1 and M_1, producers will hire capital services from the international market at the given rate w_K so as to maximize revenue minus capital costs $p_1 X_1 - w_K K_1$, where p_1 is the international price of X_1. This maximization will therefore imply that K_1 is chosen so that $w_K = p_1 \, \partial F_1(L_1, M_1, K_1)/ \partial K_1$. This equation can be solved for K_1 as a function of L_1 and M_1:

$K_1 = h(L_1, M_1; w_K/p_1)$, where the real return on capital is a parameter determined in the international markets. This function h exhibits constant returns to scale, since if L_1 and M_1 are doubled, in order to maintain the marginal product of K at the level w_K/p_1, it is necessary also to double K_1.[9] As a consequence the composite function $X_1 = F_1(L_1, M_1, h(L_1, M_1; w_K/p_1))$ also exhibits constant returns to scale. The model with mobile capital can therefore be written as

$$X_1 = F_1^*(L_1, M_1; w_K/p_1) \equiv F_1(L_1, M_1, h_1(L_1, M_1; w_K/p_1)),$$

$$X_2 = F_2^*(L_2, M_2; w_K/p_2) \equiv F_2(L_2, M_2, h_2(L_2, M_2; w_K/p_2)),$$

with labor and land conferring comparative advantage in accordance with the simple theory described in section 1.2. Factor price equalization is a consequence, which in turn implies that input intensities are the same in all countries. We may therefore write the relations between outputs and inputs as $AX = V$, where A is a fixed 3×2 matrix of factor intensities, X is the 2×1 vector of outputs, and V is the 3×1 vector of inputs including the mobile factor K. These three equations determine the three unknowns X_1, X_2, and K as linear functions of the 2 fixed factors L and M. The model with mobile factors therefore expresses outputs and trade as a function of immobile factors only and includes auxiliary relations between the mobile and the immobile factors. It is equivalent in content to the even model if the number of immobile factors is equal to the number of traded goods.[10]

Nontraded Goods Transportation costs greatly impede the international exchange of some goods and most services. Nontraded goods make up a large fraction of GNP. For the United States in 1958, for example, construction, transportation, communications, wholesale/retail trade, finance, insurance and real estate, services, and government contribute 62% of GNP (source: U.S. Department of Commerce, *The National Income and Product Accounts of the United States*, 1929–1974). At the outset, it seems unlikely that nontraded goods will greatly affect the qualitative conclusion that net exports depend on resource availability. But it is a great surprise that if we assume countries are sufficiently similar that factor prices are equalized, the existence of non-traded goods requires no adjustment at all to the Vanek equations.[11] Suppose there are m factors V, m traded goods X, and q nontraded goods Z. If factor prices are equalized, the factor intensities are equal as well, and we may write the equations of equilibrium in the factor markets as $AX + A_z Z = V$, where

A_z is the $m \times q$ matrix of factor intensities of the nontraded goods. Also, if factor prices are equalized, the zero-profit conditions imply equalization of the prices of nontraded goods, $p_z = A'_z w$, and from identical homothetic tastes we may conclude that all countries consume in the same proportions, $C = sX_w$, $C_z = sZ_w$, where X_w and Z_w are vectors of total world levels of outputs and s is the consumption share. From these, we can derive the Heckscher-Ohlin-Vanek equations:

$$AT = AX - AC = AX - sAX_w$$

$$= (V - A_z Z) - s(V_w - A_z Z_w)$$

$$= V - A_z Z_w s - s(V_w - A_z Z_w) = V - sV_w.$$

Furthermore, the consumption share can be found by imposing the trade balance condition $p'X = p'C$; then using $C = sX_w$, $X = A^{-1}(V - A_z Z) = A^{-1}(V - sA_z Z_w)$, and $X_w = A^{-1}(V_w - A_z Z_w)$, we can solve for $s = p'A^{-1}V/p'A^{-1}V_w$, which is the GNP ratio computed as if no resources were devoted to the production of nontraded goods. The reader may verify that GNP computed as if no resources were devoted to the production of nontraded goods is equal to actual GNP. This can occur because of the indeterminacy of production in this model with more goods than factors.

Transportation Costs, Tariffs, and Other Trade Impediments Transportation costs, tariffs, subsidies, and quotas impede the international flow of commodities and can alter the composition of trade. Indeed, Travis (1964) argues that tariffs on labor intensive imports can explain the Leontief finding that the United States in 1947 was a net exporter of labor services. Pre-Kennedy round tariff rates of selected countries are reported in table 1.3. Freight factors—the ratio of transport cost to value of shipments—for U.S. imports are recorded in table 1.4. Generally speaking the tariff rates are higher than the transport costs even after the Kennedy round reductions. The combined charge for importing into the United States in some cases was as high as 25%, which is a number that seems high enough to have an impact on the composition of trade.

To decide how to deal with trade impediments at an empirical level, we shall have to study their effects on our general equilibrium model. As will be shown, the effects are quite complex; this complexity, together with the difficulty of measuring trade impediments for the large number of coun-

Table 1.3
Average tariffs on dutiable, nonagricultural imports as percentage of c.i.f. value (before Kennedy round cuts)[a]

Category	U.S.	EEC	U.K.	Japan
Mineral products	9.9	9.4	9.3	12.0
Chemical products	17.8	14.3	18.8	19.7
Rubber products	11.3	15.0	13.6	15.1
Hides, furs, leather products	16.2	9.2	17.7	19.9
Wood and cork products	6.8	10.9	5.2	15.6
Pulp and paper	10.9	10.7	16.6	6.7
Textiles	21.4	16.0	20.6	23.5
Footwear and headwear	16.1	17.8	22.8	26.3
Stone, ceramic, and glass products	21.0	14.1	16.4	16.9
Base metals and metal products	8.5	9.9	12.8	11.0
Nonelectrical machinery	11.9	11.1	14.2	15.6
Electrical machinery	13.6	14.2	20.1	17.8
Transportation equipment	7.1	15.4	20.0	18.4
Precision instruments	21.1	13.3	26.4	19.1
Miscellaneous	19.5	16.5	20.1	14.7
Total	13.5	12.8	16.6	15.5

Source: Preeg (1970).
a. Final agreement on the Kennedy Round tariff reduction was signed in June 1967. Overall tariff reduction for nonagricultural dutiable imports was in 36–39% range. Tariff reduction for agricultural dutiable imports was 20%.

tries in the subsequent empirical work, forces us (reluctantly) to restrict a consideration of the effect of trade impediments to the informal study of anomalous observations.

To demonstrate the effects of price differences induced by trade impediments on the general equilibrium model, it is mathematically convenient to assume log-linear technologies and tastes. A unit-value isoquant for commodity j is assumed to be $1 = p_j \alpha_j \prod_i V_{ij}^{\theta_{ij}}$, where p_j is the product price and V_{ij} is the input of factor i. By taking the logarithm, this unit-value isoquant can be written as

$$0 = \ln p_j + \ln \alpha_j + \sum_i \theta_{ij} \ln V_{ij}. \tag{1.7}$$

Then minimizing cost, $\sum w_i V_{ij}$, subject to the unit value constraint (1.7), we obtain the first-order condition $w_i = \lambda \theta_{ij} / V_{ij}$, where λ is the Lagrange multiplier. Then using constant returns to scale $\sum_i \theta_{ij} = 1$ and zero-profit $1 = \sum_i w_i V_{ij}$, we can solve for $\lambda = 1$. Thus $w_i V_{ij} = \theta_{ij}$; in words, the value share of factor i in production of commodity j is set equal to θ_{ij}. Inserting this condition back into (1.7), we have

Table 1.4
Freight factors: averages by commodity groups[a]

SITC[b]		Average of reported freight factors
011	Meats, fresh, frozen, etc.	11
013	Meats in containers, meat preparations, etc.	4
031	Fish, fresh, frozen, etc.	7
051	Fruit, fresh, and nuts, fresh or dried	13
061	Sugar and honey	7
071	Coffee	5
081	Feeding-stuff for animals	18
112	Alcoholic beverages	9
231	Crude rubber	13
262	Wool and other animal hair	5
281	Iron ore and concentrates	26
283	Ores and concentrates, nonferrous	14
331	Petroleum, crude and partly refined	15
332	Petroleum products	14
442	Fixed vegetable oils, excluding soft	6
512	Organic chemicals	4
631	Veneers, plywood board, etc.	16
653	Textile fabrics, woven, excluding cotton	6
664	Glass	14
665	Glassware	11
666	Pottery	12
674	Iron and steel plates and sheets	11
732	Road motor vehicles	9
841	Clothing	5
851	Footwear	7
861	Scientific, medical, etc., instruments and apparatus	2
894	Toys, games, sporting goods, etc.	9
899	Manufactured articles n.e.s.	9

Source: Lipsey and Weiss (1974).
a. Freight charges as a percentage of value.
b. All groups with 30 observations or more. Some of the SITC titles are abbreviated here.

$$\sum_i \theta_{ij} \ln w_i = \ln p_j + \ln \alpha_j + \sum_i \theta_{ij} \ln(\theta_{ij}).$$

In matrix form this can be written

$$\Theta' \ln(w) = \ln(p) + \ln(X_0), \tag{1.8}$$

where Θ' is the matrix of factor shares (with rows summing to one), $\ln(w)$ and $\ln(p)$ refer to vectors with logarithms of factor prices and logarithms of commodity prices as elements, and $\ln X_0$ is a vector with the logarithms of outputs as elements: $\ln X_j(\theta_j) = \ln(\alpha_j) + \sum_i \theta_{ij} \ln \theta_{ij}$.

Since the value share of factor i in commodity j is $\theta_{ij} = w_i V_{ij}/p_j X_j$, it follows that it takes $\theta_{ij} p_j/w_i = A_{ij}$ of factor i to produce one unit of commodity j. Thus the matrix of factor intensities is

$$A = \{A_{ij}\} = \{\theta_{ij} p_j/w_i\} = W^{-1} \Theta P,$$

where W is a diagonal matrix with w on the diagonal and P is a diagonal matrix with p on the diagonal. Therefore the relation between outputs and inputs becomes

$$X = A^{-1} V = P^{-1} \Theta^{-1} W V, \tag{1.9}$$

with W a function of P according to (1.8).

We assume also that countries choose the commodity vector to maximize the Cobb-Douglas utility function $\sum_j \gamma_j \ln(X_j)$, with $\sum_j \gamma_j = 1$. Maximizing utility subject to an income constraint, $Y^* = \sum p_j C_j$, implies that the budget share $p_j C_j/Y^*$ is set equal to the elasticity γ_j. Thus the consumption vector can be written as

$$C = \begin{bmatrix} \gamma_1/p_1 \\ \gamma_2/p_2 \\ \vdots \\ \gamma_n/p_n \end{bmatrix} Y^* = P^{-1} \gamma Y^*, \tag{1.10}$$

where p_j are the internal prices. The income level Y^* is determined by the trade balance condition $1'(X - C) = 0$, where it is assumed that quantity units are selected so that the world prices are all equal to one. From the trade balance condition, we solve for the "money" income level:

$$Y^* = \sum_j X_j \Big/ \sum_j (\gamma_j/p_j).$$

Net exports may be obtained by subtracting (1.10) from (1.9). Using the result that $A_p^{-1} = P^{-1}\Theta^{-1}W_p$, where the p subscript indicates price dependent variables, we may write the trade vector in value terms as

$$PT_p = \Theta^{-1}(V_p^* - s_p^* V_w^*), \qquad\qquad (1.11)$$

where $V_p^* = W_p V$ is the vector of resources evaluated at the internal factor prices; $V_w^* = W_1 V_w$ is the vector of world resources evaluated at factor prices applicable if there were no trade impediments, $p = 1$; and $s_p^* = (\sum X_i / \sum X_{iw})/(\sum \gamma_j/p_j)$ is the GNP ratio evaluated at external prices with world outputs computed as if there were no trade impediments, all divided by a factor less than one, adjusting consumption levels upward to account for the higher internal price levels.

Equation (1.11) is surprisingly similar to the HOV equations derived when there were no trade impediments, that is, when $P = I$. The only changes that are required to allow for trade impediments are (1) trade and resources must be expressed in value terms with internal prices used for valuation, and (2) the consumption share must be adjusted to account for the distortions in production and consumption. It should be noted that trade impediments can reverse the sign of the elements of the factor abundance vector $V_p^* - s_p^* V_w^*$. For example, as Travis (1964) has argued, trade impediments could raise the return to labor, thereby increasing the internal value of labor; at the same time, the impediments would lower the consumption share, so that labor could be switched from a scarce factor to an abundant factor. [Can this happen if there are only 2 goods?]

Factor Market Distortions   According to the popular press, one of the major reasons why the U.S. markets for iron and steel and automobiles are being so effectively penetrated by foreign competitors is that unions have managed to raise wages in those industries to the point where they are no longer competitive. The effect of unions may be partially revealed by a study of the distribution of wages across industries. The first column of table 1.5 contains 1975 U.S. hourly wage rates by manufacturing sector. The highest wages are paid by refineries and the lowest are paid by the clothing industry. Much of the differences in wages across industries is probably due to skill differences, but unions or other barriers to mobility may also have an effect. If wage differences were entirely due to skill differences, then the distribution of wages across industries in other countries would be expected to be similar to the U.S. wages. Wages in four other countries may also be found in table 1.5, both in absolute

Table 1.5
Wages by manufacturing sector (average hourly earnings): 1975[a]

ISIC	Description	U.S.	Japan	France	Germany	U.K.
311–313	Food, beverage	4.57	2.85(.63)	2.69(.59)	3.60(.79)	2.54(.56)
314	Tobacco	4.51				
321	Textiles	3.40	2.25(.66)	2.45(.72)	3.34(.98)	2.32(.68)
322	Clothing	3.19	1.89(.59)	2.15(.67)	3.00(.94)	2.07(.65)
323–324	Leather, footwear	3.23	2.51(.78)	2.32(.72)	2.97(.92)	2.36(.73)
331	Wood	4.28	2.52(.59)	2.39(.59)	3.60(.84)	2.53(.63)
332	Furniture	3.75	2.50(.67)		3.95(1.05)	
341	Paper	4.99	3.39(.68)	3.01(.60)	4.03(.81)	2.82(.54)
342	Printing, publishing	5.36	3.91(.73)	3.38(.63)	4.47(.83)	
351	Industrial chemicals	5.93	4.24(.77)	3.18(.58)	4.51(.76)	2.75(.50)
352	Other chemicals	5.05			3.83(.76)	
353–354	Refineries	6.42	4.46(.69)	—	5.20[b](.81)	3.04(.47)
355–356	Rubber and plastic products	4.35	3.39[c](.78)	2.74(.63)	3.78(.87)	2.61(.60)
36	Nonmetallic	4.89	3.16(.65)	2.94(.60)	3.82(.78)	2.62(.54)
37	Basic metal industries	6.17	4.18(.68)	3.17(.51)	4.17(.68)	2.69(.44)
381	Metal products	5.04	3.34(.66)	2.79(.55)	3.74(.74)	2.51(.50)
382	Nonelectrical machinery	5.36	3.64(.68)	2.97(.55)	4.22(.79)	2.68(.50)
383	Electrical machinery	4.58	3.16(.69)	2.73(.60)	3.68(.80)	2.57(.56)
384	Transport equipment	6.02	3.65(.61)	3.11(.52)	4.40(.73)	2.92(.49)
385	Scientific, measuring, etc.	4.56	3.21(.70)	2.68(.59)	3.62(.79)	2.45(.54)
390	Other	3.79	2.98(.79)	2.69(.71)	3.40(.90)	2.22(.59)

Source: ILO, *Yearbook of Labor Statistics*, 1977.
a. Wages relative to U.S. averages in parentheses.
b. 353
c. 355.

level and relative to the corresponding U.S. wage. It is true that clothing wages are the lowest in each of these countries and refinery wages are the highest. There is generally a high degree of similarity in the wage distributions of each of these countries, and this is evidence that skill differences account for much of the cross-industry variability in wages.

But there are some subtle differences in these distributions that are revealed by the wage rates divided by the corresponding U.S. wage rates. The Japanese wage rates are relatively low (about 60% of U.S. wages) in clothing, wood, and transport equipment. The French, German, and U.K. wage rates are relatively low in the basic metal industries and in transport equipment. This seems to be pretty clear evidence of the impact of the United Auto Workers, and the United Steel Workers of America, and maybe even the Brotherhood of Textile Workers ("Look for the union label").

If unions are effective in raising wage rates and/or restricting employment, it can be expected that the composition of trade will shift to take advantage of the relatively low costs in the nonunion sectors. Factor market distortions such as unions both alter the output vector and also lower the consumption share. On the assumption that the primary effect is to distort the output vector, we concentrate here on the output changes induced by unions and other forms of distortions in the two-sector model.

This section describes the effects of unions or other labor market distortions in the two-sector general equilibrium model with prices of commodities determined exogenously in the international markets. Three kinds of distortions are considered: (1) a minimum wage with a covered sector (X_1) and an uncovered sector (X_2); (2) a license requirement for work in the X_1 sector, with the number of licenses limited; (3) a tax on labor earnings with a covered sector (X_2) and an uncovered sector (X_1). Depending on its bargaining posture, a union could be thought of as imposing any one of these three distortions. It could bargain for a high real wage, for a restricted union membership, or for a union wage higher than the nonunion wage.

Partial equilibrium analysis suggests that each of these three distortions would have the same effects: a higher wage, fewer workers, and less output in sector X_1; a lower wage, more workers, and more output in X_2. This partial equilibrium analysis fails to take into account reallocation of capital between the sectors and the consequent shifting of the labor demand schedules. When these are properly taken into account, the effects are sharply different depending on whether the union sector is capital intensive or labor intensive. What follows is a summary of the results. Derivations may be found in appendix A.

The licensing restriction and the tax on labor earnings produce the same qualitative results, but these can differ from the minimum wage. In all cases, the wage in X_1 and the wage in X_2 move in the same direction. If the unionized sector is the relatively capital intensive sector, the expected results occur, namely: wages rise, more in the union sector than in the nonunion sector; capital intensities rise; the return on capital falls; the number of workers and the level of output in the union sector fall; and the level of output in the nonunion sector rises.

But unionization of the labor intensive sector produces surprising results. If the union bargains for a minimum wage, it will, of course, receive a wage rate higher than initially but at the same time lower than the nonunion wage. Employment and output in the union sector will actually increase, while employment and output in the nonunion sector will decrease. But this equilibrium is dynamically unstable, since workers will quit the unionized industry to seek employment elsewhere at higher wage rates. If the union restricts the number of employees, or bargains for a wage higher than the nonunion wage, the union wage rate will actually fall, though by an amount less than the reduction in the nonunion wage.

The conclusion that seems warranted by this discussion is that unionization of the capital intensive sector will reduce output and decrease net exports of the unionized commodity, but that unionization of the labor intensive sector will drive it completely out of existence.

Factor Market Adjustment Costs: Short Run Models The basic model combines two extreme assumptions about the mobility of factors. Internationally factors cannot migrate at all, but internally between industries factors are perfectly mobile. These extreme assumptions are the ones most conveniently handled at a theoretical level. We have already seen that perfect international mobility of some factors does not dramatically alter the model. Similarly, complete immobility of some factors between industries can be interpreted in terms of factors so specialized that they can be used in only a single industry. However, if we assume partial mobility, the model changes dramatically. Comparative advantage in one period becomes a source of comparative advantage in another period. The effect can go either forward or backward in time, since anticipated swings in future comparative advantage necessitate anticipatory investments.

If the dynamics of comparative advantage were a concern, it is quite clear that short run adjustment costs would have to be considered, but the cross-section data analysis in this book involves no dynamics at all. Though it is not impossible that adjustment costs might substantially influence the cross-section trade pattern, this does seem unlikely. For empirical work relating to this issue see Chenery and Taylor (1968); for models of adjustment see Mayer (1974), Mussa (1974), and Leamer (1980).

1.3.4 Technology

It has been assumed that technological knowledge is free, that production functions exhibit constant returns to scale and diminishing marginal

products. Without explicitly saying so, we have ruled out also externalities, intermediate inputs, and joint products. Each of these assumptions can have important implications for international trade.

Specialized Factors Though the model summarized by equation (1.1)
appears to require that all factors be used in all industries, this is not the
case. The existence of industry-specialized factors implies that particular
elements of the factor requirements matrix A may be set to zero. If it is
known that there exists a block of elements in the A matrix that are all
zero, then there may be a corresponding block of zeros in the A^{-1} matrix.
The existence and knowledge of such specialized factors implies interesting relations between outputs and inputs. For example, suppose
that there are two inputs, labor (L) and land (M), and 2 commodities,
agricultural (X_1) and industrial (X_2). If land is not used to produce the
industrial commodity we may write the A matrix as

$$A = \begin{bmatrix} a_{L1} & a_{L2} \\ a_{M1} & 0 \end{bmatrix}.$$

The inverse of this matrix can be used to solve for the outputs as follows:

$$X = A^{-1}V = (-a_{M1}a_{L2})^{-1} \begin{bmatrix} 0 & -a_{L2} \\ -a_{M1} & a_{L1} \end{bmatrix} \begin{bmatrix} L \\ M \end{bmatrix}$$

$$= \begin{bmatrix} M/a_{M1} \\ (a_{M1}L - a_{L1}M)/a_{M1}a_{L2} \end{bmatrix}.$$

Thus even though both labor and land are used to produce agricultural
goods, the output of agricultural goods depends only upon the endowment of land. And although land is not used to produce industrial goods,
the level of output of industrial goods depends on both the endowment
of labor and the endowment of land. This apparently paradoxical result
stems trivially from the fact that full employment requires that land must
be fully utilized in the agricultural sector. This, together with the fixed
input requirement a_{M1}, determines the level of agricultural output M/a_{M1}.
Since the labor residual left over for industrial production is then
dependent upon the endowment of land (that is, $L - X_1 a_{L1} = L - Ma_{L1}/a_{M1}$), it becomes obvious that the level of industrial output is
also dependent upon the endowment of land.

     This relation suggests that resources such as agricultural land will
have a negative impact on the comparative advantage of, say, chemicals

and will be primary determinants of agricultural output. This type of relation would explain, in part, results such as those obtained by Keesing and Sherk (1971), who found that "large" less-developed countries (LDCs) have a comparative disadvantage in manufactures, where large is defined as low population density.

Public Resources   Climate is an important determinant of the location of agricultural production. Specialized knowledge is likewise critical to various manufactured products. Both climate and knowledge have the feature that the use of the factor to produce one good does not apparently reduce the stock of the factor for the production of other goods. This contrasts with the model reported previously in which the use of a certain amount of a resource for the production of one commodity implies that the quantity available for other commodities is reduced by an equal amount.

It is, not difficult, however, to treat climate conceptually and empirically as a private resource. In order to make use of a favorable climate to produce agricultural goods, it is necessary to have arable land. To give a more personal example, the purchase of a California home has made me painfully aware of the price of sunshine. The resource to which the theory refers is thus neither climate, nor arable land, but rather the physical amount of land in a particular climate zone. Then the assumption of constant returns to scale in agriculture does seem acceptable if the inputs are capital, labor, and land disaggregated by climate type.

Similarly, knowledge, which might be thought to render special technological advantages to particular countries, can be used only if it is embodied in either physical or human capital. But one may question whether constant returns to scale is a credible assumption in this case. Once a single scientist reveals the knowledge of how to produce more efficiently, a second scientist may have no marginal product.

Intermediate Inputs   There is a substantial amount of trade in raw materials and semifinished goods. As will be shown, the trade of inputs does not alter fundamentally the simplest trade theory outlined previously, and in particular, the conclusion of linearity is not affected. The production functions of a 2-good model may be written as

$$Q_1 = F(K_1, L_1, X_{21}),$$

$$Q_2 = G(K_2, L_2, X_{12}),$$

where X_{21}, X_{12} are the intermediate goods used, respectively, in the production of commodities 1 and 2, and Q_1 and Q_2 are the levels of production.

First we need to demonstrate that factor prices are equalized by trade. Profits in industry 1 are

$$p_1 F(K_1, L_1, X_{21}) - w_K K_1 - w_L L_1 - p_2 X_{21}$$

$$= p_1 L_1 f(k_1, x_{21}) - w_K L_1 k_1 - w_L L_1 - p_2 L_1 x_{21},$$

where $k_1 = K_1/L_1$ and $x_{21} = X_{21}/L_1$. Differentiating this with respect to L_1, k_1, and x_{21} yields three conditions for profit maximization: $p_1 f_1 = w_K$, $p_1 f_2 = p_2$, and $p_1 f = w_K k_1 + w_L + p_2 x_{21}$, the last condition implying zero profits. There are three equivalent equations for industry 2, and these six equations can be solved for the six unknowns, w_L, w_K, k_1, x_{21}, k_2, x_{12}, as function of the product prices.[12]

Since the prices of the inputs can be taken as given, the factor intensities can also be taken as given, and the factor exhaustion equations become

$$V = \begin{bmatrix} K \\ L \end{bmatrix} = \begin{bmatrix} a_{K1} & a_{K2} \\ a_{L1} & a_{L2} \end{bmatrix} \begin{bmatrix} Q_1 \\ Q_2 \end{bmatrix} = AQ,$$

with intermediate inputs

$$\begin{bmatrix} X_{12} \\ X_{21} \end{bmatrix} = \begin{bmatrix} 0 & b_{12} \\ b_{21} & 0 \end{bmatrix} \begin{bmatrix} Q_1 \\ Q_2 \end{bmatrix} = BQ.$$

The outputs available to meet final demand are therefore

$$X = \begin{bmatrix} X_1 \\ X_2 \end{bmatrix} = \begin{bmatrix} Q_1 \\ Q_2 \end{bmatrix} - \begin{bmatrix} X_{12} \\ X_{21} \end{bmatrix} = Q - BQ$$

$$= (I - B)A^{-1}V.$$

This establishes the result that intermediate inputs do not make essential changes in the model. Where before we had the matrix A of direct input intensities, we need only substitute the matrix $A(I - B)^{-1}$ of direct plus indirect intensities. There is one important difference, however. The cones of diversification are defined with respect to the direct requirements; that is, it is assumed that endowments V are such that $Q = A^{-1}V$ is a positive vector. It is not necessary for final output $X = (I - B)A^{-1}V$ also to be positive, since intermediate inputs can be purchased from abroad. This means that trade can have very substantial welfare benefits, since the posttrade consumption line need not be tangent to the pretrade consumption possibilities curve in the positive quadrant. (The reader is encouraged to draw a figure to illustrate this.)

Economies of Scale   The model described in section 1.2 postulates that countries, like holograms, can be divided into arbitrarily small pieces, with each piece retaining the complete image of the whole. But when countries are as small as Iceland, for example, with a work force of 100,000, it is hard to imagine automobile assembly plants or large steel mills located there. Because economies of scale at some small levels of output are obviously important, we can expect to see very small countries with trade patterns quite unlike their larger counterparts.

Another observation that forces one to think of economies of scale is the substantial amount of trade in similar products among the advanced industrialized countries. This seems hard to square with the Heckscher-Ohlin model, which seems to suggest that countries with similar resources ought to export the same products, and which consequently implies that the intensity of trade among similarly endowed countries should be less than the intensity of trade among dissimilarly endowed countries.

The level of intraindustry trade and its increase over time, documented by Balassa (1967), Kravis (1971), and Grubel and Lloyd (1975), has sparked a considerable amount of both theoretical and empirical work on scale economies. An excellent review of this literature is provided by Helpman (1982). Among the conclusions of this literature are that (1) trade can occur between identical countries, (2) commodities with identical input coefficients may be exchanged, (3) trade may make factor prices more unequal, (4) there may be multiple equilibria, (5) an increase in the supply of an endowment may increase the output of both commodities, and (6) protection may raise the return of the abundant factor and lower the return of the scarce factor.

This rapidly accumulating literature on economies of scale contains many interesting models and many interesting results. But it remains quite unsuitable as a foundation for a data analysis since it offers nothing nearly as concrete as the Heckscher-Ohlin-Vanek equations. It has been demonstrated by Markusen and Melvin (1981) that in a 2-goods model there exists an equilibrium, with the larger country exporting the good subject to increasing returns to scale and the small country exporting the good subject to constant returns to scale. But the precise relation between exports and size remains unstated; moreover, no effort is made to generalize to the case of more commodities. If there are more commodities, it is to be expected that the problem of multiple equilibria is greatly exacerbated.

The attitude that I adopt in this book concerning economies of scale combines a wish and an apology. The wish is for a fully articulated, multigood, multifactor empirically implementable model with scale economies. I really do think much of international trade is associated with scale economies, and it is a great disappointment that the empirical work presented does not deal seriously with economies of scale. The apology is that the level of aggregation and the use of net export rather than exports and imports separately reduce the possibility that scale effects are important. This statement is given theoretical support by Helpman's (1981) model of trade in differentiated products. Helpman assumes that there is one standardized product with constant returns to scale and a continuum of differentiated products, each with an identical production function subject to increasing returns. Each country then produces different varieties of the nonstandardized product, and consequently there is intraindustry trade. But *net* trade is predicted by Heckscher-Ohlin theory: If the standardized product is labor intensive, then the labor abundant country exports the standardized product and has net imports of the nonstandardized product.

Technological Differences   In common parlance, India, which uses labor intensive methods in agriculture, is said to employ a different technology than the United States, which uses capital intensive methods. This statement fails to distinguish between differences in knowledge and differences in factor prices as the cause of the differences in factor intensities in the two countries. In order to be precise, we refer to knowledge as *technology* and to the adaptation of knowledge to local factor prices as the choice of *technique*. It seems more likely that Indians choose a labor intensive technique because of low wages than that they are unaware of the capital intensive technique used in the United States.

An economist ought to be uncomfortable assuming technological differences, and Ricardo is treated unfairly when his name is associated with this idea. According to the classic Ricardian example, Portugal exchanges wine for cloth from Britain because Portugal is relatively efficient in the production of wine. The source of this comparative advantage was not Ricardo's concern, but it has been interpreted by many modern writers as "technological differences." This very superficial account of the causes of international trade seems to suppose that there are either biological differences between the Portugese and the British that preclude each from emulating the productive techniques of the other or rather effective counterintelligence agents.

The Heckscher-Ohlin model is much more satisfying, since it accounts for comparative advantage without having to appeal to the "demon" of technological differences. Namely, Portugal is relatively well endowed in land with a Mediterranean climate. The British indeed have the knowledge; but they lack the resources for efficient production of wine.

Ricardo's concern was to demonstrate the welfare gains from exchange even when one country has an absolute advantage in all commodities. For this purpose the source of the comparative advantage need not be identified, and we must suppose that he never intended to suggest that technological knowledge in Britain was different from that in Portugal. But by assuming that all countries have exactly the same technology, the Heckscher-Ohlin model goes too far, since it assumes that knowledge is free. A more satisfying viewpoint is that knowledge and the dissemination of knowledge are uncertain consequences of economic investments.

Models of knowledge formation and dissemination are currently popular. The special role in world trade played by the United States during the decades of the 1960s and 1970s gave many economists the impression that an important source of U.S. comparative advantage is technological knowledge, or knowledge capital. A "technological gap" was thought to exist, and a "product cycle" was hypothesized by which knowledge of product and production technique was disseminated to the more backward countries. Among the basic references are Kravis (1956), Hufbauer (1966), Posner (1966), Vernon (1966), Gruber, Mehta, and Vernon (1967), and Keesing (1967).

These theories tend to be descriptive rather than analytic. They also focus on dynamic questions concerning the evolution of trade patterns over time, often at a very disaggregated level. In contrast, the cross-section data analysis in this book uses highly aggregated commodity classes and ignores altogether any reasons why the intertemporal evolution of trade might not conform to the static cross-country pattern. "Technological differences" are here allowed to have an impact on trade, but only through the employment of scientists and engineers who enhance the productivity of other factors.

Exhaustible Resources   The sharp rise in the price of oil in the decade of the 1970s and the attendant cries of doom concerning the depletion of a resource essential to the well-being of mankind gave rise to a large literature on the theory of exhaustible resources. It turns out not to be very difficult to alter the HOV model to allow for exhaustible resources if there is perfect foresight. All that is required is an expansion of the list of commodities and renewable resources to distinguish the period of supply. If τ is the number of periods in the model, n is the number of goods produced in each period, m is the number of renewable resources, and q is the number of nonrenewable resources, then the number of commodities and resources are equal in the sense of the HOV model if $\tau n = \tau m + q$. If this somewhat unusual condition holds, and if the other usual assumptions hold, factor prices will be equalized, since the model is mathematically the same as the static model already discussed. Similarly, the vector of outputs and trade will be a linear function of the vector of resources. This means that the output of a commodity in any period will be a function of the original stock of the nonrenewable resource and the whole sequence of time-dated supplies of the renewable resources. This conclusion is distinctly uncomfortable from an empirical point of view, since it requires a vast increase in the list of variables that determine trade. There is fortunately one escape from this dilemma. At each instant there are $m + q$ factor market equilibrium relations that express the $m + q$ resources actually used in the period as functions of the level of production of the n goods produced in the period. If n of these equations are selected, they can be inverted to express outputs of the n commodities as linear functions of a set of renewable resources supplied in the period and a set of nonrenewable resources used in the period, n resources in total. Although this is exactly what is done in the empirical work, it should be kept in mind that the use of a nonrenewable resource in any period is properly thought to be an endogenous variable depending on the flows of the renewable resources. Moreover, this discussion has ignored what may be the most essential aspect of exhaustible resources: uncertainty about the total stock available and uncertainty about the sequence of future prices.

1.3.5   Preference Dissimilarity

Most of the structure of the general equilibrium trade model comes from the production side. The assumption of identical homothetic tastes is made to assure that results concerning production translate into results concerning the difference between production and consumption, that is, trade. The economist's euphemism "identical homothetic tastes" means that individuals facing identical commodity prices will consume commodities in the same proportions. Of course, neither individuals nor countries actually have identical budget shares, as can be seen from the data in table 1.6, which indicates the composition of private consumption expenditure for many countries. The proportion spent on food, for example, varies from the low of 14.4% for the United States to a high of 59.7% for India. What this and some of the other categories suggest is that the budget shares depend on the income level, though differences in tastes are probably required to explain the tobacco shares and the recreation shares. (For example, why does Singapore have such a high share devoted to recreation, education, and entertainment?)

Income dependent consumption can be easily introduced into the model. Suppose that within each country all citizens share equally in the ownership of all resources, and consequently each has the same level of income. Then we might write the consumption vector of a typical country as

$$C = (C_0 + C_1 y)L = C_0 L + C_1 Y,$$

where y is expenditure per worker, $C_0 + C_1 y$ is the consumption vector of a typical worker, L is the total number of workers, and Y is total expenditure. Total expenditure can also be written as $p'C$, where p is the vector of prices. From the condition $Y = p'C = p'C_0 L + p'C_1 Y$ we conclude that $p'C_1 = 1$ and $p'C_0 = 0$. To equilibrate supply and demand, we set world consumption equal to world output: $C_0 L_w + C_1 Y_w = A^{-1} V_w$. This expression allows us to write $C_1 = (A^{-1} V_w - C_0 L_w)/Y_w$. The trade vector then becomes

$$T = A^{-1} V - C$$
$$= A^{-1} V - C_0 L - C_1 Y$$
$$= A^{-1} V - C_0 L - (A^{-1} V_w - C_0 L_w) Y/Y_w \tag{1.12}$$
$$= A^{-1}(V - s V_w) - C_0 (L - s L_w),$$

Table 1.6
Composition of private consumption expenditure (%): 1975[a]

Country	1	2	3	4	5	6	7	8	9	10
AUSL	23.5		2.6	8.4	16.7	9.1	6.1	15.3	6.6	11.7
AUST	20.4	5.5	2.5	12.4	13.8	10.0	4.5	15.1	6.7	9.1
BLUX	25.5		1.8	7.2	15.2	15.0	7.2	11.4	4.3	12.4
CAN	20.1		2.2	8.4	18.1	9.1	3.0	14.6	9.5	14.9
CYPR	32.8	5.7	3.8	9.8	11.4	8.1	1.8	19.6	5.9	1.1
DEN	20.7	9.1		5.4	12.5	12.3	—	12.4	27.6	
LSAL	34.4	4.6	1.6	10.6	8.1	12.2	4.4	10.4	7.1	6.6
FIN	26.9	7.4	2.3	8.1	13.2	9.4	3.2	17.8	8.7	3.1
FRA	20.0	3.1	0.9	8.0	15.0	10.6	11.2	12.0	6.6	12.5
GER	24.8		2.3	10.7	16.3	13.0	3.1	12.6	7.2	10.0
GANA	53.7	3.8	1.2	14.2	11.5	3.7	1.4	3.3	3.8	3.4
GRCE	38.2	3.4	2.8	11.4	12.5	9.3	3.4	10.5	4.4	4.1
HOND	44.1	6.9	2.5	11.3	13.4	6.6	5.9	3.1	5.1	1.1
HOKO	32.8		1.8	8.6	14.8	8.0	7.8	7.3	7.4	11.5
ICE	20.4	5.1	2.7	9.2	15.5	11.7	7.7	14.4	6.9	6.5
INDA	59.7	2.2	2.5	7.7	7.7	3.6	2.1	7.6	3.2	3.7
IRE	26.5	14.6	5.6	8.1	12.4	7.7	2.3	9.8	8.0	5.0
ISRL	24.4	2.2	1.6	8.5	20.7	11.2	7.3	9.0	11.2	4.0
ITLY	31.3	3.1	2.3	8.6	13.4	6.0	8.5	11.0	5.6	10.2
JAMC	35.4	5.0	4.5	4.3	11.6	6.8	2.3	13.8	4.3	12.0
JAP		33.0		10.0	14.2	8.0		32.0		2.8
KORA	49.3	5.0	3.7	10.8	7.5	3.2	3.2	5.3	4.8	7.2
LIBY	34.5	1.1	2.8	10.0	18.1	4.5	3.0	12.9	3.7	9.4
MALY	37.2	2.6	5.0	5.8	13.1	6.7	2.0	13.4	5.9	8.4
MLTA	31.7	7.3	5.7	11.7	8.4	13.8	5.7	15.7	8.1	− 8.3
MAUR	26.1	8.5	3.3	4.5	—	7.3	2.2	7.8	5.8	30.5
NETH	19.7	3.3	2.4	9.2	13.5	10.8	11.2	9.7	8.5	11.6
NOR	21.6	5.0	2.4	8.6	13.1	8.9	8.6	11.9	8.1	11.8
PANM	59.2	5.6	2.1	6.6	14.7	10.4	6.1	9.4	7.8	− 21.9
PLIP	56.9	4.1	3.0	7.1	8.8	4.8	2.4	2.2	4.1	6.6
SRIL	57.7	3.2	6.6	8.0	6.8	3.4	1.7	10.0	2.6	0.0
SING	25.5	3.7	2.9	9.1	11.1	9.9	3.0	12.2	12.3	10.2
SPAN		37.7		11.1	14.9	9.2	4.4	12.0	8.4	2.5
SWE	20.1	5.4	2.6	7.2	19.9	6.6	4.1	14.2	8.7	11.3
SWIT	20.9	8.6		5.4	18.8	6.5	7.6	10.6	9.1	12.5
THAI	46.5	5.9	3.3	8.6	6.9	5.6	6.2	8.2	8.4	0.4
UK	18.4	8.6	4.4	8.6	19.3	7.3	1.0	13.5	10.0	9.0
US	14.4	1.9	1.5	7.3	19.5	7.5	10.8	15.1	8.6	13.4
YUG	38.0	8.2	3.4	11.7	—	9.9	4.2	10.8	3.9	3.3

Source: U.N., *Yearbook of National Accounts Statistics.*
a. Consumption categories: 1 = food; 2 = beverages (alcoholic and nonalcoholic); 3 = tobacco; 4 = clothing and footwear; 5 = gross rent, fuel, and power; 6 = furniture, equipment, and household operation; 7 = medical care and health expenses; 8 = transportation and communication; 9 = recreation, education, and entertainment; 10 = other (miscellaneous goods and services, statistical discrepancy, direct purchases abroad by resident HH, (—) direct purchases domestically by nonresidents, (—) net value of gifts in kind sent abroad).

where s is the GNP share Y/Y_w implied by the trade balance condition

$$0 = p'T = p'A^{-1}V - sp'A^{-1}V_w - p'C_0(L - sL_w),$$

where $p'C_0 = 0$, as noted previously.

Thus income dependent consumption shares of the linear form considered here call for a rather modest change in the model. We merely have to interpret the responsiveness of trade to the excess supply of labor $(L - sL_w)$ as arising from two sources—a production effect and a consumption effect. All other excess factor supplies have only the production effect $A^{-1}(V - sV_w)$. Countries with labor shares equal to GNP shares, or equivalently with per capita incomes equal to world per capita income, will have trade in conformance with the Heckscher-Ohlin-Vanek equations $T = A^{-1}(V - sV_w)$. Countries that have an abundance of labor will tend to import the commodities consumed by the poor, and conversely, countries that have a scarcity of labor will tend to import the commodities consumed by the rich. Regardless, trade remains a linear function of the endowments.

1.3.6   What Is Capital?

The traditional production theory that lists capital as one of the inputs often leaves capital undefined, and students who are given the task of measuring the capital used to produce a good are usually dumbfounded. One doctoral student proposed to study the textile industry at the firm level and prepared a questionnaire in which plant managers were requested to list how many workers were employed and how much capital was used. To this student, measurement of labor and measurement of capital are tasks requiring the same modest arithmetic skills—you simply add them up. A closer consideration of production processes suggests there are five classes of inputs: land, labor, other commodities, buildings, and machinery. Each one of these five categories can contain some "capital," and the problem of identifying the various components of capital and forming them into single composite is a difficult conceptual and empirical task.

Capital is listed as one of the inputs into a production process in an elliptical reference to the fact that production takes time. It might seem more realistic to write output as a function of the number of workers and the number of machines. But if machines are instantaneously produceable by labor and are completely consumed in the production process, then in fact output is an instantaneous function of labor alone. The tradition of writing capital as the input instead of machines is thus a reminder that it takes time to produce machinery and that machinery is only partially consumed by the production process. A second reason for writing capital instead of machines as the input is that there may be many alternative kinds of "machines" (also buildings, human capital, improvements to land, inventories) that under a special assumption can be aggregated into a single input, called capital. The special assumption is that the relative prices of all these inputs are constant. Any analysis by means of the static model that involves relative price changes—say, studies of technological change or analysis of tax effects—has to be viewed with great suspicion, since the capital aggregation is rendered inappropriate.

Whether the basic theorems of trade hold up when capital is treated seriously seems very doubtful, but Kemp (1973) and Ethier (1979b) have demonstrated that they do. The model considered by Ethier has two commodities and one primary input. It is assumed that it takes one period to produce commodities, with a production function depending on labor as the sole primary input and both of the commodities as intermediate inputs. The zero-profit condition if prices are constant can be written as

$$p = Bp(1 + \rho) + A_L w, \tag{1.13}$$

where $p = 2 \times 1$ vector of commodity prices, $B = 2 \times 2$ matrix of intermediate input requirements, $\rho = $ rate of interest, $A_L = 2 \times 1$ vector of labor inputs, and $w = $ wage rate paid at the end of the period. (To the student: How does this compare with the static model with intermediate inputs?)

The labor input to produce the vector of outputs X is $A'_L X$, and the full employment condition is

$$A'_L X = L.$$

The capital stock K is defined as the value of intermediate goods in process

$$p' B' X = K.$$

The row vector $p' B'$ defines the capital input requirements, and these two equations can be used to solve in the usual way for X as a function of K and L:

$$X = \begin{bmatrix} p'B' \\ A'_L \end{bmatrix}^{-1} \begin{bmatrix} K \\ L \end{bmatrix},$$ (1.14)

which is exactly the same as equation (1.1), from which we derived the Heckscher-Ohlin result. What has not been demonstrated, however, is the factor price equalization theorem, which is necessary to assure that B and A_L are the same for all countries. Because product prices are taken as given, the production functions can be written in terms of two inputs—labor and the Hicksian composite of the two intermediate goods, which we call capital. Factor price equalization then follows in exactly the same way as before—namely, there is only one wage/rental rate, $w/(1 + \rho)$, that could support the production of both commodities.

An explicit derivation of the Hicksian composite input is useful, since it emphasizes the fact that the capital composite depends on relative prices, which implies that relative prices are parameters of the production function relating output to capital and other inputs. Let the production function of X_1 be $X_1 = f(X_{11}, X_{12}, L)$, where X_{11} and X_{12} are intermediate inputs of goods 1 and 2 in the time-phased model. Efficient production requires that for every value of X_1 and L, the cost of X_{11} and X_{12} is minimized. Let this minimum cost be

$$C = \left\{ \min_{x_{11}, x_{12}} (1 + \rho)(p_1 X_{11} + p_2 X_{12}) | X_1 = f(X_{11}, X_{12}, L) \right\},$$

which is a nondecreasing function of X_1. (Minimal cost is an increasing function of output.) We may therefore invert this function to express X_1 as a function of L and C. This minimization is unaffected if instead we had minimized $C/(1 + \rho)p_2$. Thus we can write X_1 as a function of the labor input L, and the capital composite $K \equiv C/(1 + \rho)p_2 = (p_1/p_2)X_{11} + X_{12}$.

The production functions for X_1 and X_2 may therefore be written as $X_1 = F(K_1, L_1; p_1/p_2)$, $X_2 = G(K_2, L_2; p_1/p_2)$, where I have properly included the relative price p_1/p_2 as a parameter. A figure such as figure 1.1, which depicts isoquants, must implicitly be taking relative prices p_1/p_2 as given, since any change in p_1/p_2 will necessitate a change in the isoquants. This is unimportant for the factor price equalization theorem, the Heckscher-Ohlin theorem, and the Rybczynski theorem, since these results take prices as given. But the Stolper-Samuelson theorem and the Samuelson reciprocity relations deal with cases in which prices are explicitly variable. These results also apply to time-phased models, as can be seen by differentiating (1.13) and using the cost minimization conditions.[13]

As discussed by Kemp (1973) and Ethier (1979b), this model can be generalized to have any timing of inputs and any finite durabilities of capital. The basic trade theory, somewhat surprisingly, still remains unscathed by the charge that it treats capital naively.[14] But time is not an essential element in the static trade theorems, and the very difficult problems of defining and modeling capital in a dynamic world can therefore be avoided. Any study of dynamical changes would surely require a deeper treatment of capital than is evidenced by the traditional model that lists capital as an input along with other factors.

Chapter 1 has formulated the working hypothesis that serves as a foundation for the analysis of trade data to be presented and has also listed a large number of complicating factors. The impression that should have been created is that the working hypothesis summarized by the Heckscher-Ohlin-Vanek equations is extremely tidy, but also quite fragile. The set of alternative hypotheses generated by the relaxation of one or more of the unlikely assumptions underlying the HOV equations is vast, and none of the alternatives provides neat predictions of the composition of trade in a multicommodity, multifactor world. Formal statistical methods of testing hypotheses presuppose the existence of maintained and alternative hypotheses that are precisely defined, and consequently these formal methods cannot be used in our data analysis, unless they are amended to allow incredible maintained hypotheses and vague alternatives. The purpose of this chapter is to discuss what role data may play in such a setting and thereby to serve as a bridge between the theory of the previous chapter and the empirical work in the subsequent chapters. It is argued here that the HOV model is clearly incredible and can be rejected as a perfect description of reality without recourse to any data. The only credible theory entertained by economists is a vague amalgam of the many models that we use to illustrate distinct features of the workings of the economy. Though we can reject at the outset the HOV model as a complete description of reality, an empirical examination of the HOV proposition can nonetheless be fruitful if it focuses on the hypothesis that the HOV model is a sufficiently close approximation to reality that it can be useful for forecasting, for policy analysis, or for some other purpose. In order to test this hypothesis we would have to build an approximation to a complete model of the world to determine whether the simple HOV model serves our purposes as well as the more complex model or we would have to construct an alternative simple model and test to see which is the more useful. Neither of these can be done because the present state of economic theory does not allow us to articulate fully and precisely even simple alternative models of trade. As a result, the empirical analysis must focus on measuring the accuracy of the HOV model, but leave unstudied the accuracy of the unstated alternatives, and also leave untested the proposition that the HOV model is useful. However, if it were shown that the HOV model is very inaccurate, then it seems appropriate to suspect that the model is not very useful for predictions and policy. In that limited sense, the hypothesis that the HOV model is useful can and is tested.

Though the game of international economics has primarily been played at the theoretical level, there are nonetheless a fairly substantial number of recent papers that purport to offer tests of trade theories. This book may also be viewed as a test of the Heckscher-Ohlin model, though I think that is something of an overstatement. In this chapter I discuss what it would mean to test the theory, and I offer methodological comments on the empirical literature relating to testing the theory. Deardorff (1982b) and Stern (1975) also provide reviews of the empirical testing of trade theories, including summaries of the principal findings.

2.1 What Are the Hypotheses?

A careful formulation of a maintained hypothesis is the first step in a proper empirical test. This may seem so obvious that it need not be stated, but, as will be discussed subsequently, much of the literature on testing trade theory flounders precisely because inadequate effort was made to define the theory to be tested. The second step is to formulate an alternative hypothesis and to identify observable phenomena about which the maintained hypothesis and the alternative offer different predictions. As a matter of fact, the trade theories have usually been examined empirically without a clear statement of any alternative. In that event, whether the maintained hypothesis is accepted or rejected is a matter of aesthetics and judgment.

For example, suppose that there were only 2 goods and 2 factors in the world, and let us construct a program for testing the Heckscher-Ohlin hypothesis: "A country will export the commodity that uses intensively its relatively abundant factor." This is a statement about three separately measurable quantities (factor intensities, factor abundance, and trade), and a test of the theory would begin by measuring these three concepts and would then determine the extent to which they conform to the predictions of the theory. No one expects the theory to be exactly correct, and it would be mistaken to claim that the theory failed if it offered an incorrect prediction in only a single instance. Suppose that 35 out of a total of 60 countries have trade in conformance with the theory. Does the theory pass or fail? A proper answer to this question requires an alternative hypothesis, for example, the scale economy hypothesis:

"Countries with relatively large labor forces have a comparative advantage in the commodity that exhibits relatively large scale economies." Measurement difficulties may be supposed to force us to specialize this hypothesis to "There exists a critical value for the labor force, say L^*, such that all countries with labor forces in excess of L^* will export one good and all other countries will export the other good." Suppose this alternative hypothesis correctly predicts the trade pattern of only 30 of the 60 countries. Formal statistical analysis would then have us conclude that the Heckscher-Ohlin hypothesis is favored by the data as compared with the scale economies model. But let us consider whether this makes much sense. Suppose that out of the 25 incorrect predictions of the HO model, the scale economy model makes 20 correct predictions. This suggests that a combined theory would be greatly favored over either individually. When you stop to think about it, neither of the simpler hypotheses is really credible, the first since it makes the unlikely assumption that returns to scale are absolutely constant, the second since it makes the unlikely assumption that factor intensities in the two industries are identical. We therefore began this hypothesis-testing exercise with two incredible theories, and each can be rejected without appeal to any observations.

A hypothesis that cannot be rejected at the outset is the following: "The Heckscher-Ohlin model is more useful than the scale economies model." To test this kind of hypothesis, we shall have to identify the uses to which the theory is to be put. The principal function that the trade theory serves is to introduce students to the sometimes surprising implications of a general equilibrium analysis of an economic system. Without a doubt, the HO model is greatly superior to the scale economies theory for pedagogical purposes. Why else would it fill our textbooks? Another function of the HO model is the derivation of policy conclusions, especially the support of free trade, which appeals to conservative economists, who generally suppose that government intervention works to the disadvantage of some and probably all. The policy implications of the scale economy model can be quite different, which suggests this hypothesis: "The HO model serves as a more accurate guide for trade policy than the scale economy model." How is such a hypothesis to be tested? The answer is that the more general model that allows both scale economies and differences in factor intensities would have to be formulated and estimated, and the consequences of acting as if one of the simpler models were true would have to be computed. The model that is least misleading would be the one favored by the data.

The attempt to test the usefulness of the HO model properly requires us to identify a reasonably complete general model of international trade and to determine whether the restrictions implied by the simple HO model do great damage to policy decisions. The complete model includes such things as scale economies, nontraded goods, externalities, imperfect competition . . . . Unfortunately we are currently in the situation in which only the simple HO model can be fully defined. Even the inclusion of scale economies causes great difficulties in estimation. Therefore the kind of data analysis we can perform unfortunately terminates with statements about the quality of the model such as this: "The HO model correctly predicts the trade of 35 of 60 countries." To put this another way, we are able only to measure the accuracy of the HO model, when what we really want to do is to test the usefulness of this model compared with some other model. But it does seem reasonable to infer that an accurate model is likely also to be a useful model or, at least, the converse, that an inaccurate model is unlikely to be a useful model. For example, if the HO model correctly predicted the trade of 55 out of 60 countries, we may intuitively, though without a complete formal justification, conclude that the model is likely to serve as a useful guide for policy action, since there does not seem to be much role left for other factors such as scale economies. The exact degree of accuracy at which the data can be said to cast doubt on the usefulness of the HO model is a matter of judgment. It is my hope that the data analysis reported subsequently reveals that the HOV model is surprisingly accurate, so much so that the model seems more useful than it did at the outset.

2.2 Measuring the Accuracy of the Heckscher-Ohlin Predictions

If there were only 2 goods and 2 factors, the accuracy of the HO model could be easily determined. The model predicts that a country would export the commodity that uses intensively the relatively abundant resource. We could therefore measure the three concepts intensities, factor abundance, and trade and could report the number of countries that conform to the prediction. However, the multifactor, multigood model does not generate clear predictions about which goods are exported and which are imported. A convenient generalization of the HO model that applies to the 2×2 world as well as to the $n \times m$ world is summarized by the HOV equations

$$AT = V - sV_w, \tag{2.1}$$

where A is the matrix of factor intensities, T is the vector of net exports, V is the vector of factor endowments, V_w is the world's factor endowments, and s is the consumption share. A proper measure of the accuracy of the theory begins with independent measures of these three concepts and determines the extent to which they conform to the HOV equations. But what is meant by conformity? In the 2×2 model we have proposed in effect a comparison of the predicted trade vector $\hat{T} = A^{-1}(V - sV_w)$ with the actual trade vector. If the signs conform, the model is said to be perfectly accurate. Otherwise it is inaccurate. As a measure of the conformity of the data to the Vanek equations, this leaves much to be desired even in the 2×2 case, since it deals with only one aspect of the theory— namely, which good is exported—when, as a matter of fact, the theory offers much more precise predictions about the quantitative relations among the three measurable phenomena. Moreover, in more realistic settings, a measured A matrix is usually not square and it is impossible to compute the predicted trade. It is therefore essential to abandon the version of the 2×2 model that predicts which good will be exported in favor of the general HOV model.

The HOV equations are a set of relations between factor intensities and trade and resource endowments. Most studies of trade have used measures of two of these sets of variables and have inferred the third. Factor content studies, the most famous of which is Leontief (1953), take measures of trade T and factor intensities A and from them infer the factor abundance vector $V - sV_w$. Cross-section regression studies such as Baldwin (1971) also use measures of A and T to infer $V - sV_w$. Cross-section studies such as Chenery (1960) and Leamer (1974), as well as this book, use measures of trade T and endowments V and implicitly infer the inverse of the matrix of intensities A. But the way to measure the accuracy of the theory would be to obtain direct and independent measures of all three concepts and to determine the extent to which these measurements conform to the HOV equations. These studies, which use measures of only two of the three concepts, cannot be said to be measuring the accuracy of the HOV theory. Though Hufbauer (1970) does use measures of all three concepts, his method of calculating their conformity to the HOV equations is not entirely correct—actually the HOV equations are never explicitly acknowledged as the foundation for any of this work. Only Bowen, Leamer, and Sveikauskus (1982) use measures of all three concepts and explicitly refer to the HOV equations.

In addition to measuring only two of the three theoretical concepts, many studies use inappropriate generalizations of the 2×2 model to worlds with more factors and/or more goods, and these studies consequently make inappropriate inferences about the third, unmeasured, concept. The classic example is Leontief's (1953) "test," which compares the capital per man embodied in \$1 million worth of imports with the capital per man embodied in \$1 million worth of exports. This comparison is shown in Leamer (1980) not to reveal the relative abundance of capital and labor in a multifactor world.

A second measurement of the accuracy of the theory involves regressions for a given country across commodities of net exports on factor input intensities, as in Baldwin (1971), Branson and Monoyios (1977), Harkness (1978), and others. If the estimated coefficient of some factor is positive, the country is inferred to be abundantly supplied in that resource. This too is an inappropriate inference in a multifactor world, as shown in Leamer and Bowen (1981).

A third variety of study regresses net exports across countries on measures of factor endowments, as in Leamer (1974), Chenery and Syrquin (1975), and in this book. This type of study, though conceptually appropriate, cannot be said to be a complete measurement of the accuracy of the theory because it uses no data on factor intensities. The approach can be said to be measuring the accuracy of a weaker version of the theory that does not depend on factor intensities, namely: "There exists a matrix A such that $AT = V - sV_w$."

Each of these approaches is now discussed in detail.

2.2.1   Factor Content Studies

The classic empirical measurement of the accuracy of the HO model produced a result that appeared to contradict the theory. Leontief's (1953) calculation that U.S. imports were more capital intensive than her exports was interpreted to mean that trade revealed the United States to be scarce in capital compared with labor, when it was taken for granted that the reverse was true. This result was so upsetting to trade theorists at the time that it was given the provocative name "the Leontief paradox," and it spawned an enormous literature that sought to explain the finding by enlarging or altering the simple theory to include such things as tariffs, human capital, knowledge capital, monopolistic competition, and so on. It is hard to identify another empirical finding in economics that has had such an enormous impact on how economists have spent their time. Alas, the paradox rests on a simple conceptual misunderstanding, as is shown in Leamer (1980). If the correct calculations are done, the United States is revealed by trade to be relatively abundant in capital compared with labor. But, as Brecher and Choudri (1982) point out, correct calculations also imply that the United States was labor abundant, not compared with capital, but rather compared with an average of all resources. This is difficult to square with the facts, and the U.S. export of labor services embodied in trade has to be regarded as an observation in contradiction of the theory.

The impropriety of the Leontief inference is a consequence of the fact that the inference is made without benefit of a fully articulated theory.* The HOV equations (2.1) serve as a logically sound foundation for a study of trade-revealed factor abundance. Two of these equations describe the relation between capital and labor endowments and the implicit trade in capital and labor services:

$$K_T = K - sK_w, \tag{2.2}$$

$$L_T = L - sL_w, \tag{2.3}$$

where K_T and L_T are capital and labor services embodied in net exports, K and L are the factor endowments of the country in question, K_w and L_w are the world's factor endowments, and s is the country's consumption share. These two equations can be manipulated to obtain the conditions under which trade reveals the country to be capital abundant:

THEOREM 2.1   Capital is revealed by trade to be abundant relative to labor, $K/K_w > L/L_w$, if and only if

$$K/(K - K_T) > L/(L - L_T). \tag{2.4}$$

Proof   Equations (2.2) and (2.3) can be rewritten as $K/K_w = sK/(K - K_T)$ and $L/L_w = sL/(L - L_T)$, from which (2.4) is a direct consequence.   ∎

*The following material, until the end of the proof of Corollary 2, is taken in part from Leamer (1980).

There are three useful ways of rewriting (2.4). If $K_c = sK_w$ is the amount of capital embodied in the commodities used in the country, then $K - K_T = K_c$ and, similarly, $L - L_T = L_c$. Then (2.4) is equivalent to

$$K/L > K_c/L_c = K_w/L_w, \tag{2.4a}$$

which means that a country is revealed to be capital abundant if its production is more capital intensive than its consumption.

Another way to rewrite (2.3) is $K(L - L_T) > L(K - K_T)$, or

$$-KL_T > -LK_T. \tag{2.4b}$$

If L_T is positive, then this inequality becomes $K_T/L_T > K/L$, or $K_T/K > L_T/L$. Thus a country that is an exporter of both labor services and capital services is revealed by trade to be relatively capital abundant if trade is more capital intensive than production, or, equivalently, if the share of capital exported exceeds the share of labor exported. If L_T is negative, the last two inequalities are reversed.

Yet another possibility is to rewrite (2.4) as $-(K_c + K_T)L_T > -(L_c + L_T)K_T$, or

$$-K_c L_T > -L_c K_T. \tag{2.4c}$$

Thus a country that is an exporter of both labor services and capital services is revealed by trade to be relatively capital abundant if the capital intensity of net exports exceeds the capital intensity of consumption, $K_T/L_T > K_c/L_c$, and a country that is an importer of both capital and labor services is revealed by trade to be capital abundant if the capital intensity of net exports is less than the capital intensity of consumption, $K_T/L_T < K_c/L_c$.

Inequalities (2.4a), (2.4b), and (2.4c) identify three equivalent ways of computing trade-revealed factor abundance. Trade even more directly reveals relative capital abundance if the services of one factor are exported and the services of the other are imported, since inequality (2.4b) is satisfied if $K_T > 0$ and $L_T < 0$ and is violated if $K_T < 0$ and $L_T > 0$. For reference, this will be stated as a corollary.

COROLLARY 1   If the net export of capital services and the net export of labor services are opposite in sign, then the factor with positive net exports is revealed to be the relatively abundant factor.

Theorem 2.1 and corollary 1 imply that one should be examining the factor content of *net* exports, but the tradition beginning with Leontief is to distinguish exports from imports. In some cases, this is an equivalent procedure.

COROLLARY 2   Given that the net export of capital services and the net export of labor services are opposite in sign, the capital per man embodied in exports (K_x/L_x) exceeds the capital per man embodied in imports (K_m/L_m) if and only if the country is relatively abundant in capital, $K/K_w > L/L_w$.

Proof Suppose first that $K_T > 0$ and $L_T < 0$; then by corollary 1, $K/K_w > L/L_w$. But $0 < K_T = K_x - K_m$ implies $K_x/K_m > 1$, and $0 > L_T = L_x - L_m$ implies $1 > L_x/L_m$. Thus $K_x/K_m > L_x/L_m$, and $K_x/L_x > K_m/L_m$. Similarly, $K_T < 0$ and $L_T > 0$ imply both $K/K_w < L/L_w$ and $K_x/L_x < K_m/L_m$. ■

A substantial practical defect of corollary 2 is that it assumes that K_T and L_T are opposite in sign. In fact, using Leontief's 1947 U.S. data, K_T and L_T are both positive; the United States exported both capital services and labor services. In that event, the ordering $K_x/L_x < K_m/L_m$ reveals nothing about the relative magnitudes of K/K_w and L/L_w. See Leamer (1980) for an example of the paradoxical case: $K_x/L_x < K_m/L_m$ and $K/K_w > L/L_w$. A proper procedure when $K_T > 0$ and $L_T > 0$ is to compare K_T/L_T with K/L or with K_c/L_c. As it turns out, using Leontief's data and measures of endowments, we find that $K_T/L_T > K/L > K_c/L_c$, and the United States is revealed to be more abundant in capital than in labor.

Still, as Brecher and Choudri (1982) observe, it seems surprising that the United States was a net exporter of labor services. Using (2.3), we may derive the conclusion that $L_T > 0$ implies $L/L_w > s$. If the trade balance is denoted $B = p'T$, then the Vanek equations imply that the consumption share is $s = (Y - B)/Y_w$, where Y is GNP and Y_w is world GNP. The condition $L/L_w > s$ can therefore be written as $Y_w/L_w > (Y - B)/L$. Thus U.S. trade revealed that world per capita output exceeded U.S. per capita output, adjusted for the trade balance. As a matter of fact, U.S. per capita GNP was surely in excess of world per capita GNP, even after adjustment for the trade surplus, and this finding contradicts the theory. A natural explanation is Leontief's own explanation for his nonparadox: U.S. workers were more skilled than their foreign counterparts. Though aggregation across skill groups cannot explain this finding, it may be suspected that the U.S. exports the services of skilled workers but imports the services of unskilled workers. Information reported in table 2.1 from Keesing (1966) can be used to check this conjecture. The first row in this table reveals that even after disaggregation, the United States was a net exporter of labor services in every skill category. But the third row indicates that the proportion of the domestic supply embodied in net exports is large only for scientists and engineers, and technicians and draftsmen. These are consequently revealed by trade to be most abundant. Though the lower skilled categories have positive net exports, the numbers are so small that they may be explainable by the trade surplus. In another study, Stern and Maskus (1981) found that the United States was a net exporter of the services of physical capital, human capital, and labor in 1958, but a net importer of all three in 1972. The revealed abundance ordering in 1958 was human capital > labor > physical capital, and in 1972 was physical capital > human capital > labor.

Notes on the Literature   A number of other studies have applied the Leontief approach to other data sets. Tatemoto and Ichimura (1959) find that 1951 Japanese exports were more capital intensive than imports. Roskamp (1963) report that 1954 West German exports were more labor intensive than imports. Vanek (1963) finds 1947 U.S. exports to be less intensive in natural resources than imports. Keesing (1965, 1966) studies the skill content of trade of several OECD countries and reports that the U.S. exports have relatively high skill inputs compared to imports. Fareed (1972) also examines the "human capital" intensity of U.S. trade, using cost of schooling as a measure of human capital. He, like Keesing, finds exports more skill intensive than imports. Weiser (1968) for the United States and Heller (1976) for Japan report changes in factor content of trade over time. Baldwin's (1971) study of the United States is particularly noteworthy in extending the list of "resources" to include "unionization" and "concentration" and "scale economies", and also in studying the factor content of bilateral trade. But all of this research lacks a completely adequate conceptual foundation.

2.2.2   Cross-Commodity Studies of Trade and Input Intensities

Much of the empirical analysis of trade composition has sought an explanation of the trade of a particular country, often the United States,

Table 2.1
U.S. net exports of labor services by skill group (thousands of man-years; 1960 U.S. skill intensities): 1962[a]

	I	II	III	IV	V	VI	VII	VIII
(1) Net exports[b]	24.7	13.8	11.7	16.9	43.7	53.6	55.3	108.9
(2) Factor supply[c]	1,091.3	798.7	5,579.0	7,067	1,037	7,517	13,986	28,702
(1)/(2)	.0226	.0173	.0021	.0024	.0421	.0071	.0040	.0038

a. Skill classes are I = scientists and engineers, II = technicians and draftsmen, III = other professionals, IV = managers, V = machinists, electricians, and tool and diemakers, VI = other skilled manual workers, VII = clerical workers, VIII = unskilled and semiskilled workers.
b. Source: Keesing (1966, p. 257).
c. Source: U.S. Bureau of Labor Statistics, *Occupational Employment Statistics*, 1960–1967.

in terms of characteristics of the traded commodities. For example, a typical result is Baldwin's (1971) regression:

$$T_j = -1.37k_j - 421s_j + 343u_j + \cdots, \qquad R^2 = .44,$$
$$ (-4.35) \quad (-1.25) \quad (1.11)$$

where $T_j = $ U.S. net exports of commodity j in 1962, $k_j = $ capital per man in industry j, $s_j = $ scale index, and $u_j = $ unionization index. The negative sign of the capital intensity variable means that export success is negatively related to capital intensity. This seems surprising if the United States is thought of as a capital abundant country, and Baldwin uses this result as regression confirmation of the Leontief paradox. This conclusion rests on the intuitively appealing, but nonetheless false, proposition that the signs of the estimated regression coefficients are the same as the signs of the excess factor supplies $V - sV_w$. Suppose, as in Leamer and Bowen (1981), that we maintain the HOV equations and ask what can be expected if the trade vector is regressed on the factor intensities. The proposition, in the form of a regression equation, is $T = A'b$, which says that the net exports of each commodity is a linear function of the factor intensities in the production of that commodity. The least-squares estimate of the vector of coefficients b is $b = (AA')^{-1}AT$, which can be written using the HOV equations as $b = (AA')^{-1}(V - sV_w)$. The claim that b and $V - sV_w$ have the same signs is mathematically equivalent to the assertion that the transformation matrix $(AA')^{-1}$ preserves the signs of the elements of $V - sV_w$. The assumptions of the HOV theorem do imply that A is a positive matrix, but except in the 2-factor case, this is not sufficient to guarantee that b and $V - sV_w$ have the same signs. Leamer and Bowen (1981) offer a counterexample.

Aside from the fact that the cross-section regressions cannot yield reliable measures of the excess factor supply vector $V - sV_w$, it is distinctly peculiar to resort to a regression analysis to measure factor abundance when a direct computation of the factor content of trade AT is in theory exactly equal to the excess factor supply vector $V - sV_w$. But this conclusion that it makes little sense to run cross-section regressions of measures of trade performance on measures of factor intensities is derived within the context of a model in which factor prices are equalized. Hilton (1982) sketches a logic for running this type of regression when factor prices are not equalized. Suppose all countries share the same fixed input intensities but have different factor costs. The vector of zero-profit prices offered by country c is then $p_c = A'w_c$, where A is the matrix of factor intensities, assumed to be the same in all countries, and w_c is the vector of factor returns in country c. Country c will be a producer and maybe an exporter of commodity j if it is a low cost producer, that is, if $p_{jc} < p_{jc'}$, for all $c' \neq c$. If there were only two distinct possible values for the vector of factor returns, then this condition can be written as $\sum_i A_{ij}(w_{ic} - w_{ic'}) \leq 0$. If only a subset of the factor intensities is observable, then this condition can be written probabilistically as

$$\text{Prob(commodity } j \text{ is produced)} = \text{Prob}\left(\sum_{i \in I} A_{ij}(w_{ic} - w_{ic'}) \leq z \right),$$

where I is the subset of observable factor intensities with complement $\bar{I}$ and z is the unobservable "random" variable $z = \sum_{i \in \bar{I}} A_{ij}(w_{ic} - w_{ic'})$. This suggests doing an analysis with a zero-one dependent variable indicating whether the item is exported or imported, and with factor intensities as explanatory variables. The estimated coefficients are then interpreted as factor cost differences, and in that sense this type of analysis can be said to be appropriately measuring factor abundance. This is exactly the type of analysis suggested by Harkness and Kyle (1975), who argue somewhat inconclusively that the HO model should be interpreted as predicting the sign of net exports, not the level. The defects of this approach at a conceptual level should be clear from the derivation just presented. Namely, the data analysis improperly uses trade data when production data are required by the theory. At any sensible level of aggregation all products are produced, and either the sharp theory can be rejected at the outset or it must be inferred that all countries have the same factor costs. Furthermore, if there are more than two possible factor cost vectors, a more complex analysis is required.[1]

It is therefore rather difficult to provide much theoretical support for these cross-commodity regression studies, and this serves as a second illustration of the need for a fully articulated theoretical structure to support a data analysis. Though these regression equations have a surface plausibility, the need for a theory is further apparent when you try to select a precise econometric specification, a task that necessarily requires answers to questions such as the following: How should the dependent variable be scaled since there are some very large industries and some very small? To put it differently: How can I set up the analysis so that my conclusions do not depend on an arbitrarily chosen level of aggregation? Should my explanatory variables be factor intensities, factor shares, or the ratio of intensities (like capital per man)? Should I distinguish exports from imports?

Another type of ad hoc cross-section data analysis involving measures of A and T uses simple correlation rather than multiple correlation. For example, Keesing (1967) reports that the cross-commodity correlation between the variable (U.S. exports/group of 10 exports) and the variable (research and development expenditures/sales) is .90, and he uses this as evidence that the United States is abundantly supplied in knowledge capital. This is actually very close to a factor content calculation. The cross-commodity correlation between net exports and a row of the intensity matrix, say A_i, is $= \text{cov}(T, A_i)/(\sqrt{\text{var}(T)}\sqrt{\text{var}(A_i)})$, where cov is the covariance and var is the variance. If trade is measured in value terms and if trade is balanced, then average trade $\overline{T}$ is zero and $\text{cov}(T, A_i) = A_i'T_i/n - \overline{TA} = A_i'T/n$. Then the sign of the correlation is necessarily equal to the sign of the factor content $A_i'T$. In that sense, a simple cross-commodity correlation study can be said to be an indirect factor content study, but again the question needs to be asked why a direct calculation of factor content is not done instead.

The one study that comes closest to providing a proper measure of the accuracy of the HOV model is Hufbauer's (1970). Among other things, Hufbauer computes $y_1 =$ capital per man embodied in exports, $y_2 =$ capital per man embodied in imports, and $x =$ capital per man endowments for each of 24 countries. He reports that y_1 and x have a cross-country correlation of .625 and that y_2 and x have a cross-country correlation of $-.353$, and he uses this as evidence in favor of the factor abundance theory. This is not completely in harmony with the HOV model, though it is pretty close. Using the HOV model, we would not distinguish exports from imports and we would not necessarily combine capital and labor. The HOV equation (2.2) suggests regressing capital embodied in net exports on capital abundance and GNP adjusted for the trade balance. If the multiple correlation is high and if the sign of the GNP coefficient is negative, the theory can be said to be accurate.

Cross-commodity regression studies not heretofore referred to include Branson (1971), Branson and Junz (1971), Lowinger (1975), Branson and Monoyios (1977), and Stern and Maskus (1981).

2.2.3   Cross-Country Studies of Trade and Resource Endowments

The factor content studies and the cross-commodity regressions use measures of factor intensities A and trade T to infer factor endowments V.

The other major type of data analysis computes cross-country regressions with data on T and V, implicitly inferring A. Examples of cross-country regressions include Chenery (1960), Chenery and Taylor (1968), Leamer (1974), Chenery and Syrquin (1975), and Bowen (1981). This is the approach taken in this book, and a full discussion of the empirical issues is presented in chapters 5 and 6. Here it suffices to observe that the maintained hypothesis is the even model, which allows us to write the trade vector as $T = A^{-1}(V - sV_w)$. This implies that cross-country regressions of net exports on excess factor supplies $V - sV_w$ provide estimates of A^{-1}. The HOV model is then judged to be accurate if the R^2 values of these regressions are high, though it needs to be understood that this is a weakened form of the model, which makes no reference to factor intensities. In place of the hypothesis that A, T, and V fit together as predicted by the HOV equation, we substitute the hypothesis that T is a linear function of V. Interpreted as sharp hypotheses, these statements are virtually identical. The even HOV model implies linearity, and conversely, linearity almost surely implies the even HOV model. However, interpreted as approximations, these two hypotheses may be quite different. It is conceivable that trade is "approximately" a linear function of endowments, but at the same time the HOV equations do not hold, even "approximately." I shall ignore this possibility, since it depends on fuzzy notions concerning the adequacy of an approximation, and I shall proceed as if the demonstration of the accuracy of the estimated linear trade model were necessarily a demonstration of the accuracy of the HOV model.

3 Formation of the Trade Aggregates

The number of commodities that are internationally traded is enormous, and no empirical analysis with a limited time and money budget could analyze each separately. Moreover, no consumer of research results is willing to tolerate too much detail. Some method of aggregation is therefore essential. The goal of the aggregation methods discussed in this chapter is to identify a list of aggregates that is brief enough to be quickly learned and easily remembered, but not so brief that essential features of the trade data are hidden.

The 10 aggregates that are studied in this book are formed from the 61 2-digit SITC (Standard Industrial Trade Classification) commodity classes. For each year under study, the aggregation analysis begins with the 61 × 61 matrix of cross-country correlations of the net export data, using trade data from as many as 60 countries. A high correlation in a given year between two commodity classes indicates that these commodities behave similarly in international trade in the sense that if a country has large positive net exports of one, then it also has large net exports of the other. An example is SITC 24, wood, and SITC 25, pulp. Countries tend either to export both wood and pulp or to import both. When such a high correlation is found, these classes are combined into one, since the forces that determine trade in a component are likely to be the same as those that determine trade in the corresponding aggregate.

Two different aggregation methods were studied. The first uses an algorithm based on the correlation matrix alone. The second begins with a set of cross-section regressions of the net export data on a list of resources, and commodities are then aggregated that have similar regression coefficients. The 10 aggregates that are used in this book are based partly on the output of these methods and are partly the result of a certain amount of "fiddling" designed to produce a plausible set of aggregates.[1]

The correlations between the aggregates and their components are reported in section 3.1. The 10 aggregates are formed from the 61 2-digit SITC categories. The effects of beginning at a lower level of aggregation are discussed in section 3.2, where 3-digit data are explored. In several cases, it seems desirable to allocate the components of a 2-digit category to different aggregates, but overall the effort required to analyze the 3-digit data does not seem worth the effort. Finally, in section 3.3 a very interesting question is addressed: Is the theoretical model capable of generating these kinds of clusters? The disturbing answer is, "Not so easily." If factor prices are equalized, there is actually an opposite tendency; countries will tend to concentrate output in only one of several products with similar input mixes. Even if factor prices are not equalized, there is no clear-cut tendency to produce clusters of commodities. The conclusion that seems warranted is that the existence of these clusters casts a shadow on the subsequent data analysis, but not a shadow so dark that the data analysis must be ignored.

3.1 Cluster Correlations

The 10 aggregates that are used in this book are listed together with their components in table 3.1. There are 2 primary product aggregates (petroleum, raw materials), 4 crops (forest products, tropical/Mediterranean agricultural products, animal products, and cereals) and 4 manufactured aggregates (labor intensive, capital intensive, machinery, and chemicals). These 10 aggregates will henceforth be abbreviated PETRO, MAT, FOR, TROP, ANL, CER, LAB, CAP, MACH, and CHEM, respectively.

Correlations of the component net export data with the aggregate data are reported in table 3.1. Generally speaking, these correlations are high and the formation of the aggregates is successful. One of the tightest clusters is the forest product group. Three of the components of this group use forest resources rather directly to produce output. The fourth, wood and cork manufactures, combines wood inputs with capital and labor. Not surprisingly, this is the component that is least correlated with the aggregate. In fact, in 2 years, as indicated in table 3.2, this commodity is correlated more with the labor intensive manufacturing group than with the forest product group.

Table 3.2 indicates when a component is correlated more with another aggregate than with its own aggregate. For example, SITC 32, coal, is more correlated with the cereals group in every year than with the raw materials group. I have resisted reallocating this and other commodities to other aggregates because I wanted to maintain the content of the aggregate labels. A group "cereals and coal" would cause more confusion than it is worth in terms of slightly better formed aggregates in a statistical sense. Another reason why this table reveals apparent misallocations is that the movement of a component changes the aggregates, and an attempt to cure one problem often generates others. Thus the aggregates are compromises, but they capture the essential features of the trade data, without undue distortions. Still, I am not so sure that SITC 43, processed

Table 3.1
Cross-country correlations of components with aggregates, net export data

SITC	Description	1958	1960	1963	1966	1969	1972	1975
	1. Petroleum (PETRO)							
33	Petroleum, petroleum products	1.0	1.0	1.0	1.0	1.0	1.0	1.0
	2. Raw materials (MAT)							
27	Crude fertilizers, crude materials	.88	.88	.87	.80	.87	.82	.72
28	Metaliferous ores, metal scrap	.87	.89	.88	.92	.96	.96	.94
32	Coal, coke, briquettes	−.11	−.06	.03	−.02	.32	.39	.64
34	Gas, natural and manufactured	.11	.26	.57	.69	.57	.62	.62
35	Electrical energy	.37	.30	.02	.12	.07	.20	.31
68	Nonferrous metals	.86	.88	.83	.84	.85	.77	.64
	3. Forest products (FOR)							
24	Wood, lumber, cork	.92	.92	.90	.84	.82	.87	.77
25	Pulp, waste paper	.95	.94	.95	.96	.96	.93	.92
63	Wood, cork manufactures	.69	.72	.64	.61	.52	.62	.58
64	Paper, paperboard	.91	.90	.93	.91	.89	.88	.82
	4. Tropical agriculture (TROP)							
5	Fruit, vegetables	.53	.54	.60	.67	.67	.67	.62
6	Sugar, sugar preparations, honey	.79	.77	.80	.80	.78	.75	.77
7	Coffee, tea, cocoa, spices, etc.	.91	.89	.87	.88	.87	.84	.84
11	Beverages	.50	.52	.43	.46	.50	.55	.43
23	Crude rubber	.57	.52	.41	.33	.45	.28	.29
	5. Animal products (ANL)							
0	Live animals	.73	.76	.70	.70	.59	.55	.64
1	Meat, meat preparations	.95	.96	.97	.97	.96	.95	.96
2	Dairy products, eggs	.78	.90	.83	.82	.74	.77	.82
3	Fish, fish preparations	.58	.54	.56	.59	.61	.60	.55
21	Hides, skins, furskins, undressed	.80	.80	.82	.78	.70	.43	.54
29	Crude animal, vegetable minerals	.80	.81	.79	.76	.74	.70	.67
43	Animal, vegetable oils, processed	.27	.01	−.13	.18	.23	.10	.13
94	Animal, n.e.s.	.37	.02	.58	.51	.49	.49	.43
	6. Cereals, etc. (CER)							
4	Cereals, cereal preparations	.91	.93	.92	.94	.93	.95	.98
8	Feeding stuff of animals	.64	.68	.74	.79	.82	.85	.82
9	Miscellaneous food preparations	.63	.68	.71	.38	.66	.57	.52
12	Tobacco, tobacco manufactures	.83	.86	.84	.85	.86	.90	.90
22	Oil seeds, oil nuts, oil kernels	.78	.84	.87	.91	.91	.95	.94

Code	Category							
26	Textile fibers	.80	.85	.70	.58	.70	.64	.76
41	Animal oils, fats	.84	.92	.89	.91	.92	.92	.92
42	Fixed vegetable oils	.74	.65	.54	.45	.46	.38	.15
	7. Labor intensive (LAB)							
66	Nonmetallic mineral manufactures	.65	.77	.50	.83	.92	.88	.72
82	Furniture	.80	.55	.12	.45	.65	.59	.54
83	Travel goods, handbags, etc.	.45	.70	.53	.84	.96	.96	.94
84	Clothing	.55	.81	.79	.89	.91	.91	.85
85	Footwear	.35	.65	.73	.82	.91	.87	.89
89	Miscellaneous manufactured articles, n.e.s.	.70	.47	.19	.67	.80	.80	.71
91	Postal Pack. not classified according to kind	.70	.52	.31	.20	.05	.08	-.05
93	Special Trans. not classified according to kind	.16	.12	.50	.67	.78	.70	.55
96	Coin nongold, noncurrent	.00	-.01	-.32	.04	.24	-.22	-.31
	8. Capital intensive (CAP)							
61	Leather, dressed furskins	.23	.16	.19	.26	.27	.18	.11
62	Rubber manufactures, n.e.s.	.79	.68	.66	.59	.79	.68	.77
65	Textile yarn, fabrics, etc.	.78	.76	.77	.87	.90	.90	.79
67	Iron and steel	.87	.83	.83	.90	.95	.93	.98
69	Manufactures of metal	.82	.77	.70	.66	.83	.76	.87
81	Sanitary, fixtures, fittings	.72	.60	.38	.43	.39	.40	.39
	9. Machinery (MACH)							
71	Machinery, other than electrical	.99	.99	.98	.98	.88	.95	.94
72	Electrical machinery	.99	.98	.98	.94	.93	.90	.97
73	Transport equipment	.97	.98	.97	.94	.87	.92	.92
86	Professional goods, instruments, watches	.47	.62	.74	.76	.80	.81	.82
95	Firearms, ammunition	.82	.77	.72	.62	.26	.53	.51
	10. Chemicals (CHEM)							
51	Chemical elements, compounds	.93	.92	.93	.94	.89	.92	.94
52	Mineral tar and crude chemicals from coal, petroleum, natural gas	-.18	.58	.71	.48	.19	.64	-.05
53	Dyeing, tanning, coloring materials	.86	.80	.76	.75	.80	.74	.78
54	Medicinal, pharmaceutical products	.94	.92	.91	.86	.78	.85	.71
55	Essential oils, perfume materials	.76	.77	.75	.67	.57	.73	.59
56	Fertilizers, manufactured	.37	.37	.41	.59	.34	.47	.62
57	Explosives, pyrotechnic products	.76	.66	.70	.29	.48	.05	.53
58	Plastic materials, cellulose, etc.	.81	.92	.95	.93	.90	.91	.91
59	Chemical material, n.e.s.	.97	.91	.88	.94	.92	.94	.93

Table 3.2
Classification problems—component is more correlated with aggregate indicated than with its own aggregate (maximum correlation indicated by*)

SITC	1958	1960	1963	1966	1969	1972	1975
1. 33							
2. 27							
28							6
32	6, 7, 8, 9, 10*	6, 8, 9, 10*	6, 9*, 10	6, 9, 10*	6*, 9, 10	6*, 10	6
34	3*, 8	3	3	3	3	3	3
35	3	3	3*, 7, 8	3	5		1
68							2
3. 24				2	2	2	
25							
63							
64				4	4*, 7	4*, 7	
4. 5	5	5					
6							
7				7	7		
11	1		1, 2*	1, 2*		1	7
23							1
5. 0							
1							
2							
3	3	3*, 4		4	4	4	1*, 4
21						2, 6*	2, 6*
29							
43	4	6, 9, 10*	6, 8, 9, 10*	10	9, 10*	9, 10*	9, 10*
94	1*, 3, 4	7, 8*		1*, 4	1*, 2, 4	1*, 2	1, 2*, 4
6. 4							
8	5						
9					10	10	10
12							
22							
26							
41							
42				5	1, 5*	1, 2, 3, 4, 5*	

7. 66	8		8, 9, 10*	8	8	8	
82		9					
83							
84							
85							
89	9, 10*	8, 9*, 10	8, 9*, 10	8, 9*, 10	8, 9*, 10	8	8, 9*, 10
91	1, 4*	8	8*, 9	4	4	8, 9*, 10	2, 3, 5, 6, 8, 9*, 10
93	—(missing data)	1, 2, 3, 4*, 5	2	8, 9*, 10	1, 2, 3, 4, 5*, 6	2, 6, 8, 9, 10*	4, 7*
96		1, 2, 3, 4*, 5	1, 2, 3, 4, 5*, 6, 8, 9, 10				
8. 61	7, 9*, 10	9*, 10	9*, 10	4, 7*	4*, 7	4*, 7	4, 7*
62				9*, 10			
65							
67							
69	7, 9*	9	9*, 10	9*, 10	9	9	9
81	7, 9*, 10	9*, 10	9*, 10	9*, 10	9*, 10	9	9*, 10
9. 71	10	10	10				
72	10	10	10				
73							
86				6*, 10	6*, 10	6*, 10	6*, 10
95							
10. 51	1, 4, 7*, 8, 9			6	6	6	1, 2, 3, 4, 5, 6*
52	9	9	9				
53							
54							
55	9						
56	8	8					
57	9	9	9	8, 9*	7*, 8, 9	8, 9*	
58				9	9	9	
59		9					

animal and vegetable oils, ought not be put with chemicals; or that SITC 69 and 81, manufactures of metal and sanitary, fixtures and fittings, ought not be put in machinery.

The relative importance of the components in each of the aggregates is measured by the standard deviations in table 3.3. An alternative way to measure the size of these net export data is average absolute trade $\sum_{i=1}^{N} |T_i|/N$. The standard deviation $(\sum_{i=1}^{N} (T_i - \bar{T})^2/N)^{1/2}$, where $\bar{T} = \sum T_i/N$, is just another norm of the form $(\sum_i |T_i|^p/N)^{1/p}$, since $\bar{T}$ would be zero if the sample were complete. These standard deviations indicate that electric energy forms a very small part of the raw materials aggregate. Wood and cork manufactured products are unimportant in forest products. The cereals group is primarily cereals and textile fibers, the latter greatly diminishing in importance by 1975. Clothing increased its share of labor intensive products; SITC 89, miscellaneous manufactured articles, decreased its share. The capital intensive group is primarily textiles, and iron and steel, though textiles diminish greatly in importance over time.

Characteristics of the components forming the manufactured aggregates are listed in table 3.4. The data on capital per man and the skill proportions are shown in figure 3.1, in which the commodities forming the four aggregates are separated by dotted lines. It is both surprising and gratifying that the clusters based on correlations of net export data conform so well to clusters based on capital intensities and skill ratios. The extreme groups are LAB, with low capital intensities and low skill requirements, and CHEM, with high capital intensities and high skill requirements. Between these two extremes lie CAP and MACH, both with moderate levels of capital intensities and skill requirements, though with CAP leaning toward higher capital intensities and with MACH leaning toward higher skill proportions.

Figure 3.1 suggests some misclassifications. SITC 69 (manufactures of metal) might be better allocated to the machinery aggregate, than to its present position in capital intensive manufactures. Actually the trade data agree with this reallocation (see table 3.2). The commodity aggregates were formed by a study only of the trade data, and an attempt was made to choose aggregates whose labels had content. For that reason I was reluctant to include in the "machinery" aggregate a component such as SITC 69, which is composed of items such as wire, nails and tools. Because SITC 69 is highly correlated with its aggregate, CAP, this

Table 3.3
Share of components in aggregates[a]

SITC	Description	1958	1960	1963	1966	1969	1972	1975
	1. Petroleum (PETRO)							
33	Petroleum, petroleum products	1	1	1	1	1	1	1
	2. Raw materials (MAT)							
27	Crude fertilizers, crude materials	.07	.07	.07	.07	.07	.06	.06
28	Metaliferous ores, metal scrap	.36	.38	.34	.37	.38	.37	.32
32	Coal, coke, briquettes	.26	.21	.25	.17	.16	.20	.29
34	Gas, natural and manufactured	.02	.01	.03	.03	.04	.08	.17
35	Electrical Energy	.01	.01	.01	.01	.01	.01	.01
68	Nonferrous metals	.29	.32	.30	.36	.34	.27	.15
	3. Forest products (FOR)							
24	Wood, Lumber, cork	.30	.31	.33	.32	.36	.39	.34
25	Pulp, waste paper	.25	.24	.24	.24	.23	.20	.28
63	Wood, cork manufactures	.08	.09	.09	.09	.09	.11	.08
64	Paper, paperboard	.38	.36	.34	.35	.32	.30	.31
	4. Tropical agriculture (TROP)							
5	Fruit, vegetables	.24	.24	.28	.32	.30	.33	.31
6	Sugar, sugar preparations, honey	.14	.14	.18	.12	.14	.17	.26
7	Coffee, tea, cocoa, spices, etc.	.42	.38	.35	.35	.31	.29	.24
11	Beverages	.08	.07	.08	.11	.13	.15	.12
23	Crude rubber	.12	.17	.11	.10	.13	.07	.08
	5. Animal products (ANL)							
0	Live animals	.09	.08	.08	.08	.10	.15	.13
1	Meat, meat preparations	.39	.38	.37	.39	.39	.36	.33
2	Dairy products, eggs	.22	.24	.22	.19	.16	.16	.20
3	Fish, fish preparations	.14	.14	.15	.16	.16	.17	.16
21	Hides, skins, furskins, undressed	.07	.08	.08	.09	.09	.07	.06
29	Crude animal, vegetable minerals	.06	.07	.08	.08	.09	.08	.10
43	Animal, vegetable oils, fats, processed	.01	.01	.01	.01	.01	.01	.01
94	Animals, n.e.s.	.01	.00	.00	.00	.00	.00	.00
	6. Cereals, etc. (CER)							
4	Cereals, cereal preparations	.39	.38	.43	.48	.39	.42	.56
8	Feeding stuff for animals	.04	.04	.05	.06	.08	.07	.05
9	Miscellaneous food preparations	.02	.01	.01	.01	.02	.01	.02
12	Tobacco, tobacco manufactures	.10	.09	.08	.07	.10	.08	.05
22	Oil seeds, oil nuts, oil kernels	.09	.10	.11	.13	.15	.19	.17
26	Textile fibers	.30	.31	.25	.19	.21	.17	.10

Table 3.3 (continued)

SITC	Description	1958	1960	1963	1966	1969	1972	1975
41	Animal oils, fats	.03	.03	.02	.02	.02	.02	.02
42	Fixed vegetable oils	.04	.04	.03	.03	.03	.04	.04
	7. Labor intensive (LAB)							
66	Nonmetallic mineral manufactures	.16	.17	.12	.15	.12	.12	.10
82	Furniture	.03	.02	.02	.03	.05	.05	.06
83	Travel goods, handbags, etc.	.01	.02	.01	.02	.02	.02	.02
84	Clothing	.12	.18	.18	.24	.25	.29	.35
85	Footwear	.04	.09	.07	.10	.13	.16	.16
89	Miscellaneous manufactured articles, n.e.s.	.41	.28	.21	.21	.23	.22	.19
91	Postal Pack not classified according to kind	.13	.09	.08	.05	.03	.03	.02
93	Special trans. not classified according to kind	.09	.15	.30	.21	.16	.10	.10
96	Coins nongold, noncurrent	.00	.00	.00	.00	.00	.00	.00
	8. Capital intensive (CAP)							
61	Leather, dressed furskins	.02	.05	.02	.03	.03	.03	.02
62	Rubber manufactures, n.e.s.	.06	.05	.06	.05	.05	.05	.05
65	Textile, yarn, fabrics, etc.	.36	.36	.37	.35	.31	.26	.15
67	Iron and steel	.36	.36	.36	.40	.43	.49	.62
69	Manufactures of metal	.18	.16	.18	.16	.16	.15	.14
81	Sanitary, fixtures, fittings	.03	.02	.02	.02	.02	.02	.01
	9. Machinery (MACH)							
71	Machinery, other than electrical	.43	.43	.44	.44	.44	.40	.43
72	Electrical machinery	.15	.14	.15	.14	.15	.17	.14
73	Transport equipment	.35	.35	.32	.29	.30	.35	.35
86	Professional goods, watches, instruments	.04	.05	.06	.06	.07	.06	.05
95	Firearms, ammunition	.03	.03	.03	.06	.04	.02	.03
	10. Chemicals (CHEM)							
51	Chemical elements, compounds	.19	.18	.18	.25	.25	.23	.25
52	Mineral Tar and crude chemicals from coal, petroleum, natural gas	.01	.02	.01	.01	.02	.01	.01
53	Dyeing, tanning, coloring matter	.09	.10	.10	.11	.11	.14	.09
54	Medicinal, pharmaceutical products	.16	.15	.14	.13	.14	.14	.12
55	Essential oils, perfume matter	.06	.06	.06	.05	.05	.05	.05
56	Fertilizers, manufactured	.11	.09	.09	.10	.08	.08	.13
57	Explosives, pyrotechnic products	.02	.02	.01	.02	.01	.01	.01
58	Plastic materials, cellulose, etc.	.12	.16	.18	.19	.20	.21	.20
59	Chemical materials, n.e.s.	.23	.21	.22	.14	.14	.13	.14

a. Share $= \sigma_i / \sum \sigma_i$; $\sigma_i =$ standard deviation of component i.

Table 3.4
Characteristics of industries[a,b]

	Capital per man	Skill ratio	Wages per man	Scale economies	Consumer goods ratio	Trade date	Product differentiation
7. Labor intensive							
66	14,561	.0500	5,163	.048	.380	1,945.6	.7826
82	3,470	.0197	4,408	.032	.556	1,947.3	.5360
83	1,217	.0138	3,702	.031	.957	1,936.6	.6300
84	1,329	.0102	3,058	−.096	.945	1,945.5	.5273
85	1,443	.0066	3,653	.052	.957	1,927.7	.6060
89	4,845	.0730	5,004	.060	.526	1,947.9	1.3152
8. Capital intensive							
61	5,195	.0171	5,907	.104	.691	1,934.9	.5898
62	9,361	.0604	6,356	.011	.506	1,947.8	.7467
65	6,437	.0208	4,083	−.001	.603	1,948.1	.5367
67	22,547	.0502	7,183	.069	.125	1,948.5	.6959
69	6,974	.0966	5,935	.028	.378	1,945.6	1.1631
81	9,593	.0455	5,827	.065	.256	1,946.0	.9592
9. Machinery							
71	7,595	.0913	6,485	.044	.112	1,948.6	1.0199
72	5,627	.1523	6,068	.063	.494	1,947.8	1.3671
73	9,328	.1218	7,399	.137	.338	1,951.1	.7886
86	6,619	.1622	6,300	.038	.444	1,948.8	1.6355

Table 3.4 (continued)

	Capital per man	Skill ratio	Wages per man	Scale economics	Consumer goods ratio	Trade date	Product differentiation
10. Chemicals							
51	36,213	.1564	7,684	.041	.293	1,946.4	.8934
52	24,188	.1564	7,289	.027	.293	1,940.0	.8008
53	13,395	.1075	7,031	.060	.291	1,938.8	.9112
54	13,646	.1926	6,806	.083	.854	1,950.5	1.4745
55	19,506	.1564	6,273	.185	.854	1,940.5	.7488
56	17,103	.1564	4,980	.076	.293	1,933.2	.4791
57	7,703	.1564	6,190	−.079	.293	1,942.6	1.2713
58	24,788	.1564	7,126	.009	.212	1,954.6	.9093
59	19,489	.1564	6,094	.059	.293	1,945.5	.7512

Source: Hufbauer (1970).

a. SITC 91–95 not available.

b. Definitions:

Capital per man: 1963 fixed plant and equipment. Based on Leontief's 1947 estimates and capital expenditure figures from the Census of Manufactures.

Skill ratio: Percentage of work force who are professional, technical, or scientific personnel.

Wages per man: 1963 U.S. dollars; wage bill divided by total employees.

Scale economics: The coefficient β in the regression $\log v = \alpha + \beta \log r$, where v is the 1963 ratio of value added in plants employing r persons and average value added for the 4-digit U.S. Census Bureau industry.

Consumer goods ratio: Percentage of total sales appearing as consumer goods directly and indirectly after the first and second rounds of exchange among industries.

First trade date: Average date at which a commodity appeared in U.S. Census Bureau export classification list, "Schedule B."

Product differentiation: Coefficient of variation in unit values of 1965 U.S. exports destined to different countries.

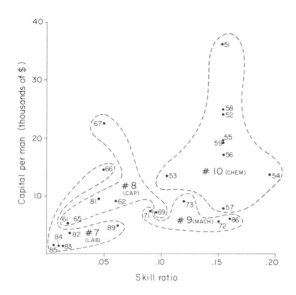

Figure 3.1
Characteristics of industries.

decision is not likely to have a major impact on the subsequent analysis.

The other reallocation suggested by figure 3.1 is the move of SITC 66 from labor intensive to capital intensive manufactures because of its high capital intensity. The trade data resist this move, although in 2 of the 8 years SITC 66 is correlated more with CAP than with LAB. Further disaggregation might resolve these aggregation conundrums. SITC 66 includes some commodities with very high capital intensities (SITC 661— lime, cement, and building materials—has a capital intensity of $41,009 per man) and some commodities with very low capital intensities (SITC 666—pottery—has a capital intensity of $2,206 per man). Hufbauer computed these capital intensities at the 3-digit level and formed the 2-digit estimates using U.S. 1965 export data as weights. The U.S. export composition in 1965 is likely to be skewed toward the capital intensive commodities compared with other countries, and the capital intensities of the aggregate may therefore be overstated when the capital intensities of the components vary significantly. What this suggests is the advisability of beginning at a lower level of aggregation. Correlations of the 1978 3-digit data with the aggregates are reported and discussed in section 3.2. As it turns out, SITC 666 (pottery) but not SITC 661 (cement) is correlated more with the capital intensive aggregate than with the labor intensive aggregate. It is true that SITC 664 (glass), which has a high capital intensity of $21,623 per man, is better placed in the capital intensive group. Thus further disaggregation seems to cure some problems but also to create others. For that reason and others discussed in section 3.2, the aggregation analysis is restricted to the 2-digit data.

Another commodity category that table 3.2 suggests could be reallocated in SITC 89, composed of such miscellaneous things as sound recorders, printed matter, plastic articles, toys, sporting goods, jewelry, and works of art. Figure 3.1 also allows this to be reallocated from LAB to either CAP or MACH, though the trade data suggest it would be better to allocate it to CAP. Again because SITC 89 is highly correlated with LAB, this apparent misallocation is not likely to cause great damage to the subsequent analysis.

Continuing the comparison between table 3.2 and figure 3.1, we note in table 3.2 that SITC 61 in several years is correlated more with LAB than CAP, and that it is also on the border in figure 3.1 between LAB and CAP. Similarly, table 3.2 suggests a reallocation of SITC 57 from CHEM to MACH, again in agreement with figure 3.1. And SITC 86 in several years is more correlated with CHEM than with its own aggregate MACH, yet again in agreement with figure 3.1. Thus figure 3.1 and the net export data yield remarkably similar clusters, down even to tiny details about the edges of the clusters. The only exception is SITC 81, which in figure 3.1 is in the middle of the CAP aggregate, but in table 3.2 is better allocated to MACH or CHEM.

The only other industry characteristic in table 3.4 that clearly separates the aggregates is wages per man, with LAB composed of industries with low wages and the other aggregates composed of industries with high wages. CAP has somewhat lower wages than MACH and CHEM, especially because SITC 65 has unusually low wages. There is no sharp distinction between the aggregates in terms of scale economies, consumer goods ratio, first trade date, or product differentiation. This may be a measurement problem. The scale economy measure, for example, seems aimed at the effect of marginal increases in plant size, but ignores average differences in plant size across commodity classes.

In summary, the commodity composition of trade is well understood in terms of 10 commodity aggregates. These 10 aggregates suggest with surprising clarity that trade can be explained by the Heckscher-Ohlin model using as resources capital, skilled labor, unskilled labor, petroleum, miscellaneous natural resources, forests, tropical/Mediterranean arable land, and temperate arable land. The 2 primary product aggregates and the 4 crops seem likely to use one of the natural resources intensively, and trade in them is expected to be explained by the abundance of the associated resource. The 4 manufacturing aggregates use capital, skilled labor and unskilled labor, and trade in them is expected to be explained by combinations of these resources: LAB uses unskilled labor; CAP uses capital and unskilled labor; MACH uses skilled labor and moderate amounts of capital; and CHEM uses skilled labor and very large amounts of capital.

3.2 Examination of 3-Digit Data

The effect of further disaggregation is suggested by table 3.5, which indicates the correlations in 1978 of the 3-digit SITC categories with the corresponding aggregates. It is clear from perusal of this table that a number of the 3-digit categories are misaggregated. For example: SITC 271 (crude fertilizers) could be moved from raw materials to chemicals; SITC 632 (wood manufactures) could be moved from forest products to labor intensive manufacturing products, as could SITC 642 (articles of paper); SITC 262 (wool and animal hair) could be moved from cereals to animal products. Glass and glassware could be moved from the labor intensive aggregate to the capital intensive. And so on.

It would be necessary to redo the aggregation with 3-digit data if it appeared that the resulting aggregates would behave quite differently from the aggregates we have already formed. There are two reasons why I think this is not likely, and why I am content with the aggregates formed from the 2-digit data. The first is that many of the misclassified 3-digit commodities are relatively unimportant in world trade as measured by the cross-country standard deviations reported in table 3.5. This is to be expected, since important misclassifications at the 3-digit level should have led to misclassifications at the 2-digit level as well.

The second reason that it is unnecessary to redo the aggregation is that many of the misclassifications would be expected if the classification scheme I have used has the content it is intended to have. The existence of these predictable misclassifications therefore both increases my confidence in the aggregation scheme and makes it unlikely that reclassifications of

Table 3.5
Correlations of 3-digit data with aggregates: 1978

SITC	Description	Corre-lation	Stan-dard devi-ation	More highly correlated with aggregates (* = max)
	1. Petroleum			
331	Crude petroleum, etc.	.98	6,297	
332	Petroleum products	.70	1,626	4
	2. Raw materials			
271	Fertilizers, crude	−.11	76	6*, 10
273	Stone, sand, and gravel	.22	21	3*, 7
274	Sulphur, etc.	.42	29	3
275	Natural abrasives	.63	12	
276	Other crude minerals	.82	113	
281	Iron ore, concentates	.86	544	
282	Iron and steel scrap	.11	180	5, 6*, 10
283	Ores and concentrates of nonferrous base metals	.94	381	
284	Nonferrous metal scrap	.53	79	
285	Silver and platinum ores	.26	51	3*, 6
286	Uranium, thorium, ores and concentrates	.42	45	3
321	Coal, coke, briquettes	.48	776	
341	Gas, natural and manufactured	.84	928	
351	Electrical energy	.50	79	3
681	Silver, platinum, etc.	.75	139	
682	Copper	.49	192	1*, 3
683	Nickel	.56	125	1*, 3
684	Aluminum	.70	233	
685	Lead	.54	56	
686	Zinc	.47	90	1*, 3, 4, 7
687	Tin	.60	144	1*, 4
688	Uranium, thorium, alloys	.28	0	1*, 3, 4, 7, 8
689	Nonferrous base metals, n.e.s.	.24	31	1*, 3, 4, 5
	3. Forest products			
241	Fuel wood and charcoal	.14	5	2, 5*, 6
242	Wood, rough	.32	660	2*, 5, 6*
243	Wood, shaped	.91	678	
244	Cork, raw and waste	.22	5	1, 2, 4*, 5
251	Pulp and waste paper	.91	428	
631	Veneers, plywood, etc.	.65	186	
632	Wood manufactures, n.e.s.	.63	80	1, 7*
633	Cork manufactures	.17	26	1, 4*
641	Paper and paperboard	.86	746	
642	Articles of paper, etc.	−.34	73	6, 7, 8, 9, 10*
	4. Tropical agriculture			
051	Fruit, fresh nuts, fresh dry	.59	420	
052	Dried fruit	.02	45	2, 3, 5, 6*
053	Fruit preserved, prepared	.64	135	
054	Vegetables, etc., fresh, simply preserved	.57	274	
055	Vegetables, etc., preserved, prepared	.77	130	
061	Sugar and honey	.56	275	
062	Sugar preparations (except chocolate)	.44	22	
071	Coffee	.86	738	1
072	Cocoa	.90	223	1
073	Chocolate and products	.61	53	1
074	Tea and Maté	.58	48	
075	Spices	.85	31	
111	Nonalcoholic beverages n.e.s.	−.18	24	6, 7, 8, 9*, 10
112	Alcoholic beverages	.55	470	7
231	Rubber, crude, synthetic	.58	193	1

Table 3.5 (continued)

SITC	Description	Corre-lation	Stan-dard devi-ation	More highly correlated with aggregates (* = max)
	5. **Animal products**			
001	Live animals	.65	230	
011	Meat, fresh, chilled, frozen	.93	629	
012	Meat, dried, salted, smoked	.37	133	
013	Meat, tinned, n.e.s. or prepared	.58	163	1, 4*
022	Milk and cream	.41	154	10
023	Butter	.56	89	
024	Cheese and curd	.74	182	
025	Eggs	.59	68	
031	Fish, fresh, simply preserved	.66	541	2
032	Fish, etc., tinned, prepared	.05	81	1*, 3, 4, 7, 8, 9
211	Hides, skins, undressed	.44	180	6
212	Fur skins, undressed	.51	68	
291	Crude animal matter n.e.s.	.79	47	
292	Crude vegetable materials n.e.s.	.63	237	
431	Processed animal veg. oil, etc.	.19	33	9, 10*
941	Zoo animals, pets	.64	5	2
	6. **Cereals, etc.**			
041	Wheat, etc., unmilled	.92	807	
042	Rice	.79	190	
043	Barley, unmilled	.23	142	2*, 3, 5
044	Maize, unmilled	.96	915	
045	Cereals n.e.s., unmilled	.83	119	
046	Wheat, etc., meal or flour	.47	58	10
047	Meal and flour, nonwheat	.64	11	10
048	Cereal, etc., preparations	.12	65	2, 5*, 10
081	Animal feeding-stuff	.87	412	
091	Margarine, shortening	.33	32	10
099	Food preparations n.e.s.	.48	54	10
121	Tobacco, unmanufactured	.83	230	
122	Tobacco manufactures	.73	142	10
221	Oil seeds, nuts, kernels	.98	1,072	
261	Silk	.18	47	2*, 3, 5
262	Wool and animal hair	.16	323	2, 3, 4, 5*
263	Cotton	.89	380	
264	Jute	.17	6	2, 3*, 4, 5
265	Vegetable fiber, except cotton and jute	−.09	15	1, 2, 3, 4, 5*, 7
266	Synthetic and regenerated fiber	.23	111	8, 9*, 10
267	Waste of textile fabrics	.70	24	10
411	Animal oils and fats	.91	108	
421	Fixed vegetable oils, soft	.79	159	
422	Fixed vegetable oil, nonsoft	−.32	140	1, 2, 3, 4*, 5, 7, 8, 9
	7. **Labor intensive**			
661	Cement, etc., building materials	.70	134	
662	Clay, refractory bldg. materials	.54	145	
663	Other nonmetal, mineral manufactures	−.26	65	6, 8, 9, 10*
664	Glass	.01	65	8*, 9, 10
665	Glassware	.21	72	8*, 9
666	Pottery	.73	126	8
667	Pearl, Precious, semiprecious stone	.57	346	1*, 4
821	Furniture	.69	300	
831	Travel goods, handbags	.94	138	
841	Clothing not of fur	.88	140	
842	Fur clothes, products	.22	61	1, 2, 3, 4*, 5
851	Footwear	.94	687	

Table 3.5 (continued)

SITC	Description	Correlation	Standard deviation	More highly correlated with aggregates (* = max)
891	Sound recorders, producers	.42	494	8*, 9
892	Printed matter	−.07	172	6, 8, 9, 10*
893	Articles of plastic n.e.s.	.68	132	
894	Toys, sporting goods, etc.	.83	206	
895	Office supplies n.e.s.	−.17	41	6, 8, 9*, 10
896	Works of art, etc.	.75	181	1*, 4
897	Gold, silverware, jewelry	.77	244	
899	Other manufactured goods	.74	90	
911	Mail not classed by kind	.04	9	9
931	Special transactions	.53	293	1
961	Coin, nongold, noncurrent	.04	8	1, 2, 3*, 4, 6
	8. Capital intensive			
611	Leather	.17	76	1, 4*
612	Leather, etc., manufactures	.28	33	1, 4, 7*
613	Fur skins tanned, dressed	−.16	31	2, 5, 6, 9, 10*
621	Materials of rubber	.51	30	9*, 10
629	Rubber articles n.e.s.	.86	225	
651	Textile yarn and thread	.43	149	
652	Cotton fabrics, woven	.38	93	
653	Woven textiles, noncotton	.83	399	
654	Lace, ribbons, tulle, etc.	.14	37	
655	Special textile, etc., prod.	.50	80	9*, 10
656	Textile, etc., products n.e.s.	.01	50	4, 6, 7*
657	Floor cover, tapestry, etc.	−.08	181	1, 2, 3, 4*, 5, 6, 7
671	Pig iron, etc.	−.11	135	1, 2, 3, 4*, 5, 7
672	Iron, steel primary forms	.68	244	
673	Iron and steel shapes	.91	464	
674	Universals, plates and sheets of iron or steel	.93	998	
675	Hoop and strip of iron and steel	.75	107	9
676	Railway rails, etc., iron, steel	.54	27	9
677	Iron, steel wire excluding wire rod	.77	91	
678	Iron, steel tubes, pipes, etc.	.94	685	
679	Iron, steel castings, unworked, n.e.s.	.14	28	9, 10*
691	Structures and parts n.e.s.	.56	226	9*, 10
692	Metal tanks, boxes, etc.	.64	52	9
693	Wire products, nonelectrical	.93	77	
694	Steel, copper nails, nuts, etc.	.84	143	
695	Tools	.53	139	9*, 10
696	Cutlery	.85	54	
697	Base metal household equipment	.58	70	7
698	Metal manufactures n.e.s.	.70	220	9
812	Plumbing, heating, lighting equipment	.36	72	9
	9. Machinery			
711	Power machinery nonelectrical	.88	733	
712	Agricultural machinery	.72	320	
714	Office machines	.42	517	6*, 10
715	Metalworking machinery	.87	433	
717	Textile, leather machinery	.79	373	
718	Machines for special industries	.72	744	10
719	Machines n.e.s. nonelectrical	.88	2,191	
722	Electrical power mach, switchgear	.95	624	
723	Electrical distributing machine	.93	135	
724	Telecommunications equipment	.71	1,186	8
725	Domestic electrical equipment	.68	225	8
726	Electrical-medical, x-ray equipment	.54	68	10

Table 3.5 (continued)

SITC	Description	Correlation	Standard deviation	More highly correlated with aggregates (* = max)
729	Railway vehicles	.90	128	
732	Road motor vehicles	.81	4,340	8
733	Road vehicles, nonmotor	.89	138	
734	Aircraft	.09	1,269	6*, 10
735	Ships and boats	.76	1,160	8
861	Instruments, apparatus	.89	568	
862	Photo, cinema supplies	.38	155	6*, 10
863	Developed cinema film	.12	10	6*, 10
864	Watches and clocks	.34	381	8
951	War firearms, ammunition	.17	322	6*, 10
	10. Chemicals			
512	Organic chemicals	.93	507	
513	Inorganic elements, oxides, etc.	.01	179	1*, 2, 3, 4, 5, 7, 8, 9
514	Other inorganic chemicals	.88	96	
515	Radioactive, etc., material	−.49	145	1, 2*, 3, 4, 5, 6, 7, 8
521	Coal, petroleum, etc. chemicals	.08	19	2, 3*, 5
531	Synthetic organic dyestuffs	.68	176	
532	Dyes n.e.s., tanning products	.44	13	
533	Pigments, paints, etc.	.88	116	
541	Medicinal, etc., products	.70	324	
551	Essential oil, perfume, etc.	.22	40	5
553	Perfume, cosmetics, etc.	.25	109	
554	Soaps, cleaning, etc., preparations	.87	80	
561	Fertilizers, manufactured	.28	167	
571	Explosives, pyrotech products	.36	18	
581	Plastic materials, etc.	.86	548	
599	Chemicals n.e.s.	.88	505	

the 3-digit categories would produce aggregates with markedly different content.

For example, SITC 271 (crude fertilizers) is, not surprisingly, better classified as a chemical product, and its small standard deviation of 76 makes it unlikely that transferring it from raw materials to chemicals would greatly affect the behavior of either aggregate. Wood manufactures (SITC 632) does not belong in the forest product aggregate because of the substantial labor and capital input requirements, but it also has a small standard deviation. Similarly, SITC 664 and 665 (glass and glassware) are relatively unimportant categories in the labor intensive aggregate.

There are several exceptions to the general rule that apparently misclassified 3-digit aggregates have small standard deviations. One is SITC 262 (wool and animal hair), which is better allocated to animal products than to cereals. Another is SITC 891 (sound recorders), which should be put in CAP, the capital intensive products. Two categories in the machinery aggregate, telecommunications equipment and road motor vehicles, could also be put in the capital intensive aggregate. These two are nonetheless highly correlated with their own aggregate, which suggests that the distinction between CAP and MACH is somewhat blurred.

3.3 Why Are There Clusters?

The clustering of commodities is a salient feature of the trade data and one should expect to have a theory of trade that can explain it. Of course, clusters could be found even in sets of random numbers, but the trade clusters are strikingly related to what we know about production functions. For example, the four commodities that use wood as an input form a tight cluster. If a country exports one, it is quite likely also to export the others. The commodity that has the lowest correlation with the aggregate is wood and cork manufactures, and is the only one of the group that is ever positively correlated with the labor intensive aggregate. What is clearly suggested by these observations is that, first, success in exporting these products is linked to the supply of a single resource, forests, and that, second, SITC63 (wood manufactures) requires also significant amounts of other resources, probably labor and possibly capital. (Note that SITC63 is labor intensive.)

At an intuitive level, it is quite unsurprising to discover these kinds of clusters of commodities, and it is quite disturbing that the traditional trade model is incompatible with this finding, as is now demonstrated. The model of trade in the $n \times n$ case is described by the set of equations $T = A^{-1}(V - sV_w)$, where T is the vector of net exports, $V - sV_w$ is the vector of excess supplies of endowments, and A is the matrix of input requirements. The correlation of trade between a pair of commodities depends, therefore, on the covariance matrix of the vector of excess factor supplies $V - sV_w$ and on the factor intensity matrix A. The proposition suggested by the observed clusters is that the correlation between a pair of commodities is positive if they use inputs in similar proportions. This statement is clearly incomplete, since it makes no reference to the correlation of factor endowments across countries. Moreover, the statement is false if you focus attention on the technology alone by assuming that the excess factor supplies are distributed independently of each other.

To see this, consider the 3×3 model with inputs capital (K), labor (L), and land (M) and with factor input matrix

$$A = \begin{bmatrix} A_{K1} & A_{K2} & A_{K3} \\ A_{L1} & A_{L2} & A_{L3} \\ A_{M1} & A_{M2} & A_{M3} \end{bmatrix}.$$

Using Cramer's rule, we can solve for the outputs of commodities 1 and 2 as functions of the endowments K, L, M:

$$X_1 = \det \begin{bmatrix} K & A_{K2} & A_{K3} \\ L & A_{L2} & A_{L3} \\ M & A_{M2} & A_{M3} \end{bmatrix} / \det A$$

$$= [K(A_{L2}A_{M3} - A_{L3}A_{M2}) + L(A_{K3}A_{M2} - A_{K2}A_{M3}) + M(A_{K2}A_{L3} - A_{K3}A_{L2})]/\det A,$$

(3.1)

$$X_2 = \det \begin{bmatrix} A_{K1} & K & A_{K3} \\ A_{L1} & L & A_{L3} \\ A_{M1} & M & A_{M3} \end{bmatrix} / \det A$$

$$= [K(A_{L3}A_{M1} - A_{L1}A_{M3}) + L(A_{K1}A_{M3} - A_{M1}A_{K3}) + M(A_{K3}A_{L1} - A_{K1}A_{L3})]/\det A.$$

(3.2)

The correlation between X_1 and X_2 is then
$\mathrm{cor}(X_1, X_2) = \mathrm{cov}(\det(A)X_1, \det(A)X_2)/(\mathrm{var}(\det(A)X_1)\,\mathrm{var}(\det(A)X_2))^{1/2}$.
Assuming that K, L, and M are distributed independently with variances σ_K^2, σ_L^2, and σ_M^2, we can write the covariance as

$$\mathrm{cov}(\det(A)X_1, \det(A)X_2)$$

$$= \sigma_K^2(A_{L2}A_{M3} - A_{L3}A_{M2})(A_{L3}A_{M1} - A_{L1}A_{M3})$$

$$+ \sigma_L^2(A_{K3}A_{M2} - A_{K2}A_{M3})(A_{K1}A_{M3} - A_{M1}A_{K3})$$

$$+ \sigma_M^2(A_{K2}A_{L3} - A_{K3}A_{L2})(A_{K3}A_{L1} - A_{K1}A_{L3})$$

$$= \sigma_K^2 A_{M1} A_{M2} A_{M3}^2 \left(\frac{A_{L2}}{A_{M2}} - \frac{A_{L3}}{A_{M3}} \right)\left(\frac{A_{L3}}{A_{M3}} - \frac{A_{L1}}{A_{M1}} \right)$$

(3.3)

$$+ \sigma_L^2 A_{M1} A_{M2} A_{M3}^2 \left(\frac{A_{K3}}{A_{M3}} - \frac{A_{K2}}{A_{M2}} \right)\left(\frac{A_{K1}}{A_{M1}} - \frac{A_{K3}}{A_{M3}} \right)$$

$$+ \sigma_M^2 A_{L1} A_{L2} A_{L3}^2 \left(\frac{A_{K2}}{A_{L2}} - \frac{A_{K3}}{A_{L3}} \right)\left(\frac{A_{K3}}{A_{L3}} - \frac{A_{K1}}{A_{L1}} \right).$$

Each of the three terms in this expression involves a comparison of the technology used to produce commodity 3 with the technologies used to produce commodities 1 and 2. If commodities 1 and 2 are similar in the sense that the labor/land ratios in 1 or 2 both exceed or both are less than the land/labor ratio in 3, then the first term is negative. The other two terms are also negative if commodities 1 and 2 are similar in an analogous sense. *Thus commodities produced by similar production processes can be expected to have outputs that are negatively correlated, not positively correlated.*

This logic can be extended to the general n-dimensional case, although it is difficult to describe the precise conditions under which commodities 1 and 2 are sufficiently similar that they are negatively correlated. In the 3-dimensional case just discussed, the commodities 1 and 2 were shown to be negatively correlated when $\partial X_1/\partial V_i$ and $\partial X_2/\partial V_i$ are opposite in sign, for $V_i = K, L, M$. More generally, these derivatives can be found by Cramer's rule and the partitioned determinant formula:

$$\partial X_1/\partial V_1 = \det \begin{bmatrix} A_{22} & A_{23} & \cdots & A_{2n} \\ A_{32} & A_{33} & \cdots & A_{3n} \\ \vdots & \vdots & & \vdots \\ A_{n2} & A_{n3} & \cdots & A_{nn} \end{bmatrix} /\det A,$$

$$\partial X_2/\partial V_1 = -\det \begin{bmatrix} A_{21} & A_{23} & \cdots & A_{2n} \\ A_{31} & A_{33} & \cdots & A_{3n} \\ \vdots & \vdots & & \vdots \\ A_{n1} & A_{n3} & \cdots & A_{nn} \end{bmatrix} /\det A,$$

where I have used the fact that switching columns of a matrix changes the sign of its determinant. The matrices in these two expressions are identical except for their first columns. The first column of the first matrix uses the input coefficients of the second commodity, and the first column of the second matrix uses the input coefficients of the first commodity. If these vectors of input coefficients are proportional to each other, then these determinants necessarily have the same signs and the derivatives are opposite in sign. Loosely speaking, if the input coefficients are "almost" proportional, then the derivatives will also be opposite in sign, and trade in the two commodities will be negatively correlated.

Although overall similarity in factor input intensities implies negative correlations, there may be other assumptions about technology that do imply positive associations. In the case of the wood cluster, it is more natural to assume that wood uses a specialized input (forest land) than to assume that the factor inputs are similar. If land is used in the first two industries but not the third, so that $A_{M3} = 0$, then (3.3) specializes to

$$\text{cov}(\det(A)X_1, \det(A)X_2) = -\sigma_K^2 A_{L3}^2 A_{M2} A_{M1} - \sigma_L^2 A_{K3}^2 A_{M2} A_{M1}$$
$$+ \sigma_M^2 A_{L1} A_{L2} A_{L3}^2 \left(\frac{A_{K2}}{A_{L2}} - \frac{A_{K3}}{A_{L3}} \right) \left(\frac{A_{K3}}{A_{L3}} - \frac{A_{K1}}{A_{L1}} \right).$$

Though the first two terms in this expression are negative, the third can offset these if the capital intensity of industry 3 is between the capital intensity of 1 and 2, and if the variance of land σ_M^2 is large enough.

Though it is not impossible for the even model with factor price equalization to produce clusters of commodities related to technologies, it does require a certain stretching of the imagination. We may, therefore, regard the clustering of commodities as evidence against the even model, especially if we can identify an alternative that more easily generates clusters. Several alternatives come to mind. An intellectually close alternative is a model in which countries specialize production in the subsets of commodities that use an abundant resource intensively. This model sensibly implies that this resource is relatively inexpensive in countries with abundant supplies. However, as is discussed subsequently, this is not a model that necessarily produces the kinds of clusters that occur in the data. The easiest way to generate such clusters is merely to assume that there are production externalities. I am not too uncomfortable explaining the chemicals cluster in terms of externalities, but I doubt that the forest products cluster and the agricultural clusters could be explained that way. Another possibility is price and/or quantity uncertainty that encourages diversification—farmland, for example, can be expected to be diversified among various crops.

The clustering implied by complete specialization can be discussed in the context of the 3×3 model with inputs K, L, and M and commodities X_1, X_2, and X_3. The intersection of the positive orthant, $K > 0$, $L > 0$, $M > 0$, with the unit value isocost plane, $w_K K + w_L L + w_M M = 1$, is a triangle, depicted in figure 3.2a. The corners of this triangle are the three coordinate axes, labeled K, L, and M. The three points in the interior of this triangle labeled 1, 2, and 3 indicate the intersection of the expansion

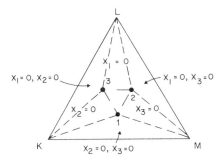

Figure 3.2a
Cones of diversification.

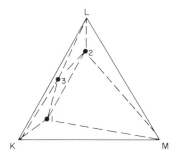

Figure 3.2b
Cones of diversification.

vectors of commodities X_1, X_2, and X_3 with the unit value isocost plane. Along the line connecting K to L the value of M is zero, and consequently commodity X_3 uses small amounts of M compared with X_1 and X_2. Also depicted in this figure are the cones of diversification. If a country has an endowment ray in the triangle with corners 1, 2, 3, then all three commodities are produced. Outside of this triangle, production concentrates on one or two commodities. Given the expansion rays depicted in figure 3.2a, there are three equally large regions in which production concentrates on two different pairs of commodities. If endowment vectors were evenly distributed over this triangle, it would be just as likely to observe clustering of X_2 and X_3 or X_1 and X_3 as X_1 and X_2 even though X_3 uses little land (M). In order to obtain the clustering of commodities X_1 and X_2 we could assume that the endowments are distributed so that few countries fall in the cones of diversification with $X_1 = 0$ or with $X_2 = 0$. Or we could assume technologies such that the region with $X_3 = 0$, $X_1 \neq 0$, $X_2 \neq 0$ is enlarged as in figure 3.2b. These are really the same assumption since figures 3.2a and 3.2b are identical after the appropriate choice of units for measuring M. Thus complete specialization can be thought to be an explanation of the clustering of commodities only if it is coupled with a special assumption about the distribution of resources among countries. It certainly is the case that the capital/labor ratio is much more constant across countries than is the land/labor ratio, and it may appropriate to suppose that, roughly speaking, most countries do fall into either the $X_3 = 0$ cone and produce both agricultural goods, the central cone and produce all three goods, or the $X_1 = 0$, $X_2 = 0$ cone and produce neither agricultural good.

4 Data Preview

One of the important goals of this book is to provide vivid and memorable images of the international economy. Four different media are used to construct these images—words, tables, graphs, and econometric data summaries. Econometric images may be viewed with suspicion because they depend on incredible assumptions and leave one wondering whether slightly different assumptions might not produce entirely different images. This concern leads to the extensive sensitivity analysis presented in subsequent chapters. The images in this preliminary chapter are formed from tables and graphs of the actual data, and the assumptions that underlie them are minimal. A considerable amount of care has gone into the selection of these displays, and it is hoped that they will prove to be an accurate and convenient source of information about the international economy. No comparable source exists.

Sections 4.1 and 4.2 discuss features such as correlation matrices and boxplots of the trade data and the resource data. Trade dependence profiles and resource abundance profiles that are located in appendix D are discussed in section 4.3. These displays clearly indicate the composition of trade and the relative abundance of resources, and they may, with some justification, leave a more lasting impression about the sources of comparative advantage than anything else in this book. Section 4.4 contains a discussion about the adequacy and the accuracy of the resource data. When exploring the first four sections it is wise to keep in mind that the data may have some serious inaccuracies. Finally, section 4.5 contains simple correlations between the trade data and the resource data. These serve as a "warm-up" for the econometric analysis of multiple correlations presented subsequently.

4.1 Net Export Data

This section reports features of the net export data of the 10 aggregates constructed in chapter 3. The questions that are answered with tables and graphs are

1. What is the relative importance of the 10 aggregates?
2. Can the data be further aggregated?
3. Which countries are the major traders?
4. How has the trade pattern changed over time?

Table 4.1
Aggregates shares[a]

AGG	1958	1960	1963	1966	1969	1972	1975
1. PETRO	.06	.06	.07	.07	.09	.10	.21
2. MAT	.06	.07	.07	.08	.10	.08	.07
3. FOR	.08	.08	.08	.07	.07	.07	.04
4. TROP	.12	.10	.10	.08	.08	.07	.05
5. ANL	.08	.08	.08	.07	.06	.07	.04
6. CER	.13	.15	.15	.15	.10	.11	.12
7. LAB	.04	.04	.04	.05	.09	.09	.06
8. CAP	.10	.09	.08	.09	.10	.11	.10
9. MACH	.28	.27	.29	.27	.27	.27	.27
10. CHEM	.06	.05	.06	.06	.06	.05	.05

a. Share $= \sigma_i / \sum \sigma_i$, $\sigma_i =$ standard deviation of aggregate i.

Table 4.2
Aggregate correlation matrix (cross-country correlations, net export data): 1958

AGG \ AGG	1	2	3	4	5	6	7	8	9	10
1. PETRO	1.0									
2. MAT	.49	1.0								
3. FOR	.43	.75	1.0							
4. TROP	.83	.46	.45	1.0						
5. ANL	.56	.48	.54	.60	1.0					
6. CER	−.06	.33	.02	−.14	.29	1.0				
7. LAB	−.65	−.87	−.74	−.64	−.60	−.19	1.0			
8. CAP	−.67	−.81	−.63	−.65	−.66	−.38	.90	1.0		
9. MACH	−.75	−.63	−.71	−.86	−.73	.08	.78	.69	1.0	
10. CHEM	−.73	−.50	−.61	−.88	−.58	.26	.63	.59	.95	1.0

These questions are also partly answered by the trade dependence profiles discussed in section 3.

4.1.1 Behavior of the Aggregates

The relative importance of the aggregates is summarized by the standard deviations in table 4.1. Machinery maintains over time approximately a 27% share of trade. Petroleum rises dramatically from 6% in 1958 to 21% in 1975. This increase is offset by a reduction in forest products, tropical agriculture, and animal products. Of course these are shares of net export *values*, and no attempt is made to separate price changes from quantity changes.

The cross-country correlations of the aggregates in 1958 and 1975 are reported in tables 4.2 and 4.3. In 1958 the four manufactured aggregates

Table 4.3
Aggregate correlation matrix (cross-country correlations, net export data): 1975

AGG \ AGG	1	2	3	4	5	6	7	8	9	10
1. PETRO	1.0									
2. MAT	.56	1.0								
3. FOR	.39	.63	1.0							
4. TROP	.70	.32	.21	1.0						
5. ANL	.49	.49	.30	.45	1.0					
6. CER	−.32	.43	.27	−.32	.04	1.0				
7. LAB	.24	−.40	−.21	.53	−.21	−.69	1.0			
8. CAP	−.60	−.87	−.55	−.42	−.45	−.46	.27	1.0		
9. MACH	−.85	−.62	−.81	−.83	−.57	.14	−.29	.69	1.0	
10. CHEM	−.70	−.29	−.42	−.84	−.81	.31	−.85	.42	.85	1.0

7–10 are positively correlated—success in exporting one tended to be associated with success in exporting the others. Similarly the first five nonmanufactured aggregates are positively correlated, cereals being the exception. In that year, it is tempting to form only three aggregates (raw materials, cereals and manufactured goods), and to conclude that countries abundant in natural resources exported raw materials, countries abundant in labor and capital exported the manufactured goods, and countries abundant in land and capital exported cereals.

By 1975 the labor intensive aggregate had broken away from the other manufactured commodities. Otherwise, the correlation matrix is much the same. What this suggests is a breaking down of the sharp distinction between developed and developing countries in terms of success in exporting manufactured products. This is further explored in tables 4.4 and 4.5, which indicate the sign of the aggregate net export data for 1958 and 1975. The manufactured aggregates are ordered to suggest a development process that begins with the export of aggregate 7, which requires primarily low skilled workers. The next rung up the ladder of commodities is aggregate 8, which requires capital. The more advanced countries, which are abundant in skills and capital, stand at the top and export 9 and 10. In 1958 a long list of countries imported all four aggregates. Seven countries exported aggregate 7 and imported the others. Austria and India exported 7 and 8 and imported 9 and 10; Belgium imported only 9. France, Germany, the United Kingdom, and the United States exported all four of these aggregates of manufactures; but the most advanced countries were Switzerland and The Netherlands. Although Chile and

Table 4.4
The ladder of development (sign of net exports of manufactured aggregates): 1958

Aggregates				
7	8	9	10	Countries
−	−	−	+	NETH
−	−	+	+	SWITZ
+	+	+	+	FRA, GER, UK, US
+	+	+	−	ITLY, JAP
+	+	−	+	BLUX
+	+	−	−	AUST, INDA
−	+	−	−	MEX
+	−	−	−	DEN, HOKO, ISRL, PORT, SLEO, SPAN, YUG
−	−	−	−	AFG, ARG, AUSL, BRAZ, BRUI, BURM, CAN, CLUM, CSTA, CYPR, DORE, ECUA, EGPT, LSAL, FIN, GANA, GRCE, HOND, ICE, INDO, IRE, JAMC, KORA, LIBR, LIBY, MALY, MLTA, MAUR, NETA, NUZE, NIGR, NOR, PANM, PERU, PLIP, SRIL, SING, SWE, THAI, TURK
−	−	−	+	CHLE, PRGY

Table 4.5
The ladder of development (sign of net exports of manufactured aggregates): 1975[a]

Aggregates				
7	8	9	10	Countries
−	−	−	+	NETH
−	−	+	+	SWITZ, US*
−	+	+	+	GER*, UK*
−	−	+	−	SWE*
+	+	+	+	FRA, JAP*
−	+	−	+	BLUX
+	+	+	−	ITLY
+	+	−	−	AUST, INDA, KOR*, SPAN*
+	−		−	BRAZ*, CLUM*, CYPR*, DEN, EGPT*, FIN*, GRCE*, HOKO, ISRL, MLTA*, PLIP*, PORT, SLEO[b], THAI*, TURK*, YUG
−	−	−	−	AFG,[b] ARG, AUSL, BRUI,[b] BRMA,[b] CHLE,[b] CSTA, CYPR,[b] ECUA,[b] LSAL,[b] GANA, HOND, ICE, INDO, IRE, LIBR, LIBY, MALY, MAUR,[b] MEX*,[b] NUZE, NIGR, NOR, PANM,[b] SRIL, SING
−	−	−	+	JAMC*

a. Asterisk indicates a change in the sign pattern since 1958.
b. Based on 1972 data.

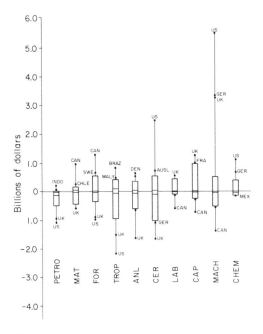

Figure 4.1
Boxplots of net export data: 1958.

Paraguay both had chemical exports in 1958, they are not placed at the top of the ladder because their chemical exports, sodium nitrate and extract of quebracho, respectively, are better classified as raw materials. Further explanation of these anomalies is provided later.

By 1975 things had changed considerably, with a large number of countries moving up this ladder of development by exporting aggregates 7 and 8 and in turn pushing the most industrialized countries out of these markets. It can be expected that the crowding of the markets of aggregates 7 and 8 causes serious adjustment problems for these most industrialized nations. The country that changed the most was Sweden, which moved from the lowest rung on the ladder to one of the highest rungs. Korea and Spain also exhibit relatively rapid changes in their trade patterns. Mexico was the only country that actually stepped down the ladder over this period. The anomalous countries in 1958, Chile and Paraguay, were no longer anomalous in 1975, but Jamaica had replaced them. Again, this is explained by the fact that the "chemical" export of Jamaica is actually a raw material (aluminum oxide).

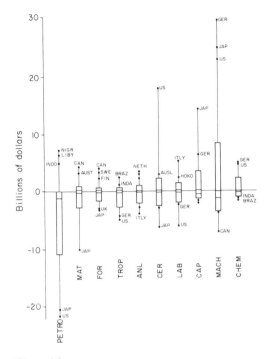

Figure 4.2
Boxplots of net export data: 1975.

The final data displays in this section are the boxplots of the net exports in figures 4.1 and 4.2. These boxplots indicate by points at least two of the extreme countries, and a third when there is a big gap between the second and the third. The remaining countries fall within or on the edge of the box. Both the upper quartile and the lower quartile of the distribution are indicated by horizontal lines. These lines are usually close to zero, which means that 75% of the countries are clustered together with relatively small net exports.

These boxplots reveal the importance of machinery trade and the increased importance of petroleum trade in 1975. The United States is often an outlier, but the trade of France, Germany, Japan (in 1975), and Canada is also very substantial in many commodities. These diagrams will be referred to again when the influence of outlying observations on the statistical inferences is discussed.

4.2 Resource Data

The collection of resource data on a large list of countries is a formidable task that necessarily involves compromises. The resources that will be used in the data analysis were selected from a longer list of potential variables on the basis of data availability, presumed economic importance (for example, polar and mountainous regions are excluded), statistical explanatory value (for example, forest area offers a poor explanation of net exports of forest products presumably because it does not distinguish tropical rain forests from cooler softwood forests), and parsimony (for example, the minerals are aggregated into a single index). A complete list of variables and a full description of sources and methods for compiling the data may be found in appendix B. The variables that have been selected are

1. *CAPITAL*. Accumulated and discounted gross domestic investment flows since 1948, assuming an average life of 15 years.

2. *LABOR 1*. Number of workers classified as professional or technical.

3. *LABOR 2*. Number of literate nonprofessional workers.

4. *LABOR 3*. Number of illiterate workers.

5. *LAND 1*. Land area in tropical rainy climate zone; comprises 30% of total area.

6. *LAND 2*. Land area in dry climate zone; comprises 30% of total area.

7. *LAND 3*. Land area in humid mesothermal climate zone (for example, California); comprises 15% of total area.

8. *LAND 4*. Land area in humid microthermal climate (for example, Michigan); comprises 17% of total area.

9. *COAL*. Value of production of primary solid fuels (coal, lignite, and brown coal).

10. *MINERALS*. Value of production of minerals: bauxite, copper, flourspar, ironore, lead, manganese, nickel, potash, pyrite, salt, tin, zinc. Table 4.6, which contains prices and values of these minerals, indicates that copper and iron ore make up about 50% of the value of minerals.

11. *OIL*. Value of oil and gas production.

This list includes measures of land, labor, capital, and natural resources. The major omission from this list is knowledge capital. Technological

Table 4.6
Prices and values of mineral resources

	Prices[a]		"World" production values (billions of current U.S. dollars)	
	1958	1975	1958	1975
Coal	9.79	35.26	11.47	40.12
Gas	3.15	35.79	1.36	41.30
Oil	9.78	49.98	6.50	67.04
Bauxite	11.37	11.32	.15	1.13
Copper	579.81	1,388.90	1.27	5.48
Fluor	55.12	104.72	.07	.30
Iron ore	8.47	18.36	.99	5.64
Lead	266.98	474.65	.42	1.01
Manganese	121.06	139.76	.21	.32
Nickel	1,631.40	4,806.03	.23	1.94
Phosphate	6.64	43.10	.11	2.02
Potash	21.00	49.21	.11	.66
Pyrite	9.84	25.29	.06	.11
Salt	11.46	15.60	.68	1.56
Tin	2,094.37	7,495.64	.22	.99
Zinc	227.29	858.91	.49	3.21
MINERALS composite[b]	.55	1.27	2.76	30.97

Source: Bureau of Mines, *Minerals Yearbook*, various years.
a. Dollars per metric ton, except for MINERALS composite, which is a 1972 quantity weighted index.
b. Excludes coal, gas, and oil.

inputs have been linked to comparative advantage in a number of studies, including Gruber, Mehta, and Vernon (1967), Keesing (1967), and Baldwin (1971, 1979). Technological inputs are here measured only by LABOR 1, the supply of professional/technical workers. The composition of this group is indicated in table 4.7, which is subsequently discussed in detail. This category is clearly too broad by its inclusion of "professionals" such as teachers and even economists. Perhaps more important, "technical" workers in advanced and in developing economies are treated as identical, but it seems quite likely that there are vast differences between them in knowledge capital. An alternative would be to use expenditure flows on education or on research and development as an indicator of knowledge capital, but the data on these expenditure flows are limited to the developed countries.

Table 4.6 reveals that the natural resources, COAL, MINERALS, and OIL, are comparable in economic value. Aggregation of COAL and OIL may seem sensible, but the distributions of these two resources across

Table 4.7
International Standard Classification of Occupations (ISCO), major group 0/1—professional, technical, and related workers (LABOR 1): 1968

0-1.	Physical scientists and related technicians
0-2/3.	Architects, engineers, and related technicians
0-4.	Aircraft and ships' officers
0-5.	Life scientists and related technicians
0-6/7.	Medical, dental, veterinary, and related workers
0-8.	Statisticians, mathematicians, systems analysts, and related technicians
0-9.	Economists
1-1.	Accountants
1-2.	Jurists
1-3.	Teachers
1-4.	Workers in religion
1-5.	Authors, journalists, and related writers
1-6.	Sculptors, painters, photographers, and related creative artists
1-7.	Composers and performing artists
1-8.	Athletes, sportsmen and related workers
1-9.	Professional, technical, and related workers not elsewhere classified

countries are quite different, and we shall let the data determine whether they have different impacts on the composition of trade. As it turns out, the distinction does seem important in 1958, though less so in 1975. Disaggregation of minerals would be desirable if the trade data were more disaggregated, but it seems unlikely that this would offer major improvements in our understanding of the determinants of our 10 trade aggregates.

Boxplots of the resource data are drawn in figures 4.3 and 4.4. These boxplots contain a horizontal line indicating the upper quartile of the distribution (75% of the countries fall below this line). These upper quartiles are all very low compared to the maximum, and all the resource data (and GNP) can be said to have a large cluster of countries near zero and a long upper tail. A few comments may be made about these boxplots.

CAPITAL. In 1958 the capital data include one extreme country (the United States) with a capital stock almost 10 times as large as the second largest country (France). The United States was still extreme in 1975, but had a capital stock only twice as large as the second largest country (Japan).

LABOR 1. The United States is an outlier in the distribution of professional workers in both 1958 and 1975. In 1958 the second most well endowed country, India, had 2.5 million workers in this category, com-

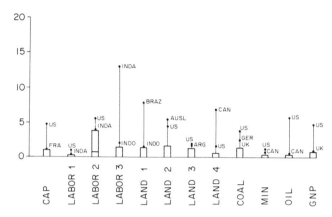

Figure 4.3
Boxplots of resource data: 1958.

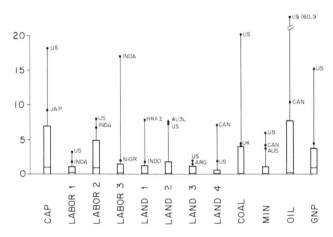

Figure 4.4
Boxplots of resource data: 1975.

pared with 7.7 in the United States. The 1975 figures are 13.6 million in United States and 7.4 in India.

LABOR 2. The United States had the greatest number of workers in the literate nonprofessional category, but Japan and India were not far behind.

LABOR 3. India was an extreme outlier in the distribution of illiterate workers, with 135 million in 1958 and 166 million in 1975. The second largest countries were Indonesia in 1958 with 21 million and Nigeria in 1975 with 18 million workers.

LAND 1. Brazil was an extreme outlier in the topical land distribution with 804 million hectares, compared with Indonesia's 167 million.

LAND 2. Australia and the United States were outliers in the distribution of LAND 2.

LAND 3. The LAND 3 distribution has a long tail including (in order) the United States, Argentina, Australia, and India.

LAND 4. Canada was the extreme outlier with 727 million hectares of LAND 4, compared with the United States's 138 million hectares, followed by Sweden's 41 million.

COAL. The United States was an outlier in coal production more so in 1975 then 1958. The other big producers were Germany, the United Kingdom, France, Japan and India in 1958, and Australia in 1975.

MINERALS. The United States was an extreme outlier. Canada also was an outlier, as was Australia in 1975.

OIL. The United States was a very extreme country, with oil production almost 20 times Canada's in 1958 and 6 times Canada's in 1975.

4.3 Trade Dependence and Resource Abundance Profiles

This section contains a discussion of the trade dependence and resource abundance profiles, which are collected together in appendix D. The form of these displays is suggested by the Heckscher-Ohlin-Vanek equations. One of the HOV equations for the $m \times m$ model takes the form $T_j = \sum_i \beta_{ji}(V_i - sV_{wi})$, where β_{ji} is an element of A^{-1}, the inverse of the matrix of factor intensities, and s is the GNP share Y/Y_w. This can be rewritten as

$$T_j/Y = \sum_i \beta_{ji}((V_i/Y) - (V_{wi}/Y_w))$$

$$= \sum_i \beta_{ji}(V_{wi}/Y_w)\left(\frac{V_i/Y}{V_{wi}/Y_w} - 1\right),$$

(4.1)

where T_j = net exports of commodity j, Y = GNP, V_i = endowment of resource i, Y_w = world GNP, and V_{wi} = world's endowment of resource i. In words, the trade dependence ratio T_j/Y is a linear function of the (centered) resource abundance ratios $(V_i/Y)/(V_{wi}/Y_w) - 1$.

This HOV equation serves as a theoretical foundation for a set of graphs that display the trade dependence ratios and the resource abundance ratios. First, the trade dependence ratios T_j/Y are collected into trade dependence profiles for each of 61 countries. These trade profiles are then sorted informally into three different groups depending on the pattern of trade in manufactures. These groups are meant to suggest the following questions: Why do all countries in a group have similar trade dependence profiles, and why do countries from different groups have dissimilar trade dependence profiles? These questions are partly answered by a study of the resource abundance ratios $(V_i/V_{iw})/(Y_i/Y_w) - 1$, which are collected into resource abundance profiles and displayed below the trade dependence profiles.

The impression I hope to leave is that exports of the natural resource products and the crops can be well explained by abundance of land or natural resources. The manufactured exports seem explainable by abundance in labor and capital. Whether this impression survives the rigors of formal statistical examination is the subject of the next chapter.

4.3.1 Trade Dependence Profiles

Trade dependence ratios (net exports relative to GNP) of the 10 commodity aggregates are collected into trade dependence profiles for 1958 and 1975, when data are available, and for other indicated years when the data are not available. In order to put all the countries on the same scale, the data have been transformed logarithmically by the function $Z = \text{sign}(T/Y) \times \ln(1 + 100|T/Y|)$. The correspondence between the numbers Z in the graphs and trade as a percentage of GNP may be found in appendix D.

These profiles, which may be found in appendix D, indicate the composition of trade. They also reveal the general level of trade dependence relative to GNP, since a country that is not very trade dependent will have short bars in the profiles. Furthermore, surplus countries will have bars primarily to the right of the profile, deficit countries primarily to the left.

The 10 aggregates that are illustrated in these profiles are described in terms of their SITC categories in the previous chapter. Roughly speaking, these 10 aggregates form a development ladder, with the most industrialized countries concentrating their exports on the manufactured commodities. Countries are accordingly sorted into three groups, depending on the sign of the net exports of the manufacturing commodities. The most advanced group is composed of exporters of machinery or chemicals in either 1958 or 1975. The middle group is composed of countries that exported labor intensive or capital intensive manufactures in 1958 or 1975, but not machinery or chemicals. Countries in the third group had net imports of all four manufactured aggregates in both years.

The following detailed comments will be most understandable if the reader refers to the relevant profiles in appendix D.

Exporters of Machinery or Chemicals   The exporters of chemicals or machinery in either 1958 or 1975 were Belgium-Luxembourg, France, Germany, Italy, Japan, The Netherlands, Sweden, Switzerland, the United Kingdom, and the United States. Chile and Paraguay had net exports of chemicals in 1958, and Jamaica had net exports of chemicals in 1975 for special reasons, and none of them is included in this category.

Generally speaking, the export earnings of these countries are concentrated in the manufactured commodities, though The Netherlands had substantial animal products exports, Sweden had forest product exports, and the United States had cereals exports. Trade profiles that are, roughly speaking, in the median of this group are France, Germany, and the United Kingdom in 1958 and Japan in 1975, each of which exported the four manufactured goods and imported all the others. Germany in 1975, Switzerland in both years, and the United Kingdom in 1975 were a step up the ladder of development, with export earnings concentrated on the last two or three manufactured aggregates. Italy in both years and Japan in 1958 were one step down the ladder, with exports concentrated on the first two or three aggregates of manufactures.

Between 1958 and 1975 these industrialized countries became somewhat more trade dependent, in particular, increasing their exports of machinery and chemicals, and either decreasing their exports or increasing their imports of labor intensive manufactures, thereby making way for the economies below them on the ladder of development. There is even some suggestion that these countries are reducing their dependence on exports of capital intensive manufactures. Another change that is apparent in these trade dependence profiles is the increase in the cost of petroleum imports.

1. *Belgium-Luxembourg.* In 1958 Belgium's exports were heavily concentrated in capital intensive manufactures. All the nonmanufactures were imported at significant rates. By 1975 Belgium had become less dependent on labor intensive and capital intensive exports, replacing these with chemicals. Labor intensive manufactures that formerly had been a source of export earnings at a rate of almost 1% of GNP fell somewhat by 1975 and actually switched to become a modest import item in 1978 (not shown). Belgium had also become much more dependent on imports of petroleum and raw materials, but somewhat less dependent on imports of cereals. An anomalous change is the switch from importing to exporting animal products.

2. *France.* France is one of the least trade dependent countries in this group. In 1958 France had positive net exports of all four manufactured products and imports of all six nonmanufactured products. In 1975 the export dependence on both labor intensive and capital intensive manufactures was less, and on machinery was more. (By 1978 France was a net importer of labor intensive manufactures.) The petroleum bill rose considerably over this period, but cereals switched from a major import item to a modest export item. This is one of the few instances of sign changes in net exports of the four crop aggregates and is suggestive of an aggressive agricultural policy.

3. *Germany.* Germany in 1958 imported all the nonmanufactured products and exported all the manufactured products, with a heavy concentration on machinery. By 1975 the petroleum bill had increased substantially, and Germany had begun importing the labor intensive manufactures and exporting more machinery and chemicals. (The 1978 data also reveal less dependence on exports of capital intensive manufactures.)

4. *Italy.* In 1958 Italy was not very trade dependent, and was a step behind many of the countries in this group on the development ladder because of her imports of chemicals. The exports of tropical/Mediterranean agricultural goods are also distinctive. By 1975 trade dependence had increased by a factor of four or five, with the biggest increase in exports of labor

intensive manufactures, suggesting a step down on the ladder of commodities.

5. *Japan*. Japan, like Italy, in 1958 had imports of chemicals and had exports of an agricultural product. The 1975 picture is quite different, with increased trade dependence and with the pattern of the most advanced economies with much less dependence on exports of labor intensive manufactures and much more dependence on machinery exports. (By 1978 capital intensive manufactures had also fallen.)

6. *The Netherlands*. The Netherlands is something of an anomaly in combining chemical exports with substantial animal products exports. From 1958 to 1975 dependence on chemical exports did increase. Further evidence of the process of development is the increased dependence on imports of labor intensive manufactures, but the switch of raw materials from the import side to the export side is another anomaly (explainable by the discovery of natural gas).

7. *Sweden*. Sweden underwent a very dramatic change in the composition of trade. In 1958 it exported only forest products and small amounts of raw materials, but in 1975 it had substantial exports of machinery and in 1978 had exports of capital intensive manufactures as well, thereby catapulting itself into the group of industrialized countries. Further evidence of this change is the increased dependence on imports of the labor intensive manufactured commodity.

8. *Switzerland*. The most advanced pattern of trade is Switzerland, with exports of only machinery and chemicals. The further advancement of Switzerland over time is evidenced by the greatly increased dependence on imports of labor intensive manufactures and the increased dependence on exports of chemicals.

9. *The United Kingdom*. The United Kingdom exported the four manufactured aggregates and imported all the others. Countering a trend, trade dependence generally fell by 1975. The pattern of exports did shift in favor of chemicals and machinery, with the labor intensive manufactures being imported in 1975.

10. *The United States*. The United States was not very trade dependent, though somewhat more so in 1975 than 1958. In 1958 it exported all the manufactured products plus cereals. The swing by 1975 toward imports of labor intensive and capital intensive imports was substantial. This,

together with increased dependence on petroleum imports, was offset by increases in machinery and cereals exports.

Exporters of Labor Intensive Manufactures and Capital Intensive Manufactures   The group of exporters of labor intensive and capital intensive manufactures can be subdivided into three categories ordered by stage of development. There were four countries that were net exporters of capital intensive manufactures in 1958 and 1975: Austria, India, Korea, and Spain. These countries can be thought to be somewhat ahead in the development process of other countries in this middle group. Denmark, Hong Kong, Israel, Portugal, and Yugoslavia were exporters of labor intensive manufactures in both 1958 and 1975, but importers of all the other manufactured aggregates. These countries form a middle subgroup. Finally, Brazil, Colombia, Cyprus, Egypt, Finland, Greece, Malta, Sri Lanka, Thailand, and Turkey show evidence of industrialization by switching from importing to exporting the labor intensive manufactured aggregate.

1. *Austria.* Austria in 1958 had exports concentrated on the labor intensive and capital intensive manufactures and also on forest products. It had heavy imports of raw materials, cereals, and machinery. By 1975 the export items fell relative to GNP, especially labor intensive manufactures, which in 1978 were imported (not shown in appendix D). The import items generally grew relative to GNP, resulting in a substantial trade deficit. Though there is evidence of movement up the ladder of development in reduced exports of labor intensive manufactures, this is not accompanied by reduced dependence on machinery or chemical imports.

2. *Brazil.* Brazil was not very trade dependent. It depended in 1958 almost entirely on exports of tropical agricultural products. In 1975 it also exported labor intensive manufactures and cereals. In 1978 capital intensive manufactures were exported as well. This is evidence of fairly rapid industrialization.

3. *Colombia.* Colombia is very similar to Brazil. In 1958 it was very dependent on exports of tropical agricultural products and petroleum. By 1975 it was exporting also animal products and labor intensive manufactures.

4. *Cyprus.* Cyprus in 1958 exported raw materials and tropical agricultural products. From 1958 to 1975 labor intensive manufactures switched from being a major import to a major export item. Cyprus is a very trade dependent country.

5. *Denmark*. Denmark had a small amount of exports of labor intensive manufactures, but its heavy dependence on exports of animal products makes it much more similar to Ireland than to the other countries in this middle group.

6. *Egypt*. Egypt is difficult to classify since its trade pattern was erratic. In 1958, exports were very concentrated in cereals; in 1975 there were heavy imports of cereals and small exports of labor intensive manufactures. In 1978 exports were completely concentrated in petroleum.

7. *Finland*. Forest products were the primary export item of Finland in 1958. By 1975 it was exporting also labor intensive manufactures.

8. *Greece*. In 1958 Greece exported agricultural products, but by 1975 was exporting labor intensive manufactures, in part paying the bill for large imports of machinery. Cereals switched from being a large export item to a moderate import item.

9. *Hong Kong*. Hong Kong is a very unusual country. It is very trade dependent, increasingly so from 1958 to 1975. Its exports are completely concentrated in labor intensive manufactures, in excess of 20% of GNP in 1975.

10. *India*. India is one of the most advanced countries in this group in the sense of having exports of capital intensive manufactures. It also had export earnings from tropical agricultural products, raw materials, and labor intensive manufactures, though it was not very trade dependent.

11. *Israel*. Israel earned export earnings both from labor intensive manufactures and from tropical/Mediterranean agricultural products. The changes over time are small, though in 1975 it did have greater dependence on exports of labor intensive manufactures and more dependence on imports of machinery and chemicals. In both years, the trade deficit is substantial.

12. *Korea*. A trade deficit in 1958 allowed Korea to import all categories except for tiny exports of animal products. By 1975 Korea was exporting very large amounts of labor intensive manufactures and large amounts of capital intensive manufactures, and animal products as well. This is evidence of a very substantial increase in industrialization.

13. *Malta*. Malta in 1958 exported small amounts of raw materials and ran a large deficit. By 1975 it was exporting large amounts of labor intensive manufactures and was very trade dependent. Hong Kong and Malta had very similar trade compositions.

14. *Portugal.* Portugal barely had positive labor intensive exports in 1958, but had substantial exports in 1975. It also has export earnings from various agricultural commodities, which were used to finance large imports of machinery, cereals, and petroleum.

15. *Spain.* Spain had small amounts of exports of labor intensive manufactures in 1958, but had virtually all export earnings from tropical/ Mediterranean agricultural products. It became substantially more industrialized by 1975, with export earnings concentrated on labor intensive manufactures and with the reduced dependence on exports of tropical/ Mediterranean agricultural products. It also had begun to export the capital intensive manufactures.

16. *Sri Lanka.* Sri Lanka in 1958 had export earnings concentrated in tropical/Mediterranean agricultural products and had a trade profile very similar to Costa Rica, Dominican Republic, and Ecuador. Although in 1975 it continued to have export earnings concentrated in TROP, it also had receipts from labor intensive manufactures, and in that sense shows evidence of substantial industrialization. Also of note is the heavy imports of cereals.

17. *Thailand.* Thailand was a substantial exporter of cereals and tropical agricultural products in both years, and in 1975 it became a substantial exporter of labor intensive manufactures. Dependence on imports of capital intensive manufactures became less over this period, and dependence on imports of machinery became much more.

18. *Turkey.* Turkey, which was not very trade dependent, exported raw materials and agricultural products in 1958. Small amounts of labor intensive manufactures were exported in 1975, and imports of the other manufactures and petroleum rose substantially.

19. *Yugoslavia.* Yugoslavia's exports of labor intensive manufactures increased greatly from 1958 to 1975. It also has export earnings from forest and animal products. Trade dependence increased substantially from 1958 to 1975.

Importers of Manufactured Commodities   The rest of the countries in the sample had net imports of all four of the aggregates of manufactured commodities in both years. Generally speaking, there is little change in their trade profiles between 1958 and 1975. They form a rather diverse group of countries, but seem sensibly separated into a subgroup of diversified countries and a subgroup of specialized countries, the latter having export earnings concentrated on one or two commodities.

The diversified countries in this group are Afghanistan, Australia, Canada, Mexico, Norway, Paraguay, Peru, and the Philippines. Mexico is classified as an importer of manufactures because of its 1972 trade profile, but in 1958 it exported capital intensive manufactures. This is one of the few examples of a country stepping down the ladder of commodities.

The specialized countries can be divided into groups depending on their export items. Costa Rica, the Dominican Republic, Ecuador, El Salvador, Ghana, Honduras, Mauritius, and Panama specialized in tropical agricultural products. Jamaica, Liberia, Malaysia, and Singapore exported both tropical agricultural products and raw materials. Chile exported raw materials. Burma exported cereals (rice). Ireland exported animal products. Indonesia, Libya, and Nigeria exported petroleum and other products. Argentina, Iceland, and New Zealand exported animal products and cereals. [Note that Iceland's animal products are primarily fish (SITC 03). Its cereals are miscellaneous food preparations (SITC 10) and animal oils and fats (SITC 26). New Zealand's cereals are primarily textile fibers (SITC 26), for example, wool.]

There are three anomalies in this group of countries. Chile and Paraguay in 1958 and Jamaica in 1975 all had positive net exports of chemicals and might be classified in the most developed group. For each of these countries, positive net exports of chemicals are a result of large exports of some peculiar product that would be better classified as a raw material than as a chemical.

The Chilean export of chemicals in 1958 is an interesting case of a commodity in transition between two of the aggregates. In 1910 64% of the world's sodium nitrate (saltpeter) was mined in Chile.[1] Saltpeter is sometimes even called Chilean nitrate. Synthetic substitutes discovered after World War I slowly replaced Chilean nitrate until by 1960 Chilean production was only 1.5% of world output. But in 1958 the mining and export of Chilean nitrate was still sufficient to give Chile a positive balance of chemical exports. Sodium nitrate is classified under SITC 51. From the standpoint of this book it would have been better to allocate Chilean nitrate to the raw materials aggregate but retain synthetic nitrates in the chemicals aggregate. Over time this misclassification corrects itself because the synthetic nitrates came to dominate the market.

The other two anomalies are also caused by deficiencies in the aggregation scheme in that items are classified as "chemicals" that are better thought to be raw materials. Paraguay had very large exports of the extract of the quebracho tree, which is used for tanning and is classified with processed chemicals that are also used for tanning. Jamaica had large exports of aluminum oxide, which is extracted from bauxite ore. (Bauxite, on the other hand, is classified as a raw material.)

4.3.2   Resource Abundance Profiles

Resource abundance profiles may be found below the trade profiles in appendix D. The first 11 horizontal bars in these profiles indicate the resource abundance ratios $(V_i/V_{wi})/(Y/Y_w)$, that is, the ratio of the share of the resource to the GNP share. The last horizontal bar, labeled SIZE, indicates the country's GNP divided by GNP averaged over all countries in the given year. Several different transformations of these data were considered, and the one that produced the clearest displays was selected. If x represents a resource abundance ratio $(V_i/V_{wi})/(Y/Y_w)$, or the relative GNP $Y/\bar{Y}$, then what is graphed is $z = (5x - 5)/(x + 5)$. This function takes on the value -1 if $x = 0$ and 0 if $x = 1$, and it has an asymptotic value of 5 as x goes to infinity. The correspondence between the numbers in the graphs and the resource ratios may be found in appendix D. In the case of a resource, the graphed value is positive if the resource is abundant in the HOV sense, $V_i/V_{iw} > Y/Y_w$. In the case of the GNP variable, the graphed value of SIZE is positive if a country's GNP exceeds average GNP.

The usefulness of the absolute resource abundance ratios as indicators of factor abundance is limited to settings in which GNP is a linear function of the endowments of productive factors, that is, when we may write GNP as $Y = \sum w_i V_i$, where w_i is the return to factor i. Then the GNP share is a weighted average of the endowment shares with weights equal to world earnings of the factors, $Y/Y_w = \sum_i (w_i V_{wi})(V_i/V_{wi})/\sum_i w_i V_{wi}$. If an endowment share V_i/V_{wi} exceeds the GNP share, the country is abundantly supplied in factor i compared with other resources on the average, and according to the Heckscher-Ohlin-Vanek theorem, the country's net exports will embody positive amounts of the resource. An abundance ratio can also be expressed as the world "productivity" divided by home "productivity," $(Y_w/V_{wi})/(Y/V_i)$. For example, if the resource is labor, the abundance ratio is world GNP per worker divided by home country GNP per worker. A country is therefore said to be abundantly supplied in labor if its labor productivity is less than the labor productivity of the world as a whole. This definition is a consequence of the fact that GNP is assumed to be a linear function of the endowments, and the only reason for relatively low labor productivity is relative scarcity of the other resources that form GNP. If GNP is a nonlinear function of the endowments, for example, if scale economies are important or if factor prices are not equalized, a comparison of a resource share with the GNP share will not reveal the abundance of the factor compared with other factors on the average. Pairwise comparisons of the abundance ratios are nonetheless appropriate, since they will reveal the relative abundance of the two resources considered.

There are measurement problems as well as conceptual problems with these resource abundance ratios. The world endowments of the resources and the world GNP are necessarily estimated inaccurately because the coverage of countries is incomplete. It may appear, for example, that a country is scarce in labor because we are overestimating world GNP per capita by excluding countries from the developing world without adequate data. It is in fact quite likely that countries that in our sample appear to have an abundance of in oil would actually be measured to have a scarcity if the major oil exporters were included. An error of this form would require proportional adjustment of the data for the selected resource of all countries.

If the GNP figure of a particular country is mismeasured, then the proper correction would be to adjust all of the resource abundance ratios upward if GNP is overestimated, or downward if GNP is underestimated. Even if GNP is measured accurately, this adjustment can be required by the Heckscher-Ohlin-Vanek theorem if there is trade imbalance, since the GNP ratio Y_i/Y_w should properly be replaced by the consumption share $(Y_i - B)/Y_w$, where B is the trade surplus. For most countries this correction is very small.

These conceptual and measurement concerns notwithstanding, a study of the resource profiles in comparison with the trade profiles is quite interesting. If the Heckscher-Ohlin model were correct, countries with similar trade dependence profiles would have similar resource abundance profiles. Indeed, this seems to be correct. Though there are many cases that seem unusual, it is exceedingly difficult to estimate multiple regressions visually, and we need to reserve judgment on the accuracy of the Heckscher-Ohlin model until the computer estimates in chapter 6 are discussed. Not surprisingly, much that can be seen visually is also detected by the formal econometrics.

The following detailed comments will be most understandable if the reader refers to the relevant profiles in appendix D.

Exporters of Machinery and Chemicals The countries with the most advanced trade dependence profiles in the sense of exporting machinery and chemicals are generally abundant in CAPITAL and in many cases scarce in everything else. The CAPITAL scarce countries in this group were Belgium-Luxembourg and Italy in 1958, the United States in 1975, and the United Kingdom in both years. The exporters of machinery and chemicals were also generally scarce in land and natural resources, but Belgium, Japan, and The Netherlands in 1958, the United States in 1975, and the United Kingdom in both years were all abundant in COAL. This hints at COAL reserves as a source of comparative advantage in manufactures, a finding that will come up again in chapter 6. An exception to the general scarcity of land is France in 1958, which was abundant in LAND 3. Sweden in both years was abundant in LAND 4 and MINERALS. This conforms nicely to the Swedish trade profiles, which have exports of forest products (associated with LAND 4) and raw materials (associated with MINERALS). (Note that although land area may remain unchanged, the land abundance ratio may change because the GNP share changes.) The countries that never exported any agricultural products (Germany, Switzerland, and the United Kingdom) seem to be among the poorest in land.

All three categories of labor were generally scarce in these most developed countries in 1975, but LABOR 1 and LABOR 2 were often abundant in 1958. The frequency with which LABOR 1 is measured to be scarce is cause for concern either about the meaning of the LABOR 1 category or about the resource abundance ratios as indicators of abundance. This finding, as discussed previously, could be summarized by saying that the productivity (output per worker) of LABOR 1 workers in the industrialized countries exceeds productivity in the developing countries. We can think of reasons why this is the case other than a relative abundance of other inputs in the industrialized countries. A comparison of the abundance ratios for the different labor groups may nonetheless be meaningful. Most countries were most abundant in the most highly skilled labor in the sense that LABOR 1 > LABOR 2 > LABOR 3, but

Germany in 1958 and Italy, Japan, and the United Kingdom in 1958 were more abundant in LABOR 2 than in LABOR 1.

The countries in this group that are smaller than the overall average (see the SIZE bar)—Belgium-Luxembourg, The Netherlands, Sweden, and Switzerland—have exports concentrated on one or two of the manufactured aggregates. This hints at scale economies as a source of comparative advantage, but because these are commodity aggregates, this suggestion should be viewed with some suspicion.

The resource abundance ratios of these countries were somewhat different in 1975 than in 1958. This is due principally to the relatively slow accumulation of capital in the United States and the rapid accumulation in the rest of the industrialized world. The effect of these differences in the rate of capital accumulation is to lower the GNP share of the United States and to increase it elsewhere. This will tend to increase the abundance ratios in the United States and to reduce them elsewhere. Labor, for example, becomes less scarce in the United States and less abundant in the other countries for this reason. Capital, however, which is the source of the changes in GNP shares, moves in the opposite direction, with the United States becoming less abundant and the other countries becoming more abundant.

The distinguishing characteristics of countries in this group are CAPITAL abundance combined with scarcity of most other resources. But there are many countries in the other two groups which according to our data also had an abundance of CAPITAL. From the list of countries that did export one or more of the manufactured commodities, the ones with a relative abundance of capital are Israel, Sweden, Cyprus, Finland, Malta in 1975, and Yugoslavia in 1958. Several countries that did not export any of the four manufactured aggregates also had CAPITAL abundance. These are Australia, Canada, Jamaica in 1958, Mauritius, New Zealand in 1958, Norway, Iceland, and Singapore in 1975. One thing that distinguishes these countries from the exporters of machinery and chemicals is the relative abundance of some other resource compared with CAPITAL. The CAPITAL abundant countries with no exports of manufactures generally have a very great abundance of land and minerals (for example, Australia, Canada, and Norway).

Exporters of Labor Intensive and Capital Intensive Manufactures The middle group of countries—the exporters of labor intensive and capital intensive manufactures—are generally abundant in LABOR. Korea is a good example. The exceptions include Austria, Denmark, and Finland, with LABOR abundance rather like the most advanced countries. Denmark is something of an overachiever in 1975 (it is scarce in everything). Israel is also an exception, with abundance in LABOR 1 but scarcity in LABOR 2 and LABOR 3.

The nonmanufactured products exported by this group seem very well explained by resource abundance. Sweden exports forest products because of abundance of LAND 4. Korea exports animal products, also because of LAND 4. Spain uses LAND 3 to produce tropical/Mediterranean agricultural products. Brazil uses LAND 1 and LAND 3 for the same. Colombia exports tropical agricultural products and petroleum because of LAND 1 and OIL resources. Cyprus has an abundance of LAND 3 and MINERALS, and exports tropical agricultural products and raw materials. Finland sells forest products grown on LAND 4. Greece has tropical agricultural exports and an abundance of LAND 3. Malta, like Hong Kong in more ways than one, is concentrated on labor intensive exports and has only labor abundance. Thailand uses LAND 1 to produce tropical agricultural products and cereals. (This is a case where rice might better have been allocated to another aggregate.) Portugal, which is well endowed with LAND 3, has exports of the tropical/Mediterranean agricultural products. Finally, Turkey, with an abundance of LAND 2 and 3, exports tropical agricultural products, animal products, and cereals.

Importers of the Manufactured Commodities It is to be suspected that a shortage of CAPITAL is the explanation for importing all the manufactured commodities. This seems correct for many of the countries, but there is a handful that had adequate CAPITAL relative to GNP or labor to justify the export of manufactured products. This list of countries includes Argentina, Australia, Canada, Denmark, Iceland, Ireland, New Zealand, and Norway. All of these countries are much more abundant in LAND than CAPITAL. CAPITAL scarcity, not necessarily relative to LABOR, therefore seems to account for dependence on imports of manufactured products. (More on this is in chapter 6.)

The diversified exporters do seem to have more balanced resource profiles than the specialized exporters. Animal product exporters have LAND 3 abundance. Tropical products exporters have LAND 1 abundance. The countries well endowed in MINERALS and/or OIL naturally export the corresponding products. Note the abundance for many of these countries of LABOR 1, a fact that makes one suspicious of the "professional/ technical" categorization. More comments on this are made in the next section.

Most countries in this group have little change in their resource profiles from 1958 to 1975. The ones with relatively rapid capital accumulation are Indonesia, Ireland, Liberia, Libya, Malaysia, and Singapore. The trade profiles of these countries do seem to conform in that dependence on imports of the labor intensive manufactures does diminish.

It would be possible to continue this discussion of the trade dependence profiles and the resource abundance profiles for many more pages. However, the intent of this section is not to provide a full examination of the relation between trade and endowments, since that is better done using multiple regression analysis, to be discussed. The intent of this relatively brief discussion is to entice the reader into a more careful study of these data displays, and to make visually clear that resource abundance is indeed a source of comparative advantage.

4.4 Notes on Data Accuracy

Both the trade data and the resource data have been carefully scrutinized over a period of several years as they have been used for a variety of purposes. Questions concerning the accuracy and usefulness of the trade data have been few and have always been resolved. (For example: Why does Iceland have animal products exports? Answer: Because fish are included in that aggregate.) The resource data, on the other hand, are a continuing source of concern. For example:

a. Many developing countries have an abundance of labor in the professional/technical category. The composition of this group is indicated in table 4.7. What probably accounts for the surprising abundance of LABOR 1 among the developing countries is the inclusion of teachers, doctors, and lawyers. These workers are likely to have a very different effect on the composition of trade than physical scientists, and disaggregation, if data permitted, would have been highly desirable.

b. Several developing countries, like Afghanistan, are more abundant in LABOR 1 than LABOR 2. LABOR 2 is a residual category formed by removing the illiterate workers and the professional workers from the total labor force. The literacy rate of the population as a whole is assumed to apply also to the labor force, whereas it seems quite likely that workers would have a higher literacy rate. Accordingly, LABOR 2 ought to be increased in many countries with low literacy rates and LABOR 3 decreased.

c. The division of labor into the three categories is intended to measure differences in human capital. The pure labor component is approximated by LABOR 3, the illiterate work force; labor embodying human capital is measured by LABOR 2 and LABOR 1. This categorization concentrates on explicit off-the-job accumulations of human capital and ignores both on-the-job training as well as experience and age-related changes in skills. The developing economies generally have a younger population and higher labor force participation rates among the young. For example, the percentage of population aged 15–30 in 1975 was 21% in Belgium, Italy, Norway, and the United Kingdom but was 26% or more in, among other countries Brazil, Costa Rica, Chile, and Nicaruaga (see table 4.8). The percentage of males aged 15–19, who are classified as "economically active," varies from lows of 32.9 in Sweden and 36.5 in Japan to highs of 71.4 in El Salvador and 77.8 in Paraguay. What this may mean is that our division of labor into the three categories fails to capture a part of human capital that happens to be positively correlated with the stage of development.

d. A further problem with the LABOR 1 category is that the censuses that are used to count the professional/technical workers are done intermittently, and the 1958 and 1975 data we have used are generally constructed by extrapolation, interpolation, and imputation; when needed, this group includes also a dash of salt and a sprinkle of pepper. (See appendix B for more details.) If you add to this the census errors, you begin to get rather uncomfortable about the division of labor into its three categories.

e. The total labor force defined by the International Labor Organization (ILO) as the "economically active" population is also questionable, since the definition of "economically active" can vary from country to country depending on the treatment of such things as

i. Casual, seasonal, part-time workers, and those engaged in looking for work.

ii. Nonmarket family labor, especially work on family owned farms in

Table 4.8
Population characteristics

	Labor force participation rates		Male, 15–19	Age composition (%)				Hours per week[a]
	Male	Female		0–15	15–30	30–60	60+	
Argentina	57.9	19.4	60.7	30	25	35	9	
Australia	56.8	26.7	55.8	29	25	34	12	40.6[b]
Austria	54.2	30.3	65.6	24	20	35	20	33.9
Belgium	54.2	21.9	41.3	24	21	36	19	35.4
Brazil	53.7	23.6	62.1	42	26	26	5	
Canada	53.4	28,3	30					
Chile	46.4	13.3	42.3	39	26	26	7	
Colombia	47.6	11.6	66.3	48	23	24	5	
Costa Rica	47.6	11.6	67.6	48	23	24	5	
Cyprus	56.3	27.5						43
Denmark	59.8	34.1	55.5	23	24	35	18	33.1
Dom. Rep.	46.1	15.9	55.1	48	24	23	5	
Egypt	51.2	4.2	58.6	43	23	27	6	
Equador	54.0	10.5						51
El Sal.	52.8	21.5	71.4	46	25	24	5	48.2[b]
Finland	55.2	37.5	43.6	24	26	35	14	38.4
France	55.9	28.0	42.8	24	22	36	19	42.7
Germany	59.2	30.0	66.9	25	21	38	16	40.5
Ghana				47	24	23	5	
Greece	54.3	20.2	46.4	25	21	38	16	42.7
Honduras				48	25	22	5	
Hong Kong	54.8	28.8	50.4	36	24	32	7	
Iceland	55.8	21.5						51.7
India	52.5	11.9	55.2	42	24	28	6	
Indonesia	46.0	22.0	48.9	44	24	32		
Ireland	55.6	19.4	50.7	31	22	31	16	41.3
Israel	50.2	18.3						37.9
Italy	54.3	19.6	52.0	24	21	38	17	
Jamaica					—			
Japan	63.2	39.1	36.5	24	28	38	11	39.7

Table 4.8 (continued)

	Labor force participation rates		Male, 15–19	Age composition (%)				Hours per week[a]
	Male	Female		0–15	15–30	30–60	60+	
Korea	42.8	23.2	45.9	42	25	28	5	50.0
Liberia					—			
Libya				44	24		32	
Luxembourg	57.3	19.5	54.9	22	21	39	19	40.9
Malta	53.4	13.4			—			
Malaysia				46		49	5	
Mauritius	50.5	12.5	64.1	40	28	26	5	
Mexico	43.6	10.2	49.9	45	25	23	6	45.6
Neta	45.3	23.4	37.7	40	26	26	7	
Netherlands				28		58	15	
New Zealand	54.9	23.3	57.1	32	24	32	13	37.2
Nicaragua	42.4	11.4	53.6	48	26	22	5	
Nigeria				43	32	22	3	
Norway	54.9	20.8	36.2	26[c]	21[d]	35	18	40.2
Panama	50.2	17.8	60.9	43	26	25	6	45.7
Paraguay	50.8	13.6	77.8	45	25	24	6	
Peru	45.3	11.8	39.8	44	26	24	6	
Philippines	46.0	21.3	52.4	43	27	24	5	46.6
Portugal	62.1	19.0	79.0	28	22	35	14	
Singapore				39	28	27	6	
Spain	57.5	13.4	65.9	28	22	36	14	42.8
Sri Lanka	49.3	18.8	48.6	39	28	26	6	
Sweden	54.7	29.9	32.9	21	23	37	20	36.6
Swiss	63.9	32.1	62.8	23	24	37	16	
Thailand	52.0	46.0	77.4	45	25	25	5	
U.K.	60.6	32.9	60.8	24	21	36	19	43.6[b]
U.S.	55.7	33.1	40.3	29	24	33	14	36.1
Yugoslavia	56.4	30.7	41.3	27	25	36	12	

Source: *Yearbook of Labor Statistics*, 1975.
a. Hours of work per week in nonagricultural sector, or manufacturing if not available.
b. Males only.
c. 0–16.
d. 16–30.

the less market-oriented economies, but also work in the home. The female labor force participation rate varies widely. For example, according to the ILO *Yearbook of Labor Statistics*, 1975, the proportion of women defined as "economically active" varied from 10.2% in Mexico to 39.1% in Japan (see table 4.8).

Furthermore, the total number of hours worked can vary depending on vacations, as well as on the number of hours worked per day. The variation of weekly hours across countries (table 4.8) is substantial, with the more developed countries having fewer hours, and probably more productive workers on the average because of reduced fatigue.

f. The capital measure is highly correlated with GNP. In 1958 the capital stock figures are virtually the same as the GNP figures, averaging across countries only 1% more. A larger wedge is driven between them by 1975, with capital averaging 50% more than GNP, but still the figures are disturbingly similar. This can also be seen in the resource profiles in which capital abundance figure rarely deviates much from zero. The capital stock figure is formed by accumulating and discounting investment flows over a 15-year period. Neither savings rates nor growth rates vary enough from country to country to drive much of a wedge between the capital data and the GNP data.

The capital estimates appear to be seriously underestimated if our 1958 number for the United States ($504 billion) is compared with Kendrick's number of $3,330 billion Kendrick (1976) goes to great lengths to include measures of all forms of wealth, many of which are excluded from the investment component of GNP. Kendrick's figure includes human intangible wealth (education, training, medical and health, and mobility), nonhuman intangibles (basic research and applied research and development), human tangibles (rearing costs of children) and nonhuman tangibles. For example, in 1966 he inflates the U.S. savings rate from the Commerce Department's number of 16.2% to 50.6%. Kendrick reports the much smaller number of $1,588.5 billion for nonhuman tangible wealth, of which $326.7 billion is land, which is wealth but not capital as we are using the term. If attention is restricted to the private domestic business economy, Kendrick's nonhuman tangible capital stock drops to $678.7 billion. If from this number the value of land is subtracted and the value of private residences is a added, a figure similar to our estimate of $504 billion might be obtained.

Table 4.9
Climate classification

A. Tropical rainy climates (LAND 1)
1. Tropical rainforest
2. Tropical savanna
B. Dry climates (LAND 2)
1. Steppe
a. Tropical and subtropical steppe
b. Middle latitude steppe
2. Desert
a. Tropical and subtropical
b. Middle latitude desert
C. Humid meso-thermal climates (LAND 3)
1. Mediterranean or dry summer subtropical
2. Humid subtropical
3. Marine west coast
D. Humid micro-thermal climates (LAND 4)
1. Humid continental, warm summer
2. Humid continental, cool summer
3. Subarctic
E. Polar climates
1. Tundra
2. Ice cap
F. Undifferentiated highlands

Another source is the Commerce Department's *Long Term Economic Growth*, which reports the following capital stock figures for 1958: consumer durables ($160.5 billion), residential structures ($304.2 billion), land ($203.2 billion), fixed business capital ($324.2 billion). Our number of $504 billion is not unlike the sum of residential structures and fixed business capital ($628.2 billion).

g. Total land area is divided into six components by inspection of the U.S. Air Force *Climatic Chart of the World* (see table 4.9). There is of course some error in this division, but there is also question whether the six categories of land are finely enough divided. LAND 4 includes humid continental land (warm summer and cool summers) and also subarctic land, much of which is not suited to agriculture. Canada and the United States are both well endowed with LAND 4, but much of Canada's is in the colder regions and is relatively unproductive. The influence of the Canadian observation on the productivity of LAND 4 is very substantial (chapter 6) and somewhat misleading because of this compositional problem. Generally speaking, two resources (for example, two categories of land) can be aggregated together if they have the same effect on trade and output, or if they are perfectly correlated across countries. Subarctic land can be expected to have a rather different effect on the composition of output than humid continental land with a warm summer. And because the Canadian observation contrasts greatly with the United States, endowments of these two land subcategories are not very highly correlated. Aggregation, as a result, is not especially desirable. The aggregation of steppe and desert into LAND 2 may also be problematical. Given our aggregation of commodities, LAND 1 and LAND 3 do not have obvious aggregation flaws.

h. No attempt is made to distinguish the fertility of land, which creates yet another aggregation problem. Some preliminary statistical work with "arable land," "forest land," and "pasture land" from the FAO *Production Yearbook* was not too promising. The "forest land" variable fails to distinguish tropical (hardwood) forests from cooler softwood forests, yet most of the value of trade in forest products comes from the cooler areas. Arable land similarly fails to distinguish climate types, which is important since the trade aggregates seem to be associated with land of different climates. The use of pasture land is avoided since the division of land into various uses is an economic decision, endogenous to our model; the same comment applies to a lesser extent to arable land and forest land.

4.5 Cross-Country Correlations

Correlations of trade relative to GNP with endowments relative to GNP are reported in table 4.10 and correlations of trade per worker with endowments per worker are reported in table 4.11. These serve initially to identify important resources and to help select the graphs that are presented in appendix C.

The correlations reported in table 4.10 are somewhat easier to understand because they compare each resource with the composite of all resources measured by GNP. Concern over the inaccuracy of the GNP measurement makes the per worker correlations in table 4.11 also of interest. In table 4.11 petroleum trade and raw material trade have the highest correlations, not surprisingly with oil production and mineral output, respectively. Forest product net exports are highly correlated with LAND 4. Animal products net exports are almost as highly correlated with LAND 3. The other products have either disappointing or puzzling correlations. Tropical agricultural exports have fairly large correlations

Table 4.10
Correlations among trade/GNP and endowments/GNP[a]

	Capital	Labor 1	Labor 2	Labor 3	Land 1	Land 2	Land 3	Land 4	Coal	Min-erals	Oil
1958											
PETRO	.05	.11	.18	.27	.25	−.02	−.09	.03	.19	.00	**.55**
MAT	−.14	.04	−.06	.16	.34	−.03	−.10	.03	−.23	**.96**	.04
FOR	.14	−.03	.02	−.02	.09	−.06	.07	**.53**	−.11	−.06	−.02
TROP	−.24	.19	.06	.24	**.28**	−.12	−.15	−.17	−.31	.30	−.01
ANL	.21	−.20	−.11	−.17	−.05	−.00	**.36**	.01	.05	−.16	−.05
CER	−.12	.20	**.38**	.29	.27	.00	.17	.05	−.04	−.03	.18
LAB	−.05	−.02	.07	−.11	−.10	−.11	−.03	−.05	.10	**−.22**	.02
CAP	.11	−.24	−.07	−.19	−.17	−.25	−.06	.04	**.55**	−.20	.16
MACH	.01	−.01	.14	−.06	−.08	**−.51**	−.03	−.01	.47	−.30	.11
CHEM	.14	−.06	.06	−.04	.07	−.25	.18	.11	**.39**	.00	.07
1975											
PETRO	−.27	.05	.01	.06	.04	.24	−.01	−.01	−.07	−.09	**.94**
MAT	−.03	.08	−.02	.11	.25	.04	−.03	.02	−.04	**.96**	.00
FOR	.10	.03	.08	.01	.15	−.05	.08	**.39**	−.06	.09	−.03
TROP	**−.28**	.19	.13	.15	.07	−.06	−.10	−.14	−.18	.08	−.10
ANL	.13	−.04	−.06	.01	−.00	.03	**.16**	−.02	.01	−.08	−.06
CER	−.04	−.01	.01	.03	**.18**	.10	.13	.12	11	.02	.06
LAB	−.04	−.04	.02	−.05	−.10	−.06	−.04	−.05	.06	−.14	**−.17**
CAP	−.01	−.06	.00	−.01	−.05	.01	.02	.06	**.31**	−.19	−.12
MACH	.10	−.02	−.01	.02	−.12	.06	−.02	.01	.25	**−.31**	−.15
CHEM	**.13**	−.10	−.08	−.05	−.03	.03	.03	.05	.09	−.00	−.01

a. Highest correlations in boldface.

with tropical land (LAND 1), but are better explained in terms of capital scarcity or mineral abundance. Cereals are associated with the land variables, but even more so with literate labor (LABOR 1 and LABOR 2) in 1975. None of the manufactured aggregates is associated positively to any great degree with any of the resources except COAL, which has its greatest impact on capital intensive manufactures (iron and steel). Machinery net exports are associated with scarcity of LAND 2 in 1958 and scarcity of minerals in 1975.

It is fair to conclude that table 4.10 promises adequate explanations of trade in the crops and raw materials, but leaves a large question mark about the source of comparative advantage in manufactured commodities.

Table 4.11
Correlations among trade per worker and endowments per worker

	Capital	Labor 1	Labor 2	Labor 3	Land 1	Land 2	Land 3	Land 4	Coal	Minerals	Oil
1958											
GNP	**.96**	.81	.59	−.64	−.24	.01	.27	.46	.53	.25	.62
PETRO	−.50	**−.68**	−.43	.46	.27	.01	−.47	−.18	−.09	−.08	.05
MAT	.08	−.09	.16	.15	.17	.00	−.12	.52	−.21	**.87**	.23
FOR	.31	.22	.15	−.16	−.06	−.05	−.19	**.61**	−.13	.23	.17
TROP	−.44	**−.46**	−.41	.43	.31	−.08	−.23	−.22	−.31	.04	−.17
ANL	.31	.26	.28	−.28	−.09	−.01	**.73**	.03	.04	−.10	−.04
CER	.29	−.03	.04	−.03	.16	.12	**.64**	.20	.11	.13	.20
LAB	−.31	−.19	−.02	.04	−.02	−.11	−.33	**−.37**	.09	−.31	−.11
CAP	−.23	−.16	−.03	.05	.04	−.13	**−.51**	−.21	.34	−.14	.03
MACH	−.28	−.23	−.05	.07	.04	−.25	**−.45**	−.31	.25	−.22	.05
CHEM	.04	−.08	.06	−.05	.03	−.17	**−.31**	−.02	.28	.06	.19
1975											
GNP	**.97**	.83	.43	−.53	−.33	.40	.21	.30	.36	.12	.40
PETRO	.15	−.05	−.34	.31	−.02	.94	−.07	−.02	−.06	−.05	**.98**
MAT	.06	.00	−.21	.19	.29	.36	.29	.32	.34	**.70**	.28
FOR	.23	.24	.07	−.11	−.05	−.14	−.16	**.49**	−.05	.16	−.10
TROP	**−.58**	−.44	−.26	.31	.28	−.27	−.21	−.23	−.06	.08	−.33
ANL	.27	.32	.22	−.25	−.09	−.10	**.69**	−.02	.01	−.05	−.12
CER	−.04	−.03	.09	−.08	.28	−.22	.45	.25	**.53**	.39	−.34
LAB	−.41	−.27	.14	−.08	−.02	−.47	−.18	−.15	−.09	−.12	**−.49**
CAP	−.15	−.19	.13	−.09	.09	−.53	−.19	−.07	.13	−.00	**−.57**
MACH	−.21	−.16	.09	−.05	.06	−.54	−.36	−.17	.06	−.10	**−.55**
CHEM	.02	−.04	.04	−.03	.02	−.15	**−.42**	−.08	.09	.06	−.15

a. Highest correlations in boldface.

5 Econometric Methods

The estimation of the Heckscher-Ohlin-Vanek equations with linear least-squares regression requires a sequence of incredible assumptions: (1) Unmeasured determinants of trade can be collected into additive error terms, which, conditional on the measured determinants, behave like a sequence of independent, identically distributed normal random variables with zero means and constant, unknown variances. (2) The observed determinants of trade are measured without error. (3) The equation is linear. (4) The data set is so informative that other sources of information can be neglected.

Because none of these claims is believable, a data analysis that makes use of them need not be taken seriously unless the consequent inferences can be demonstrated to be adequately insensitive to changes in these assumptions. In this chapter, we discuss econometric methods that are designed to determine which inferences are excessively fragile and which are adequately robust. In section 5.1 the related problems of heteroscedasticity, gross errors, and nonlinearities are discussed. Cross sections of data with vastly different countries can imply very strong inferences that can be completely reversed if observations are reweighted to adjust for heteroscedasticity, or if subsets of observations are omitted, or if a nonlinear model is used. Systematic heteroscedasticity and nonlinear models are standard fare in econometrics texts and receive brief treatment here. Econometric methods to detect and adjust for gross errors are not standard material and are discussed more intensively. The method used in this research is to determine the effect on the estimates of one-at-a-time deletion of observations. This approach is selected with some discomfort because of its unclear methodological foundation.

Chronic measurement errors in the variables are the subject of section 5.2. The proper study of regression with all variables measured with error has only recently been stated by Klepper and Leamer (1984). Because the observed variability in the explanatory variables is due partly to true variability and partly to errors in measurements, an attempt to purge the observations of measurement error can lead to a perfectly collinear set of true variables. As will be shown, the data sets in this book are so highly correlated that it is impossible to find sensible assumptions about measurement errors that would assure that the true data are not perfectly collinear.

Data sets that are perfectly collinear do not admit inferences about individual regression coefficients unless they are supplemented with additional information. In section 5.3 supplemental information in the

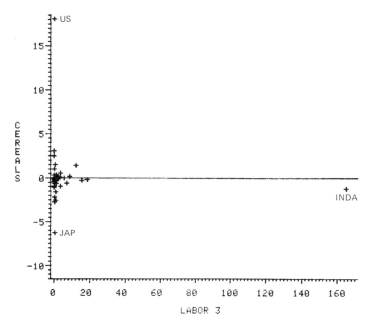

Figure 5.1
Scatter diagram, CEREALS net exports versus LABOR 3: 1975.

form of a prior distribution is assumed and Bayesian methods are discussed. Because no multivariate prior distribution is particularly believable, a study of the sensitivity of the Bayes estimates to choice of prior distribution is essential. The sensitivity analyses reported in this section allow the prior covariance matrix to vary in certain ways, and they identify the corresponding variability of the Bayes estimates.

Finally, in section 5.4 it is argued that beta values, not t-values, are the better measure of the importance of a variable.

5.1 Heteroscedasticity, Gross Errors, and Nonlinearities

The econometric study of a cross section of countries must confront the problem that individual observations can exert an uncomfortably large influence on the estimates. In that event, weighting the observations or using a nonlinear model may greatly change the inferences. Features of the data set that are cause for concern are illustrated in figure 5.1–5.3. The net export of CEREALS in 1975 is plotted against LABOR 3 in

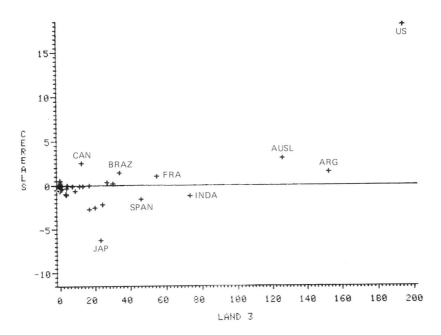

Figure 5.2
Scatter diagram, CEREALS net exports versus LAND 3: 1975.

figure 5.1. It is difficult to detect any relation between CEREALS and LABOR 3 in this figure, but a computer printout can tell a different story. Estimates and t-values as a function of the observation subset are as follows: for no excluded observations, estimated slope $= -7.9$ and t-value $= -.5$; for the United States excluded, estimated slope $= -5.1$ and t-value $= -.7$; for India excluded, estimated slope $= -5.6$ and t-value $= -.06$; and for the United States and India excluded, estimated slope $= 28.2$ and t-value $= .6$. When all observations are included, there is mild evidence of a negative relation. If the t-value of $-.5$ were treated as a posterior t-value, we could say that, given these data, the probability is approximately .8 that LABOR 3 contributes to comparative disadvantage in CEREALS. The conflict between the visual impression left by figure 5.1 and this estimated regression can be used to cast doubt either on human vision or on the method of regression. In this case, it seems clear that the method of regression is highly suspicious because its implications are extremely fragile. If the United States is excluded, the significance actually increases, but if India is excluded, the t-value falls virtually to zero. And

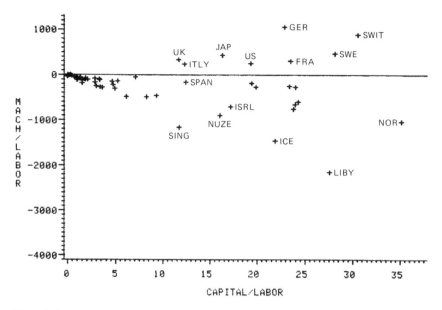

Figure 5.3
Scatter diagram, MACH net exports/LABOR versus CAPITAL/LABOR: 1975.

if both the United States and India are omitted, the sign is actually
reversed.

Figure 5.2 illustrates another case in which the United States is an
influential observation. Here when the United States is excluded, the
estimated effect of LAND 3 on CEREALS is much less, though still positive. Finally, figure 5.3, which compares 1975 MACHINERY/LABOR
with CAPITAL/LABOR, illustrates a situation in which there is no
statistically significant regression relation, but nonetheless the scatter has
an interesting feature; countries with low levels of capital abundance are
modest importers, but countries with higher levels of capital abundance
can be either exporters or importers. An ordinary regression analysis
would never reveal this feature.

This section reviews econometric methods designed to deal with these
problems. Issues concerning the weighting of observations are usually
discussed in the econometric literature under the heading "heteroscedasticity," which is the pathology of unequal residual variances, and which
requires weights on observations inversely proportional to the residual
variances. Gross errors, or outliers, which are associated with nonnormal

error terms, can also be treated by weighted regression, with relatively low weights placed on extreme observations. Because the treatment is the same, it is fair to suspect that the disease is the same. Indeed, it is the case that nonnormal errors can be thought to imply a type of heteroscedasticity.

For example, suppose we assumed that the regression residuals were drawn from a Student distribution that has relatively fat tails compared with normal and is more likely to produce outliers. A Student random variable t can be generated by selecting a random variance σ^2 from an inverse gamma distribution and then, conditional on that value of σ^2, selecting the random variable t from a normal distribution with mean zero and variance σ^2. Thus the difference between a sequence of independent identically distributed normal random variables and a sequence of independent identically distributed Student random variables is that the Student sequence allows the (conditional) variance to vary whereas the normal sequence requires a constant variance. The word "condition" is important in this sentence since the marginal distribution of the Student random variable has constant variance. Before the Student sequence is observed, there is no information about which values of the variances are largest, but once the sample is selected, it is proper to draw the inference that the most extreme observations came from normals with the largest variances. In estimating a mean, or a regression function, this form of heteroscedasticity requires exactly the same cure as all others, namely, weighted regression with weights on observations inversely proportional to the variances. Consequently, extreme observations receive less weight.

The traditional form of heteroscedasticity in contrast is systematically related to other variables; for example, the variance of residual i may be modeled as

$$\sigma_i^2 = \alpha x_i^\theta, \tag{5.1}$$

where x is an observable and α and θ are unknown parameters. Models of outliers, on the other hand, assume nonsystematic heteroscedasticity; for example, it may be assumed that σ_i^2 is drawn from an inverse gamma distribution.

Our data set is likely to exhibit systematic heteroscedasticity, since the error term is hypothesized to represent unmeasured resource endowments and since countries with relatively large GNPs are likely to have relatively large stocks of the unmeasured resources. In particular, in the next chapter we hypothesize the model (5.1) with explanatory variable x_i representing GNP. A preliminary examination of the use of total labor force as the predictor of heteroscedasticity yielded results that were significantly inferior to the GNP variable.

Maximum likelihood estimation of a regression equation with residual variances generated by equation (5.1) would require special computer programming, and I have opted instead to use the three-step approach in which the logarithms of the squared residuals from an unweighted regression of the trade equations are regressed against the logarithm of GNP to estimate the coefficients α and θ in equation (5.1). The predicted values of σ_i^2 from this auxiliary regression are then used as weights for reestimating the trade equation. This relatively inexpensive alternative to maximum likelihood estimation has been studied by Harvey (1976), who demonstrates that the estimate of θ is consistent and the corresponding weighted least-squares estimator is consistent and efficient. As a partial check of the approach, likelihood ratios of the homoscedastic model versus two heteroscedastic models were computed. This reveals that it is generally much better to weight by GNP than to use the unweighted estimates.

It can also be expected that there will be nonsystematic heteroscedasticity (outliers), possibly due to measurement errors, but also because of unusual countries that are not well described by the 11 basic resources. A formally proper way to detect and discount outlying observations is to hypothesize a family of nonnormal error distributions, say, a Student distribution, and to estimate the parameters of this distribution and the regression parameters jointly with maximum likelihood estimators (for example, see Blattberg and Gonedes, 1975.) This approach suffers from the particularity of the Student assumption as well as from its cost of implementation. Another approach is to study the asymptotic behavior of alternatives to least squares as in Huber (1972, 1973). Papers by Leamer (1981) and Gilstein and Leamer (1983a) have dealt with the issue of particularity by a global sensitivity analysis, but these are rather expensive methods as well. Instead, I adopt the relatively economical approach proposed by Belsley, Kuh, and Welsch (1980) and report the consequences of one-at-a-time deletions from the data set.[1] This informal approach does detect outliers and uncovers some sensitivities of the estimates, but it clearly cannot deal with extremes more than one-at-a-time; nor does it properly yield estimates and standard errors that account for the fact that the data have been inspected for outliers. My decision to take this path reflects my opinion that there are other, more worrisome problems.

Observations that have extreme values for the explanatory variables as well as for the dependent variable can suggest either nonlinearities, systematic heteroscedasticity, or nonsystematic heteroscedasticity. A fairly typical scatter of observations with a cross-section sample of countries is depicted in figure 5.1, which has most countries with small values of LABOR 3, but one (India) with a very large value. A regression estimate with these data has a fairly significant LABOR 3 variable. But the conclusion that LABOR 3 is a major source of comparative disadvantage is very fragile, and is completely eliminated if India is omitted. It is inappropriate merely to discard such an observation. Rather, it is desirable to identify and to report these sources of fragility and to try to find credible assumptions that eliminate it.

The reason the inference is fragile is that there are many other possibilities why India may be different from the other countries, other than a large supply of LABOR 3. If such a reason can be conjured up, the result is an equally good model for explaining CEREALS trade. One candidate variable is the square of LABOR 3. That is, suppose the relation is quadratic rather than linear. Then the effect of LABOR 3 on CEREALS trade is estimated with great inaccuracy because there are many parabolas that fit the data equally well—namely, all those that go through the center of the cluster of observations and also through the extreme observation. A pattern such as that depicted in figure 5.1 will therefore be revealed either by adding a squared term to the regression or by omitting the extreme observation. The model with systematic heteroscedasticity can also reveal the fragility of the inference, since the extreme observation can be explained by a model in which LABOR 3 has no effect on the mean value of trade, but does significantly increase the residual variance.[2]

The one-at-a-time deletions from the data set make use of a rather peculiar set of weights, with no weight put on one observation and equal weights put on all others. I have studied the sensitivity of point estimates to other choices of the weights (Leamer, 1984). In particular, if the covariance matrix Σ of the residuals is assumed to satisfy $I \leqslant \Sigma \leqslant 2I$, where the matrix inequality $A \leqslant B$ means $B - A$ is positive semidefinite, then the sign of an estimate does not depend on the choice of Σ in this range if and only if $|t| \geqslant ((n - k)/8)^{1/2}$, where $n - k$ is the degrees of freedom. For the samples considered below $n - k = 46$ and the critical value of the t-statistic is $(46/8)^{1/2} = 2.4$. If the t-statistic exceeds 2.4, the estimate can be said to be insensitive to reweighting of observations.

5.1.1 Example of the Effects of Omitting Observations

Table 5.1 indicates the effect of omitting observations from the 1975 CEREALS net export equation. The first row, labeled OLS, contains the estimates with all data included. The first column contains the t-value for country dummy variables entered one at a time into the equation. The other columns report estimates of the coefficients when one country is omitted. Consider first the LAND 3 column. The (weighted) least-squares coefficient with all the data included is 16.3. The omission of single observations generally does not have much of an impact on this estimate. The exceptions are, with estimates in parentheses, the United States (13.2), Libya (13.7), France (14.7), and Argentina (22.3). These estimates have to be interpreted with care, since they are the opposite of what you may be thinking. In particular, do not be confused into thinking that the United States data point favors the value 13.2. On the contrary, this is the estimate when the United States is excluded. Consider figure 5.2. Here all ways of excluding observations lead to large positive estimates except the omission of the United States, which produces a smaller estimate. The United States data point should be thought to favor a larger estimate, generated when it is included, not excluded. Referring now to table 5.1, we see that if the United States is included in the CEREALS equation, the estimate is 16.3, but that if the United States is excluded, the estimate is 13.2. Thus the U.S. data point makes LAND 3 appear to have a larger effect on CEREALS than the other data as a whole. Likewise, if Argentina is omitted, the coefficient increases dramatically, and Argentina is revealed to be holding down the estimate. The reason for this is easily understood. The United States and Argentina are the most abundantly endowed in LAND 3 (see the boxplot, figure 4.4) and have roughly the same endowments, but the United States has over 10 times the net exports of CEREALS of Argentina, which was nonetheless the fourth largest exporter. France also is a naturally influential observation, since it has the fifth largest endowment of LAND 3. The influence of Libya is a bit of a mystery—it has no LAND 3 and modest imports of CEREALS—but CEREALS imports per worker are greater than any other country, as can be seen in figure C.6a. It is clear from this figure that the omission of Libya makes land seem less important.

Country	t	CAPITAL	LABOR 1	LABOR 2	LABOR 3	LAND 1	LAND 2	LAND 3	LAND 4	COAL	MINERALS	OIL
OLS		-4.5	69.1	-51.0	-6.8	1.32	-4.83	16.09	-3.61	0.39	0.97	0.24
AFG	1.0	-4.4	-4.4	-45.8	-6.2	1.28	-5.45	16.83	-3.92	0.40	1.03	0.24
ARG	-0.6	-4.8	118.9	-50.5	-9.9	1.19	-5.14	20.93	-3.31	0.35	0.90	0.24
AUSL	-0.8	-4.3	-31.7	-46.8	-6.0	1.35	-3.11	16.35	-3.97	0.42	1.08	0.21
AUST	0.4	-4.5	79.1	-51.1	-7.1	1.32	-4.83	16.13	-3.62	0.39	0.97	0.24
BLUX	-0.5	-4.4	64.8	-51.3	-6.5	1.34	-4.82	16.05	-3.59	0.39	0.96	0.24
BRAZ	0.6	-4.9	70.8	-42.4	-7.7	-1.07	-4.80	15.66	-4.04	0.36	1.03	0.25
BRMA	1.4	-4.0	67.2	-59.3	-3.1	1.23	-5.15	16.42	-4.01	0.37	1.03	0.24
CAN	-1.8	-4.6	-2.5	-45.3	-5.1	1.60	-4.14	16.33	16.66	0.35	0.89	0.21
CHLE	-1.8	-4.4	64.8	-52.6	-5.0	0.80	-6.26	15.67	-5.61	0.33	1.32	0.25
CLUM	0.2	-4.4	69.8	-51.1	-6.7	1.28	-4.86	16.12	-3.65	0.39	0.98	0.24
CSTA	0.3	-4.5	73.1	-50.9	-6.9	1.32	-4.83	16.11	-3.63	0.39	0.97	0.24
CYPR	0.3	-4.5	77.3	-51.0	-7.1	1.32	-4.81	16.09	-3.61	0.39	0.97	0.24
DEN	0.5	-4.4	51.2	-50.0	-6.5	1.34	-4.85	16.10	-3.62	0.39	0.97	0.24
DORE	0.4	-4.5	84.8	-51.3	-7.2	1.31	-4.81	16.11	-3.62	0.39	0.97	0.24
ECUA	0.2	-4.5	75.2	-51.1	-6.9	1.31	-4.83	16.10	-3.63	0.39	0.97	0.24
EGPT	-0.0	-4.5	70.6	-51.1	-6.8	1.32	-4.82	16.08	-3.61	0.39	0.97	0.24
FIN	0.5	-4.5	56.0	-50.1	-6.6	1.32	-4.88	16.17	-3.68	0.39	0.98	0.24
FRA	3.5	-3.9	-809.1	-6.1	7.8	2.13	-4.55	14.70	-2.30	0.72	0.78	0.26
GANA	0.3	-4.5	69.6	-50.7	-6.9	1.31	-4.83	16.11	-3.62	0.39	0.97	0.24
GER	-1.6	-3.4	-108.1	-47.7	-2.4	1.77	-4.60	15.16	-2.89	0.51	0.86	0.22
GRCE	-0.2	-4.4	63.2	-50.8	-6.7	1.31	-4.88	16.17	-3.64	0.39	0.97	0.24
HOKO	-0.6	-4.4	58.1	-50.6	-6.6	1.32	-4.83	16.05	-3.59	0.39	0.96	0.24
HOND	0.3	-4.5	75.1	-50.9	-7.0	1.32	-4.81	16.10	-3.60	0.39	0.97	0.24
ICE	0.3	-4.5	78.2	-51.0	-7.1	1.32	-4.81	16.04	-3.62	0.38	0.97	0.24
INDA	1.7	-5.5	294.8	-49.2	-70.7	2.06	-4.11	14.87	-3.76	0.25	0.91	0.27
INDO	-1.0	-5.4	120.4	-36.8	-13.1	1.13	-4.88	15.77	-3.87	0.34	1.00	0.25
IRE	-0.1	-4.5	69.1	-51.0	-6.8	1.32	-4.84	16.10	-3.61	0.39	0.97	0.24
ISRL	-0.4	-4.5	84.2	-52.0	-7.0	1.30	-4.84	16.05	-3.64	0.38	0.97	0.24
ITLY	-1.3	-4.5	131.2	-50.3	-8.9	1.13	-4.80	16.18	-3.75	0.34	0.98	0.24

Table 5.1 (continued)

Country	t	CAPITAL	LABOR 1	LABOR 2	LABOR 3	LAND 1	LAND 2	LAND 3	LAND 4	COAL	MINERALS	OIL
JAMC	-0.1	-4.4	67.3	-51.0	-6.7	1.32	-4.85	16.08	-3.63	0.39	0.97	0.24
JAP	-1.1	-2.6	-161.0	-36.3	-1.4	1.24	-4.47	15.13	-3.75	0.32	0.95	0.24
KORA	-0.9	-4.4	-34.1	-43.6	-5.9	1.34	-4.86	16.12	-3.43	0.43	0.95	0.24
LIBR	-0.8	-4.4	53.4	-52.3	-5.5	1.21	-5.29	16.05	-4.12	0.38	1.06	0.24
LIBY	-1.8	-3.8	-26.4	-47.7	-3.2	1.67	-2.03	13.56	-2.49	0.33	0.67	0.27
LSAL	0.6	-4.5	87.4	-51.2	-7.3	1.31	-4.81	16.11	-3.63	0.38	0.98	0.24
MALY	0.3	-4.4	67.0	-50.7	-6.9	1.37	-4.71	16.11	-3.46	0.39	0.94	0.24
MAUR	0.4	-4.5	82.3	-50.8	-7.3	1.31	-4.81	16.11	-3.63	0.38	0.98	0.24
MEX	0.2	-4.4	48.6	-51.0	-6.1	1.35	-4.93	16.27	-3.59	0.40	0.97	0.24
MLTA	0.4	-4.5	79.6	-50.9	-7.1	1.32	-4.82	16.11	-3.63	0.38	0.97	0.24
NETH	-0.4	-4.5	101.5	-52.8	-7.3	1.30	-4.79	16.01	-3.63	0.38	0.97	0.24
NIGR	-3.2	-3.9	173.5	-71.9	1.8	1.52	-5.68	16.18	-4.99	0.18	1.04	0.31
NOR	-0.1	-4.4	65.2	-51.1	-6.6	1.33	-4.85	16.13	-3.61	0.39	0.97	0.24
NUZE	0.3	-4.5	72.0	-50.9	-6.9	1.33	-4.78	15.84	-3.62	0.39	0.97	0.24
PANM	0.4	-4.5	77.3	-50.9	-7.1	1.31	-4.83	16.11	-3.63	0.38	0.97	0.24
PERU	-0.4	-4.5	84.0	-52.0	-6.9	1.30	-4.93	15.95	-3.81	0.38	1.01	0.24
PGRY	-0.3	-4.4	50.0	-50.8	-6.3	1.36	-4.91	16.41	-3.58	0.39	0.96	0.24
PLIP	1.0	-3.7	-72.8	-52.5	-0.9	1.62	-4.79	16.45	-3.35	0.42	0.91	0.24
PORT	-0.8	-4.4	44.2	-50.2	-6.2	1.32	-4.90	16.28	-3.61	0.39	0.97	0.24
SING	0.1	-4.5	70.2	-50.9	-6.8	1.32	-4.83	16.10	-3.61	0.39	0.97	0.24
SPAN	-1.9	-3.9	-89.2	-43.8	-3.5	1.22	-5.52	17.99	-3.92	0.39	1.01	0.24
SRIL	0.1	-4.4	70.8	-51.3	-6.7	1.33	-4.83	16.10	-3.62	0.39	0.97	0.24
SWE	0.4	-4.4	28.5	-48.8	-6.2	1.37	-4.80	16.20	-3.54	0.40	0.95	0.24
SWIT	0.3	-4.5	68.4	-50.5	-7.0	1.32	-4.84	16.13	-3.61	0.39	0.97	0.24
THAI	2.7	-5.1	608.2	-92.7	-11.6	1.25	-4.61	16.16	-3.83	0.27	1.00	0.23
TURK	0.5	-4.4	72.1	-51.7	-6.7	1.34	-4.89	15.84	-3.69	0.39	0.98	0.24
UK	-4.6	-9.5	1,168.7	-67.4	-50.4	1.28	-2.81	14.18	-0.19	0.65	0.56	0.11
US	6.6	-5.9	538.8	-47.8	-16.0	1.94	0.86	13.16	2.38	-0.14	0.51	-0.03
YUG	-0.5	-4.8	146.8	-52.3	-9.4	1.24	-4.79	15.97	-3.57	0.38	0.97	0.23

a. Listing of coefficients produced by dropping observations one at a time.

Although Argentina has a major impact on the estimate of the coefficient of LAND 3, it is not an unusual country when judged by its t-value of $-.8$ (in the first column). The United States, on the other hand, has significantly more CEREALS exports than would be predicted on the basis of the behavior of the other countries (t-value of 6.0). France, with a t-value of 4.0, is the other major outlier on the high side. The United Kingdom and Nigeria, on the other hand, have significantly more imports (or fewer exports) than the other data would predict. All of these unusual countries tend to make the estimate of the coefficient of LAND 3 somewhat lower and create the impression that the (weighted) least-squares estimate may be a slight overestimate.

Though the LAND 3 coefficient is reasonably insensitive to the omission of observations one at a time, the LABOR 3 coefficient is very sensitive. The least-squares estimate is -4.1, but if India is omitted, the estimate jumps to -70.3, whereas if France is omitted, the estimate becomes 12.5. The influence of India on the LABOR 3 coefficient derives from its very extreme endowment of LABOR 3 (see the boxplot, figure 4.4). The LABOR 3 variable therefore behaves much like a dummy variable for India.

Perusal of table 5.1 reveals that the following coefficients have signs and values that are insensitive to these one-at-a-time omissions: CAPITAL, LAND 3, and MINERALS. These coefficients have t-values (not shown) of -2.1, 3.5, and 3.0, respectively. The other coefficients with large t-values are LAND 2 (-2.1) and OIL (6.1), both of which are greatly influenced by the U.S. observation, and only the U.S. observation. Thus a large t-value does seem to make it more likely that the coefficient is insensitive to observation omissions, but there is no guarantee.

To conclude, the inferences about many of the coefficients in the CEREALS equation are very sensitive to the U.S. observation. If I had to pick point estimates, I would probably omit the United States. The land coefficients seem then to take on sensible values, COAL, MINERALS and OIL have small effects, and CAPITAL and LABOR 2 have negative coefficients, suggesting comparative advantage in manufacturing rather than agriculture.

5.2 Chronic Measurement Errors

It is beyond the wildest stretch of the imagination to suppose that the data on resources, trade, and GNP are perfect measures of their corresponding hypotheticals. God (and very few others) knows how all these countries collect information on GNP, savings flows, labor force and so on. In a world of changing relative prices the measurement of capital as an accumulation of savings flows is not even conceptually correct. Endowments of oil, coal, and minerals are proxied by production data, but for various reasons some countries may exhaust their known supplies more quickly and/or look for new supplies more intensively than other countries.

The study of nonsystematic heteroscedasticity described in the previous section is intended partly to identify and to treat gross errors in the data by determining the effect of reducing the weights on observations that may be subject to gross measurement errors. This would not adequately deal with chronic errors. There is, however, an econometric tradition for dealing with chronic measurement errors. If it is assumed that there is a linear relation between two variables η_i and χ_i, $\eta_i = \alpha + \beta\chi_i$, and if it also assumed that there are independent measures of η_i and χ_i, $y_i = \eta_i + \varepsilon_{yi}$, $x_i = \chi_i + \varepsilon_{xi}$, where the measurement errors ε_{yi} and ε_{xi} and the true variables χ_i are independent serially uncorrelated random variables with means $(0, 0, \bar{\chi})$ and variances $(\sigma_y^2, \sigma_x^2, \sigma_\chi^2)$, then the joint distribution of the observables y and x has mean vector and covariance matrix

$$E(y, x) = (\alpha + \beta\bar{\chi}, \bar{\chi}),$$

$$V(y, x) = \begin{bmatrix} \beta^2\sigma_\chi^2 + \sigma_y^2 & \beta\sigma_\chi^2 \\ \beta\sigma_\chi^2 & \sigma_\chi^2 + \sigma_x^2 \end{bmatrix}.$$

Estimates of the parameters may be found by setting these theoretical moments equal to observed sample moments:

$$\hat{\alpha} + \hat{\beta}\hat{\bar{\chi}} = \bar{y},$$

$$\hat{\bar{\chi}} = \bar{x},$$

$$\hat{\beta}^2\hat{\sigma}_\chi^2 + \hat{\sigma}_y^2 = s_y^2,$$

$$\hat{\beta}\hat{\sigma}_\chi^2 = s_{xy},$$

$$\hat{\sigma}_\chi^2 + \hat{\sigma}_x^2 = s_x^2.$$

There are, however, seven unknown parameters, but only six equations. In a word, the model is underidentified. An arbitrary selection of one parameter may be made, and we may then solve for the others. If $\hat{\beta}$ is arbitrarily selected, then estimates of the other parameters are

$$\hat{\alpha} = \bar{y} - \hat{\beta}\bar{x},$$

$$\hat{\bar{\chi}} = \bar{x},$$

$$\hat{\sigma}_\chi^2 = s_{xy}/\hat{\beta},$$

$$\hat{\sigma}_y^2 = s_y^2 - \hat{\beta}s_{xy},$$

$$\hat{\sigma}_x^2 = s_x^2 - (s_{xy}/\hat{\beta}).$$

Of course, it is known that the variances are positive, and values of $\hat{\beta}$ must be selected that imply positive estimates of these parameters. The restriction $\hat{\sigma}_\chi^2 > 0$ implies that $\hat{\beta}$ and s_{xy} must have the same sign. The other two inequalities may be written either as $s_{xy}/s_x^2 \leqslant \hat{\beta} \leqslant s_y^2/s_{xy}$ or as $s_y^2/s_{xy} \leqslant \hat{\beta} \leqslant s_{xy}/s_x^2$, depending on the sign of s_{xy}.

The ratio s_{xy}/s_x^2 is the "direct" regression, formed by regressing y on x. The ratio s_y^2/s_{xy} is the "reverse" regression, formed by first regressing x on y and then by inverting the estimated equation to express y as a function of x. Alternatively, the direct regression can be found by minimizing the sum of squared residuals with distance between an observation point and the regression line measured in the direction of the y axis (vertically), and the reverse regression may be found by measuring the distance in the direction of the x axis (horizontally).

The inequalities for $\hat{\beta}$ in the previous paragraph can then be summarized by the statement that the set of estimates of β compatible with the observed means, variances, and covariances is the interval between the direct regression $\hat{\beta}^D = s_{xy}/s_x^2$ and the reverse regression $\hat{\beta}^R = s_y^2/s_{xy}$. This interval of estimates is also the set of maximum likelihood estimates if normal distributions are assumed, and it will capture the true value of β with probability approaching one as sample size increases. The length of the errors-in-variable interval is a decreasing function of the squared correlation; in particular, the ratio $\hat{\beta}^D/\hat{\beta}^R$ is the squared correlation $s_{xy}^2/s_x^2 s_y^2$. This is one of the few cases in econometric theory in which the size of the squared correlation really matters.

The treatment of chronic errors in variables therefore begins with the computation of the direct and the reverse regressions. If this interval of estimates is narrow enough to be useful, then it can be reported that chronic measurement errors are revealed by the data to be inconsequential. If the interval of estimates is uselessly large, then an attempt may be made to narrow the interval by appeal to prior information about either of the two measurement error variances. If credible restrictions on the error variances do not produce usefully narrow sets of estimates, then we are forced to conclude that measurement errors may be so severe that these data by themselves are useless.

This approach to the treatment of chronic measurement errors has been extended to the multiple regression setting by Klepper and Leamer (1984). If there are k explanatory variables, then there are $k + 1$ ways of estimating the regression, depending on the direction in which the residuals are measured, or, equivalently, depending on which variable is used as the left-hand-side variable. If these $k + 1$ regressions have the same sign pattern (after normalization) then any weighted average of these $k + 1$ regressions is a maximum likelihood estimate, and any point that is not a weighted average is not a maximum likelihood estimate. This is the straightforward generalization of the bivariate errors-in-variables bound. But if these $k + 1$ regressions have sign changes, then the set of maximum likelihood estimates is unbounded. The reason the set is unbounded is the following. The measured covariance matrix is equal to the true covariance matrix plus the (diagonal) measurement error covariance matrix. To recover the true covariance matrix from the measured covariance matrix, we must subtract out the measurement error covariance matrix. The result can be a singular matrix. If the result is a singular matrix, the normal equations based on this estimated covariance matrix do not admit a unique solution, the set of all least-squares solutions is unbounded, and standard errors may be thought to be infinite. If the $k + 1$ regressions all have the same sign patterns, no choice of the measurement error covariance matrix that is compatible with the first two observed moments can imply a singular true covariance matrix, and the set of possible estimates is consequently bounded. But when the observed variables are sufficiently collinear that the signs of the estimates depend on the direction in which the sum-of-squared residuals is minimized, then, using the data alone, we cannot rule out the possibility that the true variables are perfectly collinear.

If the set of estimates compatible with the first two moments of the data is too large to be useful, then some prior information on the measurement error variances may prove helpful. Klepper and Leamer (1984) consider in particular two forms of prior restrictions: (a) the minimum squared correlation between the true variable and its measurement and (b) the maximum value for the squared multiple correlation if the measurement errors in the explanatory variables were removed.

In the typical case when the $k + 1$ regressions are not all in the same orthant and the set of maximum likelihood estimates is unbounded, a restricted set of estimates will be bounded if one of the following restrictions is imposed:

a. The squared correlation between each true explanatory variable and its measurement exceeds $1 - \lambda_1$, where λ_1 is the minimum eigenvalue of the correlation matrix of the measured explanatory variable.

b. The squared multiple correlation between the dependent variable and the true explanatory variable does not exceed

$$R_m^2 = R^2 + (1 - R^2)\left(\max_{i,j}(1 - \hat{\beta}_{ij}/b_j)\right)^{-1},$$

where R^2 is the squared multiple correlation based on the measured variables, b_j is the usual least-squares estimate of coefficient j, and $\hat{\beta}_{ij}$ is the reverse regression estimate of coefficient j with residuals minimized in the direction of variable i. For comparison across equations with different R^2 values, it is convenient to report the proportion of the gap between R^2 and 1 that can be attributed to measurement errors without destroying the usefulness of the data:

$$g = (R_m^2 - R^2)/(1 - R^2) = \left(\max_{i,j}(1 - \hat{\beta}_{ij}/b_j)\right)^{-1}.$$

These two diagnostics, $1 - \lambda_1$ and R_m^2, are constructive in the sense that they indicate assumptions that are sufficient to imply that the true data are not perfectly collinear. Leamer (1983) suggests destructive diagnostics, which are sets of measurement error variances that would imply that the true explanatory variables are perfectly collinear. If error variances in the neighborhoods of these cannot be ruled out on an a pirori basis, then the data alone are useless, and prior information that restricts the values of the coefficients either absolutely or probabilistically would have to be employed.

The preceding discussion is slightly modified if a subset of variables is known to be measured perfectly. Then only the reverse regressions corresponding to the mismeasured variables need to be computed, and only the coefficients on the mismeasured variables need to be inspected for sign changes.

Parenthetically, it may be noted that the Heckscher-Ohlin-Vanek model defines a system of equations with the same set of hypothetical variables in each. The foregoing discussion is applicable to a single equation, but the evidence can be much stronger if the whole system is analyzed because the same hypothetical variables enter each equation. The proper treatment of underidentified systems of equations with errors in variables has not been worked out, and we consequently study the data one equation at a time. Another shortcoming of this treatment is that the measurement error variance is assumed to be the same for all countries—large and small. A better model or errors in measurement might be the logarithmic model $\log x_i = \log \xi_i + \varepsilon_{xi}$, where x_i is the measurement and ξ_i is the true variable. This, too, creates econometric theory problems that have not been fully worked out.

5.2.1   Example of Estimation with Chronic Measurement Errors

Direct and reverse regressions for the 1975 machinery equation are reported in table 5.2. The first column in table 5.2 contains the usual least-squares estimates. The second column contains a reverse regression estimate formed by regressing CAPITAL on machinery net exports and the other resource variables and then solving the estimated equation for machinery in terms of all the resource endowments. Equivalently, the size of each residual is measured as the difference between an observation point and the regression plane in the direction of the CAPITAL axis. A feature of this regression is that the coefficient of the CAPITAL variable is enlarged; in fact, it is multiplied by the inverse of the squared partial correlation between MACH and CAPITAL. If it is thought that CAPITAL is the only variable (other than MACH) that is measured with error, then only these first two regressions need to be considered, and the set of maximum likelihood estimates is just the interval of estimates between these two. It could then be concluded that chronic measurement errors in CAPITAL would greatly limit the inferences that can be made about the effect of LAND 4, since either sign is possible. The other coefficients do retain their signs and many change little in magnitude.

If CAPITAL and LABOR 1 are both suspected to be contaminated by measurement errors, then the first three columns in this table must be considered. Because neither the CAPITAL coefficient nor the LABOR 1 coefficient changes sign in the first three columns, the set of maximum likelihood estimates remains bounded. The set of estimates is still bounded even if CAPITAL and all three LABOR variables are possibly measured with error, since the subset of coefficients corresponding to these variables

Table 5.2
Direct and reverse regressions, MACHINERY equation: 1975[a]

	MACH	CAPITAL	LABOR 1	LABOR 2	LABOR 3	LAND 1	LAND 2	LAND 3	LAND 4	COAL	MINERALS	OIL
CAPITAL	32.2	67.6	130.2	33.1	373.6	443.7	2.6	31.4	-12.1	38.8	33.6	13.0
LABOR 1	-2,118	-8,850	-42,548	-37,154	-77,848	-81,277	14,686	2,321	3,158	-10,321	-2,572	4383
LABOR 2	107	110	1,874	3,452	405	-847	-229	-53	600	524	205	-129
LABOR 3	25	285	905	93	3,261	2,453	-514	-252	-642	115	-41	-182
LAND 1	.6	8.5	24	-5	62	817	41	2.7	105	13	26	-.1
LAND 2	7.1	.6	-49	-15	-147	466	382	70	403	4	100	24
LAND 3	-33	-33	37	16	34	-145	-330	-299	-51	-26	-39	-52
LAND 4	3.4	-1.3	-5.0	19	-87	569	191	5.1	507	27.6	88.9	20.4
COAL	7.9	9.5	39	39	37	165	4.5	6.1	65	31	17	15
MINERALS	-4.2	-4	-5	-8	7	-177	-60	-5	-111	-9	-30	-5
OIL	-2.6	-1	5	3	20	.4	-9	-4	-16	-5	-3	-9

a. Each column contains a set of estimates formed by minimization of the residuals in the direction indicated. $R^2 = .91$, $g = .037$, $1 - \lambda_1 = .9934$.

do not change sign in the first five columns. If, however, any one of the other variables is thought also to be measured with error, then the set of feasible estimates becomes unbounded, since relevant estimates change in sign.

Prior information may be useful in restricting these unbounded sets of estimates. The smallest eigenvalue of the correlation matrix is rather small, and in order for a bounded set of estimates to be obtained by appeal to information about the error variances, it would have to be assumed that the squared correlation between true variables and measured variables exceeds .9934. This seems to me to be an unreasonable assumption. Another form of prior information that may be entertained is the maximum value that the multiple correlation coefficient can be expected to attain if the explanatory variables were perfectly measured. If this number is not much higher than the R^2 based on the mismeasured variables, then the set of maximum likelihood estimates is also bounded. The statistic g indicates the proportion of the difference between the measured R^2 and 1 that could be attributed to measurement errors without causing the sets to become unbounded. This number is only .037, which means that if it is thought that the elimination of the measurement error could not increase the R^2 by more than $(1 - .91) \times .037 = .003$, then the set is bounded. That seems to be an unreasonable assumption.

Destructive diagnostics are reported in table 5.3. Entries in this table indicate pairs of measurement error variances that would imply that the true data are perfectly collinear. As discussed in Leamer (1983), this form of collinearity affects all of the coefficients, not just the two measured with error. The numbers in table 5.3 are the destructive error variances divided by the observed sample variances, reported in pairs, with the row variance first and the column variance second. (The squared correlation between a measured variable and the true variable is equal to one minus this variance ratio.) Variance ratios less than .0005 are rounded off to .000. Pairs of asterisks indicate that perfect collinearity cannot be induced by assuming measurement error only in those two variables (for example, CAPITAL and LABOR 1). The numbers in this table are disturbingly small, and the possibilities for perfect collinearity seem abundant. For example, if the noise variance were .1% of the total variance for CAPITAL and LABOR 2, or for LABOR 1 and LABOR 2, or for LABOR 3 and LAND 2 . . . , the true variables would be perfectly collinear.

The conclusion that is suggested by this example is that sensible assump-

Table 5.3
Destructive diagnostics, MACHINERY equation: 1975[a]

	CAPITAL	LABOR 1	LABOR 2	LABOR 3	LAND 1	LAND 2	LAND 3	LAND 4	COAL	MIN-ERALS	OIL
CAPITAL	(*,*)	(.001,.001)	(.001,.001)	(*,*)	(*,*)	(*,*)	(*,*)	(.000,.003)	(.001,.001)	(.001,.001)	(*,*)
LABOR 1		(*,*)	(.001,.001)	(*,*)	(*,*)	(.000,.031)	(.000,.003)	(.000,.003)	(*,*)	(.000,.001)	(.000,.000)
LABOR 2			(*,*)	(.001,.001)	(.000,.008)	(.001,.002)	(.001,.003)	(.001,.003)	(*,*)	(.001,.001)	(.001,.001)
LABOR 3				(*,*)	(.005,.009)	(.001,.001)	(.001,.003)	(.001,.003)	(*,*)	(.001,.001)	(.001,.000)
LAND 1					(*,*)	(*,*)	(.008,.007)	(*,*)	(*,*)	(*,*)	(.008,.001)
LAND 2						(*,*)	(*,*)	(*,*)	(*,*)	(*,*)	(.002,.037)
LAND 3							(*,*)	(.004,.003)	(*,*)	(.004,.001)	(.004,.001)
LAND 4								(*,*)	(*,*)	(*,*)	(*,*)
COAL									(*,*)	(.001,.001)	(.001,.001)
MINERALS										(*,*)	(.001,.001)
OIL											(*,*)

a. Noise variance divided by total variance. If these noise variances are subtracted from the observed variances, the covariance matrix becomes singular. (*, *) indicates that no singular matrix is producible.

tions about the errors of measurement preclude estimation from these data alone, since we cannot rule out the possibility that the true explanatory variables are perfectly collinear. This same conclusion holds for every one of the estimated regressions.

5.3 Prior Information and the Collinearity Problem

Data sets with perfectly collinear explanatory variables cannot be used to estimate individual regression coefficients unless credible restrictions on the coefficients of some form are imposed. A fairly typical approach is to identify a set of "doubtful" variables and to see what happens to the regression equation as subsets of these doubtful variables are omitted. To say that a variable is doubtful is equivalent to announcing the opinion that the corresponding coefficient is small, and this approach thus implicitly supplements the given data set with another set of information about the coefficients. A Bayesian analysis is a formally proper way of supplementing the information in the given data set. The critical defect of a Bayesian analysis is that it presupposes that users can characterize their opinions about the regression coefficients in the form of probability distributions. The impossibility of making a credible selection of such a distribution forces practicing Bayesians to perform extensive sensitivity analyses to determine whether the precise choice of prior distribution matters very much.*

As an introduction, consider a regression model in which it is generally agreed that a set of variables "belongs" in the equation, but there exists also a set of variables that "may or may not belong." (Quotation marks surround ambiguous words.) The variables that are certainly included in the equation will be symbolized by x; the doubtful variables will be denoted z. A three-variable linear regression model with one certain and two doubtful variables can be written as

$$y_t = \beta x_t + \gamma_1 z_{1t} + \gamma_2 z_{2t} + u_t, \tag{5.2}$$

where t indexes a set of T observations, u_t is assumed to be a sequence of independent normal random variables with mean zero and unknown variances σ^2, $(y_t, x_t, z_{1t}, z_{2t})$ is a sequence of observable vectors, and

*The following material, up to section 5.3.1, is taken in part from Leamer and Leonard (1983). For a more extensive treatment consult Leamer (1978).

$(\beta, \gamma_1, \gamma_2)$ is an unobservable vector of regression coefficients. Inferences are to be drawn from a data set about the effect β of the variable x on the dependent variable y. In an ideal experiment, the variables z_1 and z_2 would have been controlled at some constant level. As a substitute for experimental control, the variables z_1 and z_2 are included in the equation.

A researcher wishing to show that β is large or finding it difficult to estimate γ_1 and γ_2 accurately might estimate the four different regressions using different subsets of the "control" variables (z_1, z_2) and select for reporting purposes the most favorable result. The alternative procedure, which is advocated here, is, first, to enlarge the search and, second, to require reporting of both the most favorable and the least favorable outcomes. The search may be enlarged by defining a composite control variable

$$w_t(\theta) = z_{1t} + \theta z_{2t},$$

where θ is a number to be selected by the researcher. The regression model is now

$$y_t = \beta x_t + \eta w_t(\theta) + u_t. \tag{5.3}$$

Each value of θ selects a different constraint of the form $\gamma_2 = \theta \gamma_1$ and consequently a different method for estimating β. Allowing θ to take any value contrasts with the usual search procedure, in which θ is implicitly permitted to take one of only four values. The usual procedure has the virtue of historical acceptance and the additional merit that it is comparatively easy to carry out computationally in the context of the existing econometric technology. As is discussed subsequently, there are settings is which the method is completely justifiable. This is not always the case, and we now expand the search to include all values of θ.

To each value of θ there is a least-squares estimate of β, $\hat{\beta}(\theta)$. The most "favorable" value of θ, for the researcher who wishes to show β is large, is found by maximizing $\hat{\beta}(\theta)$ with respect to θ, and the least favorable value is found by minimizing $\hat{\beta}(\theta)$. These extreme values, $\hat{\beta}_{min}$ and $\hat{\beta}_{max}$, delineate the ambiguity in the inferences about β induced by the ambiguity in choice of model. If the interval $[\hat{\beta}_{min}, \hat{\beta}_{max}]$ is short in comparison with the sampling uncertainty, or if all estimates in the interval imply the same decision, the ambiguity in the model may be considered irrelevant, since all models lead to essentially the same inferences. But if the bound is wide, an effort should be made to narrow the family of models, and, it is hoped, to sharpen the inferences. One way to narrow the family of models is to constrain the parameters γ_1 and γ_2 to lie within the ellipse

$$\gamma_1^2 a^2 + \gamma_2^2 \leqslant r^2, \tag{5.4}$$

where a is the relative length of the two principal axes and r is the radius. This may seem to be a peculiar thing to do, but this constraint is the foundation of the voluminous literature on "biased estimation."[3] It can be justified in the following way. The only compelling reason for the omission of the z variables is that they are thought to be doubtful. If they truly do not belong in the equation, then a better estimate of β can be produced by an equation with the z variables omitted. To say that the z variables are doubtful is to say that the parameters γ_1 and γ_2 are small. One precise definition of smallness is given by equation (5.4), and a natural way to estimate the parameter β is to use least squares subject to the constraint (5.4). Henceforth, this constraint will be called the prior ellipse in reference to the fact that it represents information about γ_1 and γ_2 that is available prior to the data analysis.

If the parameters of the prior ellipse, a^2 and r^2, were known, this procedure would generate a unique estimate, but we are unaware of any real data analysis in which the values a^2 and r^2 could sensibly be taken as given. For any value of a^2 and r^2, there is a constrained least-squares estimate, $\hat{\beta}(a^2, r^2)$, computed by minimizing the sum of squared residuals subject to the constraint (5.4). We now turn to an examination of the function $\hat{\beta}(a^2, r^2)$.

Consider first the case when a^2 is known, taken without loss of generality to be equal to one. For each value of r^2, equation (5.4) defines a circle located at the origin, depicted in figure 5.4. Also depicted in figure 5.4 are the unconstrained least-squares estimates of γ_1 and γ_2, (g_1, g_2), and the contours of equal residual sums of squares around (g_1, g_2). It should be noted that the sum-of-squared residuals depends on the estimate of β as well as on the estimates of γ_1 and γ_2. But $\hat{\beta}$ is selected by regressing $y - \gamma_1 z_1 - \gamma_2 z_2$ on x, which implies that $\hat{\beta}$ is linear function of $\hat{\gamma}_1$ and $\hat{\gamma}_2$. With this estimate of β, the residual sum of squares can be expressed as a function of $\hat{\gamma}_1$ and $\hat{\gamma}_2$ only.

The estimation problem of minimizing the residual sum of squares subject to the constraint (5.4) can be described graphically in terms of a tangency point between a sum-of-squares ellipse and the prior circle

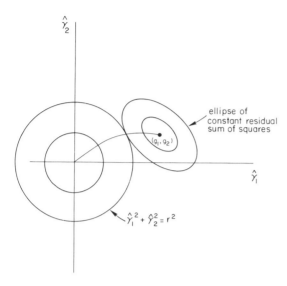

Figure 5.4
An information contract curve.

located at the origin. As the radius of the circle is varied, a curve of estimates is formed that we call an *information contract curve*.[4] This language is selected to suggest the Edgeworth-Bowley analysis of trade between a pair of consumers, a setting that is analogous to our own problem both mathematically and substantively. In the Edgeworth-Bowley analysis, a contract curve represents the Pareto efficient allocation of a pair of commodities to a pair of consumers with conflicting desires. Here, the information contract curve represents the "Pareto efficient" set of estimates given two conflicting sources of information.

The choice of a point on the contract curve in the Edgeworth-Bowley analysis requires cardinal utility and a social welfare criterion. To put it differently, there has to be a way of comparing the utilities of the two consumers. Analogously, the choice of a point on the information contract curve requires us to compare the strength of the two information sources, a problem to which we shall return.

Next consider the case when neither a^2 nor r^2 can be taken as known. For any a^2 there will be a contract curve, two of which are depicted in figure 5.5. The hull of all such curves is the shaded area in figure 5.5, which has been shown by Leamer and Chamberlain (1976) to be a subset of the

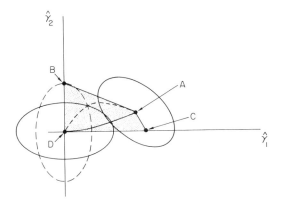

Figure 5.5
Contract curves in the hull of 2^q regressions: A = unconstrained least-squares estimate; B = least squares given $\hat{\gamma}_1 = 0$; C = least squares given $\hat{\gamma}_2 = 0$; D = least squares given $\hat{\gamma}_1 = 0$ and $\hat{\gamma}_2 = 0$.

set of all weighted averages of the four regressions formed by omitting or including the two z variables. This brings us back to the traditional procedure. Now we have a justification for it: If, in the researchers' opinion, γ_1 and γ_2 are thought to be small in the sense of the ellipse (5.4), but neither a nor r is known, then the extreme estimates that can be generated from the sample are the four regressions formed by omitting the z variables. We would then recommend, in fact require, that *both* the minimum and the maximum estimate of β from among this set of four regressions be reported.

The widest bound for β swept out by the parameter θ can also be depicted graphically. The prior ellipses so far considered all have axes in the coordinate directions. If the quadratic form were, more generally,

$$\gamma_1^2 a^2 + \gamma_2^2 + c\gamma_1\gamma_2 \leqslant r^2,$$

then the ellipse is tilted, and estimates can lie outside the shaded area in figure 5.5. The hull of all contract curves, with all families of prior ellipses, is the shaded area in figure 5.6. The boundary of this region, which is an ellipse, is the set of constrained least-squares points subject to constraints of the form $\gamma_2 = \theta\gamma_1$, where θ varies from $-\infty$ to ∞.

We have now considered three bounds for the estimates of β that can be generated from a given data set. The choice among these bounds depends on how precisely the researcher is willing to define the vague

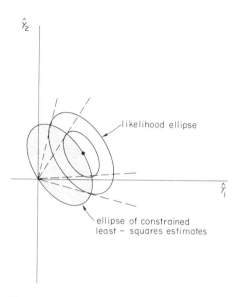

Figure 5.6
Ellipse of constrained estimates.

notion that the z variables are doubtful. If it can only be said that the z variables are doubtful, the widest set of estimates, depicted in figure 5.6, applies. If it can be agreed that the definition of doubtful should be restricted to mean that $\gamma_1^2 a^2 + \gamma_2^2$ is likely to be small, where a^2 is left undetermined, then the shaded area in figure 5.5 is the bound. Finally, if doubtful is even more precisely defined to mean that $\gamma_1^2 + \gamma_2^2$ is small, then the contract curve in figure 5.4 defines the bound.

To narrow the bounds further, it will be necessary to devise a method for choosing points from a contract curve. As in the Edgeworth-Bowley analysis, this will require a comparison of the strengths of the two sources of information. If the sample information is relatively precise, it will be better to select points relatively close to the least-squares point. Conversely, if the prior information is relatively precise, we shall prefer points in the neighborhood of the prior point, the origin in the example. One way to make the prior information comparable to the sample information is to act as if the prior information came from a previous set of observations. Suppose we observed the process

$$y_t^* = \gamma_1 z_{1t}^* + \gamma_2 z_{2t}^* + u_t^*,$$

with u_t^* normally distributed with variance σ_1^2. Suppose also that

$$\sum_t z_{1t}^* z_{2t}^* = 0, \qquad \sum_t z_{it}^{*2} = 1, \qquad \text{and} \qquad \sum_t z_{it}^* y_t^* = 0. \tag{5.5}$$

Then the least-squares estimate of γ_1 and γ_2 based on these data would be $(0,0)$ with variance matrix $\sigma_1^2 I$.

Now consider pooling this "prior" sample with the sample generated by equation (5.2). The pooled estimates are computed using the usual formula with pooled sample moments:

$$\begin{bmatrix} \hat{\beta} \\ \hat{\gamma}_1 \\ \hat{\gamma}_2 \end{bmatrix} = \left(\sigma_1^{-2} \begin{bmatrix} 0 & 0 & 0 \\ 0 & 1 & 0 \\ 0 & 0 & 1 \end{bmatrix} + \sigma^{-2} \begin{bmatrix} x'x & z_1'x & z_2'x \\ z_1'x & z_1'z_1 & z_1'z_2 \\ z_2'x & z_2'z_1 & z_2'z_2 \end{bmatrix} \right)^{-1} \cdot \sigma^{-2} \begin{bmatrix} x'y \\ z_1'y \\ z_2'y \end{bmatrix}. \tag{5.6}$$

Using the partitioned inverse rule, we can obtain

$$\begin{bmatrix} \hat{\gamma}_1 \\ \hat{\gamma}_2 \end{bmatrix} = \left(\sigma_1^{-2} \begin{bmatrix} 1 & 0 \\ 0 & 1 \end{bmatrix} + \sigma^{-2} \begin{bmatrix} z_1'Mz_1 & z_1'Mz_2 \\ z_2'Mz_1 & z_2'Mz_2 \end{bmatrix} \right)^{-1} \cdot \begin{bmatrix} z_1'My \\ z_2'My \end{bmatrix} \sigma^{-2},$$

where $M = I - x(x'x)^{-1}x'$. This equation describes the pooled estimates of γ_1 and γ_2 as a function of the variance ratio σ_1/σ^2. If this variance ratio is small, the estimates will be close to the "prior" estimates $(0,0)$, and if this variance ratio is large, the estimates will be close to the least-squares estimates from the second data set (g_1, g_2). Moreover, as the variance ratio is varied from zero to infinity, the estimates $(\hat{\gamma}_1, \hat{\gamma}_2)$ will sweep out exactly the contract curve depicted in figure 5.4, where the contours (5.4) of the prior ellipse are the likelihood contours implied by the prior sample y^*, z_1^*, z_2^*.

To the extent that the prior information can be considered as coming from a hypothetical normal experiment, and to the extent that we can select the variance ratio σ_1^2/σ^2, we are now able to pick a particular point from the contract curve. The variance σ^2 can be estimated from the data y, x, z_1, z_2. The prior variance σ_1^2 presents greater difficulty. This number determines the size of the prior confidence intervals for γ_i since a 95% interval, for example, is $|\gamma_i| \leqslant 1.96\sigma_1$. In selecting a value of σ_1, it is therefore necessary to indicate the degree of confidence in the statement that γ_i is small. If $|\gamma_i| \leqslant 1.96$ is believed with considerable confidence, then $\sigma_1 = 1$ may be a useful starting point.

It seems unlikely that a precise number for σ_1 could ever be selected. A sensitivity analysis in which several different values of σ_1 are selected is therefore desirable. A researcher might sensibly constrain σ_1 to an interval such as $.5 \leqslant \sigma_1 \leqslant 2$. As σ_1 is varied in this interval, a subset of points on the contract curve is selected. Often this subset of points will be so narrow that the ambiguity that remains will be for practical purposes irrelevant.

A sensitivity analysis can be applied to other features of the prior covariance matrix. Let Ω denote the 3×3 prior covariance matrix that above has been taken to be the 3×3 diagonal matrix $\sigma_1^2 \cdot \text{diag}\{\infty, 1, 1\}$. Then Ω^{-1} replaces the 3×3 diagonal matrix $\sigma_1^{-2} \cdot \text{diag}\{0, 1, 1\}$ in equation (5.6). Leamer (1982) has shown how restrictions on Ω imply restrictions on the pooled estimate $(\hat{\beta}, \hat{\gamma}_1, \hat{\gamma}_2)$. It is required that Ω be bounded from above, $\Omega \leqslant \Omega_U$, or from below, $\Omega_L \leqslant \Omega$, where $A \leqslant B$ means $B - A$ is positive semidefinite. An alternative to the interval of values for σ_1, $.5 \leqslant \sigma_1 \leqslant 2$, is the interval of matrices, $\text{diag}(\infty, .25, .25) \leqslant \Omega \leqslant \text{diag}(\infty, 4, 4)$. The interval of matrices restricts the prior standard error for γ_i to be between .5 and 2, but does not restrict the prior standard error of γ_1 to be equal to the prior standard error of γ_2, nor does it restrict the covariances to be zero.

Though this example has made use of the prior information that some of the coefficients are close to zero, merely by choice of origin it applies equally well to prior information that some or all of the coefficients are close to selected nonzero values. It needs to be emphasized that a credible selection of a precise and complete multivariate prior distribution cannot be made, and the choice of some particular distribution to characterize prior information is inherently whimsical. The sensitivity analyses that have just been discussed are designed to control the whimsy. In principle, the sensitivity analysis should encompass all arbitrary assumptions about the prior distribution, including (1) the form of the distribution, (2) the location of the distribution, and (3) the dispersion of the distribution. I do not possess computer software that can do a sensitivity analysis of the choice of distributional form, but the effect of the choice of location and the choice of variance-covariance matrix given a normal distribution can be studied. In this book the location and the form of the prior will be taken as known, and the effect of changing the prior variance-covariance matrix on the point estimates will be studied. A particular hypothetical prior covariance matrix Ω_0 will be selected. First, this prior covariance matrix is multiplied by a scalar σ_1 and the point estimates of the coefficients are expressed as functions of σ_1. This shows how the estimates

Table 5.4
Prior means and standard errors for the GNP regressions[a]

	1958		1975	
	Mean	Standard error	Mean	Standard error
CAPITAL	500	500	500	500
LABOR 1	7,100	3,550	13,000	6,500
LABOR 2	1,700	850	5,200	2,600
LABOR 3	170	85	520	260
LAND 1	3.3	6.7	10	20
LAND 2	1.7	3.3	5	10
LAND 3	33.3	8.3	100	25
LAND 4	16.7	8.3	50	25
COAL	1.0	.1	1.0	.1
MINERALS	1.0	.1	1.0	.1
OIL	1.0	.1	1.0	.1

a. All variables are measured in thousands—dollars, workers or hectares—except CAPITAL, which is measured in millions of dollars.

change as the prior is diluted or concentrated in one special way. Next it is assumed that the prior variance matrix Ω lies in an interval of matrices $\lambda_1 \Omega_0 \leqslant \Omega \leqslant \lambda_2 \Omega_0$, for some values of the scalars λ_1 and λ_2. Corresponding to this interval of prior covariance matrices is an ellipsoid of pooled (posterior) estimates. Extreme estimates of parameters of interest are then selected from the ellipsoid of possible estimates. If this interval of estimates is small, it is reported that the choice of estimates is insensitive to choice of Ω in the interval $\lambda_1 \Omega_0 \leqslant \Omega \leqslant \lambda_2 \Omega_0$. If the interval of estimates is too large to be useful, then a smaller interval of λ values is selected. If the λ interval is so small already that it cannot credibly be narrowed, then it is reported that the point estimates are so sensitive to the choice of prior covariance matrix that the data cannot be used to draw useful inferences about this parameter. For further discussion of these methods, consult Leamer (1978, 1982) or Leamer and Leonard (1983).

5.3.1   Choice of Priors for the GNP Regression

Prior means and standard errors for the coefficients in the GNP regressions are reported in table 5.4. These are meant to be guesses about the annual earnings of each of the factors. An explanation of the choice of these numbers follows.

The coefficient of the CAPITAL variable in principle is the real interest rate plus the rate of depreciation. The capital stock figures we are using assume a 15-year life and a 13.3% rate of depreciation. If to this is added a real rate of interest of, say, 3–4%, a coefficient of around .17 is obtained. However, there are two reasons why it would be unsurprising to obtain an estimate higher than .17. First, because we assume only a 15-year life, and because the CAPITAL figure excludes certain forms of human capital that may not be adequately captured by the LABOR 1/LABOR 2/ LABOR 3 distinction, the capital stock number is likely to be a serious underestimate. Second, unmeasured resources that contribute to GNP cannot sensibly be assumed to be uncorrelated with capital because by generating product they allow greater total savings and consequently contribute to capital formation. For these reasons, we set the prior estimate of the capital coefficient to .5, with a large standard error of .5, thereby indicating not much more than the opinion that the coefficient is likely to be between zero and one.

We take information about the annual earnings of the other factors from U.S. sources, remembering that factor price equalization is presently assumed. Farm workers in the United States received annual earnings of $1,700 in 1958 and $5,200 in 1975. Workers in radio and television broadcasting earned $7,100 in 1958 and $13,000 in 1975.[5] These numbers serve as a basis for the prior means for the labor coefficients. Most agricultural workers in the United States fall into the LABOR 2 category: literate but not professional. Accordingly I use the U.S. agricultural earnings as the prior mean for the LABOR 2 coefficients. The radio and television broadcasting workers are the highest paid among the categories reported in the U.S. National Income and Products Accounts. In the United States there are technical and professional workers who are paid more, but the LABOR 1 categories also include lower-paying occupations such as teachers. Thus I will take the prior mean of LABOR 1 coefficients to be the earnings of U.S. broadcast workers. Table 1.1 indicates that agricultural workers in developing countries earn about a tenth of U.S. workers, and I will take the prior mean for the illiterate workers to be a tenth of the U.S. agricultural annual earnings. The prior standard deviations are all set equal to half the prior means to represent a high degree of confidence in the signs of the coefficients.

The USDA (1978) reports figures on rent per acre of cropland and pasture. In 1975 these numbers varied for cropland from a high of $70 an acre for irrigated land in Nebraska to $14.9 for land in Texas. Pastureland varied from a high of $26.70 per acre in Iowa to $5.30 in Texas. A hectare of land (100 square meters) is 2.47 acres, and the highest rental value that could be expected for either LAND 3 or LAND 4 is $70 \times (2.47) = \$173$. Keeping in mind that much of the land is not high quality Nebraska farmland, my expectation is that LAND 3 (California) on the average would yield around \$100 per hectare, but that LAND 4 (Michigan) is much less productive, with rental value of \$50 per hectare. The standard errors for these numbers mean that, roughly speaking, I think that there is a 50% chance that the LAND 3 coefficient is between 75 and 125 and that there is a 50% chance that the LAND 4 coefficient is between 25 and 75. For no especially compelling reasons, the prior means for LAND 1 and LAND 2 are set to 10 and 5, respectively, with relatively large standard errors to reflect my relative ignorance of these coefficients. I was unable to find comparable rental values for 1958 U.S. farmland, but indexes of asset values increased by a factor of approximately three over the period from 1958 to 1975. The 1958 prior means and standard deviations therefore are one-third of the 1975 means and standard deviations.

Every dollar in coal, minerals, and oil produced by the economy can be expected to add approximately \$1 to GNP, if these resources are freely traded and if the production of these items does not use other inputs. There are several reasons why the coefficients of these variables might not be exactly equal to one. First, these are not homogeneous products, and the prices used to convert physical to value units may not be completely appropriate. Second, if international transportation costs are significant and cannot be avoided by the exchange of finished products (that is, factor prices are not equalized) then exporters will have access to cheaper resources on the margin than importers (who pay the transportation costs), and the marginal value of the resource will be lower in the exporting countries than the importing country. Third, a dollar in resource extracted does not contribute exactly a dollar to GNP because extraction requires labor and capital inputs, which are consequently double counted in the GNP equation. Nonetheless, the prior means are selected as if these natural resources were costlessly extracted and freely traded, and are set equal to one. The standard errors on these numbers are selected to reflect considerable confidence in these prior means.

5.3.2 Choice of Prior Distribution for the Net Export Equations

The choice of a prior distribution for the net export equations is much more difficult than the choice for the GNP equations because the coefficients do not have observable counterparts and because they are in theory a consequence of a rather complex computation. The GNP coefficients do determine the rough order of magnitude of the net export coefficients, since it is fair to expect a resource to contribute less to net exports than to GNP. This kind of thinking leads to the prior means for the net export equations reported in Tables 5.5 and 5.6. Prior standard errors are set equal to these prior means to represent a fairly high degree of uncertainty. In order to select these prior means it is necessary first to consider the effect that nontraded goods have on the derivatives of net exports with respect to factor endowments. As discussed in section 1.3.3, the even model with nontraded goods and factor price equalization can be written either as $T = A^{-1}(V - sV_w)$ or as $T = A^{-1}(V^* - sV_w^*)$, where the asterisks indicate resources devoted to the traded goods sector. The second form is the easier one to think about, since the consumption effect is $sA^{-1}V_w^* = A^{-1}V_w^* Y/Y_w$, which is GNP times the share of the commodity in final output. The derivative of this consumption effect with respect to a factor endowment is just the consumption share times the effect of the resource on GNP, the latter predicted by the prior means in table 5.4. To find the prior means for the net export equations, the consumption shares have all been set to 1/20, on the assumption that roughly half of final output is nontraded goods and services and that each of the 10 aggregates comprise roughly the same proportion of final output. If there were no production effect, then the expected effect of a resource on net exports would be the negative of its effect on GNP divided by 20. This number is used as the prior mean in cases when the production effect of a resource is expected to be small. The means for the other coefficients are set equal to each other and large enough that the coefficients sum to zero across equations, as implied by balanced trade. For example, $1 of COAL is expected to contribute $1 to GNP. Half of that dollar in earnings is expected to be spent on nontraded goods, and of the remaining half, one-tenth is expected to be spent on each of the 10 traded aggregates. Thus the pure consumption effect is $1 \times .5 \times .1 = .05$. The negative of this number serves as the prior mean for all of the COAL coefficients except the coefficient in the MAT equation, on the expectation that COAL does not contribute to the production of any product except coal itself, which is included in the MAT aggregate. The prior mean of .45 in the MAT equation assures that the means add to one across equations. To put this differently, the production effect of COAL on MAT net exports is .5 offset by a consumption effect of .05, the latter a consequence of the

Table 5.5
Prior means, net export equations: 1958[a]

	CAPITAL	LABOR 1	LABOR 2	LABOR 3	LAND 1	LAND 2	LAND 3	LAND 4	COAL	MINERALS	OIL
PETRO	-25	-355	-85	-8.5	-.17	-.09	-1.7	-.84	-.05	-.05	.20
MAT	-25	-355	-85	-8.5	-.17	-.09	-1.7	-.84	.45	.45	.20
FOR	-25	-355	21	8.5	-.17	-.09	-1.7	3.4	-.05	-.05	-.05
TROP	-25	-355	21	8.5	.68	.21	4.0	-.84	-.05	-.05	-.05
ANL	-25	-355	21	8.5	-.17	.21	4.0	-.84	-.05	-.05	-.05
CER	-25	-355	21	8.5	.68	.21	4.0	3.4	-.05	-.05	-.05
LAB	37.5	-355	21	8.5	-.17	-.09	-1.7	-.84	-.05	-.05	-.05
CAP	37.5	-355	21	-8.5	-.17	-.09	-1.7	-.84	-.05	-.05	-.05
MACH	37.5	1,420	21	-8.5	-.17	-.09	-1.7	-.84	-.05	-.05	-.05
CHEM	37.5	1,420	21	-8.5	-.17	-.09	-1.7	-.84	-.05	-.05	-.05

a. Standard errors equal to means.

Table 5.6
Prior means, net export equations: 1975[a]

	CAPITAL	LABOR 1	LABOR 2	LABOR 3	LAND 1	LAND 2	LAND 3	LAND 4	COAL	MINERALS	OIL
PETRO	-25	-650	-260	-26	-.5	-.25	-5	-2.5	-.05	-.05	.20
MAT	-25	-650	-260	-26	-.5	-.25	-5	-2.5	.45	.45	.20
FOR	-25	-650	65	26	-.5	-.25	-5	10	-.05	-.05	-.05
TROP	-25	-650	65	26	2.0	.58	11.7	-2.5	-.05	-.05	-.05
ANL	-25	-650	65	26	-.5	.58	11.7	-2.5	-.05	-.05	-.05
CER	-25	-650	65	26	2.0	.58	11.7	10	-.05	-.05	-.05
LAB	37.5	-650	65	26	-.5	-.25	-5	-2.5	-.05	-.05	-.05
CAP	37.5	-650	65	-26	-.5	-.25	-5	-2.5	-.05	-.05	-.05
MACH	37.5	2,600	65	-26	-.5	-.25	-5	-2.5	-.05	-.05	-.05
CHEM	37.5	2,600	65	-26	-.5	-.25	-5	-2.5	-.05	-.05	-.05

a. Standard errors equal to means.

Table 5.7
Bayes estimates, MACHINERY equation: 1975

σ_1	0	.5	1	2	∞
R^2	−2.2	.79	.83	.86	.91
Confidence[a]	1.0	.999	.999	.98	0
CAPITAL	37.5	24.5	29.1	32.3	37.2
LABOR 1	2,600	−821	−1,177	−1,008	−3,519
LABOR 2	65	77	78	37	142
LABOR 3	−26	−13	8	25	65
LAND 1	−.5	−.6	−.7	−1.1	1.9
LAND 2	−.25	−.27	−.30	−.37	5.2
LAND 3	−5.0	−7.2	−11.7	−21.1	−30.2
LAND 4	−2.5	−4.5	−7.5	−10.6	5.5
COAL	−.05	−.05	−.05	.00	2.1
MINERALS	−.05	−.06	−.08	−.12	−3.0
OIL	−.05	−.10	−.17	−.25	−.49

a. One minus the significance level at which the hypothesis that the coefficients equal their indicated values is rejected.

increased GNP induced by increases in COAL resources. Similar calculations apply to all of the other coefficients.

From tables 5.5 and 5.6 it will be observed that I expect LABOR 1 to contribute to comparative advantage in the last two manufactured aggregates—the most skill intensive products. LABOR 2 contributes to all the manufactured commodities plus all the agricultural commodities. LABOR 3, the illiterate work force, has a positive effect on the labor intensive manufactured product and on the agricultural products. Tropical land (LAND 1) is expected to contribute to the tropical agricultural products and to cereals (including rice). The dry land (LAND 2) is associated with the agricultural products, but not forest products or cereals. COAL, MINERALS, and OIL contribute positively to their corresponding trade categories. (OIL includes natural gas, which is included in MAT.)

5.3.3 Example of the Use of Prior Information

Estimates of the 1975 MACHINERY regression using the prior information described in table 5.6 are recorded in table 5.7. The first row of this table contains values for σ_1, the scalar that multiplies all the prior standard errors. If $\sigma_1 = \infty$, the prior standard errors are infinite and the estimates are based on the data alone. These numbers are recorded in the last column of the table. If $\sigma_1 = 0$, the prior standard errors are all set to zero and the coefficients are constrained to equal their prior means. These numbers are recorded in the first column. The column headed by $\sigma_1 = 1$ contains the compromise estimates built on the prior defined in table 5.6. The value $\sigma_1 = 2$ uses a prior that is twice as diffuse, and the value $\sigma_1 = .5$ uses a prior that is twice as dogmatic.

There is little difference between the least-squares estimate of the CAPITAL coefficient (37.2) and the prior estimate (37.5). The pooled estimate, with $\sigma_1 = 1$ is similar, though it is smaller than both. Similarly, there is relatively little disagreement over the estimates of the coefficients of LABOR 2, LAND 3, MINERALS, and OIL, in the sense that the signs of the prior and data estimates conform. For the other coefficients there is apparent conflict between the prior and the data. Highly skilled workers (LABOR 1) are estimated by the data to have a negative effect on MACHINERY net exports. This negative sign is retained even if σ_1 is as small as .5. The LABOR 3 coefficient is estimated with the data alone to be positive, though this turns negative if the prior is sharpened and σ_1 is set to .5. The LAND 1, LAND 2, LAND 4, and COAL coefficients, which are positive at the least-squares estimate, all turn negative even with the fairly small dose of prior information with $\sigma_1 = 2$.

A reasonable interval of values for σ_1 is $.5 < \sigma_1 < 2$. This allows the prior to be either twice as informed or twice as uninformed. The estimates corresponding to this interval generally conform in sign to their prior values and any a priori implausible least-squares estimates are eliminated. An example is the least-squares estimate of the MINERALS coefficient, which suggests that each extra dollar in MINERALS output generates $3 of MACHINERY imports. A little bit of prior information is enough to produce a sensibly small coefficient. The coefficient for LABOR 3 changes sign within the $.5 < \sigma_1 < 2$ interval, and in this case we may conclude that the data and prior are jointly inconclusive about the sign of the effect of illiterate workers on the net exports of MACHINERY. The major finding suggested by table 5.7 is that LABOR 1 has a negative effect, contrary to the sign of the prior, regardless of the value of σ_1 in the interval $.5 < \sigma_1 < 2$. The surprising influence of human capital on comparative advantage is discussed further in the next chapter.

This sensitivity analysis considers the effect of simultaneous, proportional increases or reductions of all elements in the prior covariance matrix; the next form of sensitivity analysis allows all elements of the prior variance matrix to change independently. The intervals of estimates

Table 5.8
Estimates and bounds,[a] MACHINERY equation: 1975[b]

	Prior estimate	Least squares	Bayes estimate[a]	Lower bound[b]	Upper bound[b]
CAPITAL	37.5(37.5)	37.2(5.5)	29.1(3.2)	18.1	38.9
LABOR 1	2,600(2,600)	−3,519(1,460)	−1,177(582)	−3,250	1,420
LABOR 2	65(65)	142(82)	78(45)	−117	231
LABOR 3	−26(26)	65.1(45)	8(20)	−82.8	95.1
LAND 1	−.5(.5)	1.9(3.4)	−.7(.5)	−3.8	2.1
LAND 2	−.25(.25)	5.2(7.7)	−.3(.2)	−1.9	1.3
LAND 3	−5(5)	−30(14)	−12(5)	−37	8
LAND 4	−2.5(2.5)	5.5(6.9)	−7.5(1.9)	−15	.2
COAL	−.05(.05)	2.1(4.3)	−.05(.05)	−.33	.28
MINERALS	−.05(.05)	−3.0(1.1)	−.08(.05)	−.40	.22
OIL	−.05(.05)	−.49(.11)	−.17(.04)	−.38	.02

a. This is the Bayes estimate implied by the prior covariance matrix defined in table 5.6. The same estimates may be found in table 5.7 in the column headed $\sigma_1 = 1$.
b. Standard errors in parentheses.
c. These bounds let the prior covariance matrix lie between $\Omega_0/4$ and Ω_0, where Ω_0 is the covariance matrix defined in table 5.6. If the interval of prior variance is made smaller, $\Omega_0/(1.5)^2$ to $1.5^2\,\Omega_0$, the LAND 4 interval becomes -12 to -3 and the OIL interval becomes $-.29$ to $-.06$. Except for these and CAPITAL, the sensitivity intervals overlap zero.

implied by intervals of prior covariance matrices $.25\Omega_0 \leqslant \Omega \leqslant 4\Omega_0$ are reported in table 5.8. In this interval, only the CAPITAL coefficient takes on a single sign. If one is unable or unwilling to define the prior more sharply, then it must be concluded that there is little to be learned from these data about the determinants of MACHINERY net exports. But if the interval of prior covariance matrices is narrowed to $\Omega_0/(1.5)^2 \leqslant \Omega \leqslant (1.5)^2\Omega_0$, then the LAND 4 coefficient and the OIL coefficient are necessarily negative.

5.4 Beta Coefficients as Measures of Significance

Beta coefficients are used in chapter 6 to rank variables. A beta coefficient is the estimated regression parameter after all variables have been standardized to have unit variance. If b_i is the ordinary least-squares estimate of the ith coefficient, then the corresponding beta coefficient is $b_i\,\mathrm{sd}(x_i)/\mathrm{sd}(y)$, where $\mathrm{sd}(x_i)$ is the standard deviation of variable i and $\mathrm{sd}(y)$ is the standard deviation of the dependent variable. A beta coefficient indicates the number of standard deviation changes in y induced by a one standard deviation change in x_i.

In applied econometric studies it is much more common to rank variables by their t-values rather than their beta values. A large t-value does indicate four things:

1. If all the standard assumptions hold, the sign of the coefficient is determined with high confidence by the data. Formally speaking, a t of, say, 2.2 or more, with degrees of freedom in excess of 10, indicates that there is less than a 2.5% chance that the coefficient has a sign opposite its estimate, assuming the researcher is not otherwise informed (that is, the prior is diffuse).

2. The estimated coefficient is insensitive to the omission of variables. Leamer (1975) has shown that if you omit a variable, then there will be no sign changes to any coefficient with a t-value higher than the coefficient of the omitted variable.

3. The estimated coefficient is insensitive to the reweighting of observations. Leamer (1983) demonstrates that the sign of a coefficient is insensitive to the doubling of weights on selected observations if $|t| > ((n - k)/8)^{1/2}$, where $n - k$ is the degrees of freedom.

4. If all of the standard assumptions hold, then the data cast doubt on the hypothesis that the coefficient is exactly zero. A weighted likelihood ratio (or Bayes factor) against the hypothesis that the coefficient is zero is $(1 + t^2/(n - k))^{n/2}n^{1/2}$ (see Leamer, 1978, p. 114.)

Although there are settings in which it is appropriate to identify the coefficients that are (1) most likely to be positive, (2) most insensitive to selection of variables, (3) most insensitive to the reweighting of observations, or (4) most likely not to be exactly zero, our desire here is to select the most important variables. It is perfectly possible for a coefficient to have a large t-value but to take on an infinitesimal value, so small that it surely is insignificant in any sense but statistical.

If it is wished to select the most important variables, then the purposes for which a model is being constructed have to be identified. Forecasting and control are the usual decision problems, neither of which is apparently pertinent to the present study. What is sought is a simple model that offers a reasonably complete "explanation." This rather vague objective can be given many interpretations. Here I imagine the problem is to "predict" a randomly selected country's net exports (or GNP) given its endowments. The best "prediction" is offered by the least-squares regression with all the endowment variables included. The unimportant endowment variables are those that can be expected not to have much impact on this prediction. Suppose an estimated trade equation were $\hat{T} = a + b_1 V_1 + b_2 V_2$. If V_2 were not observed, then a prediction of T would be $\tilde{T} = a + b_1 V_1 + b_2 \bar{V}_2$, where $\bar{V}_2$ is the mean value of V_2. The expected squared prediction error due to not observing V_2 is then $E(\hat{T} - \tilde{T})^2 = E(b_2 V_2 - b_2 \bar{V}_2)^2 = b_2^2 \operatorname{var}(V_2)$, which is just the squared beta value times $\operatorname{var}(T)$. Therefore a large beta value indicates that the variable ought to be used for prediction. This prediction does not use information about the correlation between V_1 and V_2. Given suitable assumptions, the optimal prediction of V_2 given V_1 is formed by regressing V_2 on V_1: $\tilde{V}_2 = r_1 + r_2 V_1$. Then the optimal predictor of T based on V_1 alone is $\tilde{T}^* = a + b_1 V_1 + b_1(r_1 + r_2 V_1)$, and the expected squared increment to prediction error is $b_2^2 \operatorname{var}(V_2 | V_1)$, which uses the conditional variance. This criterion as shown in Leamer (1978) ranks variables the same as t-statistics, and the choice between beta values and t-statistics as indicators of importance comes down to the way in which omitted variables are predicted. I prefer beta values because the theory associated with the model $\tilde{T}^*$ is complex: V_1 has a direct and an indirect effect on T. The model $\tilde{T}$ is simpler since it includes only the direct effect. For further discussion, see Leamer (1978, chapter 6).

6 Estimates of the Trade Dependence Model

A data analysis based on the linear Heckscher-Ohlin-Vanek trade model is presented in this chapter. Section 6.1 comments on the reasons for doing this empirical work when there is no adequately articulated alternative theory. This summarizes and extends some of the material in chapter 2. Section 6.2 contains a discussion of whether it is better to express the model in terms of supplies of resource endowments or in terms of excess supplies of resource endowments, the former being selected for econometric reasons. Section 6.3 is a map through the thicket of econometric problems. The estimates are then discussed in section 6.4, and the performance of certain nonlinear alternatives are summarized in section 6.5. A conclusion is offered in section 6.6.

6.1 Purposes of the Empirical Analysis

The maintained hypothesis of this empirical work is that trade and GNP are linear functions of the resource endowments. This model is a consequence of a long list of incredible assumptions identified in chapter 1, together with a particular selection of a set of resource endowments. Formal testing of the adequacy of an incredible but simple model requires us either to articulate the more general theory from which it is extracted, and to determine whether the benefits from simplicity outweigh the costs of inaccuracy, or to define an alternative simple model and determine which works best for the stated purposes. However, the most general theory discussed in chapter 1 is so complex that it can never be articulated with the mathematical precision necessary for formal statistical study. Even simple alternatives currently defy attempts at precise formulation. In the absence of fully articulated alternative models, the best we can do is to measure the accuracy of the maintained hypothesis. A "test" of the adequacy of this simple maintained hypothesis will remain a matter of aesthetics. Are you surprised by how well these 11 resources explain the 10 trade aggregates? Do you think you can do much better with a more complex model or a simple alternative?

There is one class of alternatives that is investigated here. These allow trade to be nonlinear functions of the resource endowments. The need to consider nonlinear functions seems clearly suggested by the disparity in average agricultural wage rates among countries reported in table 1.1. Part of the differences in these wage rates might be explained by skill differences, but it seems doubtful that all can be explained that way. The same assumptions that imply the linear trade model also can be used to prove factor price equalization. The apparent failure of wages to be equal everywhere in the world thus casts doubt on these assumptions and, as a consequence, on the linear trade model. There are many reasons why factor prices may fail to equalize, but most seem likely to have only a small effect on trade patterns. Two assumptions may be badly violated and may have major consequences for factor prices and trade. These are incomplete specialization and constant returns to scale.

One potential source of important nonlinearities is complete specialization. If endowments are sufficiently dissimilar, countries will specialize in production of a subset of all goods. All countries that produce the same subset of goods will have the same factor prices, but countries that produce different subsets will have different factor prices. Outputs will be linear functions of endowments within each cluster of countries, but will be different linear functions for each cluster. This possibility could be handled at an empirical level by estimating separate trade functions for each cluster of countries, but in the absence of knowledge of what those clusters may be, this presents formidable estimation problems, especially because many clusters may have too few countries for ordinary least-squares estimation. Instead, I will deal with this problem by searching for nonlinearities in the data set as a whole. In particular, I am looking for relations between trade and endowments similar to that depicted in figure 1.9, which has a sequence of piecewise linear segments of opposite slopes. Since formal statistical methods are not well suited to discovering complex nonlinearities, I resort to inspection of graphs as well as to estimation of specific nonlinear models. One scatter of points that is very suggestive of this form of nonlinearity is the plot of 1958 capital intensive net exports per workers versus capital per worker in figure C.8a. This is very similar to figure 1.9 with exporters generally confined to the middle region of capital abundance.

Another source of nonlinearities is increasing returns to scale. At the outset I did not expect to find evidence of scale economies, but the failure of bivariate scatter plots of the last three manufactured aggregates to reveal resources that determine comparative advantage in these commodities forced some reconsideration of initial expectations, and led to the suspicion that scale economies are important. For example, the plot of 1975 machinery net exports per worker versus capital per worker in figure C.9a indicates that countries with capital abundance are either net exporters or net importers. The large industrial countries are all net exporters (as are Sweden and Switzerland), a fact that is suggestive of economies of scale.

This search for nonlinearities is clearly deficient on account of its lack of a firm foundation in economic theory, and it is offered only as an addendum to the main body of empirical work. Some readers may be tempted to make the harsh judgment that much of this empirical exercise is irrelevant, since it depends critically on linearity, and implicitly on factor price equalization. This, I believe, would be an erroneous conclusion, since the hypothesis of linearity is taken only as an approximation, and since factor prices may be much more similar than the first glance suggests. Krueger (1968), in particular, challenges the traditional viewpoint that factor prices are greatly disparate and concludes, "That more than half of the difference between United Nations estimates of *per capita* income of each of the less-developed countries in the sample and the United States is explained by demographic variables alone must surely cast some doubt on the degree of conviction with which the factor-price equalization model is held to be unrealistic."

Except for these vague, nonlinear hypotheses, no explicit alternative hypotheses are considered here, and there is a serious risk that this analysis, like many empirical studies, will degenerate into an elaborate exercise in econometric journalism. Traditional journalism might report that, on the average, women earn 20% less than men. Econometric journalism would add that, controlling for education, the number is 10%. Traditional journalism might report that one in three families in the United States has two or more automobiles. Econometric journalism would report that the income elasticity of the demand for automobiles is .92. A journalist's primary concern is to find facts that the consuming public will find amusing and/or useful. Knowledge of the fact that women earn less than men is interesting to me, as is the econometric observation that part of the difference can be accounted for by education. I also find somewhat amusing the fact that one in three families has two or more cars. But the income elasticity of automobiles is of little current interest to me, and I wish not to spend my time reading about it, unless it can be demonstrated, that it is far from what I regard to be a reasonable value. If it is shown to be negative, I shall certainly sit up and take notice.

The coefficients in a model explaining trade as a function of resource endowments seems initially to be uninteresting. Who would want to know by how much exports of machinery can be expected to increase if capital were to increase by $1 million? Uses of this number might be imagined by forecasters, investors, and policymakers, but the general readers of this book are not likely to be amused. There are five questions that I suppose will be of interest to the general reader:

1. How well do the 11 measured resources explain trade? I suppose there are many doubters who may be impressed by how well these resources do and who will conclude that the Heckscher-Ohlin model has more content than imagined.

2. Do the coefficients take on values that are surprising? My expected values of the coefficients are the prior means reported in the last chapter. Major differences between estimates and these prior means are worth noticing.

3. Has the structural relation between trade and endowments changed much over time? We have already seen that a large number of countries have begun to export the manufactured products. Has this been accompanied by a demonstrable shift in the sources of comparative advantage? If so, serious adjustment problems could be expected.

4. Which are the most important resources? This question is studied in this chapter by referring to beta (standardized) coefficients and in the next chapter by studying the trade-reducing impact of resource reallocations.

5. What impact do tariff structures have on the functional distribution of income? This is found in the next chapter by first purging the consumption effect from the trade coefficients and then appealing to the duality between the Stolper-Samuelson effects and the Rybczynski effects.

6.2 Choice of Model

The Heckscher-Ohlin-Vanek equation can express trade in terms of endowment supplies or in terms of excess endowment supplies. In order to comment on the choice between these two forms of the model, we may write the 2-good 2-factor version as

$$T_1 = \beta_{1L}(L - YL_w/Y_w) + \beta_{1K}(K - YK_w/Y_w), \tag{6.1}$$

$$T_2 = \beta_{2L}(L - YL_w/Y_w) + \beta_{2K}(K - YK_w/Y_w), \tag{6.2}$$

$$Y = w_L L + w_K K, \tag{6.3}$$

where T_1 and T_2 are net exports of the two commodities, Y is GNP, L is labor, K is capital, w_L and w_K are the factor returns, the w subscript indicates world totals, and β_{ji} is a Rybczynski coefficient, namely, the derivative of output j with respect to input i. In this form, trade is expressed in terms of the excess supplies of factors, $L - YL_w/Y_w$ and $K - YK_w/Y_w$.

In order to draw inferences about the coefficients β_{ji} in this model, it is necessary to describe the links between the hypotheticals (T, Y, K, and L) and corresponding observable variables. It is easy to reject the composite hypothesis that the model given by (6.1)–(6.3) holds and that all variables are measured perfectly, since no real data conform to these exact linear restrictions. We can still maintain the model if we allow measurement error in some or all variables. Two forms of measurement error are naturally considered: One or more of the resources may be assumed to be completely unobservable, or one or more of the variables may be assumed to be measured with errors having finite variances. Both of these are sensible assumptions, the first because many resources are clearly not measured and the second because measurements of trade, GNP, and resources are surely subject to measurement errors.

The conclusion that can be reached from a consideration of the econometric issues raised by (6.1)–(6.3) is that it is wildly optimistic to expect to recover the Rybczynski coefficients from data on trade and endowments by a regression of trade on a subset of excess factor supplies. Because each of the excess factor endowments is a linear function of all factor supplies, $L - YL_w/Y_w = L - (w_L L + w_K K)L_w/Y_w$ and $K - YL_w/Y_w = K - (w_L L + w_K K)K_w/Y_w$, for almost all distributions of K and L these excess supplies are correlated, and a regression of trade on a subset of the excess supplies yields biased and inconsistent estimates because variables are excluded that are necessarily correlated with the included variables. This problem is only compounded if the observed factor supplies are measured with error. Because of these econometric difficulties, we opt for estimation of the reduced form found by inserting (6.3) into (6.1) and (6.2):

$$T_1 = \theta_{1L}L + \theta_{1K}K, \tag{6.4}$$

$$T_2 = \theta_{2L}L + \theta_{2K}K, \tag{6.5}$$

$$Y = w_L L + w_K K, \tag{6.6}$$

where $\theta_{ji} = \beta_{ji} - Q_{jw}w_i/Y_w$, with Q_{jw} equal to world output of commodity j, $Q_{jw} = \beta_{jL}L_w + \beta_{jK}K_w$. [Econometric tests of (6.4) versus (6.1) also strongly favor (6.4), possibly because world endowments and world GNP are not accurately measured.]

Factor endowments that are unmeasured are (optimistically) assumed to be distributed independently of the measured endowments, and regression of net exports on measured endowments would then yield estimates $\hat{\theta}_{ji}$ of the Rybczynski effects β_{ji} minus the product of the wage rate w_i times the consumption share Q_j/Y_w. Regression estimates of equations such as (6.4) can be used to recover the Rybczynski coefficients if we have other information on the consumption shares Q_j/Y_w and on the wage rates w_i, the latter obtainable from a regression (6.6) of GNP on the observed factors.[1]

6.3 Econometric Strategy

Chapter 5 identified a sequence of econometric modeling problems (heteroscedasticity, gross errors, chronic measurement errors, multicollinearity, and nonlinearities) and discussed how each can be treated. It is beyond our technical capabilities to deal with all of these issues in a single comprehensive analysis, and we are forced to use an approach that is piecemeal, though defensible. The approach that will be taken is first to estimate the model using ordinary least-squares methods. Second, these estimates are corrected for systematic heteroscedasticity that is assumed to be a function of GNP. Third, the sensitivity of the heteroscedasticity-adjusted estimates to the deletion of observations is studied to detect gross errors. Fourth, the sensitivity of the ordinary least-squares regression to chronic measurement errors is explored. Fifth, a Bayesian analysis of the homoscedastic model is performed, including a study of the fragility of the Bayes estimates. Last, nonlinear functional forms are tested.

This sequence of procedures has an underlying logic. The sensitivity of estimates to the omission of individual observations can be expected to be less after adjustment for heteroscedasticity, since the large countries, which are likely to be most influential, are expected to receive less weight after heteroscedasticity adjustment. By first purging the estimates of this form of systematic heteroscedasticity we leave for the analysis of observation omissions the job of detecting purely nonsystematic heteroscedasticity. For absence of econometric theory dealing jointly with chronic measurement errors and systematic heteroscedasticity, we are forced to perform our errors-in-variables analysis on the homoscedastic model. As it turns out, the collinearity in the measured explanatory variables is so high that the true variables might be perfectly collinear, and this data set by itself would then be useless for estimating individual coefficients. It seems quite unlikely that this conclusion would change if heteroscedasticity were allowed. Because these data are so collinear that they cannot by themselves produce estimates, a Bayesian analysis with a proper prior distribution is essential. The Bayesian analysis presented here makes use of the homoscedastic model and therefore ignores systematic heteroscedasticity, gross errors, and chronic errors. It is unlikely that treatment of systematic heteroscedasticity would have much effect on the Bayes estimates, since the Bayes estimates involve prior information and are therefore less sensitive to changes in the sample information than the sample estimates themselves, and since adjusting for heteroscedasticity in this case does not cause apparent substantial changes in the sample estimates. For the same reason that the Bayes estimates are relatively insensitive to sample information, omitting observations or correcting the sample moments for measurement errors will have less impact. Moreover, the Bayesian sensitivity analysis to some extent encompasses measurement error problems.[2] Finally, I have saved for last the testing of nonlinear forms basically because I have no adequately articulated nonlinear theory and do not really know how to react to the nonlinear estimates that are obtained.

6.4 Discussion of the Estimates

The net exports of the 10 aggregate commodities measured in thousands of dollars are explained in terms of the following 11 measured resources:

CAPITAL = millions of dollars of discounted and accumulated investment flows,

LABOR 1 = thousands of professional/technical workers,

LABOR 2 = thousands of nonprofessional literate workers,

LABOR 3 = thousands of illiterate workers,

LAND 1 = thousands of hectares of tropical land,

LAND 2 = thousands of hectares of dry land (desert and steppe),

LAND 3 = thousands of hectares of humid mesothermal land,

LAND 4 = thousands of hectares of humid microthermal land,

COAL = value in thousands of dollars of production of primary solid fuel,

MINERALS = value in thousands of dollars of production of minerals,

OIL = value in thousands of dollars of production of oil and gas.

Incidentally, the use of 10 trade aggregates and 11 resources should not be a cause for concern about the theoretical model that supposes equal numbers of factors and goods because goods have been aggregated to 10 and because only 11 resources out of a larger set are observed. (In fact, there are exactly 2,118 goods and 2,118 factors. You did know that, didn't you?)

Weighted regression estimates of the trade equations and the GNP equations are reported in table 6.1. The abbreviations in this table for the 10 commodity aggregates will be used repeatedly. The 3 that take some getting used to are MAT for raw materials, LAB for labor intensive manufactures, and CAP for capital intensive manufactures. The squared multiple correlations (R^2) reported in this table are pleasantly high. The exceptions are ANL and LAB in 1975. (The unweighted R^2 values for these equations are higher—.34 and .59). Generally the R^2 values are lower in 1975 than 1958, indicating diminished importance of these resources as determinants of trade. The heteroscedasticity adjustment factors, θ in the formula $\sigma^2 = \alpha GNP^\theta$, are reported in the last column of this table and are lower than expected. (For the GNP equation, the model is $\sigma^2 = \alpha CAPITAL^\theta$.) If the standard error were proportional to GNP, then θ would be 2. In no case does the estimate of θ exceed 1, and in one case it is actually negative.

Because of the seriousness of chronic measurement errors, the estimates in this table need not be treated too seriously. Nonetheless, there are a number of interesting general findings that apply also to the Bayes estimates to be discussed. The natural resources MINERALS and OIL contribute to comparative advantage in the natural resource products PETRO and MAT; CAPITAL and LABOR 1 are sources of comparative disadvantage. One or more of the LAND variables create comparative advantage in the four crops: FOR, TROP, ANL, and CER. Abundance of LAND is a source of comparative disadvantage in manufactures. The sources of comparative advantage in manufactures are unclear for the 1958 data, though LABOR 3 was clearly a source of disadvantage and

Table 6.1
Weighted least-squares estimates[a]

	CAPITAL	LABOR 1	LABOR 2	LABOR 3	LAND 1	LAND 2	LAND 3	LAND 4	COAL	MIN-ERALS	OIL	R^2	$wt(\theta)$
1958													
GNP	775**	4,310	-89	54*	5.2*	-4.5	20.7*	-2.3	5.6**	-6.1*	3.3	.998	.13
PETRO	-7.95**	-126*	2.5	1.8*	-0.12*	-0.01	-0.6*	-0.3**	-0.02	0.19*	0.58**	.84	.43
MAT	-3.7*	-403**	5.0*	5.2**	.11*	-0.00	-.1	.9**	.04	.89**	.43**	.90	.81
FOR	3.9	130	-5.8	.3	-.02	.01	-1.2*	1.8**	-.39**	.11	-.36*	.67	.44
TROP	-8.3*	-305*	18.5*	2.4	1.00**	.02	.1	-.6**	-.36**	.48*	.63**	.90	.10
ANL	.83	169	-5.8	-.9	-.12	.10	2.3*	.3	-.56**	-.01	-.05	.55	.19
CER	1.4	-520*	-.8	6.5**	.08	.60**	3.8**	.4*	-.31**	.29*	.90**	.89	.36
LAB	1.2	190*	2.4	-3.8**	-.09*	-.11	-.4	-.8**	.02	-.14*	-.23**	.86	.03
CAP	3.2	671**	-6.1	-7.3**	-.25*	.10	-2.5**	-.9**	.07	-.89**	-.76**	.80	.17
MACH	-4	68	-2.6	-5.5*	-.32*	-.65*	-2.5**	-1.4**	1.5**	-.94**	.28*	.97	.08
CHEM	1.3	17	-4.5*	-.1	-.07	-.15*	-.4*	-.1	.25**	-.11*	.01	.82	.51
1975													
GNP	452.7**	15,683**	-445*	-479.7**	30.1**	-49.1**	80.6*	-26.6*	9.0**	2.8*	2.1**	.997	.42
PETRO	-18.4**	-248	-.8	33.7*	0.5	7.9**	-5.4	0.3	-1.0**	-.4	.6**	.92	.41
MAT	-8.9**	127	-31.2*	-2.3	.89	.47	1.1	3.3**	.45**	.86**	.04*	.86	.46
FOR	-1.7	34	-18.8	8.4	-.45	-2.7*	.3	3.3**	-.17	.53*	.08*	.53	.34
TROP	-2.9**	-30.1	8.9	5.6	2.0**	-1.1	4.5*	-3.9**	-.30**	.44**	.05*	.72	.39
ANL	-.5	-42	-29.3	14.0	.09	-.34	5.6*	-1.3	-.17	.28	.05	.22	.27
CER	-4.5**	70	-51.0*	-6.8	1.3*	-4.8**	16.1**	-3.6*	.39**	.97**	.24**	.86	.31
LAB	1.9	-397	41.6*	7.4	-.97	.00	-.6	-1.6	-.10	-.09	-.07*	.13	.99
CAP	17.9**	-1,900**	115.9**	49.0**	-.89	3.2*	-12.4**	-.63	-.12	-.46*	-.17**	.86	.26
MACH	29.1**	-1,471*	38.2	33.3	-1.6	-1.5	-23.5**	-7.9*	1.0**	-1.1*	-.27**	.76	.59
CHEM	4.1**	-154	-16.0	3.0	-.57	-.30	-6.0*	-1.0	.3**	-.15	-.04*	.51	.66

a. GNP is scaled in thousands of dollars; CAPITAL is in millions. * indicates that $|t| > 1$, ** that $|t| > 2$.

Table 6.2
Bounds for weighted least-squares estimates formed by omitting observations one at a time[a]

	CAPITAL	LABOR 1	LABOR 2	LABOR 3	LAND 1
1958					
GNP	**716/840**	**1,364/6,452**	−157/235	−63/198	−2.7/6.0
PETRO	**−9.5/−2.5**	**−298/−67**	**.07/5.3**	**1.2/6.5**	−.17/.44
MAT	**−9.1/−2.6**	**−457/−254**	**3.6/7.1**	**3.2/7.6**	**.08/.15**
FOR	−2.3/6.0	−46/219	−9.7/1.4	−2.2/1.1	−.04/.17
TROP	**−13/−5**	**−391/−133**	**9.8/22.0**	**.26/3.1**	**.82/1.06**
ANL	−4.1/3.3	**30/395**	**−18.8/−.9**	−11.9/3.7	**−.47/.001**
CER	−6.1/12.4	**−1,018/−253**	−13/12	**3.4/30.4**	−.19/1.22
LAB	−1.2/2.0	**60/252**	**.12/9.0**	**−6.4/−3.5**	**−.16/−.06**
CAP	−6.0/6.7	**322/1,094**	−15/6	**−28/−5**	**−1.01/−.02**
MACH	−3.1/8.5	−290/335	−11.9/10.7	−9.9/7.0	−.46/.43
CHEM	**.45/4.37**	−85/50	**−5.7/−3.0**	−.4/2.3	−.09/.14
1975					
GNP	**424/510**	**9,627/21,895**	**−666/−25**	**−719/−311**	−65.9/32.0
PETRO	**−22.5/−14.3**	−1,151/396	−60/34	**16/125**	−1.0/16.2
MAT	**−10.5/−5.1**	−303/472	**−47/−6.2**	−15.6/9.1	**.55/2.88**
FOR	**−4.8/.46**	−379/698	−29/3.1	−18/15	−1.8/.34
TROP	**−4.2/−1.7**	−264/268	−6.4/25.8	−23.0/10	−1.5/2.5
ANL	−3.6/.12	−400/625	**−40/−10**	−13/19	−.50/.80
CER	**−9.5/−2.6**	−809/1,169	**−93/−6**	−71/8	−1.1/2.1
LAB	.24/2.74	**−608/−90**	**21.5/54.7**	**.7/28.6**	**−4.1/−.6**
CAP	**13.5/19.3**	**−2,420/−1,162**	**68/148**	**36/73**	−1.6/3.8
MACH	**22.6/33.8**	**−2,361/−652**	−25/95	**13/69**	−3.7/14.0
CHEM	**2.9/5.2**	−304/17	**−35/−6**	−11.4/7.7	−.9/3.9

a. Intervals excluding zero are in boldface.

LABOR 1 a source of advantage at least in CAP. The 1975 data tell quite a different story. CAPITAL and to some extent LABOR 2 and LABOR 3 are sources of comparative advantage, but LABOR 1 is a source of disadvantage in manufactures.

If a t-value in excess of 2 is taken to mean that the coefficient is measurable in the sense of taking on the sign of its least-squares value with high probability, then the COAL effects on trade are most often measurable (12 out of 20). OIL has 10 measurable effects, LAND 4 has 9, and CAPITAL has 8. Among the effects with t-values greater than 2 in absolute value, the surprises in terms of signs are LABOR 1 (−) for 1975 CAP, LAND 4 (−) for TROP, COAL (+) for MACH, MINERALS (+) for 1975 TROP, OIL (+) for CER, and 1975 TROP. Most distressingly, several of the resources are estimated to have negative effects on GNP.

LAND 2	LAND 3	LAND 4	COAL	MIN	OIL
−6.6/7.0	**6.8/24.4**	−71.5/1.7	**.3/10.1**	**−12.1/−1.2**	**1.1/6.5**
−.08/.03	−.8/.0	−1.4/−.2	−.18/.13	.07/.29	.43/.86
−.01/.04	−.1/.1	.5/1.2	−.003/.07	**.83/.98**	.17/.51
−.12/.08	−.1/−.4	**1.7/15.5**	−.55/−.23	−.03/.19	**−.55/−.18**
−.67/.13	−.28/2.4	−2.1/−.5	−.56/−.18	.21/.88	.31/.82
−.13/.20	**1.9/3.1**	.1/1.1	−.86/−.26	−.17/.12	−.24/.11
.32/1.03	**3.0/4.2**	.3/1.2	−.50/−.15	.15/.40	**.50/1.13**
−.16/.07	−.6/−.3	−3.1/−.7	−.06/.12	−.20/−.07	−.26/.01
.02/.48	**−2.88/−2.3**	**−7.3/−.8**	−.06/.29	−.56/−.17	**−.83/−.43**
−.79/−.33	**−4.7/−2.2**	−3.1/−1.2	**1.39/1.59**	**−1.19/−.66**	−.04/.39
−.30/−.09	−.91/−.07	−1.8/−.0	**.18/.29**	−.24/−.06	−.12/.08
−59.2/−8.1	**54/142**	−46/74	**5.4/10.6**	**.9/5.6**	**1/2.8**
−1.6/10.8	**−8.6/−.7**	−33.7/3.1	−1.4/.08	−.94/.22	**.49/1.07**
−.36/1.04	−.7/3.5	**1.8/4.3**	**.30/.55**	**.75/.94**	−.003/.05
−3.5/−.38	−.9/1.4	**2.2/62.6**	−.40/−.01	**.29/.72**	−.03/.11
−2.0/1.2	**3.4/13.2**	−6.4/−1.5	**.55/−.17**	**.28/.68**	−.06/.07
−1.5/1.8	**4.1/13.9**	−2.2/6.9	−.36/−.01	**.02/.45**	−.06/.07
−6.3/.9	**13.2/20.9**	−5.6/16.7	−.14/.72	**.51/1.32**	−.03/.31
−.50/.71	−1.2/.5	**−2.1/−.1**	−.26/.06	−.15/−.02	−.09/−.06
1.6/4.3	**−30/−10**	−19.9/.4	.40/.04	−.64/−.2	−.20/−.10
−5.2/3.2	**−66/17**	−63/−5	**.48/1.62**	**−1.51/−.66**	−.34/−.09
.92/.31	**−11.1/−4.9**	−23/−.2	**.22/.43**	−.27/−.08	−.06/−.01

The extreme estimates after individual observations are omitted are reported in table 6.2. Estimates that have signs insensitive to these one-at-a-time omissions are printed in boldface. The coefficients that are most insensitive in this sense to the choice of observations are MINERALS, with a total of 19 of 22 insensitive coefficients. LAND 3 and LAND 4 have a total of 16 insensitive coefficients each. The most sensitive coefficients apply to LAND 1 and LAND 2, each of which has only 6 insensitive signs. Among those coefficients with t-values in excess of 2 (indicated by double asterisks in table 6.1), the following can be reversed in sign by omission of a single observation: LAND 1 in 1975 TROP, LAND 2 in 1975 PETRO and 1975 CER, OIL in 1975 LAB and 1975 CER, and COAL in 1975 CER. But generally speaking, the coefficients with high t-values are insensitive to the omission of observations. Parenthetically, note that of the eight coefficients in the GNP equation with negative signs, four can be made positive (corrected) by the omission of a suitable observation.

Often, the omission of a country will generate an extreme estimate for a coefficient in many different equations. The following list contains countries that critically influence the estimates in the sense of often implying an extreme estimate if omitted. The number of times (out of 20) that the variable generates an extreme estimate in a trade equation is given in parentheses, where a minimum of 5 is required to make the list:

CAPITAL: UK (7), GER (6), JAP (5);

LABOR 1: UK (6), FRA (5);

LABOR 2: THAI (8), FRA (6);

LABOR 3: INDA (17), JAP (5);

LAND 1: BRAZ (19), INDA (8), GER (5);

LAND 2: AUSL (12), US (8), LIBY (5);

LAND 3: ARG (13);

LAND 4: CAN (20), CHLE (6);

COAL: GER (13), UK (10), US (8);

MINERALS: CHLE (16), UK (5);

OIL: US (11), NIGR (7), FRA (6), INDO (6).

The most frequently influential countries not surprisingly are among the extremes in the boxplots of the resource variables in chapter 4. Canada is most abundant in LAND 4, India in LABOR 3, Brazil in LAND 1, and the United States in OIL. Argentina is second in LAND 3, and Chile is either third or fourth in MINERALS. Some of the less frequently influential observations are not among the extremes, and their influence has to be attributed to subtleties in the multivariate distribution of the data that are not revealed by looking at the distributions of the variables one at a time.

The reaction that seems appropriate to these extreme and influential observations is one of suspicion. For example, as is discussed in chapter 4, LAND 4 is an aggregate that includes land with subarctic climates. The LAND 4 figure for Canada, therefore, is likely to overestimate the economically productive land, and the extreme influence that Canada has on the LAND 4 coefficient can be regarded as primarily due to a gross aggregation error. In another case, India is so extreme in LABOR 3 that our conclusions about its effect are very dependent on the Indian observation. Though I cannot think of a specific reason why this observation should be discarded, I am confident that a little bit of thought could produce one. Some form of nonlinearity would certainly do. Accordingly, inferences about the LABOR 3 coefficient have to be regarded with great suspicion, since they are almost certainly extremely fragile. In most of the other cases there are ways of omitting countries that produce estimates similar to the extreme and the inference is not so dependent on a single observation. The other coefficients that are heavily dependent on a particular country and that may be viewed with special suspicion are LAND 1 (Brazil), LAND 3 (Argentina), MINERALS (Chile), and OIL (United States).

The extreme t-statistics of dummy variables that select out a single country and that are included in the equation only one at a time are reported in table 6.3. The most unusual observations have t-statistics 6 or more. By this criterion, in 1958 the United Kingdom had an unexplainably high GNP and unexplainably low net exports of PETRO. Canada had unusually low net exports of FOR in both years. In 1975 Sweden had unusually large net exports of FOR, the United States of CER, and Hong Kong of LAB. The United States had peculiarly negative net exports of PETRO. This table is meant to stimulate thinking about defects in the model. The forest product results make me think again of the defect in measuring LAND 4—that is, the inclusion of subarctic climate. The source of comparative advantage in forest products is LAND 4, but the Canadian observation makes LAND 4 appear less productive than it ought to. The compromise estimate of LAND 4's productivity accordingly badly underestimates net exports of Finland and Sweden, and badly overestimates net exports of Canada. Similarly, the unexplainable dependence of the United States on CEREALS exports may be due to conceptual errors in measurement of LAND 3 and LAND 4, since no attempt has been made here to measure the fertility of land, and since the United States may be endowed with especially fertile land. A more exotic explanation is nonlinearities associated with factor intensity reversals—the United States uses capital intensive techniques in agriculture, whereas many other countries use labor intensive techniques. Hong Kong's concentration on labor intensive manufactures may also be explained by nonlinearities. Hong Kong may be so scarce in land that it completely specializes in

Table 6.3
t-statistics of extreme countries, weighted regressions[a]

$t < -2$		$t > 2$
1958		
GNP	GER(-5.4), JAP(-4.0)	ITLY(3.1), UK(7.9)
PETRO	SWE(-2.8), UK(-6.8)	GER(4.8)
MAT	AUST(-2.4), ITLY(-2.5), YUG(-3.3)	MALY(2.2), US(2.7)
FOR	CAN(-10.8)	FIN(5.8), SWE(4.4)
TROP	CHLE(-2.1), UK(-3.8)	GER(3.4), MALY(3.6)
ANL	ITLY(-2.2), UK(-4.6)	DEN(4.3), GER(3.5), NETH(3.1)
CER	INDA(-3.2), UK(-2.6)	BRMA(2.5), EGPT(2.9), GER(2.6), NIGR(3.1), THAI(2.4)
LAB	GER(-4.4), NETH(-2.7), SWE(-2.1)	CAN(2.1), FRA(3.0), HOKO(4.2), UK(4.0)
CAP	GER(-3.3)	BLUX(5.5), CAN(2.5), INDA(2.3), UK(2.1)
MACH	BLUX(-3.1), NOR(-2.4)	ITLY(3.2), SWIT(3.0)
CHEM		CAN(2.1), CHLE(2.3), GER(2.1), SWIT(3.3)
1975		
GNP	AUSL(-2.8), JAP(-4.1), NIGR(-2.9) UK(-3.0)	BRAZ(3.3), SPAN(2.5), TURK(2.5), US(3.1)
PETRO	BRAZ(-3.1), US(-11.9)	AUSL(2.9), GER(5.0), INDO(2.7) LIBY(2.4), NIGR(3.6), UK(2.4)
MAT	BLUX(-2.2), HOKO(-2.5), JAP(-3.6)	GER(2.2), NETH(4.9)
FOR	CAN(-10.1), UK(-2.9)	FIN(4.5), SWE(6.1), US(2.3)
TROP	GER(-3.0), INDO(-2.1)	ITLY(2.1), US(3.7)
ANL	ITLY(-3.9)	DEN(3.0), NETH(5.1)
CER	NIGR(-3.2), UK(-4.6)	FRA(3.5), THAI(2.7), US(6.6)
LAB		HOKO(8.3), ITLY(2.7), KORA(2.4)
CAP	FRA(-2.5), THAI(-2.6)	ARG(2.3), BLUX(4.2), JAP(2.8)
MACH		ARG(2.9), GER(4.9)
CHEM	BRAZ(-2.1)	CAN(2.8), GER(2.7), NETH(3.9)

a. t-value applies to dummy variable selecting the country.

manufacturing, and the linear model used here is rendered inappropriate because it assumes incomplete specialization. An explanation of the U.K. dependence on petroleum imports in 1958, as well as that of the United States in 1975, eludes me. If the United Kingdom were not included, one might think of gas-guzzling U.S. automobiles.

Errors-in-variables diagnostics are reported in table 6.4. In every case, the $k + 1$ regressions formed by minimizing the sum of squares in the $k + 1$ possible orthogonal directions fail to conform is sign (not shown). This implies that after purging the data of measurement errors, a perfectly collinear data set may remain. Some restriction on the measurement error variances is necessary if perfect collinearity among the true variables is to be ruled out (see chapter 5). The diagnostics in table 6.4 suggest

Table 6.4
Errors-in-variables diagnostics (g and $1 - \lambda_1$)[a]

	1958	1975
g: GNP	.0013	.2300
PETRO	.015	.0088
MAT	.0022	.0019
FOR	.0041	.0038
TROP	.0020	.0029
ANL	.0003	.0015
CER	.0065	.0044
LAB	.0294	.0003
CAP	.0009	.0040
MACH	.0234	.0370
CHEM	.0205	.0019
$1 - \lambda_1$	.995	.993

a. g = proportion of gap between estimated R^2 and one that can be attributed to measurement error without allowing perfect collinearity in the data. $1 - \lambda_1$ = minimum squared correlation between true variables and their measurements to assure that the true variables are not perfectly collinear.

restrictions on the error variances that could be used to rule out the problem of perfect collinearity. One way to restrict the error variances is to select a maximum value for the multiple correlation coefficient that would be achieved if the measurement errors were completely eliminated. If this maximum R^2 is not much larger than the estimated R^2, then the error variances cannot be very large. The statistic g indicates the proportion of the difference between the measured R^2 and 1 that could be attributed to measurement error and still leave the data set less than perfectly collinear. Except for GNP in 1975, these g-statistics are very small, which means that it would have to be claimed that eliminating the measurement error could increase the R^2 by at most a very small amount. I am uncomfortable with such a claim. The statistic $1 - \lambda_1$ in table 6.4 indicates an assumption about the squared correlation between true and measured explanatory variables that could rule out perfect collinearity. However, I am quite unwilling to claim that the squared correlation between the true and the measured explanatory variables certainly exceeds .995 in 1958 and .997 in 1975. We are accordingly in a situation of high enough correlation among the measured explanatory variables that the true explanatory variables may be virtually perfectly collinear, and these data cannot by themselves yield reliable estimates of the parameters. Estimates can nonetheless be obtained if a proper prior distribution is employed because the prior is like a previous data set that is not perfectly collinear, and because adding more data to this hypothetical prior data set is useful even if the new data are ill-conditioned.

Bayes estimates and t-statistics based on the priors described in section 5.3 are reported in tables 6.5 and 6.6 and the corresponding beta values are reported in table 6.7. Bounds for the Bayes estimates are indicated in table 6.8. These intervals of estimates are generated by intervals of prior covariance matrices from one-fourth to four times the covariance matrices used to obtain the Bayes estimates in table 6.5. Most of the discussion is based on this Bayesian analysis because minor chronic measurement errors would render the least-squares estimates totally irrelevant, but leave the Bayes estimates relatively intact. Discussion of the GNP equation is saved for the end of this section.

The pattern of Bayes estimates and t-values in tables 6.5 and 6.6 is quite interesting, though, as discussed subsequently, many of these estimates are rather fragile. In discussing these results it is useful to group the 10 commodity aggregates into three groups. The first group is composed of the natural resource products, PETRO and MAT, which are expected to be related to the natural resources COAL, MINERALS, and OIL. The next 4 aggregates are crops, and are expected to be positively related to the LAND variables. The last 4 aggregates are manufactured commodities and are expected to be related positively to CAPITAL and to the LABOR variables. Generally speaking, the Bayes estimates conform to these expectations.

The sign patterns of all the 1958 coefficients for all four manufactured aggregates are identical except that LABOR 2 is negative for MACH and CHEM, and CAPITAL is positive for CHEM. There are some surprises in these results in the sense that they do not all conform in sign to the prior means in table 5.5. It was expected that CAPITAL would contribute to comparative advantage in all four of the manufactured commodities, but it actually contributes positively in 1958 only to CHEM. The most highly skilled workers, LABOR 1, whose effects were expected to be concentrated on MACH and CHEM actually in 1958 contribute positively to all four. LABOR 2, which was expected to contribute to all four, actually creates comparative disadvantage in MACH and CHEM. Finally, the least skilled workers (LABOR 3) were expected to contribute positively to comparative advantage in LAB, but in fact in 1958 all four coefficients are negative. It is then interesting to observe the sharp changes in all but the CHEM coefficients in 1975. By then CAPITAL was playing its expected

Table 6.5
Bayes estimates

	CAPITAL	LABOR 1	LABOR 2	LABOR 3	LAND 1	LAND 2	LAND 3	LAND 4	COAL	MIN	OIL
1958											
GNP	774	7,556	−142	23.7	3.1	−1.6	27	−4.2	1	.99	.99
PETRO	−4.8	−133.5	1.4	2.4	−.12	−.04	−.67	−.25	−.07	−.01	.43
MAT	−3.3	−494.3	8.7	5.5	.09	−.03	.03	.99	.07	.82	.48
FOR	2.8	−249.6	6	3.1	−.08	−.08	−.81	1.9	−.14	−.04	−.05
TROP	6.9	−826	22.2	9.8	1.2	.2	−.46	−.42	−.21	−.03	.02
ANL	6.4	−534.5	9.3	5.8	−.11	.16	2.4	.28	−.16	−.04	−.03
CER	20.8	−1,068.5	−1.8	15	.26	.46	3.5	.43	−.22	−.03	.05
LAB	−.9	195.3	4.5	−4.5	−.12	−.1	−.38	−.84	.02	−.06	−.11
CAP	−6.5	614.1	9.8	−11	−.27	−.1	−1.6	−.1	.04	−.06	−.11
MACH	−8.1	1,570	−30.8	−20.3	−.39	−.12	−4.3	−2.2	.35	−.09	−.1
CHEM	1.1	158.5	−8.9	−1.1	−.1	−.14	−.47	−.14	.18	−.07	−.07
1975											
GNP	423.2	40,295.9	−1,752.7	−850.2	22.9	9.3	93.4	−2.5	1	1	1.3
PETRO	−20.4	−507.6	8.9	18.9	−.4	−.2	−2.7	−.07	−.07	−.04	.38
MAT	−8.8	303.1	−59.4	2.5	−.1	−.26	−.79	1.4	.4	1.1	.04
FOR	−1.3	−81.2	−17.1	11.5	−.2	−.22	−.79	6	−.04	−.02	.07
TROP	−2.7	−301.3	22.6	7.9	2.9	.56	6.8	−1.3	−.11	−.02	.05
ANL	.04	−279.4	−17.3	17.9	−.31	.67	7.4	−.04	−.05	−.03	.03
CER	−4.3	946.3	−97.4	−18.8	2.3	.96	19.1	1.5	.03	−.01	.24
LAB	1	−699.7	78.9	4.8	−.49	−.26	−1.7	−2.1	−.07	−.05	−.04
CAP	16.5	−1,947.9	126.7	39.1	−.77	−.25	−9.4	−2.4	−.08	−.07	−.17
MACH	29.1	−1,177.4	77.7	8.3	−.69	−.3	−11.7	−7.5	−.05	−.08	−.17
CHEM	3.8	481.7	−53.4	−4.4	−.83	−.21	−6.9	−1.6	.03	−.05	−.04

Table 6.6
t-values for the Bayes estimates[a]

	CAPITAL	LABOR 1	LABOR 2	LABOR 3	LAND 1	LAND 2	LAND 3	LAND 4	COAL	MIN	OIL
1958											
GNP	**24.3**	2.7	-1.2	.8	1.0	-.6	3.7	-1.2	10.3	9.9	10.0
PETRO	-2.0	-1.0	.3	1.8	-1.4	-.5	-1.6	-2.1	-2.1	-.2	**4.6**
MAT	-2.0	-5.3	2.6	6.2	1.5	-.4	.1	**10.4**	2.6	8.5	7.4
FOR	1.2	-1.3	.8	1.7	.6	-.9	-1.2	**9.8**	-3.6	-.7	-1.1
TROP	3.0	-4.4	3.0	5.3	**7.0**	1.2	-.6	-2.2	-5.2	-.7	.4
ANL	2.4	-2.4	1.0	2.4	-.8	.9	2.3	1.1	**-3.7**	-.8	-.6
CER	**9.3**	-5.9	-.3	8.7	1.7	2.8	4.9	2.4	-5.6	-.7	1.0
LAB	-.6	1.8	1.1	-4.5	-1.7	-1.5	-1.1	**-8.8**	.8	-1.3	-2.5
CAP	-2.7	3.1	1.2	**-5.6**	-2.1	-1.1	-2.3	-4.7	1.0	-1.2	-2.3
MACH	-2.7	6.1	-3.1	-8.7	-2.9	-1.3	-5.4	**-9.2**	8.3	-1.9	-2.0
CHEM	.9	1.8	-2.8	-1.4	-1.7	-2.0	-1.7	-1.9	**8.2**	-1.7	-1.7
1975											
GNP	**29.9**	17.7	-8.0	-8.3	2.7	1.2	4.4	-.3	10.8	10.1	13.4
PETRO	**-9.9**	-1.2	.2	1.2	-.8	-.8	-.7	-.0	-1.5	-.9	8.6
MAT	**-7.3**	1.0	-2.9	.3	-.2	-1.1	-.3	1.2	3.6	7.0	1.4
FOR	-1.0	-.3	-.8	1.1	-.5	-.9	-.3	**6.2**	-.8	-.4	2.9
TROP	-2.6	-1.4	1.5	1.0	**5.0**	1.1	2.8	-1.9	-2.5	-.4	2.4
ANL	.0	-.9	-.7	1.4	-.7	1.2	**1.7**	-.0	-.9	-.7	1.2
CER	-2.9	3.2	-4.3	-1.7	2.6	1.8	5.2	1.4	.7	-.1	**9.2**
LAB	.6	-2.1	**2.9**	.4	-1.0	-1.1	-.5	-1.7	-1.4	-1.0	-1.4
CAP	**11.1**	-6.5	5.6	3.4	-1.7	-1.0	-3.1	-2.4	-1.7	-1.4	-6.5
MACH	**9.2**	-2.0	1.7	.4	-1.4	-1.2	-2.6	-3.9	-1.0	-1.6	-4.2
CHEM	**3.1**	1.8	-2.8	-.4	-2.0	-.9	-2.7	-1.9	.6	-1.1	-1.9

a. Largest value in row is in boldface.

Table 6.7
Beta values based on Bayes estimates[a]

	CAPITAL	LABOR 1	LABOR 2	LABOR 3	LAND 1	LAND 2	LAND 3	LAND 4	COAL	MIN	OIL
1958											
GNP	**.85**	.13	-.02	0	0	0	.01	0	.01	0	.01
PETRO	-1.51	-.69	.07	.2	-.06	-.01	-.1	-.11	-.21	0	**1.69**
MAT	-1.01	**-2.51**	.44	.45	.04	-.01	0	.44	.2	.72	1.84
FOR	.66	**-.98**	.23	.19	-.03	-.02	-.09	.65	-.32	-.02	-.14
TROP	1.05	**-2.07**	.56	.4	.3	.04	-.03	-.09	-.31	-.01	.03
ANL	1.47	**-2.03**	.36	.35	-.04	.05	.28	.09	-.35	-.02	-.08
CER	**2.84**	-2.41	-.04	.55	.05	.09	.24	.08	-.29	-.01	.08
LAB	-.38	**1.38**	.32	-.51	-.08	-.06	-.08	-.52	.08	-.07	-.59
CAP	-1.24	**1.94**	.31	-.56	-.08	-.02	-.15	-.27	.07	-.03	-.26
MACH	-.53	**1.72**	-.34	-.36	-.04	-.01	-.14	-.21	.22	-.01	-.08
CHEM	.36	**.86**	-.49	-.09	-.05	-.06	-.08	-.06	.58	-.06	-.29
1975											
GNP	.64	**1.2**	-.38	-.26	.03	.01	.04	0	.03	.01	.14
PETRO	-.45	-.22	.02	.08	0	0	-.02	0	-.04	0	**.63**
MAT	-.55	.36	-.53	.03	0	-.01	-.01	.07	.64	**.66**	.18
FOR	-.14	-.17	-.26	.24	-.02	-.02	-.02	**.58**	-.11	-.02	.56
TROP	-.25	**-.56**	.3	.15	.28	.05	.22	-.11	-.27	-.01	.35
ANL	0	**-.6**	-.27	.39	-.03	.07	.27	0	-.14	-.03	.24
CER	-.17	**.74**	-.55	-.15	.09	.03	.26	.05	.03	0	.72
LAB	.08	**-1.13**	.93	.08	-.04	-.02	-.04	-.15	-.14	-.03	-.24
CAP	.78	**-1.8**	.85	.37	-.03	-.01	-.15	-.1	-.09	-.03	-.6
MACH	**.49**	-.39	.18	.02	-.01	0	-.06	-.11	-.02	-.01	-.21
CHEM	.35	**.87**	-.71	-.08	-.07	-.01	-.22	-.13	.07	-.04	-.28

a. Largest value in row is in boldface.

Table 6.8
Bounds for Bayes estimates[a]

	CAPITAL	LABOR 1	LABOR 2	LABOR 3	LAND 1
1958					
GNP	**632/913**	−4,710/20,300	−627/319	−61.2/123	−5.24/11.5
PETRO	−9.71/.439	−407/132	−6.61/9.39	.0597/4.84*	−.305/.0503
MAT	−7.05/.783	**−673/−284**	**2.41/13.7**	**3.74/7.24***	−.0658/.202
FOR	−3.31/8.43	−643/222	−10.1/20.1	−.430/6.17	−.371/.204
TROP	−4.60/14.8	−1,430/14.1	−6.06/44.1	**3.18/14.2**	**.864/1.42**
ANL	−3.93/14.8	−1,190/310	−20.0/34.5	−.815/10.6	−.611/.377
CER	**6.98/30.0***	**−1,760/−99.5**	−33.4/23.8	**7.14/20.0**	−.0353/.566
LAB	−4.53/4.29	−94.0/384	−.969/13.8	**−6.20/−2.01***	−.277/.0229
CAP	−14.3/4.08	−166/1,230	−12.9/36.6	**−15.5/−4.99**	−.720/.208
MACH	−27.1/18.5	−599/2,920	−82.5/45.4	**−30.7/−3.50**	−1.58/.873
CHEM	−4.21/5.79	−18.5/389	**−14.4/3.73***	−3.61/.677	−.252/.0418
1975					
GNP	**370/518**	**22,000/50,700**	**−2,500/−880***	**−1,260/−133***	−20.3/65.5
PETRO	**−24.6/−15.7**	−1,604/521	−46.5/73.5	−20.1/56.6	−2.11/1.51
MAT	**−11.4/−5.88**	−587/1,030	**−88.2/−18.9**	−20.9/26.4	−1.83/1.84
FOR	−4.15/2.24	−956/731	−60.5/31.8	−14.7/39.7	−1.99/1.73
TROP	**−4.58/−.909**	−775/288	−4.59/45.8	−8.82/23.1	**1.84/3.71**
ANL	−3.29/3.92	−1,220/569	−66.3/40.8	−12.1/49.2	−1.95/1.54
CER	−11.6/4.95	−1,320/2,880	−203/30.3	−84.8/55.3	−2.22/6.72
LAB	−1.01/3.24	**−1,190/−144**	**42.9/107**	−12.4/23.5	−1.51/.478
CAP	**10.9/20.5**	**−3,100/−633**	**56.3/197**	−6.48/75.2	−3.40/1.75
MACH	**18.1/38.9**	−3,250/1,420	−117/231	−82.8/95.1	−3.81/2.13
CHEM	**1.39/5.95**	−210/1,030	**−76.8/−9.52***	−26.3/14.1	−2.33/.712

a. Intervals excluding zero are in boldface; * indicates intervals not intersecting the prior one-standard-error interval. GNP is scaled in thousands of dollars; CAPITAL is in millions of dollars.

role of creating comparative advantage in manufactures. LABOR 1 contributed positively only to CHEM, while LABOR 2 and LABOR 3 contributed positively to all but CHEM. This suggests a rather dramatic change in the role of knowledge capital as a source of comparative advantage. In 1958 countries abundant in LABOR 1 were the exporters of manufactured commodities, but in 1975 CAPITAL and LABOR 2 were the resources generally associated with comparative advantage in manufactures. This change in the inferences about the effects of labor and capital may be due partly to the accumulation of capital in the developing countries and partly to the shift of the world's work force from the lower to the higher skilled categories. In 1958 the world percentages in LABOR 1, LABOR 2, and LABOR 3 were 4.3, 57.5, and 38.2, respec-

LAND 2	LAND 3	LAND 4	COAL	MIN	OIL
−15.7/11.9	−12.5/65.4	−11.3/7.02	**.377/1.73**	**.304/1.67**	**.311/1.68**
−.329/.258	−1.50/.00529	−.446/−.113	−.149/.0179	−.189/.215	**.217/.616**
−.360/.313	−.747/.687	**.833/1.12***	**.0255/.100**	**.632/1.01**	**.312/.621**
−.387/.252	−2.05/.153	**1.77/2.09**	**−.267/−.0448**	−.221/.171	−.245/.120
−.590/1.01	−2.06/1.43	**−.813/−.0621**	**−.406/−.0379**	−.341/.296	−.250/.344
−.604/.922	**.527/4.30**	−.255/.642	**−.372/−.0214**	−.289/.213	−.267/.215
−.441/1.44	**1.41/5.45**	**.146/.781**	**−.437/−.00303**	−.423/.374	−.279/.454
−.410/.189	−1.13/.241	**−1.01/−.681**	−.0604/.0853	−.285/.154	−.297/.0612
−.566/.380	−3.48/.151	**−1.38/−.633**	−.133/.216	−.348/.222	−.404/.132
−1.31/1.02	−8.80/1.09	**−3.09/−1.03**	**.00254/.910***	−.809/.575	−.750/.567
−.514/.224	−1.29/.320	−.361/.0646	**.0778/.236***	−.370/.222	−.285/.165
−63.5/78.3	−118/297	−42.5/43.6	−.216/2.43	−.319/2.35	**.240/2.51**
−1.22/.879	−13.2/8.08	−3.56/2.79	−.284/.108	−.250/.160	**.299/.465**
1.68/1.15	−8.42/6.46	−1.77/4.31	**.179/.661**	**.631/1.52**	**.00621/.0850**
−1.60/1.14	−9.14/6.62	**4.50/7.79**	−.274/.181	−.268/.253	**.00688/.134***
−1.46/2.57	**2.98/11.2**	**−2.97/−.0548**	−.314/.0281	.210/.225	**.000941/.0861***
−1.64/3.00	**.0383/15.6**	−2.79/2.14	−.254/.145	−.245/.190	−.0479/.107
−5.18/6.96	**2.29/36.4**	−2.14/5.74	−.485/.563	−.575/.611	**.0406/.396***
−.900/.349	−6.72/3.52	**−3.57/−.666**	−.196/.0284	−.175/.0665	−.0875/.00183
−1.98/1.55	−20.9/2.63	−5.78/.765	−.377/.230	−.409/.266	**−.265/−.0562**
−1.89/1.25	36.6/8.32	−15.2/.201	−.330/.281	−.399/.223	−.377/.0197
−1.40/.996	**−13.0/−.792**	−3.24/.251	−1.26/.260	−.283/.166	−.103/.00566

tively. In 1975 these had changed to 7.0, 60.5, 32.5, indicating increased literacy and an increased proportion of professional/technical workers. This change can also be seen in the boxplots given in figures 4.3 and 4.4.

The other surprising result among these four aggregates of manufactures is the positive effect of COAL in 1958, coupled with its generally negative effect in 1975. For example, each dollar in COAL extracted is estimated to generate $.35 of MACH exports in 1958 but $.05 in MACH imports in 1975. The delivered price of COAL includes a heavy transportation charge; in retrospect, therefore, it is not surprising to see COAL as a source of comparative advantage in manufactures. It is interesting that this effect reverses or diminishes by 1975. This is suggestive of the increased importance of OIL as a source of energy. OIL does not replace COAL as a source of comparative advantage in manufactures, possibly because the transportation component of the delivered price of OIL is much less than COAL.

The two natural resource products, as expected, have their sources of comparative advantage in the natural resources COAL, MINERALS, and OIL. The CAPITAL variable seems clearly to create demand for these natural resource products, since the coefficients are large negative numbers, with large t-values and large beta values. Although the prior estimates of the coefficients on the LAND variables are negative, in retrospect it is unsurprising to obtain positive effects on the net exports of raw materials, since the coverage of the MINERALS variable is incomplete and since land is where raw materials are found. LAND 4, in particular, seems to be a source of mineral wealth. The significant positive effect of several of the labor variables on these two natural resources is a surprise. In the case of LABOR 3 it might be supposed that abundance of the least skilled workers creates comparative disadvantage in manufactures and consequently reduced demand for raw material inputs. The changing role of LABOR as a source of comparative advantage in manufactures seems to be paralleled by a changing role in PETRO and MAT. Namely, those variables that were sources of comparative advantage in manufactures in a given year tend to be sources of disadvantage in these natural resource products in the same year.

The group of crops—FOR, TROP, ANL, CER—is, as expected, positively related to the land variables. FOR is associated with LAND 4, TROP with LAND 1, ANL with LAND 2, 3, or 4, and CER with all the LAND variables. A major surprise is that in 1958 CAPITAL is a source of comparative advantage in these crops. This surprise parallels the conclusion that in 1958 CAPITAL was a source of comparative disadvantage in manufactures. These results "correct" themselves in 1975, though LABOR 1 then becomes a source of comparative advantage. Though the prior for LABOR 2 was positive for these crops, in retrospect it is not surprising to find LABOR 2 creating comparative disadvantage in CEREALS in both years and in FOR and ANL in 1975 through a demand effect. The natural resources, COAL, MIN, and OIL, do generally contribute to comparative disadvantage in these crops, though OIL has a positive effect in 1975.

The beta values in table 6.7 indicate the amount of change in standard deviation units of the net export variable induced by a change of one standard deviation in the resource variable. A beta value of .1 is small, since a change of one standard deviation in the resource would have a hardly perceptible effect on net exports, but a beta value of one can be regarded to be rather large. LABOR 1 most often has the largest beta value. If we (arbitrarily) select .5 to define a significant beta value, then LABOR 1 is significant fifteen (of twenty) times, CAPITAL ten, LABOR 2 six, OIL five, LABOR 3 and LAND 4 three, COAL and MIN two, and LAND 1, LAND 2, and LAND 3 never. Generally speaking, it is knowledge capital embodied in LABOR 1 and physical capital that can be said to explain the composition of trade, though their estimated effects have shifted dramatically from 1958 to 1975.

The foregoing inferences, which in many respects are quite pleasing, can be fragile for a variety of reasons, including gross errors, chronic errors, and improper specification of the prior. Ideally, a sensitivity study involving all of these assumptions would be performed. Technical limitations allow us at this stage only to study the effect of perturbations of the prior distribution. I have already discussed important sensitivities of least-squares estimates to gross and chronic errors, but because the Bayes estimates pool the data information with another source of information, the Bayes estimates will be relatively insensitive to these problems.

The bounds in table 6.8 indicate the sensitivity of the Bayes estimates to choice of prior variance matrix. The prior variance matrix is allowed to be any matrix between one-fourth and four times the matrix we have so far been using. This interval allows the standard error of any linear combination of parameters to be reduced or to be increased by a factor of two. This is a rather wide interval of variance matrices, reflecting great ambiguity in the choice of prior. Each such matrix in this interval implies a Bayes estimate, and from among this set of estimates the most extreme are selected and reported in table 6.8. Not many of the coefficients can be said to be insensitive to the choice of the prior variance matrix, since most can be either positive or negative depending on the variance matrix selected from the hypothesized interval of matrices. Estimates in boldface in table 6.8 are not sensitive to the choice of prior distribution and take on a single sign, independent of the choice of prior variance matrix. The least sensitive coefficients apply to LAND 4, which has 11 of 20 sets of estimates with unique signs. COAL and OIL have 8 insensitive coefficients and CAPITAL and LABOR 3 have 7. LAND 2 has the most sensitive estimates—none of the estimates has a unique sign. LAND 1 and MINERALS have only 2 insensitive coefficients. These sensitivity results weaken, in particular, the finding about the changing role of capital and human capital, since the

1958 results are found to be sensitive to the choice of prior. Nonetheless, in 1975 LABOR 1 clearly contributes to comparative disadvantage in LAB and CAP.

The number of sensitive coefficients is somewhat discouraging but also predictable. It is naively optimistic to expect that a cross section of countries would yield sharp, robust inferences about all questions concerning the sources of comparative advantage because the many potential explanatory variables are highly collinear and because the prior distribution cannot be selected with much precision. As a consequence it is difficult to disentangle one effect from another. Still, there are many forces so strong that even the collinearity in the data set and the ambiguity in the prior distribution cannot disguise their effects. These robust determinants of comparative advantage are identified for each of the commodity aggregates in appendix C. For example, the influence of OIL on PETRO net exports is clearly perceptible, as are the effects of MINERALS on MAT, LAND 4 on FOR, LAND 1 on TROP, LAND 3 on CER, and LABOR 2 on LAB. These are examples of findings that are consistent with the stated prior information, but there are some surprises as well.

When the prior distribution and the posterior distribution are significantly different, the data can be said to force a surprising revision of opinion. For example, it is surprising to find the Bayes estimates in table 6.5 more than one prior standard error away from the prior estimates in tables 5.5 and 5.6. Since the prior standard errors and means are equal, estimates in table 6.5 that are opposite in sign to the prior means in tables 5.5 and 5.6 are surprising in this sense. It is even more surprising if none of the estimates in the intervals in table 6.8 are within a prior standard error of the prior means, since then the surprise is demonstrated not to be sensitive to the choice of prior variance matrix. These robust surprises are indicated by an asterisk in table 6.8.

In retrospect one of the surprises is not surprising at all. Although the prior estimate of the effect of LAND 4 on MAT is negative, the data indicate quite clearly that the coefficient is positive. But it is unsurprising that a land variable contributes positively to the export of raw materials, since natural resources are found on land and since the coverage of the three natural resource variables is incomplete. This is an example of a self-correcting feature of Bayesian inference; mistaken priors are ignored if the data evidence is strong enough.

It is likewise not especially surprising that LABOR 2 contributes negatively to chemical exports because of the extreme skill and capital intensity of chemical production. The 1958 positive effect of LABOR 3 on PETRO and MAT and negative effect on labor intensive manufactures suggests that the illiterate work force at that time was not suited to manufacturing production, and countries with large numbers of the most unskilled workers were forced to depend on raw material and agricultural exports. This is somewhat surprising, and it is of interest to note that the same conclusion does not apply to the 1975 data.

Perhaps the most interesting surprise is the effect of COAL on the last two aggregates of manufactured goods in 1958. If COAL were costlessly transportable, availability of COAL resources would have no effect on the production of any other product. Earnings from the sale of COAL would create demand for all of these products. Consequently, net exports of everything but COAL would be negatively related to COAL resources. The positive effect of COAL on MACH and CHEM can therefore be taken as evidence that COAL is not costlessly transportable or as evidence that the model is badly misspecified.

What remains as a surprise in hindsight as well as foresight is the positive effect of CAPITAL on CEREALS in 1958 and the positive effect of OIL on FOR, TROP, and CER in 1975.

Finally, in this section we may discuss in detail the GNP equations. The reason the GNP equation is of special interest is that the same assumptions that imply our linear trade model also imply the linear GNP equation with coefficients equal to factor returns. If these coefficients turn out to be negative, we have clear evidence of a deficiency in the basic model. Either resources are left out or mismeasured or the model should be nonlinear. In several cases the weighted regression estimates in table 6.1 have negative coefficients. LABOR 3 and LAND 2 in 1975 even have t-values less than -2. Table 6.2 reveals that these results are not due to a gross error in a single observation, since many of the negative estimates remain even if individual observations are omitted. The Bayes results in table 6.5 do indicate that some of the negative least-squares estimates are due to collinearity in the data, but six coefficients remain negative even after the dose of prior information. Most distressing of all, the posterior t-value for LABOR 2 in 1975 is -8.0 and for LABOR 3 is -8.3. LABOR 2 and LAND 4 in 1958 also have significantly negative coefficients, with t-values of -1.2. The Bayes bounds in table 6.8 allow most of the coefficients to be positive. What this means is there is a prior distribution close to the one under consideration that implies positive marginal products. But neither LABOR 2 nor LABOR 3 in 1975 can have positive coefficients regardless of the prior in this interval of priors. Another disturbing feature is the very large estimate in 1975 of the marginal product of LABOR 1. Nonlinearities may well be the explanation for these peculiar results.

6.5 Nonlinearities

Concerns about nonlinearities have been stimulated by the wage rate data in table 1.1, by figures C.8a and C.9a, and by the negative coefficients of the GNP equations. The maintained hypothesis of the previous section is that trade and GNP are linear functions of the measured endowments. Factor returns that are the derivatives of GNP with respect to the endowments are thereby assumed constant across countries. But the wage data in table 1.1 hardly seem compatible with this assumption, and some study of nonlinearities of the GNP equation may be required. Models that imply nonlinear GNP equations will also imply nonlinear trade equations.

The general hypothesis of nonlinearity is much too broad to admit a sensible statistical analysis, and some attempt has to be made to select some better defined specific nonlinearities to explore. The first form of nonlinearity considered here is motivated by the model with more goods than factors illustrated in figures 1.7, 1.8, and 1.9, which summarize consequences of a model with 3 goods and 2 factors. The wage rate is a monotone nondecreasing function of capital per worker (figure 1.8), and GNP per worker is correspondingly a concave function of capital abundance (figure 1.7). The "middle" commodity is exported at moderate levels of capital abundance, but imported at both high and low levels of capital abundance. First look at figure 1.9, where this relation between net exports and capital per man is illustrated, and then look at figure C.8a. Setting aside a couple of exceptional countries, figure C.8a conforms remarkably well to the predictions offered by figure 1.9. (Much the same picture emerges for the labor intensive manufactures in 1958.)

The exact form of the nonlinearities suggested by figure 1.9 is exceedingly difficult to work with because the "join points" of the pieces of the function are unknown and because things get much more complex if there are more than 3 commodities and more than 2 goods. As an approximation to the simplest case, I allow GNP to depend on $(\text{CAPITAL})^2/(\text{LABOR } 1 + \text{LABOR } 2 + \text{LABOR } 3)$ in addition to the

11 resources entering linearly. This allows the function to have the kind of curvature depicted in figure 1.9. Scatter plots of GNP per worker versus capital per worker in figure C.11 also suggest some curvature of this form, especially in 1958. The same sort of logic leads one to include K^2/L and K^3/L^2 in the trade equation ($K = $ CAPITAL, $L = $ LABOR 1 + LABOR 2 + LABOR 3). This makes net exports per worker a cubic function of capital per man and allows the kind of curvature suggested by figures 1.9 and C.8a.

There is now an extra parameter in the equation, and the prior distribution has to be extended to encompass it. This is done by distinguishing the marginal products of LABOR in a capital abundant country (the United States) and a capital scarce country (Korea). A part of the nonlinear GNP equation is

$$\text{GNP} = \beta_1 \text{ CAPITAL} + \beta_2 \text{ LABOR 1} + \beta_3 \text{ LABOR 2} + \beta_4 \text{ LABOR 3}$$

$$+ \beta_5 \text{ CAPITAL}^2/(\text{LABOR 1} + \text{LABOR 2} + \text{LABOR 3}).$$

The marginal products of CAPITAL and of the three forms of labor are

$$\partial\,\text{GNP}/\partial\,\text{CAPITAL} = \beta_1 + 2\beta_5 k,$$

$$\partial\,\text{GNP}/\partial\,\text{LABOR 1} = \beta_2 - \beta_5 k^2,$$

$$\partial\,\text{GNP}/\partial\,\text{LABOR 2} = \beta_3 - \beta_5 k^2,$$

$$\partial\,\text{GNP}/\partial\,\text{LABOR 3} = \beta_4 - \beta_5 k^2,$$

where $k = $ CAPITAL/(LABOR 1 + LABOR 2 + LABOR 3). These marginal products of CAPITAL and each of the LABOR variables depend on the capital per man. In selecting a prior for this nonlinear equation I act as if the previously selected prior in table 5.4 referred to U.S. marginal products, that is, to these linear combinations of coefficients evaluated at the U.S. value of k. The other element of prior information I use is the marginal product of LABOR 2 in a capital scarce country— Korea selected as the representative. Korean agricultural wage rates were about 1/40 of U.S. wage rates in 1950 and about 1/6.4 in 1975. The prior mean and standard error for the Korean marginal product of LABOR 2 is set equal to the corresponding fraction of the U.S. marginal product. [This may be objected to if the agricultural wage rate is thought of as referring in the United States to skilled workers (LABOR 2) and in Korea to unskilled workers (LABOR 3).] Incidentally, the prior mean for the $(CAPITAL)^2/LABOR$ coefficient implied by these mean values of the marginal products is negative, implying that all the wage rates are increasing functions of k and that the marginal return on capital is a decreasing function of k.

Tables 6.9a and 6.9b contain estimates and bounds implied by the nonlinear GNP equations. The factor σ_1 multiplies the prior standard error. Thus the column headed $\sigma_1 = 0$ contains the prior estimates, the column $\sigma_1 = \infty$ contains the least-squares estimates, and the column headed $\sigma_1 = 1$ contains the Bayes estimates based on the prior just discussed. The other value of σ_1 was selected to yield as many positive coefficients as possible. Note that information is provided about the marginal products in the United States and Korea instead of the coefficients individually. These tables can be compared with tables 6.1–6.8, which contain the linear GNP estimates. It can be seen that this form of nonlinearity does not cause large changes to the inferences about the capital, land, or natural resource coefficients, but it does cause substantial changes in the labor productivities.

In 1958 the least-squares estimate of the nonlinear coefficient is negative (with a t-value of -1.06), and the data in that sense conform to the prior belief that labor productivity increases with capital abundance. This effect is so great that labor in countries as capital scarce as Korea is actually estimated to have a negative marginal product. The Bayes estimate, however, indicates a small positive marginal product of labor in Korea in 1958. It is surprising that the least-squares estimate of LABOR 3's productivity exceeds the estimate of LABOR 2's productivity. Though the order is reversed with the Bayes estimates, these two labor categories are estimated to have essentially the same wage in the United States, with LABOR 1 almost 20 times as productive. The Bayes bounds for the nonlinear equations are often wider than the bounds for the linear equation because the family of priors is enlarged to include an extra parameter. It is possible to find a prior close to the one specified that implies a positive marginal product for any of the inputs. An example in which they are all positive is given in the table with $\sigma_1 = .5$. Here the estimates are little different from the prior except that LABOR 2 is sharply lower.

The least-squares estimates with the 1975 data in table 6.9b are quite different because the nonlinear term has a positive coefficient. Korean labor productivity is accordingly higher than that of the United States,

Table 6.9a
Estimates and bounds, nonlinear GNP equation; 1958[a]

	$\sigma_1 = 0$	$\sigma_1 = .5$	$\sigma_1 = 1$	$\sigma_1 = \infty$	Lower bound	Upper bound
CAPITAL (US)	500	783	768	584	710	843
LABOR 1 (US)	7,100	5,550	4,280	1,390	145	9,070
LABOR 2 (US)	1,700	229	203	1,460	−239	674
LABOR 2 (KOR)	42.5	40.6	36	−172	−87	152
LABOR 3 (US)	170	182	186	1,690	−278	678
LAND 1	3.3	3.1	3.0	4.5	−3.9	10.2
LAND 2	1.7	.7	−1.4	−4.2	−13.4	10.0
LAND 3	33.3	30.9	26.5	18.9	−7.3	58.9
LAND 4	16.7	3.4	−4.3	1.3	−10.0	5.5
COAL	1.0	1.0	1.0	4.9	.48	1.6
MINERALS	1.0	1.0	1.0	−10.7	.40	1.6
OIL	1.0	1.0	1.0	3.6	.42	1.6
R^2	.8031	.9971	.9975	.9983		

a. This is a nonlinear equation with $CAPITAL^2/(LABOR\ 1 + LABOR\ 2 + LABOR\ 3)$ as a variable with a t-value of -1.1. The factor σ_1^2 multiplies the prior variance-covariance matrix. The lower and upper bounds allow the prior to be twice as diffuse or twice as dogmatic.

Table 6.9b
Estimates and bounds, nonlinear GNP equation: 1975[a]

	$\sigma_1 = 0$	$\sigma_1 = .25$	$\sigma_1 = 1$	$\sigma_1 = \infty$	Lower bound	Upper bound
CAPITAL (US)	500	459	432	476	341	542
LABOR 1 (US)	13,000	13,400	37,600	15,100	15,800	50,500
LABOR 2 (US)	5,200	267	−1,150	−561	−2,410	520
LABOR 2 (KOR)	810	142	−1,110	−506	−2,540	687
LABOR 3 (US)	520	−80	−1,010	−493	−1,750	41
LAND 1	10	95	18	32	−33	68
LAND 2	5	8.1	12	−89	−75	93
LAND 3	100	102	97	120	−153	338
LAND 4	50	39	−1.2	−55	−49	54
COAL	1.0	1.0	1.1	3.3	−.5	2.7
MINERALS	1.0	1.0	1.0	6.5	−.6	2.6
OIL	1.0	1.0	1.3	2.8	.1	2.7
R^2	−13.1	.9893	.9971	.9989		

a. This is a nonlinear equation with $CAPITAL^2/(LABOR\ 1 + LABOR\ 2 + LABOR\ 3)$ as a variable with a t-value of 1.42. The factor σ_1^2 multiplies the prior variance-covariance matrix. The lower and upper bounds allow the prior to be twice as diffuse or twice as dogmatic.

Table 6.10
Weighted nonlinear net export regressions: selected coefficients

	K	K^2/L	K^3/L^2	Stable points	$wt(\theta)$	R^2
1958						
PETRO	$-11.71(1.2)$	$5.33(1.6)$	$-.69(2.1)$	$1.6*,3.6**$	$-.12(.6)$	.91
MAT	$-13.52(3.1)$	$.47(.3)$	$.13(.7)$	$-7.2,4.8**$	$.65(2.8)$	.94
FOR	$-8.28(.6)$	$5.46(1.0)$	$-.55(1.0)$	$.9*,5.7**$	$.44(2.7)$	.68
TROP	$7.79(.5)$	$-6.18(1.1)$	$.59(1.0)$	$.7**,6.3*$	$-.03(.1)$	.93
ANL	$-14.21(.6)$	$6.53(.9)$	$-.66(.8)$	$1.4*,5.2**$	$.15(.6)$	.57
CER	$-38.78(2.8)$	$11.73(2.4)$	$-.91(1.8)$	$2.2*,6.4**$	$.35(1.6)$	.89
LAB	$6.11(.8)$	$-1.70(.7)$	$.15(.6)$	$2.9**,4.6*$	$.05(.3)$	.86
CAP	$17.45(1.0)$	$-6.45(1.1)$	$.66(1.1)$	$1.9**,4.6*$	$.22(1.1)$	.79
MACH	$4.42(.2)$	$-.05(.01)$	$-.080(.1)$	$-4.5,4.1**$	$-.07(.3)$	.98
CHEM	$-7.03(1.4)$	$4.12(2.4)$	$-.43(2.4)$	$1.0*,5.4**$	$.12(.6)$	.95
1975						
PETRO	$-20.97(1.5)$	$-.74(.6)$	$.04(1.2)$	$-8.4,20.8*$	$.37(2.8)$	.94
MAT	$-15.07(2.9)$	$.09(.2)$	$.01(.8)$	$-25.6,19.6*$	$.83(4.8)$	.85
FOR	$-8.44(1.1)$	$.17(.2)$	$.007(.3)$	$-29.7,13.5*$	$.62(4.2)$	.51
TROP	$-2.94(.5)$	$.19(.3)$	$-.009(.6)$	$-,-$	$.34(2.2)$	.76
ANL	$-27.35(2.3)$	$2.29(2.0)$	$-.05(1.6)$	$8.1,22.4**$	$.14(1.1)$	.40
CER	$-28.98(3.1)$	$2.00(2.2)$	$-.04(1.7)$	$10.6*,22.7**$	$.24(1.9)$	.91
LAB	$22.90(2.0)$	$-1.25(1.1)$	$.011(.4)$	$21.3**,65.1$	$.91(4.5)$	.29
CAP	$2.52(.3)$	$1.86(2.1)$	$-.058(2.4)$	$-.7,22.0**$	$.65(4.0)$	.74
MACH	$-13.32(.5)$	$4.12(1.7)$	$-.099(1.6)$	$1.7*,26.0**$	$.50(3.7)$	.81
CHEM	$-11.38(1.8)$	$1.20(2.0)$	$-.022(1.4)$	$5.6*,30.8**$	$.70(4.5)$	.59

a. t-statistics are in parentheses. *indicates local minimum; **, a local maximum.

though both are negative. In order to obtain a more sensible result it is necessary to sharpen the prior to $\sigma_1 = .25$, which implies results not much different from the prior, though with an R^2 not much less than least squares. The major adjustment to the prior is to lower substantially the estimated productivities of LABOR 2 and LABOR 3. The 1958 data likewise suggest a greatly reduced estimate of the productivity of LABOR 2.

One of the unresolved anomalies was that the Bayes bounds for LABOR 2 and LABOR 3 productivities implied by a linear model were strictly negative. A consideration of nonlinearities in table 6.9b allows positive estimates of all productivities. This, together with the t-value of the nonlinear term in 1958, is taken as some evidence of nonlinearities in GNP.

Estimates of selected coefficients from the nonlinear trade regression are reported in table 6.10. If net exports per man were to take the shape illustrated in figure 1.8 and suggested by the scatter in figure C.8a, then the signs of the coefficients of K, K^2/L, and K^3/L^2 would be $-$, $+$, and $-$, respectively. In that case the derivative of net exports per man would be negative for small values of K/L, positive for moderate values, and negative again for large values. Such a function has a local minimum at a small value of K/L and a local maximum at a large value. The local minima and maxima of the estimated cubic relation between net exports per man and K/L are indicated in table 6.10 under the heading "Stable points." One function, TROP in 1975, is a strictly decreasing function of K/L and has no stable points. Several functions have stable points outside the observed range of K/L, ($0 \leqslant K/L \leqslant 7.5$ in 1958, and $0 \leqslant K/L \leqslant 36$ in 1975), and therefore have only a single relevant stable point. (In table 6.10, the relevant minima are indicated by an asterisk, and the relevant maxima by a double asterisk.)

Nine of the estimated functions have the shape suggested by figure 1.8; but LAB and CAP do not. In 1975 LAB and CAP do have the feature that they decrease for high values of K/L, but they are estimated in 1958 to increase for high values. The commodities that do have this shape— with net exports increasing with K/L for moderate values of K/L and decreasing for large—are a surprise: PETRO, FOR, ANL, CER, MACH and CHEM. These happen also to be the commodities with the largest t-values for the nonlinear terms.

The nonlinearities thus far considered have their theoretical support in models with constant returns to scale but unequal numbers of factors and goods. Another possible source of serious nonlinearities is increasing returns to scale. The review of the data in chapter 4 hints at scale economies in chemicals and machinery, since what seems to distinguish exporters from importers is country size as measured by either capital or labor. For example, the machinery exporters, illustrated in figure C.9a (France, Germany, Italy, Japan, Sweden, Switzerland, the United Kingdom and the United States), are not distinguished from the importers in terms of capital abundance. Country size is a possible explanation. Proper theoretical modeling of the scale economy effect is a prerequisite for a sensible data analysis. But models with scale economies are sufficiently unwieldy that they do not yield a clear-cut equation describing the determinants of trade. What I will do, with considerable discomfort, is merely to add the square of capital as an explanatory variable. These

Table 6.11
t-statistics for nonlinear terms of weighted regressions[a]

	K	K^2/L	K^3/L^2	K^2	$wt(\theta)$	R^2
1958						
PETRO	-1.6	2.0	-2.2	1.7	.27	.88
MAT	-1.5	-1.9	2.9	-2.8	.84	.94
FOR	-1.8	2.3	-2.4	2.2	.16	.79
TROP	.4	$-.8$	.4	.03	$-.04$	.93
ANL	$-.5$	.4	$-.05$	$-.3$	.13	.58
CER	-3.0	3.4	-3.0	2.4	$-.13$	.97
LAB	.4	.1	$-.6$	1.0	.11	.85
CAP	1.0	-1.0	.8	$-.5$	.08	.83
MACH	$-.9$	1.3	-1.5	1.6	.25	.96
CHEM	-1.5	2.1	-1.5	.7	.23	.93
1975						
PETRO	-5.2	3.4	-2.6	-8.8	.76	.97
MAT	-2.7	$-.02$	.9	.4	.80	.86
FOR	$-.4$	$-.8$	1.3	2.2	.23	.67
TROP	.04	$-.6$	.4	1.8	.41	.74
ANL	-2.6	1.7	-1.3	2.2	$-.18$	.58
CER	-3.2	$-.2$	1.1	7.5	.16	.97
LAB	1.9	$-.9$	.2	$-.2$	.87	.30
CAP	.4	1.9	-2.3	$-.8$	.49	.81
MACH	$-.6$	1.7	-1.6	$-.8$	.45	.83
CHEM	-2.1	2.3	-1.8	-1.1	.72	.59

a. CAPITAL^2 term included.

results are summarized in table 6.11. The scale economy variable does not have a statistically significant positive effect on MACH in 1958, but the t-value is small for CHEM in 1958 and negative for MACH and CHEM in1975. The t-values are, somewhat mysteriously, highest for PETRO and CER.

This brief examination of the ill-defined nonlinear alternatives to the linear maintained hypothesis has uncovered some evidence of non-linearities in the GNP equation, but the anticipated nonlinearities of the trade equation generally failed to emerge. It is possible that a repeat of the sensitivity analyses and the Bayesian analysis could resolve the peculiarities with these nonlinear equations, but because these nonlinear equations have a very unclear foundation in economic theory, none of these results would or should be taken very seriously.

6.6 Conclusions

What emerges from this data analysis is a surprisingly good explanation
of the main features of the trade data in terms of a relatively brief list of
resource endowments. There are apparent problems with measuring some
of the resources, and there is some evidence of nonlinearities, but overall
the simple linear model does an excellent job. It explains a large amount
of the variability of net exports across countries, and it also identifies
sources of comparative advantage that we all "know" are there, thereby
increasing the credibility of the results in cases when we do not "know"
the sources of comparative advantage. Perhaps the most interesting
finding is the altered role from 1958 to 1975 of knowledge capital as a
source of comparative advantage in manufactured products: In 1958
the most highly skilled laborers (LABOR 1) contributed to comparative
advantage in all four manufactured aggregates, but in 1975 these workers
contributed positively to only the most skill intensive manufactured
aggregate (CHEM). CAPITAL, on the other hand, goes through an
exactly opposite transformation: in 1958 contributing to comparative
advantage in only CHEM, but in 1975 contributing positively to all
four of the manufactured products. The other LABOR categories have
undergone a shift that parallels this switch in the roles of physical and
knowledge capital. In 1958 LABOR 2 contributed to comparative advantage in the first two manufactured products, CAP and LAB, and
LABOR 3 contributed to none of the four. But in 1975 LABOR 2 and
LABOR 3 were sources of comparative advantage in all but CHEM. In
summary, in 1958 success in exporting manufactured products was linked
to abundance of knowledge capital embodied in the professional/technical
work force. In 1975, however, knowledge capital continued to be the
most important source of comparative advantage in chemicals, but physical capital and skilled and unskilled labor were the sources of comparative
advantage in machinery and labor intensive and capital intensive manufactures.

    Another interesting finding is that COAL in 1958 was a source of
comparative advantage in manufactured products, but that by 1975
this effect had reversed itself. Otherwise, the results are pretty much what
would be expected: Unskilled labor and land are sources of comparative
advantage in the agricultural products, and natural resources are sources
of comparative advantage in the natural resource products.

7 Counterfactuals

Econometric models can be used to answer counterfactual questions or to form predictions of the effects of policy actions. In this chapter the econometric model of net exports that has been reported in the previous chapter is used to estimate the effect of a rearrangement of the world's resources on trade flows and to predict the influence of price changes on the returns to factors.

The resources that have the greatest effect on world trade are identified in section 7.1. Based on the estimated model, the change in each resource endowment is computed that would reduce trade dependence as much as possible, holding fixed the levels of the other resources. Then by comparing the predicted reduction in trade dependence corresponding to each resource, the resources are identified that are the most important determinants of trade. Intellectual amusement is the primary reason for identifying the most important resources, since in the linear model with factor price equalization, there are no efficiency consequences of an uneven distribution of the world's resources. If the model is nonlinear, however, commodity trade is not a complete substitute for factor mobility, and the resources that are most influential in determining trade can also be expected to be the resources that have the greatest economic reward for international migration. Without formal justification, we might imagine that the identification of the most important resources for the nonlinear model would be similar to the identification for the linear model. The principal findings reported in section 7.1 are that in 1958 LABOR 1 was the most influential resource overall, followed closely by LABOR 3, LABOR 2, and LAND 4. In 1975 CAPITAL was by far the most influential, with OIL in second place, trailed considerably by LAND 4. The finding that the uneven distribution of the most highly skilled workers was the primary cause of trade in 1958 conforms with the conclusion reached in the previous chapter about the relative importance of LABOR 1. The finding about the importance of CAPITAL in 1975 seems initially surprising, since this was a period of increased international capital mobility. But much of the net trade that occurs in 1975 appears to be CAPITAL abundant countries paying the bill for petroleum imports with large amounts of manufactured exports. A leveling of the CAPITAL/OIL ratio around the world could be expected to have a dramatic effect on reducing trade.

Estimates of the elasticities of factor returns to changes in product prices are reported in section 7.2. These estimates are based theoretically on the duality between the Stolper-Samuelson effects and the Rybczynski effects. The Rybczynski effects are computed by purging consumption effects from the estimated derivatives of net exports with respect to factor endowments. This amusingly subtle way of estimating the income distributional consequences of tariffs turns out to be rather suspicious for a variety of reasons outlined subsequently.

7.1 Most Important Resources

In the model with constant returns to scale, trade of commodities compensates for an uneven geographical distribution of the world's productive resources. It is an intellectually interesting problem to determine which resource is most unevenly distributed in the sense of being the primary cause of trade. This can be studied in a limited way using the estimated model described in the previous chapter. This model is based on the assumption that commodity prices are fixed, and we are consequently restricted to counterfactual questions that could sensibly be assumed to leave commodity prices undisturbed. The even model (with factor price equalization) does have the feature that small reallocations of the world's productive resources would leave product prices unchanged. We may therefore legitimately use it to ask this counterfactual: By how much would trade diminish if a particular resource were reallocated?

Let us write the counterfactual net export vector of some country as a function of some hypothetical change in the country's endowment of a particular factor, ΔV_i:

$$T^* = T + \beta(\Delta V_i),$$

where T is the actual trade vector and β is the vector of coefficients that indicate how resource i affects the net export vector. A measure of the amount of trade is the squared length of the trade vector

$$T^{*\prime}T^* = (T + \beta(\Delta V_i))'(T + \beta(\Delta V_i))$$
$$= T'T + 2T'\beta(\Delta V_i) + \beta'\beta(\Delta V_i)^2.$$

The vector of coefficients β is unknown, though estimates of it have been discussed in the previous chapter. To allow for this uncertainty we can find the ΔV_i that minimizes the expected amount of trade:

$$T'T + 2E(T'\beta)\Delta V_i + E(\beta'\beta)(\Delta V_i)^2.$$

This value for ΔV_i is

$$\Delta V_i = -T'E(\beta)/E(\beta'\beta), \tag{7.1}$$

and the square root of the corresponding percentage reduction in expected trade is

$$r = (T'T - T^{*\prime}T^{*})^{1/2}/(T'T)^{1/2} = |T'E(\beta)|/(T'T)^{1/2}(E(\beta'\beta))^{1/2}. \tag{7.2}$$

Expression (7.1) for ΔV_i can be less than $-V_i$, where V_i is the original resource supply, and the country can be left with negative amounts of the resource. If this occurs, we restrict ΔV_i to $-V_i$, and the reduction in expected trade becomes

$$r = (2T'E(\beta)V_i - E(\beta'\beta)V_i^2)^{1/2}/(T'T)^{1/2}. \tag{7.3}$$

Values for $E(\beta)$ and $E(\beta'\beta)$ that are required to compute these numbers are taken from the Bayes estimates $\hat{\beta}_j$ and Bayes standard errors $\hat{\sigma}_j$ reported in the previous chapter. The mean $E(\beta_j)$ is the Bayes estimate $\hat{\beta}_j$, and the expected sum of squares of the coefficients is $E(\beta'\beta) = \sum_j(\hat{\beta}_j^2 + \hat{\sigma}_j^2)$.

It should be noted that this formulation will yield a ranking of resources that depends not only on the estimated coefficients but also on the uncertainty in the estimates because $E(\beta'\beta)$ depends on the estimated variances. If the coefficients attaching to a particular resource are very uncertain, then $E(\beta'\beta)$ will be large, ΔV_i will be small, and the reduction in expected trade is correspondingly small. In that sense, the reported numbers are similar to F-statistics for testing the joint significance across equations of a particular variable.

Notice also that the change in a resource (7.1) takes the opposite sign of $T'E(\beta)$. This means, for example, that a country with positive net exports of commodities that have positive capital coefficients and negative net exports of the commodities with negative capital coefficients would have a reduction in capital to reduce trade dependence. In that sense, the country is revealed to be abundant in capital.

This notion of factor abundance need not conform to the physical definition that a country is abundant in a factor if its endowment share exceeds it consumption share. The model we have used as a basis for this empirical work is summarized by the vector of equations $T = A^{-1}(V - sV_{\rm w})$, where A is the matrix of input intensities, V is the endowment vector, $V_{\rm w}$ is the world's endowment, and s is the consumption share. If trade is balanced, the consumption share is the GNP ratio $s = p'A^{-1}V/p'A^{-1}V_w$, where p is the vector of product prices. In the cross-section empirical work, with prices p and world endowments V_w fixed across countries, we imagine that we are estimating $\partial T/\partial V = A^{-1} - V_w p'A^{-1}/p'A^{-1}V_w \equiv B$. The inner product of this matrix with the vector T is used in formula (7.1) to define the revealed factor abundance vector:

$$(\partial T/\partial V)'T = B'T = B'A^{-1}(V - sV_w).$$

This vector will not necessarily have the same sign as the excess factor supply vector $V - sV_w$, since the transformation $B'A^{-1}$ need not preserve the signs of $V - sV_w$. What this means is that it is possible to find a factor that is abundant in the physical sense, yet in order to reduce trade the country would have to be provided even more of the factor. There is mathematical and conceptual similarity between this observation and Leamer and Bowen's (1981) comment that cross-section regressions of net exports on factor intensities need not reveal the sign of the factor abundance vector $V - sV_w$.

Tables 7.1 and 7.3 contain the expected percentage reduction of the square root of the sum of squares of the net export vectors induced by an optimally selected reallocation of resources. The corresponding reallocations of resources are reported in tables 7.2 and 7.4, where 99.9 indicates that the original level of the resource was zero so that the percentage change is $+\infty$.

Consider, for example, the U.S. numbers in tables 7.3 and 7.4. The CAPITAL columns of table 7.3 and 7.4 indicate that a reduction of the capital stock by 36% in the United States in 1975 would have been expected to reduce the size of the net export vector by 68%. No other resource offers a reduction as large. In that sense, U.S. trade in 1975 can be thought to have been primarily a consequence of CAPITAL abundance. Other important variables are OIL (scarce), LAND 4 (scarce), and LABOR 3 (scarce), where the words "scarce" and "abundant" refer to the signs of the resource changes in table 7.4. The 1958 results are rather different. LABOR 2 (scarce) was the most important variable, followed closely by LABOR 1 (abundant), LAND 4 (scarce), LABOR 3 (scarce), and COAL (abundant).

These conclusions compare interestingly with the findings of the rest of the empirical literature, as summarized by Deardorff (1982b): "It is

Table 7.1
Percentage trade reduction: 1958[a]

Country	CAPITAL	LABOR 1	LABOR 2	LABOR 3	LAND 1	LAND 2	LAND 3	LAND 4	COAL	MINERALS	OIL
AFG	52	75	41	**75**	0	63	0	0	75	8	9
ARG	67	66	23	20	0	31	**90**	0	61	12	13
AUSL	77	82	29	5	29	65	**90**	0	70	12	0
AUST	19	9	28	14	28	32	6	19	22	34	**38**
BLUX	42	42	14	**50**	31	35	28	33	20	25	40
BRAZ	39	62	67	50	**88**	8	29	0	62	5	3
BRMA	41	52	10	**58**	31	0	0	0	39	0	8
CAN	44	68	25	5	0	7	19	**97**	52	39	24
CHLE	4	48	38	19	13	1	0	0	13	**86**	18
CLUM	23	49	54	31	**71**	5	0	0	53	0	19
CSTA	23	54	38	15	37	0	0	0	54	1	0
CYPR	5	47	31	20	0	0	23	0	16	**61**	0
DEN	20	18	13	2	5	0	17	0	**25**	15	21
DORE	31	**58**	42	29	31	0	0	0	55	1	0
ECUA	25	51	51	32	**57**	0	0	0	52	1	6
EGPT	26	63	19	**63**	0	49	0	0	58	0	4
LSAL	25	60	40	38	24	0	0	0	**61**	1	0
FIN	11	16	14	2	8	13	0	**46**	30	7	14
FRA	53	77	35	**82**	68	51	46	50	43	36	59
GER	60	**92**	70	91	54	49	78	72	70	20	32
GANA	22	53	37	49	**53**	0	0	0	48	14	0
GRCE	52	**75**	46	40	0	0	65	0	65	11	0
HOND	30	**64**	44	45	52	0	0	0	62	5	0
HOKO	34	12	15	16	10	**39**	8	2	0	2	9
ICE	31	52	16	2	0	0	**67**	0	49	0	4
INDA	3	36	**75**	28	41	0	19	0	44	8	6
INDO	15	38	33	39	**68**	0	5	2	32	8	37
IRE	23	41	32	4	0	0	44	0	**46**	6	12
ISRL	2	33	**36**	13	0	7	12	0	29	4	10

JAMC	11	56	41	17	13	0	0	0	31	**65**	0
JAP	63	67	4	**76**	42	56	54	46	34	29	53
KORA	**63**	43	14	43	22	54	32	12	33	6	20
LIBR	11	**64**	16	47	57	0	0	0	41	60	0
LIBY	16	**63**	18	37	0	20	0	0	56	0	0
MALY	7	**48**	33	25	24	0	0	0	38	29	0
MLTA	15	12	3	10	3	**17**	6	0	0	0	0
MAUR	12	**42**	5	32	10	0	0	0	41	1	0
MEX	35	74	74	50	32	26	0	0	72	29	27
NETH	5	9	**26**	2	0	5	12	0	15	18	25
NUZE	49	**68**	18	3	0	0	67	0	64	1	0
NIGR	45	83	31	**88**	61	0	0	0	70	5	10
NOR	34	**64**	32	3	0	0	40	42	57	11	0
PANM	31	**62**	47	32	58	0	0	0	54	2	0
PGRY	48	55	31	49	16	0	52	0	**56**	9	14
PERU	39	**82**	58	55	54	25	0	0	59	63	39
PLIP	64	**81**	47	63	46	0	0	0	72	15	0
PORT	7	42	**60**	36	0	6	33	0	52	2	13
SRIL	16	39	**46**	26	23	0	1	0	39	0	0
SING	8	7	19	6	2	15	0	0	0	0	**30**
SPAN	6	31	**57**	25	0	3	11	0	36	3	23
SWE	4	1	2	1	20	5	3	**43**	9	6	22
SWIT	53	**84**	75	81	52	48	66	54	0	20	38
THAI	25	**84**	41	78	56	0	0	0	73	12	0
TURK	79	88	51	**90**	0	47	80	0	75	21	8
UK	68	92	64	**95**	56	56	76	70	62	17	37
US	7	9	**74**	56	46	5	35	58	54	17	27
YUG	33	68	63	48	0	0	34	58	**70**	10	8
WORLD	20	**54**	42	50	23	13	30	40	32	4	10

a. Largest value for each country is in boldface.

Table 7.2
Percentage resource change: 1958

Country	CAPITAL	LABOR 1	LABOR 2	LABOR 3	LAND 1	LAND 2	LAND 3	LAND 4	COAL	MINERALS	OIL
AFG	-100	8	-100	-13	0	-49	0	0	6,928	120	∞
ARG	-100	53	-60	-100	0	-100	-74	0	68,666	476	194
AUSL	-100	115	-100	-100	-100	-100	-100	0	398	-58	0
AUST	42	-6	-65	3,817	∞	100	∞	-100	205	699	428
BLUX	160	-43	-90	16,843	∞	100	1,220	∞	-100	1,811	67,400
BRAZ	-100	47	-100	-100	-84	-100	-100	0	9,196	-64	115
BRMA	-100	15	5	-76	-51	0	0	0	∞	0	-100
CAN	-93	111	-100	-100	0	-100	-100	-96	2,213	-100	-100
CHLE	-21	54	-100	-100	-99	-16	0	0	426	-100	-100
CLUM	-100	60	-100	-100	-100	-100	0	0	1,536	-25	-100
CSTA	-100	162	-100	-100	-100	0	0	0	∞	-100	0
CYPR	-24	66	-100	-100	0	0	-100	0	∞	-100	0
DEN	-100	40	-100	-100	∞	0	-100	0	1,363	33,781	∞
DORE	-100	131	-100	-100	-100	0	0	0	∞	-100	0
ECUA	-100	75	-100	-100	-100	0	0	0	∞	615	-100
EGPT	-100	40	-80	-100	0	-100	0	0	∞	-24	-26
LASL	-100	132	-100	-100	-100	0	0	0	∞	196	0
FIN	-57	28	-100	-100	∞	∞	0	-100	42,312	165	∞
FRA	58	-37	74	13,351	∞	∞	227	∞	-100	280	6,488
GER	150	-88	251	38,163	∞	∞	2,716	10,017	-100	549	2,555
GANA	-100	84	-100	-100	-100	0	0	0	∞	-93	0
GRCE	-100	67	-77	-100	0	0	-100	0	2,226	-100	0
HOND	-100	81	-100	-100	-100	0	0	0	∞	-100	0
HOKO	508	-29	-100	419	∞	∞	3.500	∞	0	-100	∞
ICE	-100	196	-100	-100	0	0	-100	0	100	0	∞
INDA	5	4	-28	-5	-100	-2	-30	0	132	-41	999
INDO	-67	11	-32	-32	-100	0	100	∞	4,742	-54	-84
IRE	-100	53	-100	-100	0	0	-100	0	765	4,422	∞
ISRL	4	25	-100	-100	0	1,117	-100	0	∞	-100	1,656

ITLY	66	−29	23	1,008	∞	∞	428	4,436	−100	529	1,889
JAMC	−68	95	−100	−100	−100	0	0	0	∞	−96	0
JAP	101	−26	4	?,956	∞	∞	587	1,567	−100	401	17,287
KORA	98	−10	6	65	∞	∞	149	65	−100	−100	∞
LIBR	−100	155	−100	−100	−100	0	0	0	∞	−100	0
LIBY	−100	187	−100	−100	0	−13	0	0	∞	0	0
MALY	−100	119	−100	−100	−100	0	0	0	555,560	−100	0
MLTA	104	12	−19	−100	∞	∞	−100	0	0	0	0
MAUR	−100	94	−100	−100	−100	0	0	0	∞	−100	0
MEX	−78	50	−100	−100	−100	−100	0	0	4,955	−100	−100
NETH	13	8	−100	−100	0	∞	−100	0	159	1,712	1,049
NUZE	−100	201	−100	−100	0	0	−100	0	2,258	1,331	−100
NIGR	−100	28	−88	−59	0	0	0	0	7,299	−100	−100
NOR	−100	151	−100	−100	0	0	−100	−100	20,021	−100	0
PANM	−100	58	−100	−100	−100	0	0	0	∞	−100	0
PGRY	−100	25	−29	−100	08	0	−8	0	∞	100	∞
PERU	−100	104	−100	−100	−100	−100	0	0	9,124	−100	−100
PLIP	−100	37	−37	−100	−100	0	0	0	33,148	−100	0
PORT	−29	35	−100	−100	0	8,333	−94	0	2,179	26	∞
SRIL	−100	35	−100	−100	−100	0	∞	0	∞	−100	0
SING	405	11	−100	−100	−100	∞	0	0	0	0	∞
SPAN	−5	9	−41	−100	0	−100	−11	0	121	10	∞
SWE	−10	1	14	−100	∞	∞	100	−100	4,091	−42	∞
SWIT	122	−95	382	47,382	∞	∞	7,405	∞	0	46,454	∞
THAI	−100	59	−27	−100	−100	0	0	0	34,432	−100	0
TURK	−89	39	−41	−63	0	−100	−70	0	414	−100	−100
UK	258	−100	288	50,078	∞	∞	2,232	∞	−100	2,025	177,781
US	4	−22	177	7,804	124,563	103	221	827	−100	106	42
YUG	−19	17	−56	−100	0	0	−100	−100	146	−9	−100

Table 7.3
Percentage trade reduction: 1975[a]

Country	CAPITAL	LABOR 1	LABOR 2	LABOR 3	LAND 1	LAND 2	LAND 3	LAND 4	COAL	MINERALS	OIL
AFG	44	39	47	15	0	**55**	0	0	15	10	34
ARG	29	51	46	45	0	34	**86**	0	11	21	43
AUSL	56	48	64	23	23	34	**66**	0	45	62	33
AUST	8	3	14	1	13	2	0	19	22	30	**34**
BLUX	47	43	35	2	27	11	29	15	35	40	**60**
BRAZ	34	45	33	33	**62**	6	44	0	4	12	5
BRMA	70	**71**	69	44	57	0	0	0	3	12	57
CAN	70	53	65	19	0	5	18	**87**	19	50	48
CHLE	45	30	36	10	2	14	0	0	22	**91**	10
CLUM	54	13	7	3	**62**	6	0	0	18	1	35
CSTA	**37**	20	10	9	27	0	0	0	11	1	0
CYPR	27	**33**	11	31	0	0	20	0	0	22	19
DEN	6	**22**	20	13	0	0	18	0	2	7	20
DORE	**42**	27	19	14	41	0	0	0	1	12	0
ECUA	**57**	16	13	2	52	0	0	0	16	1	39
EGPT	**46**	13	7	6	7	7	0	0	4	4	2
LSAL	**44**	21	16	9	30	0	0	0	13	1	0
FIN	24	32	25	15	0	0	0	**41**	3	8	0
FRA	**90**	21	29	9	3	0	17	47	16	26	78
GER	**91**	41	32	1	29	24	52	68	8	13	65
GANA	31	18	12	7	**45**	0	0	0	5	9	0
GRCE	**44**	36	20	22	0	0	34	0	8	7	3
HOND	**46**	32	25	12	36	0	0	0	0	20	0
HOKO	4	12	28	11	19	23	13	13	29	**30**	23
ICE	40	28	40	8	0	0	**53**	0	0	0	0
INDA	13	22	35	17	14	0	2	0	1	14	**52**
INDO	76	3	12	18	4	2	0	0	9	3	76
IRE	17	19	22	0	0	0	**32**	0	1	2	5
ISRL	29	**39**	16	32	0	2	9	0	0	1	23

ITLY	78	43	55	2	15	26	41	52	26	27	**82**
JAMC	20	**41**	36	31	6	0	0	0	0	23	19
JAP	**98**	49	50	2	26	19	47	62	26	31	85
KORA	2	16	35	7	15	9	0	7	13	8	**41**
LIBR	44	33	41	11	14	2	0	0	0	**92**	0
LIBY	66	1	10	4	7	9	1	0	7	0	**73**
MALY	**68**	44	46	15	23	0	0	0	0	29	0
MLTA	35	41	16	**43**	12	14	4	0	0	0	9
MAUR	**24**	8	0	2	10	0	0	0	15	0	0
MEX	**69**	35	31	8	35	28	6	0	6	11	35
NETH	4	23	**34**	0	6	0	**64**	0	0	6	17
NUZE	46	43	49	19	0	0	0	0	5	1	7
NIGR	**76**	8	16	13	2	2	0	0	8	1	76
NOR	**74**	53	59	21	0	0	34	40	5	17	37
PANM	**56**	55	41	34	37	0	0	0	0	4	0
PGRY	64	57	58	22	25	0	**65**	0	0	4	0
PERU	53	42	52	20	37	16	0	0	9	**84**	37
PLIP	43	**45**	35	27	28	0	0	0	2	25	0
PORT	18	7	13	1	16	19	6	0	6	6	**33**
SRIL	2	13	25	11	17	2	7	6	12	2	**30**
SING	**69**	45	53	47	1	0	0	0	0	0	0
SPAN	17	5	20	14	0	1	5	0	17	22	**58**
SWE	**51**	2	1	4	10	10	12	17	0	4	42
SWIT	**77**	11	10	9	31	21	46	53	0	11	58
THAI	**42**	42	32	28	39	0	0	0	1	8	1
TURK	55	55	39	37	0	17	**59**	0	10	6	13
UK	**87**	19	31	14	28	24	46	60	2	15	81
US	**68**	11	13	29	1	9	6	30	14	0	42
YUG	**49**	48	29	33	0	0	20	36	9	1	3
WORLD	**69**	13	13	3	5	3	14	28	3	4	43

a. Largest value for each country in boldface.

Table 7.4
Percentage resource change: 1975

Country	CAPITAL	LABOR 1	LABOR 2	LABOR 3	LAND 1	LAND 2	LAND 3	LAND 4	COAL	MINERALS	OIL
AFG	135	-3	32	2	0	-31	0	0	-100	-100	-22
ARG	20	-43	48	1,604	0	-100	-38	0	2,554	476	-79
AUSL	60	-100	339	59,769	-100	-100	-100	0	-100	-96	-100
AUST	-5	6	-34	-100	∞	∞	0	-100	1,244	782	381
BLUX	-60	155	-100	-100	∞	∞	1,481	∞	1,736	12,997	223,942
BRAZ	42	-46	42	232	-100	-100	-100	0	-100	-53	-68
BRMA	108	-5	3	28	-20	0	0	0	-100	-80	-100
CAN	77	-100	359	51,623	0	-100	-100	-100	-100	-100	-91
CHLE	81	-50	48	226	-10	283	0	0	-100	-57	-49
CLUM	94	-10	6	-19	-100	-100	0	0	283	38	-87
CSTA	149	-48	34	628	-100	0	0	0	∞	-100	0
CYPR	44	-58	22	1,191	0	0	-76	0	0	-100	∞
DEN	-9	-63	123	39,337	0	0	-100	0	∞	4,651	6,616
DORE	158	-46	18	86	-100	0	0	0	∞	-100	0
ECUA	211	-16	12	-16	-100	0	0	0	∞	-100	-67
EGPT	119	-8	-13	15	∞	46	0	0	∞	123	5
LSAL	165	-33	17	42	-100	0	0	0	∞	-100	0
FIN	33	-100	177	51,237	0	0	0	-100	∞	159	0
FRA	-51	27	-81	11,764	∞	0	128	∞	600	499	3,030
GER	-100	139	-100	-100	∞	∞	3,536	24,836	126	947	3,118
GANA	118	-23	29	26	-100	0	0	0	∞	-100	0
GRCE	72	-100	65	1,067	0	0	-100	0	-100	-64	∞
HOND	161	-50	52	81	-100	0	0	0	0	-69	0
HOKO	-35	120	-100	2,460	∞	∞	12,227	∞	∞	47,617	∞
ICE	121	-100	549	57,768	0	0	-100	0	0	0	0
INDA	-11	3	-6	-4	-58	-0	2	0	0	-42	326
INDO	45,176	-3	10	-96	-34	∞	0	0	13,996	-35	-100
IRE	51	-76	124	-100	0	0	-100	0	-100	-40	∞
ISRL	41	-74	97	4,586	0	-100	-100	0	0	11	182

ITLY	−91	107	−100	−100	∞	∞	856	13,633	42,278	1,488	2,466
JAMC	73	−100	150	2,445	−100	0	0	0	0	−80	∞
JAP	−97	145	−100	−100	∞	∞	2,653	14,886	3,114	2,515	36,656
KORA	−6	39	−49	−84	∞	∞	4	−100	147	314	∞
LIBR	370	−100	688	107	−100	∞	0	0	0	−66	0
LIBY	676	25	2,362	−100	∞	179	∞	0	∞	−100	−100
MALY	226	−100	143	247	−100	0	0	0	0	−73	0
MLTA	150	−100	88	13,469	∞	∞	−100	0	0	−100	∞
MAUR	219	−17	−100	15	−100	0	0	0	∞	−100	0
MEX	53	−18	17	52	−100	−100	0	0	−100	−21	−39
NETH	4	−56	183	−100	∞	0	−100	0	0	−100	1,737
NUZE	101	−100	361	68,631	0	0	−100	0	−100	−100	−100
NIGR	621	−19	106	−80	−40	∞	0	0	12,086	114	−100
NOR	65	−100	386	66,736	0	0	−100	−100	−100	−100	−100
PANM	153	−96	95	930	−100	0	0	0	0	−100	0
PGRY	113	−23	16	69	−8	0	−5	0	0	−7	0
PERU	142	−32	55	127	−75	−100	0	0	−100	−63	−100
PLIP	90	−29	20	345	−100	0	0	0	−100	−89	0
PORT	31	−19	−32	22	∞	67,956	28	0	1,764	194	∞
SRIL	11	12	−16	−74	−100	∞	∞	∞	∞	−100	∞
SING	236	−100	539	5,827	−100	0	0	0	0	0	0
SPAN	−12	−10	−39	1,014	0	−100	−18	0	509	267	3,272
SWE	−58	6	−10	12,720	∞	∞	∞	−100	−100	33	∞
SWIT	−72	31	−57	26,757	∞	∞	8,166	∞	0	9,220	∞
THAI	93	−64	16	205	−100	0	0	0	−100	−80	−100
TURK	77	−57	47	128	0	−100	−100	0	−100	−92	−100
UK	−90	26	−78	17,390	∞	∞	823	∞	10	793	1,148
US	−36	−11	28	45,864	−100	−100	−45	645	−57	1	51
YUG	87	−37	35	668	0	0	−100	−100	−60	−7	−32

now quite clear that U.S. comparative advantage derives from the knowledge possessed by its workers or its firms . . . . As for the role of capital, it seems to have shifted over time to become positively related to U.S. net exports in recent years." Our findings are partly in agreement and partly to the contrary: Abundance of human capital was important in 1958 but not very important in 1975. Capital was actually scarce in 1958, though unimportantly so. In 1975 capital abundance was the primary determinant of U.S. trade.

The percentage trade reductions in tables 7.1 and 7.3 seem rather large. If, in 1958, Canada were to lose 96% of LAND 4, then its trade would be reduced by 97%. If, in 1975, Japan were to lose 97% of CAPITAL, then its trade would be reduced by 98%. These numbers do seem rather ridiculous, but there are two possible explanations for their magnitudes. (a) What is being reduced is not the ratio of trade to GNP but total trade. A reduction of the Japanese capital stock by 97% would lower GNP considerably and doubtlessly would have a dramatic effect on total trade. (b) The model can only be assumed to hold for variations of resources within the given "cone of diversification." Many of the resource changes that are considered would certainly move the country into another cone and alter the relation between trade and resources. In light of this observation it is probably best to focus on the ranking of resources rather than the predicted absolute trade changes.

The last rows of tables 7.1 and 7.3 indicate the reduction in trade in the world overall induced by optimally selected changes in the resources, where it needs to be repeated that it is assumed that these adjustments leave product prices unchanged. In 1958 the most important determinant of trade overall was LABOR 1, followed by LABOR 3, LABOR 2, and LAND 4. In 1975 CAPITAL was most important by a wide margin, with OIL and LAND 4 placing second and third. It is a rather interesting finding that the uneven distribution of highly skilled workers in particular and workers in general were the primary causes of trade in 1958; but keep in mind that LAND 4 was also quite important.

It is not surprising to find OIL having an increased impact in 1975, but it is surprising that CAPITAL was by far the most important variable, since this was a period in which the world's financial markets were more integrated than before. There is an interesting explanation for this that derives from a consideration of equation (7.2). The importance of a resource is found by taking the inner product of the coefficient vector and

Table 7.5
Estimated capital coefficients and U.S. net exports

	1958		1975	
	Coefficient	U.S. trade	Coefficient	U.S. trade
PETRO	−4.8	−1,098	−20.4	−23,858
MAT	−3.3	−437	−8.8	499
FOR	2.8	−946	−1.3	−11
TROP	6.9	−2,220	−2.7	−4,987
ANL	6.4	−606	.04	−1,625
CER	20.8	2,484	−4.3	18,096
LAB	−.9	377	1.0	−6,188
CAP	−6.5	849	16.5	−1,636
MACH	−8.5	5,544	29.1	23,929
CHEM	1.1	1,230	3.8	4,985

the trade vector. The estimated CAPITAL coefficient vectors and the U.S. net export vectors are reported in table 7.5. There have been substantial changes in the signs and relative magnitudes of these coefficients. The changes that are most important for these calculations occur for those commodities with large trade values: PETRO, TROP, CER, and MACH for the United States. To make it simple, suppose a country imported x of PETRO, exported an equivalent amount of MACH, and otherwise did not trade. The inner product of the trade vector and the net export vector would then be $(4.8-8.1)x = -3.3x$ in 1958 and $(20.4 + 29.1)x = 49.5x$ in 1975. It would be inferred that this country was capital scarce in 1958 but capital abundant in 1975. The importation of PETRO makes the country appear capital abundant in both years, but in 1958 this is offset by the exportation of MACH, which is estimated to be associated with capital scarce countries. Thus the change in the sign of the MACH coefficient and the increased size of the PETRO coefficient both contribute to the conclusion that the scarcity of CAPITAL reversed itself.

The increased importance of CAPITAL as a source of trade is due partly to the increased negative CAPITAL coefficient on PETRO and the shift in sign of the coefficients of CHEM and MACH. It is also due partly to the change in the composition of trade. The big change that occurred in the trade of the United States and many other countries was a substantial increase in the relative importance of petroleum imports. These coefficient changes and the trade changes together have increased CAPITAL as a cause of trade especially for the petroleum importers.

But this is entirely sensible: CAPITAL abundance creates a demand for petroleum to fuel manufacturing facilities and a consequent need to earn export receipts from manufactured products. Reduction in CAPITAL in any given country could indeed be expected to reduce greatly petroleum imports as well as manufactured good exports.

Some of the other factor scarcities suggested by these calculations seem surprising. If the sign of a change in resource in tables 7.2 and 7.4 is positive, the country is revealed to be scarce in the resource, since trade would be reduced if more were available. In that sense the United States in 1958 was revealed to be scarce in CAPITAL, LABOR 2, LABOR 3, LAND 1, LAND 2, LAND 3, LAND 4, MINERALS, and OIL and abundant in LABOR 1 and COAL. In 1975 several of these changed. CAPITAL, LAND 1, LAND 2, and LAND 3 were abundant. These findings do not conform well with the abundant resources illustrated in the resource abundance profiles, where the United States is abundant only in CAPITAL and OIL in 1958, and only in COAL and OIL in 1975. But keep in mind that the physical definition of abundance is not linked directly to the trade-reducing definition used here, and also keep in mind that the United States is difficult to classify because of its unusual combination of exports of CER and MACH. For example, LAND 1 may appear abundant in 1975 because some countries use LAND 1 to produce rice, which is classified in CER. Because LAND 1 contributes positively to CER and because the United States has great exports of CER, there is a tendency to infer that the United States is abundant in LAND 1. This is best thought to be an error of aggregation—it would have been better to separate rice from CER. However, when one considers both the conceptual differences in these abundance definitions and also the measurement differences, the degree of conformity of results is remarkably high for most countries.

For ease of study, the most important resource for each country for each year is listed in tables 7.6a and 7.6b, together with the sign of the change needed to reduce trade. Thus a minus sign means that the country is abundant in the resource, and a plus sign indicates scarcity. This table also includes the abundance ratio (endowment share divided by GNP share) of each of the most influential resources. If this number exceeds one, the country is abundant in the resource and we may expect that the change in the endowment needed to reduce trade would be negative. For example, Afghanistan in 1958 is very abundant in LABOR 3, with an

Table 7.6a
Most important resources: 1958[a]

	Resource	Resource change	Abundance ratio	Trade change
AFG	LABOR 3	−13	6.6	75
ARG	LAND 3	−74	12.0	90
AUSL	LAND 3	−100	10.0	90
AUST	OIL	+428	1.0	38
BLUX	LABOR 3	+16,843	.0	50
BRAZ	LAND 1	−84	23.8	88
BRMA	LABOR 3	−76	11.8	58
CAN	LAND 4	−96	20.4	97
CHLE	MINERALS	−100	13.3	86
CLUM	LAND 1	−100	16.8	71
CSTA	COAL	+∞	0	54
CYPR	MINERALS	−100	15.4	61
DEN	COAL	+1,363	.4	25
DORE	LABOR 1	+131	1.1*	58
ECUA	LAND 1	−100	11.9	57
EGPT	LABOR 3	−100	5.4	63
LSAL	COAL	+∞	0	61
FIN	LAND 4	−100	7.9	46
FRA	LABOR 3	+13,351	.0	82
GER	LABOR 1	−88	1.0	92
GANA	LAND 1	−100	11.6	53
GRCE	LABOR 1	+67	1.2*	75
HOND	LABOR 1	+81	1.7*	64
HOKO	LAND 2	+∞	0	39
ICE	LAND 3	−100	22.3	67
INDA	LABOR 2	−28	3.9	75
INDO	LAND 1	−100	10.3	68
IRE	COAL	+765	1.3*	46
ISRL	LABOR 2	−100	.7*	36
ITLY	LABOR 3	+1,008	.3	72

Table 7.6a (continued)

	Resource	Resource change	Abundance ratio	Trade change
JAMC	MINERALS	−96	28.8	65
JAP	LABOR 3	+5,956	.1	76
KORA	CAPITAL	+98	.7	63
LIBR	LABOR 1	+155	1.9*	64
LIBY	LABOR 1	+187	1.1*	63
MALY	LABOR 1	+119	1.5*	48
MLTA	LAND 2	+∞	0	17
MAUR	LABOR 1	+94	1.9*	42
MEX	LABOR 1	+50	1.1*	74
NETH	LABOR 2	−100	1.1	26
NUZE	LABOR 1	+201	.8	68
NIGR	LABOR 3	−59	19.1	88
NOR	LABOR 1	+151	.8	64
PANM	LABOR 1	+58	1.4*	62
PGRY	COAL	+∞	0	56
PERU	LABOR 1	+104	1.3*	82
PLIP	LABOR 1	+37	1.5*	81
PORT	LABOR 2	−100	2.4	60
SRIL	LABOR 2	−100	4.5	46
SING	OIL	+∞	0	30
SPAN	LABOR 2	−41	1.9	57
SWE	LAND 4	−100	3.4	43
SWIT	LABOR 1	−95	.9*	84
THAI	LABOR 1	+59	2.3*	84
TURK	LABOR 3	−63	3.6	90
UK	LABOR 3	+50,078	.0	95
US	LABOR 2	+177	.4	74
YUG	COAL	+146	1.8*	70
WORLD	LABOR 1			54

a. *indicates a discrepancy between the two measurements of resource abundance: the negative of the sign of the resource change and the abundance ratio minus one.

Table 7.6b
Most important resources: 1975[a]

	Resource	Resource change	Abundance ratio	Trade change
AFG	LAND 2	−31	100.2	55
ARG	LAND 3	−38	13.9	86
AUSL	LAND 3	−100	6.6	66
AUST	OIL	+381	.3	34
BLUX	OIL	200,000	.0	60
BRAZ	LAND 1	−100	16.9	62
BRMA	LABOR 1	−5	17.2	71
CAN	LAND 4	−100	20.5	87
CHLE	MINERALS	−57	16.5	91
CLUM	LAND 1	−100	17.9	62
CSTA	CAPITAL	+149	.8	38
CYPR	LABOR 1	−58	2.0	33
DEN	LABOR 1	−63	.8*	22
DORE	CAPITAL	+158	.5	42
ECUA	CAPITAL	+211	.7	57
EGPT	CAPITAL	+119	.6	46
LSAL	CAPITAL	+165	.6	44
FIN	LAND 4	−100	5.6	41
FRA	CAPITAL	−51	1.2	90
GER	CAPITAL	−100	1.1	91
GANA	LAND 1	−100	10.3	45
GRCE	CAPITAL	+72	.9	44
IIOND	CAPITAL	+161	.9	46
HOKO	MINERALS	+47,617	.0	30
ICE	LAND 3	−100	15.3	53
INDA	OIL	+326	.4	52
INDO	CAPITAL	+45,176	.0	76
IRE	LAND 3	−100	4.0	32
ISRL	LABOR 1	−74	1.3	39
ITLY	OIL	+2,466	.2	82

Table 7.6b (continued)

	Resource	Resource change	Abundance ratio	Trade change
JAMC	LABOR 1	−100	1.2	41
JAP	CAPITAL	−97	1.3	98
KORA	OIL	+∞	0	41
LIBR	MINERALS	−66	100.7	92
LIBY	OIL	−100	20.1	73
MALY	CAPITAL	+226	.8	68
MLTA	LABOR 3	+13,469	.2	43
MAUR	CAPITAL	+219	.7	24
MEX	CAPITAL	+53	.7	69
NETH	LABOR 2	+183	.5	34
NUZE	LAND 3	−100	9.9	64
NIGR	CAPITAL	+621	.6	76
NOR	CAPITAL	+65	1.5*	74
PANM	CAPITAL	+153	.8	56
PGRY	LAND 3	−5	135.0	65
PERU	MINERALS	−63	21.6	84
PLIP	LABOR 1	−29	4.1	45
PORT	OIL	+∞	0	33
SRIL	OIL	+∞	0	30
SING	CAPITAL	+236	1.2*	69
SPAN	OIL	+3,272	.1	58
SWE	CAPITAL	−58	1.1	51
SWIT	CAPITAL	−72	1.2	77
THAI	LABOR 1	−64	1.9	42
TURK	LAND 3	−100	3.7	59
UK	CAPITAL	−90	.96*	87
US	CAPITAL	−36	.9*	68
YUG	CAPITAL	+87	.5	49
WORLD	CAPITAL			69

a. *indicates a discrepancy between the two measurements of resource abundance: the negative of the sign of the resource change and the abundance ratio minus one.

endowment share 6.6 times the GNP share. This conforms with the finding reported in tables 7.1 and 7.2 that an 18% reduction in LABOR 3 would reduce trade dependence by 75%. Conflicts in these two measures of factor abundance are indicated in table 7.6, with an asterisk following the abundance ratio. For example, the Dominican Republic in 1958 is measured to be slightly abundant in LABOR 1, with an abundance ratio of 1.1, but nonetheless trade is reduced if the LABOR 1 endowment were increased by 131%. There are only 22 such conflicts out of a total possible of 116. Fourteen of these conflicts involve LABOR 1: the Dominican Republic, Greece, Honduras, Liberia, Libya, Malaysia, Mauritius, Mexico, Panama, Peru, the Philippines, and Thailand in 1958 have abundance ratios in excess of one but need increases in LABOR 1 to reduce trade. Switzerland in 1958 and Denmark in 1975 have abundance ratios less than one, but require a reduction of LABOR 1 to reduce trade. It seems clear that the abundance ratio is misleading in all of these cases. This may be due partly to the extrapolation/interpolation/imputation schemes used to measure LABOR 1, and partly to the fact that the composition of LABOR 1 is likely different in the developing countries, with relatively many doctors, lawyers, and teachers, and relatively few scientists and engineers. Other problems may be mismeasurement of GNP or a "world" that excludes too many countries. Four of the other conflicts in table 7.6 involve CAPITAL in 1975. These conflicts generate a reaction similar to the LABOR 1 conflicts—it is the abundance ratio that is at fault. (Singapore is best thought to be capital scarce, the United States and the United Kingdom capital abundant.) Overall, the surprising conformity of the two measurements of factor abundance contributes considerably to the credibility of the method by which the most important trade-reducing resources are identified.

7.2 Tariffs and the Functional Distribution of Income

Tariffs and trade restrictions are most often used for purposes of income redistribution, yet there is hardly any quantitative information that indicates the size of the redistributional effects. The redistributional consequences of trade restrictions can be studied either with a long run model in which factors are costlessly mobile between industries or with a short run model in which some mobility may occur but not without cost. Examination of the political pressure for trade restrictions as in Brock and Magee (1978) suggests that the short run model is the more suitable, since workers and owners ordinarily lobby for protection only in their own industries. If the long run model were a completely accurate description of reality, the interest of a class of workers would focus on a set of industries regardless of the industry in which workers happened to be located. Whatever gains might accrue to workers in the protected industry would be partly, if not completely, competed away by workers moving to the affected industry. In such a world we would not expect often to see workers or owners organize to exert political pressure, since the gains would be relatively small and the organizational costs relatively large.

The model that has been used in this book is a long run model, and it can be used to study the long run distributional consequences of tariffs. In light of the preceding comments it is fair to ask who might be interested in these long run effects. An answer is that the political process is likely to be myopic and possibly poorly informed as well. Workers and owners may be unaware how quickly gains would be competed away through the mobility of factors, or they may be relatively unconcerned about future events because of high discount rates. The length of time it takes for the long run model adequately to approximate reality is not something I care to conjecture seriously about; nor do I believe there exists much information about it. If the answer were as short as 5 years, I believe the long run consequences of trade restrictions could and should have a more noticeable effect on the political processes. I therefore present some estimates of the long run consequences of tariffs with the hope that future quantitative analysis will reveal the practical relevance of these effects in the sense of demonstrating that the speeds of adjustment are rather more than the current political processes seem to assume.

The approach to estimating the tariff effects rests on the reciprocity between the Stolper-Samuelson effects and the Rybczynski effects,

$$\partial X_j / \partial V_i = \partial w_i / \partial p_j, \tag{7.4}$$

which asserts that the derivative of final output X_j with respect to the total supply of the ith primary factor is equal to the derivative of the return to that factor with respect to the price of that good. Direct econometric estimation of the Stolper-Samuelson effects, $\partial w_i / \partial p_j$, could proceed by regressing a time series sample of factor rewards (or internal prices) for a particular country on time series of external product prices, as in Chipman (1977/1978). This approach is rendered difficult by the high degree of collinearity among the many product prices and the consequent need to use prior information about the coefficients. The approach is also questionable because the relation between factor prices and product prices will change with the technology, which is not credibly assumed constant for long periods of time.

The indirect econometric estimates of the Stolper-Samuelson effects that are reported in this section begin with cross-section estimates of the effects of factor endowments on net exports, $\partial T_j/\partial V_i$. In the trade model with equal numbers of factors and goods, this derivative is equal to

$$\partial T_j/\partial V_i = \partial X_j/\partial V_i - (X_{jw}/Y_w)(\partial Y/\partial V_i),$$

where X_j is output, Y is GNP, and the w subscript indicates the world totals. The net export data we are using are expressed in value terms, and we may multiply this expression by p_j and rearrange to obtain

$$p_j \partial X_j/\partial V_i = p_j(\partial T_j/\partial V_i) + (p_j X_{jw}/Y_w)(\partial Y/\partial V_i)$$
$$= \beta_{ji} + \gamma_j w_i,$$
(7.5)

where β_{ji} is the coefficient of resource i in the net export equation for commodity j, γ_j is the share in final consumption of commodity j, and w_i is the wage rate of factor i. Then by appealing to the Samuelson reciprocity relations (7.4), we have the elasticity of factor earnings with respect to product prices:

$$(\partial w_i/w_i)/(\partial p_j/p_j) = p_j(\partial X_j/\partial V_i)/w_i = \beta_{ji}/w_i + \gamma_j.$$
(7.6)

The trade regressions are the source of estimates of the trade derivatives β_{ji}, and the GNP regressions may be used to obtain estimates of the factor returns w_i. The final product consumption shares are derived from BEA estimates as described subsequently.

Before proceeding with discussion of the actual estimates, it is wise to pause a bit to reflect on the believability of the approach. The reciprocity relations are reasonably insensitive to the form of the model. As Chang (1979) demonstrates, they apply in uneven models as well as even ones. It does seem entirely sensible to suppose that those industries that would increase exports most in response to the accumulation of a particular resource are the very same industries for which protection would be most beneficial to that resource. But equation (7.5), which purges the consumption effect from the trade effect to obtain the output effect, is specific to the even model, as is the assumption used in most of the previous chapters that $\partial T_j/\partial V_i$ is a constant independent of factor supplies V. For these reasons, the estimates that are now to be presented should be thought to have very large standard errors, partly because of estimation uncertainty in the computation of β_{ji}, γ_j, and w_i, but, more important, because of conceptual uncertainty attaching to formula (7.6). This is perhaps expressed most clearly by pointing out that formula (7.6) is used as if it applied to all countries, which means, for example, that a 10% tariff on steel imports in India is estimated to have the same impact on wages as a 10% tariff on steel imports in the United States.

In addition to these conceptual concerns, the numbers implied by equation (7.6) turn out to be disconcertingly dependent on the consumption shares, since the estimates of the trade sensitivities β_{ji} are often very small compared to estimates of the factor returns w_i (taken from the cross-section GNP regressions). This can be corrected mechanically by either reducing the consumption shares or the factor returns or increasing the trade sensitivities. I have unfortunately been unable to find a theoretical justification for doing any of these.

My first instinct was to reduce the consumption shares to adjust for the fact that part of income is spent on nontraded goods and services. It is somewhat surprising that this adjustment is groundless in theory. As is explained in chapter 1, if factor prices are equalized, the model with nontraded goods can be written, as always, as $T = A^{-1}(V - sV_w)$, where V and V_w refer to total supplies of factors, not just supplies to the traded goods sector. The relation between prices and wages is as before $w = A'^{-1}p$, and it is desired to recover A'^{-1} from the trade regressions. It is true that output of the traded goods is less sensitive to factor accumulation because part of the factors is used in the nontraded goods sector, and it is also true as a consequence that the reciprocity between the Stolper-Samuelson effects and the Rybczynski effects no longer holds unless the Rybczynski derivatives are taken with respect to factors allocated to the traded goods sector. Nonetheless, the trade equations remain exactly as before because the reduced sensitivity of production is offset by reduced sensitivity of consumption. There is one minor adjustment to (7.6) necessitated by the existence of nontraded goods. The consumption vector $A^{-1}V_w$ is the vector of world outputs of traded goods if all resources were devoted to the production of traded goods. The consumption shares in table 7.6 would therefore have to be adjusted for the hypothetical output changes associated with reallocating all resources from nontraded goods to traded goods. These shares would still add to one; thus whatever adjustment might be made, the shares would still dominate formula (7.6).

There is another model discussed in chapter 1 that may also account for the fact that trade seems too insensitive to factor supplies compared with the sensitivity of GNP. The model to which I refer has trade impediments in the form of transportation costs, tariffs, or other ad valorem charges, and what I expect is that these costs that discourage trade would have a relatively large effect on the sensitivity of trade to factor supply changes. In particular, if log-linear production functions and log-linear utility functions are assumed, then the model is summarized by equations (1.6) and (1.8), which are repeated here:

$$\Theta' \ln(w) = \ln(p) + \ln(X_0),\tag{7.7}$$

$$PT = \Theta^{-1}WV - \gamma 1'P^{-1}\Theta^{-1}WV/1'P^{-1}\gamma,\tag{7.8}$$

where commodity units are assumed so that international prices are all equal to one, and p = vector of internal prices (exceeding one), P = diag$\{p\}$, w = vector of internal factor prices, W = diag$\{w\}$, Θ = matrix of fixed input value shares with column sums equal to one ($1'\Theta = 1'$), $\ln(z)$ = vector with elements $\ln(z_i)$, X_0 = vector of constants, γ = vector of fixed consumption shares, summing to one ($1'\gamma = 1$), T = vector of net exports, and V = vector of factor endowments. What we wish to do is to recover Θ'^{-1}, the matrix of elasticities of factor returns with respect to product prices, from a cross-section regression of trade on endowments. Assume that the internal prices p and w are approximately the same in all countries, so that a regression of trade on factor endowments would yield estimates of the trade sensitivities:

$$\partial PT/\partial V = \Theta^{-1}W - \gamma 1'P^{-1}\Theta^{-1}W/1'P^{-1}\gamma.$$

We may symbolize the matrix of derivatives $\partial PT/\partial V$ by B (thinking of regression coefficients) and rewrite (7.8) as

$$\Theta^{-1} = BW^{-1} + \gamma 1'P^{-1}\Theta^{-1}/1'P^{-1}\gamma,\tag{7.9}$$

which is a generalization (7.6). If there are no trade impediments and internal prices are all equal to one, then P is the identity matrix, and $1'P^{-1}\Theta^{-1}/1'P^{-1}\gamma = 1'$, since $1'\Theta = 1'$ implies $1' = 1'\Theta^{-1}$ and $1'\gamma = 1$. In this case (7.9) and (7.6) are identical expressions. Otherwise, the adjustment necessary for trade impediments involves substitution of the vector $1'P^{-1}\Theta^{-1}/1'P^{-1}\gamma$ for the vector $1'$. This would tend to correct the problem caused by the fact that the shares γ are generally an order of magnitude larger than trade estimates BW^{-1} if the vector $1'P^{-1}\Theta^{-1}/1'P^{-1}\gamma$ were less than the vector of ones. There is no reason for this to be the case. A typical element in this vector is the ratio of a weighted average of the elements of a column of Θ^{-1} divided by a weighted average of the elements in γ. Both simple averages are equal to one, and it is unclear whether the weights will make the numerator or the denominator larger.

It should be clear from the preceding discussion that I have been unable to find a logic for altering the elasticity formula, but nonetheless I remain uncomfortable with the implied elasticities, since they seem unduly influenced by the consumption shares γ_j in the several cases when the estimated wage rates are much higher than the estimated trade coefficients. Estimates of the trade derivatives β_{ji} are taken from the table of Bayes estimates, table 6.5. In order to get positive factor productivities for all resources, the prior for GNP was concentrated around the prior means. The estimated factor rewards that result are basically the prior means except for the returns to CAPITAL and LABOR 2. Consumption shares were formed from final consumption estimates[1] of the United States in the 1967 input-output table, using a concordance between the SITC categories and the SIC categories.

The wages, consumption shares, and the estimated elasticities are reported in table 7.7. The predominance of positive numbers in this table is a result of the influence of the consumption shares. For example, the CAPITAL column in 1958 is virtually identical to the consumption shares because the estimated derivatives of trade with respect to changes in CAPITAL are much smaller than the estimated derivatives of GNP. Because of the influence of the consumption shares, it is best to restrict comparisons to numbers in the same row of this table. It is particularly interesting to identify the factors that are estimated to have prices most sensitive to the price of each commodity. These are listed in table 7.8. Not surprisingly, if a petroleum tariff is imposed, OIL is the factor with the greatest percentage increase in factor price. The other results seem similarly sensible, and it is interesting to observe the changing effect of prices of manufactures on the labor categories in light of our earlier discussion of the reduced role of knowledge capital in trade in manufactures. In 1958 the estimated elasticities of the returns to the three labor

Table 7.7
Estimated elasticities of factor rewards with respect to changes in product prices

	Consumption share	CAP	LABOR 1	LABOR 2	LABOR 3	LAND 1	LAND 2	LAND 3	LAND 4	COAL	MINERALS	OIL
1958												
PETRO	.02	0.02	0.00	0.03	0.04	-0.02	-0.00	0.00	0.01	-0.04	0.01	0.45
MAT	.04	0.04	-0.04	0.11	0.09	0.07	0.03	0.04	0.11	0.11	0.86	0.52
FOR	.01	0.02	-0.03	0.06	0.04	-0.01	-0.04	-0.01	0.14	-0.13	-0.02	-0.04
TROP	.09	0.10	-0.05	0.26	0.16	0.50	0.21	0.07	0.06	-0.12	0.05	0.11
ANL	.13	0.14	0.04	0.20	0.17	0.09	0.23	0.20	0.15	-0.03	0.08	0.10
CER	.09	0.12	-0.09	0.08	0.21	0.18	0.38	0.20	0.12	-0.13	0.06	0.14
LAB	.15	0.14	0.18	0.18	0.11	0.10	0.08	0.13	0.09	0.17	0.09	0.04
CAP	.05	0.04	0.15	0.12	-0.04	-0.05	-0.01	-0.00	-0.02	0.09	-0.01	-0.06
MACH	.36	0.35	0.63	0.12	0.20	0.23	0.28	0.23	0.21	0.71	0.27	0.26
CHEM	.04	0.05	0.07	-0.03	0.04	0.01	-0.04	0.03	0.03	0.22	-0.03	-0.02
Wage		754.0	5,875.0	128.0	127.0	2.9	1.6	33.0	15.1	1.0	1.0	1.0
1975												
PETRO	.02	-0.02	-0.02	0.06	0.07	-0.02	-0.02	-0.00	0.02	-0.05	-0.02	0.40
MAT	.04	0.03	0.07	-0.17	0.05	0.03	-0.01	0.03	0.07	0.44	1.14	0.08
FOR	.01	0.01	0.01	-0.05	0.04	-0.01	-0.03	0.01	0.14	-0.02	-0.01	0.08
TROP	.09	0.08	0.06	0.17	0.11	0.39	0.19	0.15	0.06	-0.02	0.07	0.13
ANL	.13	0.13	0.10	0.06	0.17	0.09	0.26	0.20	0.13	0.08	0.09	0.16
CER	.09	0.08	0.18	-0.26	0.05	0.33	0.28	0.28	0.12	0.12	0.09	0.33
LAB	.15	0.15	0.08	0.43	0.16	0.09	0.10	0.13	0.10	0.08	0.09	0.10
CAP	.05	0.08	-0.13	0.50	0.14	-0.03	-0.00	-0.05	-0.00	-0.03	-0.02	-0.12
MACH	.36	0.41	0.25	0.64	0.38	0.29	0.30	0.24	0.21	0.31	0.28	0.19
CHEM	.04	0.05	0.09	-0.15	0.03	-0.04	0.00	-0.03	0.01	0.07	-0.01	-0.00
Wage		533.0	11,034.0	279.0	402.0	9.6	5.2	99.9	49.0	1.0	1.0	1.0

Table 7.8
Most sensitive factor returns

Protected commodity	Most sensitive factor return
PETRO	OIL
MAT	MINERALS
FOR	LAND 4
TROP	LAND 1
ANL	LAND 2
CER	LAND 2 (1958), LAND 1 (1975)
LAB	LABOR 2
CAP	LABOR 1 (1958), LABOR 2 (1975)
MACH	LABOR 1 (1958), LABOR 2 (1975)
CHEM	LABOR 1

categories with respect to the change in the price of CAP where .15, .12, and −.04. Thus it was slightly in the interest of both LABOR 1 and LABOR 2 to have tariff protection for CAP, but the return to LABOR 3 would have been slightly reduced by such a policy. In 1975 the elasticities changed sharply to −.13, .50, and .14. The return to LABOR 1 would have been reduced by protection of CAP, and the return to LABOR 2 would have been greatly increased. A similar change occurred for MACH, though the estimated elasticity of LABOR 1 with respect to MACH in 1975 remained positive. Although great uncertainty attaches to the elasticities in table 7.7, it is quite interesting that the period 1958–1975 witnessed a sharp change in the expressed desire for protection by labor unions such as the United Automobile Workers. In 1958 these unions were decidely on the side of free trade, but by 1975 and thereafter were activity seeking trade protection. This is quite consistent with the numbers presented in table 7.7.

Appendix A

Factor Market Distortions in the 2 × 2 Model

The usual 2 × 2 model can be completely described by the following sets of conditions:

a. factor market equilibrium:

$$a_{K1} X_1 + a_{K2} X_2 = K,$$

$$a_{L1} X_1 + a_{L2} X_2 = L;$$

b. zero profits:

$$a_{K1} r + a_{L1} w_1 = p_1,$$

$$a_{K2} r + a_{L2} w_2 = p_2;$$

c. unit isoquants, constant returns to scale:

$$1 = F(a_{K1}, a_{L1}) = a_{L1} f(a_{K1}/a_{L1}),$$

$$1 = G(a_{K2}, a_{L2}) = a_{L2} g(a_{K2}/a_{L2});$$

d. cost minimization:

$$w_1/r = (f/f') - (a_{K1}/a_{L1}),$$

$$w_2/r = (g/g') - (a_{K2}/a_{L2});$$

e. no factor market distortion:

$$w_1 = w_2.$$

Comparative static exercises can be done by differentiating each of these equalities. For example, differentiating the first factor market equation yields

$$a_{K1} dX_1 + a_{K2} dX_2 + X_1 da_{K1} + X_2 da_{K2} = dK.$$

If this in turn is divided by the same equation, we obtain an expression in terms of percentage changes as in Jones (1965):

$$\frac{a_{K1} X_1 \hat{X}_1 + a_{K2} X_2 \hat{X}_2 + a_{K1} X_1 \hat{a}_{K1} + a_{K2} X_2 \hat{a}_{K2}}{a_{K1} X_1 + a_{K2} X_2} = \hat{K}.$$

If λ_{Kj} is the proportion of capital allocated to industry j and λ_{Lj} is the proportion of labor, then the factor market equations can be written in differential form as

$$\lambda'_K \hat{X} + \lambda'_K \hat{a}_K = \hat{K} = 0,$$
$$\lambda'_L \hat{X} + \lambda'_L \hat{a}_L = \hat{L} = 0,$$

(A1)

where a_K and a_L are rows of the factor intensity matrix A.

Next, differentiating the first unit isoquant, we obtain

$$0 = f' \, da_{K1} + (f - (a_{K1}/a_{L1})f') da_{L1},$$

but using the cost minimization condition this can be written as

$$0 = r \, da_{K1} + w_1 \, da_{L1},$$

or

$$0 = \theta_{K1} \hat{a}_{K1} + \theta_{L1} \hat{a}_{L1},$$

where $\theta_{K1} = ra_{K1}/(ra_{K1} + w_1 a_{L1})$ is capital's value share in industry one and $\theta_{L1} = 1 - \theta_{K1}$. A similar expression results from differentiating the equation of the other unit isoquant. Thus

$$0 = \theta'_1 \hat{a}_1,$$
$$0 = \theta'_2 \hat{a}_2.$$

(A2)

Differentiating the zero profit conditions yields a set of equations like (A1), except (A2) implies that the second terms to the left of the equality can be eliminated. Thus

$$\theta_{K1} \hat{r} + \theta_{L1} \hat{w}_1 = \hat{p}_1 = 0,$$
$$\theta_{K2} \hat{r} + \theta_{L2} \hat{w}_2 = \hat{p}_2 = 0.$$

(A3)

These can be rewritten as

$$\hat{r} + \theta_{L1}(\hat{w}_1 - \hat{r}) = 0,$$
$$\hat{r} + \theta_{L2}(\hat{w}_2 - \hat{r}) = 0.$$

(A4)

Last, we may differentiate the cost minimization conditions and express them as

$$\hat{w}_1 - \hat{r} = \sigma_1^{-1}(\hat{a}_{K1} - \hat{a}_{L1}),$$
$$\hat{w}_2 - \hat{r} = \sigma_2^{-1}(\hat{a}_{K2} - \hat{a}_{L2}),$$

(A5)

where σ_j is the elasticity of the capital intensity a_{Kj}/a_{Lj} with respect to be relative factor price w/r.

By selecting pairs of equation from (A2) and (A5), we can solve for $\hat{a}_1$ and $\hat{a}_2$:

$$\begin{bmatrix} \hat{a}_{K1} \\ \hat{a}_{L1} \end{bmatrix} = \begin{bmatrix} \theta_{K1} & \theta_{L1} \\ 1 & -1 \end{bmatrix}^{-1} \begin{bmatrix} 0 \\ \sigma_1(\hat{w}_1 - \hat{r}) \end{bmatrix}$$

$$= \begin{bmatrix} \theta_{L1} \\ -\theta_{K1} \end{bmatrix} \sigma_1(\hat{w}_1 - \hat{r}) = \begin{bmatrix} -\theta_{L1} \\ \theta_{K1} \end{bmatrix} \sigma_1 \hat{r}/\theta_{L1},$$

$$\begin{bmatrix} \hat{a}_{K2} \\ \hat{a}_{L2} \end{bmatrix} = \begin{bmatrix} -\theta_{L2} \\ \theta_{K2} \end{bmatrix} \sigma_2 \hat{r}/\theta_{L2}.$$

Inserting these into (A1), we obtain

$$\hat{X} = \lambda^{-1} \begin{bmatrix} \lambda_{K1}\sigma_1 + \lambda_{K2}\sigma_2 \\ -(\lambda_{L1}\theta_{K1}\theta_{L1}^{-1}\sigma_1 + \lambda_{L2}\theta_{K2}\theta_{L2}^{-1}\sigma_2) \end{bmatrix} \hat{r}. \tag{A6}$$

If prices were constant and factors growing, we would have $\hat{X} = \lambda^{-1}\hat{V}$, an equation that can be interpreted in terms of the Rybczynski theorem: If $\hat{V} = (+, -)$, output of the capital intensive section grows and output of the labor intensive sector contracts. Therefore equation (A6) can be interpreted to mean that whatever the form of the labor market distortion, if it raises the return to capital, outputs will adjust as if capital had increased and labor decreased.

The labor allocated to sector one is a $a_{L1}X_1$, and using the preceding results, the percentage change in this quantity is

$$\hat{L}_1 = \hat{a}_{L1} + \hat{X}_1$$

$$= \hat{r}[(\sigma_1\theta_{K1}\theta_{L1}^{-1} + |\lambda|^{-1}(\lambda_{L2}(\lambda_{K1}\sigma_1 + \lambda_{K2}\sigma_2)$$
$$+ \lambda_{K2}(\lambda_{L1}\theta_{K1}\theta_{L1}^{-1}\sigma_1 + \lambda_{L2}\theta_{K2}\theta_{L2}^{-1}\sigma_2))] \tag{A7}$$
$$= \hat{r}|\lambda|(\sigma_1\lambda_{K1}\lambda_{L2}(1 + \theta_{K1}\theta_{L1}^{-1}) + \sigma_2\lambda_{K2}\lambda_{L2}(1 + \theta_{K2}\theta_{L2}^{-1})),$$

where $|\lambda|$ is the determinant of the share matrix and is positive if sector one is capital intensive. What this implies is that the sign of $\hat{L}_1$ and the sign of $\hat{X}_1$ are identical.

From (A3) we obtain another basic relation that holds regardless of the form of the distortion:

$$\hat{w}_1/\hat{w}_2 = (\theta_{K1}/\theta_{L1})/(\theta_{K2}/\theta_{L2}). \tag{A8}$$

This implies that the wages in the two sectors must move in the same direction and that the wage in the capital intensive sector (in the value sense) must change more than the wage in the labor intensive sector. This causes certain peculiarities if unionization is attempted in the labor intensive sector. Namely, either the nonunion sector ends up with a higher wage or unionization causes both wages to fall. It may also be noted that the fate of capital is opposite to that of labor, since (A3) can be written as $\hat{r} = -(\theta_{L1}/\theta_{K1})\hat{w}_1$. This, together with (A6), implies that successful unionization ($\hat{w}_1 > 0$) is associated with a fall in the capital return ($\hat{r} < 0$), a reduction in output of the capital intensive sector, and an increase in output in the labor intensive sector, regardless of which sector is unionized.

What remains is to study the effects of the three possible distortions. First, suppose the wage rate is raised in sector one $\hat{w} = c$, and sector one is capital intensive, $|\theta| > 0$. Then from (A3) and (A8), $\hat{w}_1 > \hat{w}_2 > 0 > \hat{r}$. And from (A6) and (A7), $\hat{X}_1 < 0$, $\hat{L}_1 < 0$. These are all intuitive results. But suppose sector one is labor intensive; then the comparative statics equations imply that the nonunion workers are relatively better off, $\hat{w}_2 > \hat{w}_1 > 0 > \hat{r}$. This strange result of Carruth and Oswald (1982), together with a plausible story of adjustment, leads to the conclusion that the union sector goes completely out of existence.

Next, suppose $\hat{w}_1 = \hat{w}_2 + t$, a case considered by Johnson and Mieszkowski (1970), Jones (1971), Magee (1971, 1980), and Neary (1978). This condition, together with (A3), implies

$$\begin{bmatrix} \hat{r} \\ w_2 \end{bmatrix} = \begin{bmatrix} \theta_{K1} & \theta_{L1} \\ \theta_{K2} & \theta_{L2} \end{bmatrix}^{-1} \begin{bmatrix} -\theta_{L1} \\ 0 \end{bmatrix} t$$

$$= |\theta|^{-1} \begin{bmatrix} -\theta_{L2} \\ \theta_{K2} \end{bmatrix} \theta_{L1} t.$$

If X_1 is capital intensive in the value sense, $|\theta| > 0$, then $\hat{w}_1 > \hat{w}_2 > 0 > \hat{r}$, $\hat{X}_1 < 0$, and $\hat{L}_1 < 0$. But if $|\theta| < 0$, then $\hat{r} > 0 > \hat{w}_1 > \hat{w}_2$, $\hat{X}_1 > 0$, and $\hat{L}_1 > 0$. Here relative wage bargaining has made all workers worse off, though there is an increase in union membership.

Last, suppose there is a licensing arrangement that restricts employment in sector one. Then from (A7), $\hat{L}_1 < 0$ implies $\text{sign}(\hat{r}) = -\text{sign}|\lambda|$. Thus if sector one is capital intensive, $|\lambda| > 0$, then $\hat{w}_1 > \hat{w}_2 > 0 > \hat{r}$ and $\hat{X}_1 < 0$. But if sector one is labor intensive, $\hat{r} > 0 > \hat{w}_2 > \hat{w}_1$ and $\hat{X}_1 < 0$. These results are summarized in table A.1.

Table A.1
Effects of labor market distortion[a]

	Factor intensity	Factor rewards	sign $\hat{X}_1$ (= sign $\hat{L}_1$)
Minimum wage	$s_\theta > 0$	$\hat{w}_1 > \hat{w}_2 > 0 > \hat{r}$	$-s_\lambda$
$\hat{w}_1 > 0$	$s_\theta < 0$	$\hat{w}_2 > \hat{w}_1 > 0 > \hat{r}$	$-s_\lambda$
Earnings tax	$s_\theta > 0$	$\hat{w}_1 > \hat{w}_2 > 0 > \hat{r}$	$-s_\lambda$
$\hat{w}_1 = \hat{w}_2 + t$	$s_\theta < 0$	$\hat{r} > 0 > \hat{w}_1 > \hat{w}_2$	s_λ
License requirement	$s_\lambda > 0$	$\hat{w}_1 > \hat{w}_2 > 0 > \hat{r}$	—
$\hat{L}_1 < 0$	$s_\lambda < 0$	$\hat{r} > 0 > \hat{w}_1 > \hat{w}_2$	—

a. $s_\lambda = \mathrm{sign}|\lambda|$; $s_\theta = \mathrm{sign}|\theta|$. $\hat{X} = dX/X$. λ is the matrix of factor shares in a physical sense. $s_\lambda = \mathrm{sign}|\lambda| > 0$ implies that the unionized sector is capital intensive, $k_1 > k_2$. θ is the matrix of factor shares in a value sense. $s_\theta = \mathrm{sign}|\theta| > 0$ implies that the union sector is capital intensive, after accounting for wage differences, $k_1/w_1 > k_2/w_2$. Neary (1978) has shown that dynamic stability requires $|\lambda||\theta| > 0$.

Appendix B

Data Sources and Methods

This appendix describes the data set used in this book. A larger data set including intervening years and other country characteristics was originally collected by Harry P. Bowen, Graduate School of Business Administration, New York University, when he was a student at UCLA. Much of this appendix was prepared by Bowen.[1] The subset of the data that is used here was selected for reasons of simplicity and country coverage. Some analysis of the years between 1958 and 1975 suggests that the changes over time have been gradual and monotonic. Little of interest is lost by focusing on the end years. It would have been desirable to extend the sample either forward or backward in time, but much of the data are unavailable before 1958, and a complete data set for a year after 1975 could not be assembled at the time this project commenced.

The data are listed in table B.1. Abbreviations for the 60 countries form the first column. With several possible exceptions these abbreviations need not be spelled out. The exceptions are MALA, which refers to (West) Malaysia; INDA, to India; INDO, to Indonesia; and SRIL, to Sri Lanka (Ceylon). The next column contains the year of the data. A year close to 1958 and 1975 has been substituted when data in those years are unavailable. The columns labeled AGG 1–AGG 10 refer to the net export data in thousands of U.S. dollars; the other columns indicate country attributes, which are described in table B.2. Units and primary sources are also listed in table B.2. Secondary sources and various notes comprise table B.3.

CAPITAL Estimates of the net stock of capital for each country were made by summing gross domestic investment[2] flows over the period 1948–1975, applying depreciation factors based on assumed average asset lives. Gross domestic investment measures the outlays for the addition of reproducible capital goods to the fixed assets of both private and public enterprises, private nonprofit institutions, and general government and to the value of the net change in inventories. This includes all new items whether produced domestically or purchased abroad as well as all new dwellings, expenditures or the improvement of durable goods, and nonreproducible tangible assets such as land, mineral deposits, and additions to livestock herds. Excluded are increases in natural resources due to growth, such as forests, and new discoveries, such as mineral deposits.

Table B.1
Data Set

NAME	YEAR	AGG1	AGG2	AGG3	AGG4	AGG5	AGG6	AGG7	AGG8	AGG9	AGG10
AFG	60	−5,994	−3,121	0	5,341	15,555	8,604	−4,426	−6,159	−12,470	−1,668
ARG	58	−215,400	−141,754	−141,188	−78,040	379,805	515,635	−10,194	−228,460	−397,000	−44,619
AUSL	58	−193,740	72,803	−99,433	73,962	255,611	736,034	−105,929	−246,923	−507,001	−106,357
AUST	58	−20,577	−131,878	201,079	−81,115	−6,521	−116,329	40,889	140,915	−142,763	−39,402
BLUX	58	−147,812	−217,117	−93,228	−132,604	−52,273	−292,492	96,846	847,710	−118,529	26,288
BRAZ	58	−257,140	11,300	−1,060	879,537	44,510	−46,967	−7,704	−75,286	−533,090	−121,625
BRMA	58	−3,632	1,086	6,945	9,053	−14,521	142,038	−3,079	−53,701	0	0
CAN	58	−329,723	1,027,838	1,300,702	−376,169	293,049	578,588	−595,818	−721,239	−1,397,433	−69,832
CHLE	58	−31,887	267,390	−6,161	−29,764	−5,224	−11,909	−3,461	−27,688	−168,590	27,175
CLUM	58	64,274	−6,895	−17,148	356,326	0	−41,701	−5,986	−63,722	−98,378	−61,557
CSTA	58	−6,650	−793	−1,575	81,839	130	−7,664	−8,082	−23,052	−26,193	−14,656
CYPR	60	−10,237	23,820	−5,698	10,099	−6,582	−10,854	−13,168	−18,877	−20,729	0
DEN	58	−134,407	−115,557	−71,456	−30,155	671,474	−112,572	13,178	−190,112	−46,070	−79,980
DORE	58	−10,230	−960	−3,848	115,490	−3,890	3,480	−1,714	−30,420	−38,370	−7,510
EUCA	58	−3,312	−2,523	−1,281	120,814	657	−5,363	−4,515	−16,287	−30,802	−8,867
EGPT	60	−52,206	−12,548	−48,071	−9,965	−12,979	307,805	−1,665	−22,256	−133,760	−69,876
LSAL	58	−7,340	−3,808	−3,904	84,716	−3,852	12,400	−11,648	−16,712	−25,656	−16,536
FIN	58	−62,175	−55,124	592,938	−76,232	16,492	−75,237	−15,538	−116,248	−113,201	−49,431
FRA	58	−497,947	−571,272	−115,632	−857,273	−92,825	−573,437	444,445	1,055,842	513,070	202,812
GER	58	−356,163	−438,754	−370,276	−966,519	−611,185	−1,083,490	250,847	757,203	3,351,668	668,252
GANA	58	−15,946	22,272	28,307	161,906	−19,429	−16,411	−6,761	−67,046	−44,252	−18,487
GRCE	58	−54,370	−2,345	−35,286	20,773	−34,125	68,438	−8,821	−88,382	−172,941	−47,010
HOND	58	−4,837	2,044	5,022	46,932	1,828	1,566	−7,024	−15,968	−16,663	−8,048
HOKO	60	−30,612	1,464	−33,674	−47,304	−96,673	−131,352	208,973	−45,451	−102,653	−50,493
ICE	58	−11,640	−2,257	−7,476	−5,326	49,803	8,777	−6,725	−19,174	−22,366	−4,269
INDA	58	−150,612	8,397	−41,972	322,081	26,397	−295,635	2,210	244,647	−533,601	−127,808

NAME	YEAR	GNP	CAPITAL	LABOR 1	LABOR 2	LABOR 3	LABOR 4	LAND 1	LAND 2	LAND 3	LAND 4	COAL	MINERALS	OIL
AFG	60	2,815.0	195	100.71	141.3	4,579		0	45,325	0	0	470	1,971	0
ARG	58	13,944.5	11,222	443.29	6,406.2	847		0	97,191	152,729	0	1,331	24,841	78,178
AUSL	58	13,742.4	17,084	301.13	3,629.1	48		85,324	557,297	126,064	0	312,986	242,307	0
AUST	58	5,257.5	5,850	210.72	3,125.8	41		0	0	3,310	6,186	64,957	20,087	44,115
BLUX	58	10,890.2	9,320	397.68	3,182.5	92		804,381	0	0	0	264,937	15,257	822
BRAZ	58	17,900.2	13,395	597.87	10,973.8	9,857		67,803	12,768	34,048	0	12,844	96,612	39,616
BRMA	58	1,318.6	673	222.07	6,227.9	3,837		0	0	0	0	0	11,754	7,226
CAN	58	33,903.1	44,229	639.12	5,442.1	118		0	39,905	0	727,560	103,803	622,799	383,429
CHLE	58	4,224.6	2,258	119.45	1,884.4	419		31,572	20,922	12,470	0	17,896	292,317	13,476

Table B.1 (continued)

NAME	YEAR	GNP	CAPITAL	LABOR 1	LABOR 2	LABOR 3	LAND 1	LAND 2	LAND 3	LAND 4	COAL	MINERALS	OIL
CLUM	58	3,189.8	3,153	133.71	2,927.7	1,441	101,363	2,278	0	0	23,888	5,578	97,575
CSTA	58	430.5	338	12.81	278.9	62	5,070	0	0	0	0	344	0
CYPR	60	300.4	340	13.17	167.7	57	0	0	925	0	23,937	23,968	0
DEN	58	4,971.1	3,971	142.76	1,913.3	25	0	0	4,307	0	0	381	0
DORE	58	710.1	685	23.66	498.2	317	4,873	0	0	0	0	699	0
ECUA	58	795.6	553	36.02	816.1	492	17,893	0	0	0	0	281	6,465
EGPT	60	4,103.2	545	230.96	1,709.7	5,438	0	100,145	0	0	0	6,853	49,868
LSAL	58	552.0	257	17.85	344.7	420	2,104	0	0	0	0	573	0
FIN	58	4,036.3	4,306	151.07	1,841.7	24	0	0	0	0	0	32,627	0
FRA	58	58,263.1	61,620	1,579.02	17,731.0	354	0	0	54,703	33,701	793	271,668	23,633
GER	58	55,120.1	57,766	1,711.54	22,831.4	298	0	0	16,637	8,094	587,782	165,492	70,210
GANA	58	1,086.4	664	50.03	629.3	1,954	23,854	0	0	0	2,401,076	33,998	0
GRCE	58	3,136.9	2,594	107.02	2,799.8	796	0	0	13,194	0	0	18,833	0
HOND	58	357.9	248	17.91	224.5	323	6,138	0	0	0	11,699	1,343	0
HOKO	60	988.9	747	53.68	775.8	356	0	0	104	0	0	0	0
ICE	58	201.8	249	6.85	73.2	1	0	0	4,120	0	0	682	0
INDA	58	29,798.0	15,340	2,547.26	42,978.3	135,131	140,076	95,429	73,384	0	450,957	175,747	6,778

NAME	YEAR	AGG1	AGG2	AGG3	AGG4	AGG5	AGG6	AGG7	AGG8	AGG9	AGG10
INDO	60	195,121	47,629	−19,578	441,084	−902	−53,654	−5,948	−207,340	0	0
IRE	58	−46,654	−31,165	−20,140	−10,454	182,650	−45,402	−19,996	−64,733	−107,690	−39,606
ISRL	58	−46,714	−10,436	−22,910	40,296	−23,856	−72,546	10,109	−39,030	−109,758	−14,532
ITLY	58	−285,158	−417,116	−181,244	181,981	−292,225	−405,393	167,968	320,452	325,964	−27,966
JAMC	60	−15,988	70,831	−12,438	61,815	−18,420	−21,203	−14,930	−37,009	−54,352	−15,732
JAP	58	−407,865	−416,354	27,671	−221,573	122,469	−1,020,362	440,212	1,023,410	316,942	−28,485
KORA	58	−34,745	−1,517	−28,159	−18,699	123	−97,893	−7,621	−25,773	0	0
LIBR	60	−2,788	35,577	−812	37,415	−2,415	−2,771	−6,967	−12,358	−23,332	−2,424
LIBY	60	−6,337	−793	−2,646	−8,073	1,150	−5,526	−10,620	−30,220	−70,975	−12,191
MALY	60	−45,347	165,149	3,201	508,511	−42,274	−60,854	−44,743	−80,681	−104,282	−40,780
MLTA	60	−5,760	980	−1,520	−7,803	−8,751	−8,025	−4,573	−10,729	−11,891	−4,113
MAUR	60	−2,709	−714	−1,911	32,361	−4,179	−12,621	−7,413	−13,881	−12,957	−6,888
MEX	58	−9,531	113,650	−23,456	86,462	64,276	57,759	−15,465	88,941	−502,276	−137,214
NETH	58	−123,232	−155,034	−121,917	54,440	532,287	−360,026	−89,469	−35,081	−190,880	72,573
NUZE	58	−55,569	−21,974	−8,151	−33,043	388,816	219,590	−47,846	−189,987	−216,835	−48,443
NIGR	60	−19,136	−5,833	14,370	119,982	−14,666	196,362	−72,781	−166,803	−144,590	−16,884
NOR	58	−98,880	44,263	138,622	−98,740	127,863	−24,198	−44,113	−123,461	−487,443	−1,036
PANM	58	−9,388	216	−3,110	17,154	816	−5,436	−7,055	−16,938	−20,289	−7,004

NAME	YEAR	GNP	CAPITAL	LABOR 1	LABOR 2	LABOR 3	LAND 1	LAND 2	LAND 3	LAND 4	COAL	MINERALS	OIL
PGRY	58	-2,980	-1,360		9,110	923	9,560		1,897	0	-5,630	-5,768	2,770
PERU	58	5,231	109,614		-10,936	46,519	-5,478		43,678	-3,853	-43,969	-129,821	-33,666
PLIP	58	-37,259	28,198		61,963	139,700	-54,824		133,636	-14,598	-100,669	-132,034	-34,686
PORT	58	-34,875	-19,230		59,686	15,300	25,722		-70,008	1,367	-17,241	-125,642	-27,095
SRIL	58	-27,120	-5,419		-3,115	267,799	-32,278		-52,318	-22,669	-61,500	-54,079	-18,184
SING	60	-65,008	-826		-11,316	17,033	-20,057		-49,607	19,663	-41,614	-35,477	-13,729
SPAN	58	-128,328	-34,729		-16,490	192,405	-24,027		-132,924	4,102	-32,506	-153,075	-61,291
SWE	58	-309,549	31,840		673,417	-212,081	-7,007		-89,596	-99,131	-139,295	-23,352	-103,611

NAME	YEAR	GNP	CAPITAL	LABOR 1	LABOR 2	LABOR 3	LAND 1	LAND 2	LAND 3	LAND 4	COAL	MINERALS	OIL
INDO	60	8,600	4,381	768.57	11,345.2	20,626.8	167,202	0	0	0	6,442	93,296	331,698
IRE	58	1,649	1,189	77.02	1,058.6	13.8	0	0	7,028	0	25,199	384	0
ISRL	58	1,967	2,720	85.08	496.3	127.6	0	1,345	724	0	0	3,227	1,340
ITLY	58	29,344	24,534	891.56	17,222.0	2,057.4	0	0	19,972	4,127	14,049	95,604	43,633
JAMC	60	644	718	30.31	468.3	109.4	1,096	0	0	0	0	96,208	0
JAP	58	31,531	38,404	1,832.70	39,719.7	675.6	0	0	23,083	14,148	501,796	140,951	7,340
KORA	58	4,144	2,675	195.02	5,558.2	2,372.8	0	0	3,644	6,204	26,149	6,927	0
LIBR	60	178	62	10.26	26.9	394.8	11,137	0	0	0	0	30,415	0
LIBY	60	335	150	11.40	62.6	296.0	0	175,954	0	0	0	0	0
MALY	60	2,123	275	95.11	1,255.0	1,382.9	13,159	0	0	0	69	146,550	0
MLTA	60	144	121	9.66	63.8	24.5	0	0	32	0	0	0	0
MAUR	60	137	177	7.74	2.3	190.0	186	0	0	0	0	11	0
MEX	58	10,176	9,153	346.72	6,197.9	3,713.4	61,814	104,763	0	0	14,391	185,377	210,589
NETH	58	9,457	10,834	348.51	3,745.8	49.7	0	0	3,613	0	118,802	9,111	24,343
NUZE	58	3,178	4,044	76.41	762.4	10.2	0	0	26,868	0	27,060	263	10
NIGR	60	3,340	1,606	410.85	2,367.6	15,744.5	92,377	0	0	0	5,590	16,607	13,633
NOR	58	4,012	6,842	100.24	1,283.0	16.8	0	0	11,179	18,448	2,849	23,909	0
PANM	58	371	272	15.71	224.5	94.8	7,565	0	0	0	0	69	0
PGRY	58	273	171	15.07	361.2	150.7	23,998	0	16,677	0	0	0	0
PERU	58	1,649	1,966	63.22	1,644.5	288.3	64,261	25,190	0	0	2,183	116,773	40,756
PLIP	58	5,606	4,021	250.85	7,244.7	2,498.5	30,000	0	0	0	1,057	35,636	0
PORT	58	2,153	1,487	83.71	1,932.7	305.5	0	178	8,716	0	7,078	11,758	0
SRIL	58	1,238	885	136.66	2,076.1	980.3	6,561	0	0	0	0	206	0
SING	60	715	80	29.32	319.1	187.6	58	0	0	0	0	0	0
SPAN	58	13,079	13,165	444.29	9,227.5	1,720.2	0	4,543	45,935	0	167,575	101,744	0
SWE	58	11,201	13,063	369.40	2,793.2	38.4	0	0	0	40,496	3,123	133,365	0

Table B.1 (continued)

NAME	YEAR	AGG1	AGG2	AGG3	AGG4	AGG5	AGG6	AGG7	AGG8	AGG9	AGG10
SWIT	58	−125,587	−75,798	−32,709	−158,460	−39,128	−192,607	−32,333	−48,333	413,551	132,205
THAI	60	−48,233	20,817	9,129	132,541	5,920	161,223	−20,606	−132,419	−118,477	−45,711
TURK	58	−40,348	28,467	−11,746	54,204	6,848	99,698	−11,468	−50,514	−110,855	−32,131
UK	58	−932,915	−576,333	−868,092	−1,530,900	−1,621,966	−1,665,225	561,647	1,307,577	3,324,624	401,329
US	58	−1,097,693	−437,049	−945,785	−2,219,942	−606,331	2,483,841	377,290	848,628	5,543,967	1,230,064
YUG	60	−13,614	−1,497	48,626	−152	63,034	−26,192	23,554	−68,193	−233,042	−48,481
AFG	72	−6,518	16,953	−449	24,082	24,685	10,776	−951	−18,780	−13,354	−8,143
ARG	75	−290,377	−533,545	−280,855	142,170	321,733	1,482,531	−22,317	−700,758	−480,569	−622,896
AUSL	75	−729,183	3,577,839	−340,530	663,183	1,120,086	3,053,162	−980,064	−514,166	−3,438,718	−366,067
AUST	75	−775,752	−554,678	514,260	−358,449	−4,638	−192,514	59,993	576,243	−873,539	−265,019
BLUX	75	−1,879,851	−1,883,563	−359,957	−512,980	222,373	−933,779	310,149	3,720,583	−1,059,099	945,864
BRAZ	75	−3,131,393	285,913	−14,254	2,415,743	98,948	1,418,083	365,651	−1,109,389	−3,683,624	−1,554,629
BRMA	72	−6,505	4,569	26,692	12,867	−3,505	55,298	−4,630	−45,163	−66,882	−14,052
CAN	75	−83,558	4,675,575	4,154,816	−1,293,199	238,493	2,503,998	−2,171,806	−1,800,662	−7,168,515	−708,689
CHLE	72	−76,594	692,605	19,093	−30,673	−102,061	−88,039	−38,926	−76,848	−298,609	−89,680
CLUM	75	87,279	−47,757	−57,078	770,426	76,212	17,593	49,302	−75,192	−578,087	−272,583
CSTA	75	−71,383	−12,660	−45,674	292,537	32,516	−37,548	−15,650	−72,097	−179,567	−90,374
CYPR	75	−45,502	15,050	−13,251	41,271	−12,776	−39,889	13,412	−47,705	−38,615	−26,615
DEN	75	−1,462,329	−300,278	−437,264	−119,515	−2,244,350	−24,329	57,386	−771,286	−426,373	−423,529
DORE	69	−17,860	13,884	−13,452	134,943	−7,972	−6,250	−9,068	−37,997	−68,910	−13,528
ECUA	72	48,971	−4,549	−1,959	220,269	20,022	−26,690	−11,884	−52,349	−137,698	−42,953
EGPT	75	−57,476	−149,824	−275,859	−53,197	−69,608	−573,914	37,808	−124,604	−808,916	−456,524
LSAL	72	−11,477	−3,792	−10,560	121,628	5,507	29,419	−1,054	−15,969	−73,505	−41,003
FIN	75	−1,124,150	−412,416	2,265,241	−356,665	65,487	−161,883	221,458	−687,768	−1,470,063	−449,873
FRA	75	−9,336,568	−2,944,869	−894,998	−299,209	67,420	980,340	259,424	2,257,183	6,838,689	671,282
GER	75	−10,706,121	−2,241,214	−1,636,917	−4,388,522	−2,051,564	−2,714,761	−2,274,144	6,786,680	29,810,943	5,229,252

NAME	YEAR	GNP	CAPITAL	LABOR 1	LABOR 2	LABOR 3	LABOR 4	LAND 1	LAND 2	LAND 3	LAND 4	MINERALS	COAL	OIL
SWIT	58	7,335	8,447	195.50	2,162.9	29		0	0	702		263	0	0
THAI	60	2,533	400	170.58	8,994.6	4,373		51,400		0		28,472	1,067	0
TURK	58	9,010	5,815	169.00	4,555.3	8,079			47,811	30,247		27,871	57,105	4,949
UK	58	64,716	46,668	1,528.76	22,257.3	289				24,404		47,245	2,151,568	1,434
US	58	455,000	503,860	7,731.17	59,171.8	1,575		1,800	455,510	162,587	137,929	1,249,911	3,833,353	6,345,565
YUG	60	10,496	16,691	447.56	6,174.0	1,728				3,722	21,858	341,841	222,360	14,101
AFG	72	991	377	246.96	299.6	5,664			45,325	0		593	4,795	137,970
ARG	75	49,140	69,568	807.76	8,151.0	832			97,191	152,729		77,469	17,736	2,024,558
AUSL	75	85,172	140,302	648.91	5,079.5	35		85,324	557,297	126,064		3,482,718	2,693,582	1,833,126

NAME	YEAR												
AUST	75	33,347	64,792	299.42	2,932.1	20	0	0	0	6,186	59,907	53,870	263,492
BLUX	75	59,321	93,700	464.43	3,385.7	43	0	0	3,310	0	210,573	13,274	2,470
BRAZ	75	107,479	115,654	1,965.79	20,149.4	12,494	804,381	12,768	34,048	0	83,178	1,213,019	744,832
BRMA	72	2,064	1,624	505.33	9,579.8	2,490	67,803	0	12,470	727,560	564	13,235	798,42
CAN	75	139,766	227,522	1,311.49	8,183.2	57	0	39,905	0	0	783,301	4,166,671	10,245,627
CHLE	72	11,406	10,600	162.75	2,533.7	514	31,572	20,922	0	0	47,248	1,114,926	307,271
CLUM	75	12,734	14,256	427.55	5,175.9	2,073	101,363	2,278	0	0	137,549	22,664	771,794
CSTA	75	1,864	2,306	54.21	499.3	81	5,070	0	0	0	0	234	0
CYPR	75	709	1,509	20.07	229.0	40	0	0	925	0	0	16,272	0
DEN	75	31,596	46,585	342.34	2,037.3	14	0	0	4,307	0	0	3,806	16,779
DORE	69	1,302	1,039	32.09	736.5	373	4,873	0	0	0	0	13,819	0
ECUA	72	1,775	1,823	91.77	1,243.7	626	17,893	0	0	0	0	726	304,752
EGPT	75	11,749	10,881	664.61	2,658.4	7,193	0	100,145	0	0	0	35,806	965,164
LSAL	72	1,142	985	33.63	605.7	471	2,104	0	0	0	0	452	0
FIN	75	23,770	53,987	329.71	1,902.8	13	0	0	0	0	0	135,213	
FRA	75	297,780	525,489	3,215.44	18,933.9	134	0	0	54,703	33,701	679,707	556,681	595,231
GER	75	372,844	641,369	3,376.34	24,428.8	168	0	0	16,637	8,094	4,311,699	392,395	1,312,231

NAME	YEAR	AGG1	AGG2	AGG3	AGG4	AGG5	AGG6	AGG7	AGG8	AGG9	AGG10
GANA	75	-110,345	43,519	51,786	535,540	-39,346	-49,892	-62,601	-115,952	-203,234	-109,490
GRCE	75	-871,225	-32,400	-218,083	339,889	-127,596	-101,122	209,004	-41,085	-1,872,439	-328,019
HOND	75	-56,247	27,980	23,333	126,392	22,534	-26,953	-15,613	-49,320	-116,964	-46,461
HOKO	75	-395,491	-886,639	-151,227	-341,933	-577,121	-615,989	2,463,682	-472,557	-276,991	-283,901
ICE	75	-61,628	30,202	-31,088	-27,484	212,003	12,068	-33,945	-60,812	-155,392	-64,559
INDA	75	-1,397,496	280,926	-78,327	1,071,795	212,079	-1,208,763	346,838	537,136	-695,802	-1,003,146
INDO	75	5,085,039	155,233	434,201	438,949	72,417	-285,402	-133,383	-847,852	-1,775,999	-783,424
IRE	75	-458,724	-14,006	-138,815	-38,296	1,126,348	-111,104	-30,262	-184,984	-553,779	-186,563
ISRL	75	-637,494	-114,031	-191,392	136,198	-55,008	-365,649	200,628	-312,668	-860,174	-34,639
ITLY	75	-7,295,534	-2,977,522	-974,038	741,081	-3,750,174	-2,549,647	5,332,116	3,497,922	4,996,721	-123,648
JAMC	75	-201,151	99,757	-63,210	185,925	-77,574	-127,651	-50,184	-141,189	-210,120	280,707
JAP	75	-20,839,833	-10,248,177	-3,052,227	-2,742,320	-1,923,788	-6,287,291	1,651,651	14,459,793	25,045,207	1,825,153
KORA	75	-1,243,918	-311,753	-110,129	-119,319	338,941	-961,025	1,793,976	362,507	-1,224,375	-721,283
LIBR	75	-47,949	308,783	6,088	45,128	-5,911	-24,841	-26,222	-56,130	-116,682	-19,351
LIBY	75	6,537,937	180,615	-109,305	-194,304	-126,969	-294,815	-525,006	-787,241	-1,256,404	-131,698
MALY	75	80	343,205	471,154	728,007	-29,885	346,476	-63,747	-333,955	-867,491	-258,645
MLTA	75	-35,399	-4,526	-11,668	-26,690	-22,657	-41,360	46,524	-70,056	-55,252	-21,279
MAUR	72	-9,401	-1,470	-3,407	95,905	-9,420	-21,804	-8,289	-19,981	-23,362	-13,095

Table B.1 (continued)

NAME	YEAR	AGG1	AGG2	AGG3	AGG4	AGG5	AGG6	AGG7	AGG8	AGG9	AGG10
MEX	72	-61,098	59,846	-77,098	401,101	184,025	79,138	-81,905	-25,900	-1,273,651	-294,860
NETH	75	-1,636,903	1,119,261	-824,429	508,719	3,582,415	-1,088,912	-1,738,220	-330,621	-1,310,506	2,398,994
NUZE	75	-425,799	-69,319	100,083	-103,154	1,091,817	339,736	-143,197	-492,093	-1,102,814	-297,227
NIGR	75	7,286,681	-75,565	-139,576	139,032	-156,117	-162,427	-500,774	-1,258,995	-2,645,204	-538,934
NOR	75	16,440	288,178	236,311	-364,482	427,512	-107,149	-637,555	-577,343	-1,572,706	-208,803
PANM	72	-51,607	-2,632	-23,319	62,294	4,816	-17,244	-43,735	-69,382	-132,678	-43,792
PGRY	69	-4,688	-1,061	9,220	-1,392	13,168	6,858	-3,263	-9,720	-27,353	-2,172
PERU	69	-14,479	465,325	-18,690	60,972	-35,762	203,641	-24,578	-72,685	-207,592	-90,700

NAME	YEAR	GNP	CAPITAL	LABOR 1	LABOR 2	LABOR 3	LAND 1	LAND 2	LAND 3	LAND 4	COAL	MINERALS	OIL
GANA	75	5,219	3,887	163.6	1,060.7	2,486	23,854	0	0	0	0	28,594	0
GRCE	75	21,601	31,620	249.8	2,917.3	658	0	0	13,194	0	208,316	198,568	0
HOND	75	974	1,383	44.0	426.6	434	6,138	0	0	0	0	51,157	0
HOKO	75	7,609	8,700	96.8	1,588.0	187	0	0	104	0	0	1,616	0
ICE	75	1,204	2,324	14.3	91.1	1	0	0	4,120	0	0	0	0
INDA	75	80,307	73,350	7,448.0	67,272.2	165,538	140,076	95,429	73,384	0	3,391,518	751,030	765,214
INDO	75	26,290	229	1,853.7	29,750.4	15,426	167,202	0	0	0	7,299	386,348	5,372,262
IRE	75	7,849	11,105	119.5	1,062.4	7	0	0	7,028	0	2,398	75,299	0
ISRL	75	11,490	21,006	220.5	873.9	126	0	1,345	724	0	0	86,970	293,597
ITLY	75	150,812	256,438	1,672.1	18,234.7	916	0	0	19,972	4,127	15,761	194,844	765,890
JAMC	75	2,599	3,305	45.6	530.3	96	1,096	0	0	0	0	130,984	0
JAP	75	450,588	930,860	4,438.5	52,025.7	513	0	0	23,083	14,148	666,661	412,911	165,318
KORA	75	19,069	22,982	388.2	8,746.4	3,552	0	0	3,644	6,204	539,125	67,877	0
LIBR	75	707	992	31.8	90.0	533	0	0	0	0	0	422,280	0
LIBY	75	12,319	16,111	57.8	125.6	401	11,137	0	0	0	0	156	6,520,287
MALY	75	8,312	10,225	183.4	1,945.4	1,299	13,159	0	0	0	0	494,350	0
MLTA	75	424	703	13.9	95.3	6	0	0	32	0	0	16	0
MAUR	72	271	278	16.1	0.6	249	186	0	0	0	0	78	0
MEX	72	40,410	43,750	905.6	11,042.8	3,273	61,814	104,763	0	0	127,394	676,040	2,288,397
NETH	75	72,963	121,257	763.6	4,375.4	31	0	0	0	0	0	41,964	102,859
NUZE	75	12,179	19,603	163.7	1,049.9	7	0	0	3,613	0	83,460	2,139	30,677
NIGR	75	25,379	23,686	1,116.4	5,049.8	18,499	92,377	0	26,868	0	11,072	34,973	7,820,608
NOR	75	23,769	53,475	227.5	1,284.3	9	0	0	11,179	18,448	15,373	116,760	876,719
PANM	72	1,264	1,633	35.7	344.0	100	7,565	0	0	0	0	1,585	0
PGRY	69	554	474	29.2	538.0	162	23,998	0	16,677	0	0	15,428	0
PERU	69	5,248	5,182	252.2	2,352.1	1,330	64,261	25,190	0	0	5,712	671,520	306,157

NAME	YEAR	AGG1	AGG2	AGG3	AGG4	AGG5	AGG6	AGG7	AGG8	AGG9	AGG10
PLIP	75	-776,661	295,459	207,240	746,452	-100,982	155,152	-13,506	-337,189	-1,147,337	-409,651
PORT	75	-481,784	-145,593	227,488	-45,372	-96,556	-639,608	235,194	-3,391	-741,226	-225,392
SRIL	75	-123,561	22,037	-17,173	370,553	-15,012	-283,138	36,905	-49,178	-66,485	-61,948
SING	75	-206,570	-33,293	-5,721	139,911	-110,484	-171,060	-217,069	-888,182	-993,368	-272,142
SPAN	75	-3,462,076	-1,334,393	-110,641	445,143	-326,874	-1,570,519	835,853	228,748	-1,963,141	-967,185
SWE	75	-2,626,496	-228,099	3,253,072	-781,765	-267,547	-34,688	-916,162	-54,178	1,731,380	-668,174
SWIT	75	-1,290,882	-272,537	-225,672	-735,896	-184,156	-469,918	-1,075,292	-162,641	2,769,277	1,327,176
THAI	75	-691,561	29,566	-8,213	737,019	73,126	528,515	213,709	-253,496	-1,149,755	-428,198
TURK	75	-753,222	-89,187	-41,419	236,076	74,620	172,420	78,595	-645,785	-1,650,321	-621,262
UK	75	-7,644,434	-1,767,170	-2,913,012	-2,573,301	-2,769,122	-2,192,727	-600,952	743,557	8,617,358	1,702,078
US	75	-23,858,143	498,527	-10,893	-4,987,105	-1,624,613	18,095,530	-6,187,519	-1,635,670	23,923,543	4,984,966
YUG	75	-730,530	-161,511	17,852	-230,928	168,511	-308,877	373,471	-729,358	-1,570,819	-454,561

NAME	YEAR	GNP	CAPITAL	LABOR 1	LABOR 2	LABOR 3	LAND 1	LAND 2	LAND 3	LAND 4	COAL	MINERALS	OIL
PLIP	75	15,483	19,831	898.0	12,776.7	2,025.30	30,000.0	0	0	0	3,561	421,434	0
PORT	75	15,519	16,197	137.6	2,153.2	1,123.21	0.0	178	8,716	0	7,828	31,630	0
SRIL	75	1,880	2,058	184.4	3,499.3	1,057.24	6,561.0	0	0	0	0	1,856	0
SING	75	5,663	10,025	80.9	601.5	170.60	58.0	0	0	0	0	0	0
SPAN	75	102,695	153,243	775.0	10,572.7	973.36	0.0	4,543	45,935	0	323,687	338,456	157,623
SWE	75	61,959	102,201	694.8	2,911.5	21.77	0.0	0	0	40,496	388	553,901	0
SWIT	75	49,979	95,224	429.1	2,668.2	18.70	0.0	0	702	0	0	3,697	0
THAI	75	14,332	18,883	387.7	15,274.6	3,551.70	51,400.0	47,811	30,247	0	5,395	157,757	450
TURK	75	36,526	35,773	671.9	7,514.0	155.54	0.0	0	24,404	0	277,355	110,125	241,897
UK	75	206,130	303,695	3,315.6	22,451.9	377.38	0.0	0	0	0	4,446,251	214,567	1,716,016
US	75	1,332,099	1,831,020	13,556.4	80,535.7	377.38	2,153.5	544,840	194,472	164,978	20,317,059	6,029,738	60,939,361
YUG	75	33,383	27,783	900.9	7,393.0	1,498.18	0.0	0	3,722	21,858	637,007	332,664	364,869

Table B.2
Variables and sources: country attributes

Variable	Description	Units	Primary Source
GNP	Gross national product at current market prices	Millions of U.S. dollars	World Bank, *World Tables 1976*
GDP	Gross domestic product at current market prices	Millions of U.S. dollars	World Bank, *World Tables 1976*
LABOR	Number of economically active population	Thousands	ILO, *Labor Force Projections 1965–1985*
CAPITAL	Capital stock at current market prices assuming 15 year average life of assets	Millions of U.S. dollars	Derived from World Bank, *World Tables 1976*
SKILL 1	Professional technical and related workers as a percentage of economically active population	Percentage	ILO, *Yearbook of Labour Statistics*, various years
PYRITE	Production of pyrite (sulfur content)	Metric tons	Bureau of Mines, *Minerals Yearbook*, various years
SALT	Production of salt	Thousands of metric tons	Bureau of Mines, *Minerals Yearbook*, various years
TIN	Production of tin	Metric tons	U.N., *Growth of World Industry*, various years
LEAD	Production of lead-bearing ores	Metric tons	U.N., *Growth of World Industry*, various years
OIL	Crude oil production plus production of natural gas	Thousands of U.S. dollars	American Petroleum Institute, *Petroleum Facts and Figures*, various years; U.N., *World Energy Supplies*, various years
COPPER	Production of copper-bearing ores	Metric tons	U.N., *Growth of World Industry*, various years
IRONORE	Production of iron ore (metal content)	Thousands of metric tons	U.N., *Growth of World Industry*, various years
PHOSPHATE	Production of phosphate rock (and guano)	Metric tons	Bureau of Mines, *Minerals Yearbook*, various years
BAUXITE	Production of bauxite	Thousands of metric tons	U.N., *Growth of World Industry*, various years
NICKEL	Production of nickel-bearing ores	Metric tons	U.N., *Growth of World Industry*, various years
POTASH	Production of potash (potassium oxide equivalent)	Thousands of metric tons	Bureau of Mines, *Minerals Yearbook*, various years

Table B.2 (continued)

Variable	Description	Units	Primary Source
FLUOR	Production of fluorspar	Metric tons	Bureau of Mines, *Minerals Yearbook*, various years
ZINC	Production of zinc-bearing ores	Metric tons	U.N., *Growth of World Industry*, various years
MANGANESE	Production of manganese-bearing ores	Metric tons	U.N., *Growth of World Industry*, various years
COAL	Production of primary solid fuels (coal, lignite, and brown coal) plus natural gas	Thousands of U.S. dollars	U.N., *World Energy Supplies*, various years
CLIM 1	Percentage of total country area designated as a tropical rainy climate	Percentage	U.S. Air Force, *Climatic Chart of the World*
CLIM 2	Percentage of total country area designated as a dry climate	Percentage	U.S. Air Force, *Climatic Chart of the World*
CLIM 3	Percentage of total country area designated as a humid mesothermal climate	Percentage	U.S. Air Force, *Climatic Chart of the World*
CLIM 4	Percentage of total country area designated as a humid microthermal climate	Percentage	U.S. Air Force, *Climatic Chart of the World*
CLIM 5	Percentage of country area designated as a polar climate	Percentage	U.S. Air Force, *Climatic Chart of the World*
CLIM 6	Percentage of country area designated as undifferentiated highlands	Percentage	U.S. Air Force, *Climatic Chart of the World*
LAREA	Land area	Thousands of hectares	FAO, *Production Yearbook*, various years
LIT	Literacy rate	Percentage	Banks (1973)
LABOR 1	LABOR × SKILL 1	Thousands	
LABOR 2	LABOR − LABOR 1 − LABOR 3	Thousands	
LABOR 3	LABOR × LIT	Thousands	
$LAND_j$	$LAREA \times CLIM_j$	Thousands of hectares	
MINERALS	Index of minerals (see table 4.6)	Thousands of U.S. dollars	

Table B.3
Secondary sources and notes: country attribute data[a]

1. Gross National and Domestic Product (GNP and GDP)

1958. Secondary source: all countries—U.N., *Yearbook of National Accounts Statistics*, various years.

a. For Austria, Mauritius, Portugal, and Brazil, GNP = GDP.

b. Belgium-Luxembourg includes Luxembourg.

c. Yugoslavia, GNP = GDP = gross material product.

d. Nigeria and Hong Kong estimates from World Bank data.

e. Egypt, estimate from 1959 data.

f. Liberia, Libya—GNP estimated from GNP/GDP ratio, 1960, World Bank data.

1960–1975. Secondary source: Luxembourg, Netherlands Antilles—U.N., *Yearbook of National Accounts Statistics*, were available.

1975. Secondary source: Australia, Austria, Canada, Denmark, Finland, France, Germany, Italy, Japan, Netherlands, New Zealand, Norway, Sweden, Switzerland, United Kingdom, and United States—U.N., *Yearbook of National Accounts Statistics*.

2. Labor Force (LABOR)

1958–1975.

a. Brunei, Netherlands Antilles are estimates based on trend, 1960 and 1971 data.

b. Other countries based on growth rates given in ILO, *Labor Force Projections 1965–1985*, and applied as follows:

1. 1958—used 1955–1960 rate from 1960 base.

2. 1963, 1966—used 1960–1965 rate on 1965 base.

3. 1969, 1972—used 1970–1975 rate on 1970 base.

3. Implicit GDI Deflator (PRGDI)

1958.

a. Derived from U.N., *Yearbook of National Accounts Statistics* data on nominal GDI and estimated real GDI from World Bank data.

b. For El Salvador, France, Honduras, Hong Kong, India, Indonesia, Italy, Malta, Mauritius, Mexico, Sri Lanka, and Turkey, nominal GDI derived from GDI/GDP ratio, *Chenery Data Base*.

c. For Burma, Jamaica, Japan, Nigeria, Paraguay, Philippines, and Sweden, index derived by taking change in implicit index given in U.N., *Yearbook of National Accounts Statistics*, applied to implicit 1960 index from World Bank data.

1975. Secondary source: Australia, Austria, Belgium-Luxembourg, Canada, Denmark, Finland, France, Germany, Italy, Japan, Netherlands, Norway, Sweden, Switzerland, United Kingdom, and United States—U.N., *Yearbook of National Accounts Statistics*. Series were linked where necessary.

4. Implicit GDP Deflator (PRGDP)

1958. Secondary source:

a. Netherlands Antilles, U.N., *Yearbook of National Accounts Statistics*;

b. All others derived by linking implicit GDP deflator in U.N., *Yearbook of National Accounts Statistics*.

1975. Secondary source: see (4), 1975 source.

5. Exchange Rate (CEXCH)

1958. Secondary source:

a. Average annual exchange rates (conversion factors)—IMF, *International Financial Statistics, 1972 Supplement*;

b. Iceland, Malta, Mauritius, Netherlands Antilles—U.N., *Yearbook of National Accounts Statistics*.

Turkey, average of conversion factor and 1960 buying rate.

Table B.3 (continued)

6. Pyrite

Sulfur content estimates derived from crude pyrite figures for the following: 1963, 1966, Australia, Canada, France, Greece, Italy, Japan, Philippines, Turkey, U.S., Yugoslavia; 1969, Canada; 1972, U.S. 1975. Korea—figure is for 1974.

7. Gas

1958–1975. Figures converted to coal equivalent using conversion: one thousand million cubic meters = 1,332,000 coal equivalent metric tons.

8. Salt

1963. Indonesia—estimate based on interpolation, closest available year

1966. Indonesia, Italy—estimate based on interpolation, closest available year.

9. Tin

1958–1972. All zero's obtained from Bureau of Mines, *Minerals Yearbook*.

10. Lead

1975. Secondary source: all countries, Bureau of Mines, *Minerals Yearbook*.

11. Oil Production

1975. Secondary source: all countries, Bureau of Mines, *Minerals Yearbook*.

1958–1975. Figures converted to coal equivalents using conversion: one barrel = .2127 coal equivalent metric tons.

12. Copper

1975. Secondary source: all countries, Bureau of Mines, *Minerals Yearbook*.

13. Iron Ore

1975. Secondary source: all countries, Bureau of Mines, *Minerals Yearbook*.

14. Bauxite

1975. Secondary source: all countries, Bureau of Mines, *Minerals Yearbook*.

15. Nickel

1975. Secondary source: all countries, Bureau of Mines, *Minerals Yearbook*.

16. Manganese

1975. Secondary source: all countries, Bureau of Mines, *Minerals Yearbook*. Figures derived from gross amounts and yields.

17. Coal

1975. Secondary source: all countries, Bureau of Mines, *Minerals Yearbook*.

a. Data were converted to coal equivalent tons by use of conversion factors in U.N., *World Energy Supplies*.

b. Korea and Norway—figures are for 1974.

18. Gross Domestic Investment (GDIGDP)

1975. Secondary source: Australia, Austria, Canada, Denmark, Finland, France, Germany, Italy, Japan, Netherlands, New Zealand, Norway, Sweden, Switzerland, United Kingdom, United States—U.N., *Yearbook of National Accounts Statistics*.

a. Citation of the World Bank, *World Tables 1976*, as a primary or secondary source refers in general only to the following countries: Australia, Austria, Canada, Denmark, Finland, France, Germany, Italy, Japan, The Netherlands, New Zealand, Norway, Sweden, Switzerland, the United Kingdom, and the United States. Data on remaining countries were taken, as much as possible, from that appearing in the associated *Economic Data Sheet I—National Accounts and Prices*, derived from the World Bank's *Economic and Social Data Bank Master File* which was generously supplied by the staff of the Economic and Social Data Division of the World Bank.

Also excluded are government outlays for construction and durable goods for military purposes.

Ideally, estimates of the net stock of capital would be obtained by using disaggregated investment series with the appropriate depreciation and deflation factors, such as that done by Kendrick (1976) in his estimation of the U.S. capital stock. However, data limitations make such an approach impossible in the present study. The alternative is to use aggregate gross investment flows along with assumptions concerning the average life of the assets in order to arrive at rough estimates. This approach assumes away relative price changes, which would cause revaluations of existing assets, and it also ignores the possibility that some countries may concentrate their investments on either short- or long-lived assets.

The basic data for computing the capital stocks were taken from World Bank National Accounts data sheets, which provided figures in domestic currency on gross domestic investment (GDI) in both real and nominal terms. Data were given for 1950 and 1955 and yearly for the period 1960–1975. Average annual growth rates of real GDI computed over the subperiods 1950–1955 and 1955–1960 were used to obtain yearly data between 1948 and 1959. To check the effect of the missing investment data, we compared the resultant capital stock figures with figures based on complete series for the countries with adequate national income accounts. No appreciable differences in the statistical conclusions seemed to arise. Implicit GDI deflators were computed directly from the data given in 1960, 1963, 1966, 1969, 1972, and 1975. Data on nominal GDI in 1958 were obtained by using the GDI share in GDP from the Chenery and Syrquin (1975) data set and the associated GDP figure.

In order to use these figures to form estimates of capital stocks, it is necessary to translate them into a common currency and to select an asset life and a rate of depreciation. Three different asset lives were considered— 10, 15, and 20 years—but because the asset life seemed to make little difference in the statistical analysis and because the longer life causes missing data problems, the asset life of 15 years was selected. The corresponding rate of depreciation commensurate with the double declining balance method is 13.3%.

A critical issue is how to translate GDI in home currency into the common currency, the U.S. dollar. Three alternative formulas based on the following data are possible:

I_t = gross domestic investment in year t in units of home currency;

P_t^b = implicit gross domestic investment deflator at time t with base year b, $P_b^b = 1.0$;

e_t = exchange rate in time period t, dollars per unit of home currency;

δ = rate of depreciation.

The first formula accumulates the GDI in home currency and then converts it into dollars at the current exchange rate. The real capital stock at the end of year t in year b home currency is

$$K_{it}^b = \sum_{j=0}^{t} (1 - \delta)^{t-j}(I_j/P_j^b).$$

This stock evaluated at base year prices is converted to current home prices by multiplying by P_t^b, which is converted into U.S. dollars by multiplying by e_t to form capital stock in current U.S. dollars:

$$K_{1t}^\$ = K_t^b P_t^b e_t.$$

One defect of this method is that exchange rate changes that are not offset by price changes can cause substantial changes in this measurement of the capital stock. A more stable measure, which is probably more suitable in a period of great exchange rate variability, is

$$K_{2t}^\$ = K_t^b P_t^b(\$)e_b,$$

where $P_t^b(\$)$ is the U.S. implicit GDI deflator. If exchange rate variability compensated exactly for differential rates of inflation, we would have $P_t^b e_t = P_t^b(\$)e_b$, and these two measures would be the same.

A third possibility is to convert the investment flows year by year into dollars and to use the U.S. GDI deflator to convert to constant dollars:

$$K_{3t} = P_t^b(\$) \sum_{j=0}^{t} (1 - \delta)^{t-j}(I_j e_j/P_j^b(\$)).$$

This method implicitly treats the bundle of investment goods in each country as if it were the same. It, like $K_{2t}^\$$, is relatively unaffected by exchange rate gyrations. The formula that is actually used to construct the CAPITAL data is K_{1t}^b, though some study of K_{2t}^b indicates little difference in the statistical conclusions drawn from these two numbers. Balassa (1979) uses the same formulation.

Of all the variables included in this study, CAPITAL is the one that causes this author the greatest discomfort, both for conceptual and measurement reasons. But the problem of translating home currency figures into dollars exists also for GNP. In retrospect, the substantial work done by Kravis, Heston, and Summers (1978a, b), Kravis et al. (1975), and Summers, Kravis, and Heston (1980) at translating GNP figures into dollars using purchasing power parities could have been of considerable value.

SKILL 1, LABOR   Data on the number of economically active people in ISCO major labor force group 0/1 were taken from various issues of the *Yearbook of Labor Statistics* published annually by the International Labor Office. The composition of this group is described in table 4.9. These data are derived from national sources based on industrial censuses and labor force sample surveys. Due to the intermittent nature of these data, observations for the years under study were often unavailable and had to be estimated or imputed. Utilizing the available data, the occupational shares were estimated on the basis of trend regression equations. The specification of the relation (for example, log-linear) in each category was chosen after visual examination of the data for each country. Table B.4 lists, for each country, the years upon which the estimates were based. Although the time span between observations for some countries is large, the relative stability of the share data in the observed years suggests that the estimates can be considered as acceptable. Of course, this applies mainly to interpolation as opposed to extrapolation. For countries with missing data altogether, skill ratios were imputed from a regression of skill ratios on capital per man. The data set includes imputed skill ratios for Afghanistan, Burma, Honduras, Indonesia, Iceland, Liberia, Libya, Cyprus, Jamaica, and Nigeria.

CLIM   The classification of climate used here is a simplified and otherwise modified version of the Köppen (1931) classification as given by Trewartha (1943). This quantitative system of classification defines climatic boundaries based on numerical values of temperature and rainfall. The simplified classification involves 5 major climates with 12 subclimates. Table 4.11 gives the 6 major climate types employed in this research (variable name is indicated in parentheses) and indicates the subclimates that comprise each type. In order to use this classification, it was necessary to obtain, for each country, the percentage of its area of each climate type. Unfortunately, no published data of this kind could be

Table B.4
Occupational data availability

Country	Years data available
Australia	1966, 1971
Austria	1961, 1971, 1974, 1975
Argentina	1960, 1970
Belgium-Luxembourg	1961, 1970
Brazil	1960, 1970
Brunei	1960, 1971
Canada	1961, 1970, 1971, 1975, 1976
Chile	1960, 1971
Colombia	1964, 1973
Costa Rica	1963, 1973
Denmark	1960, 1965, 1970
Dominican Republic	1960, 1970
Ecuador	1962, 1974
Egypt	1960, 1966
El Salvador	1961, 1971
Finland	1960, 1970, 1975
France	1962, 1968
Germany	1961, 1970
Ghana	1960, 1970
Greece	1961, 1971
Hong Kong	1961, 1966, 1971, 1976
India	1961, 1971
Ireland	1961, 1966, 1971
Israel	1961, 1964, 1969, 1973, 1975
Italy	1961, 1964, 1965, 1971
Japan	1960, 1964, 1965, 1970, 1974, 1975
Korea	1960, 1964, 1966, 1968, 1970, 1974, 1975
Malaysia (Peninsula)	1957, 1970
Malta	1957, 1967
Mauritius	1962, 1972
Mexico	1960, 1970, 1975
Netherlands	1960, 1971
Netherlands Antilles	1960, 1972
New Zealand	1961, 1966, 1971
Norway	1960, 1970, 1974, 1975
Panama	1960, 1970
Paraguay	1962, 1972
Peru	1961, 1972
Philippines	1960, 1965, 1970, 1974, 1975
Portugal	1960, 1970
Sri Lanka	1963, 1971
Singapore	1951, 1970, 1974, 1975

Table B.4 (continued)

Country	Years data available
Spain	1960, 1969, 1970
Sweden	1960, 1965, 1970, 1974, 1975
Switzerland	1960, 1970
Thailand	1960, 1970, 1973
Turkey	1960, 1965, 1970
United Kingdom	1966, 1971
United States	1960, 1969, 1970, 1974, 1975
Yugoslavia	1961, 1971

located. As a consequence, the percentages were estimated based on the delineation of the climate regions on a climatic map of the world. To measure the percentages a planimeter was used. This device is specifically designed to measure area contained within irregular boundaries and is a standard tool of geographers. For each region within a country corresponding to a climate type, three measurements were taken and then averaged. The resulting numbers were normalized to sum to one across climate types and treated as percentages applicable to measurements of total land area.

MINERALS, OIL, and COAL   The minerals composite is formed from a list of minerals identified in table 4.6. Conversion factors into metric tons are 1 metric ton = .984196 long ton = 1.1023 short ton = 2,204.6 pounds = (35.31/1.332) cubic meters. Manganese, which is measured in long ton units (LTU), is converted to pounds by 1 LTU = 220 pounds; for potash (K_2O), 1 unit K_2O = 33.61 pounds; for OIL, 1 barrel = .2127 coal equivalent tons.

The price of Arabian medium grade oil was taken from *The Petroleum Economist*, volume 42 (1975), #9 (p. 358) and #11 (p. 438); and volume 25 (1958), #1–12. The price of natural gas was taken from Braeutigan (1981). All other prices are from the *Minerals Yearbooks*.

Trade Data

Data were collected on the net exports of each country in each sample year, at the 1- and 2-digit levels of the Standard International Trade Classification, Revised (SITC). For a complete description of the SITC categories, see Statistical Office of the United Nations, *Standard Interna-*

Table B.5
Correspondence between
original SITC and SITC revised

ORIGINAL	REVISED
026	06
311	32
312	33
313	33
314	34
315	35
412	42
413	43
591	57
599-01	58
599-02	59
671	68
672	66
673	89
681	67

tional Trade Classification, Revised, series M, No. 2, 1961. All trade flow data were derived from United Nations sources and converted to thousands of U.S. dollars. Data for 1958 were taken from the U.N. publications *Commodity Trade Statistics, Series D* and *Yearbook of International Trade Statistics* in various years. Data for 1975 were taken, in general, from the U.N. Trade Data tapes, although exceptions may be noted. Conversion factors ($/unit foreign), used to convert the trade data to dollars, were taken directly from the U.N. sources.

Primarily due to a change in the SITC classification around 1960, some reclassification was necessary in order to make the data comparable across years. In addition, a comparison between *Yearbook* and *Series D* data indicated anomalies that required some adjustment. Data for most countries in 1958 and 1960 required reclassification from the original SITC classification to the revised. At the 2-digit level this required minor modification from the existing classification. Table B.5 indicates the concordance used to reclassify the data. In addition, a few countries reported data on principal commodities that then had to be classified according to the SITC. These adjustments are noted in table B.6, where they apply. Further adjustments were required due to the apparent omissions in reporting at the 2-digit level, particularly in the early years, of data appearing in the U.N. *Yearbooks*. One-digit section totals were often

Table B.6

Trade data notes

Afghanistan
1960. (a) Imports: divisions 05, 07, 55, 67, 69, 86, and 89 based on 1966 percentages. (b) Exports: division 89 based on 1966 percentages.

Argentina
1958. (a) Exports: sections 1 and 6 based on 1963 percentages. (b) Imports: section 6 and division 12 based on 1963 percentages.

Brazil
1958. (a) Imports: section 1 estimated from 1961 percentages. (b) Exports: sections 5, 7, and 8 estimated from 1961 percentages.

Brunei
1958. (a) Imports: sections 1, 4, and 5 estimated from 1963 percentages. (b) Imports: section 5 and divisions 22, 25, 26, 27, 28, and 29 based on 1963 percentages.

Chile
1958. (a) Data reclassified to SITC revised based on principal commodities. (b) Exports: section 1 and division 42 based on 1963 percentages. (c) Imports: section 1 based on 1963 percentages.

Colombia
1958. (a) Imports: original division 59 allocated based on 1964 percentages to 57 and 59. (b) Exports: section 6 based on 1959 percentages; section 5 based on 1960 percentages.

Costa Rica
1958. (a) Imports: sections 1, 2, 4, and divisions 00, 32, 33, 34, 58, 83, 84, and 85 based on 1966 percentages. (b) Exports: sections 4–8 and divisions 01, 03, 21, 22, 23, 24, 27, 28, and 29 based on 1966 percentages.

Cyprus
1958. (a) Imports: original division 59 allocated to revised 57, 58, and 59 based on 1969 percentages. (b) Exports: original division 68 allocated to 67 and 68 based on 1969 percentages.

Dominican Republic
1958. (a) Imports: data reclassified from principal commodity to SITC revised, section 4 and divisions 61, 62, and 64 based on 1968 percentages. (b) Exports: sections 3–8 based on 1963 percentages.

Ecuador
1958. (a) Exports: sections 5 and 6 based on 1959 percentages. (b) Imports: divisions 82, 83, 84, 85, and 89 based on 1969 percentages.

Egypt
1958. (a) Imports: original division 59 allocated to 57, 58, and 59 based on 1962 percentages. (b) Exports: sections 1 and 5 based on 1962 percentages.

El Salvador
1958. (a) Imports: section 4 and divisions 83, 85, and 89 based on 1960 percentages. (b) Exports: divisions 42, 82, 83, 85, and 89 based on 1960 percentages.

Honduras
1958. (a) Imports: sections 2 and 4 based on 1963 percentages. (b) Exports: section 8 and division 12 based on 1963 percentages.

India
1958. (a) Imports: sections 1 and 4 and divisions 01, 05, 06, 09, 21, 29, 52, 55, 57, 61, 63, 64, 81, 82, and 86 based on 1960 percentages. (b) Exports: section 7 and divisions 00–05, 09, 22, 24, 43, 51, 52, 53, 54, 59, 62–66, 68, 69, 81–84, 86, and 89 based on 1960 percentages.

Indonesia
1960. (a) original division 59 allocated to 57, 58 and 59 based on 1967 percentages.

Jamaica
1958. (a) Exports: sections 3, 4, and 5 based on 1959 percentages; section 8 and divisions 64, 65, 66, and 69 based on 1963 percentages.

Table B.6 (continued)

Korea
1958. (a) Imports: section 3 based on 1963 percentages.

Libya
1958. (a) Imports: sections 1 and 4 based on 1963 percentages. (b) Exports: section 1 based on 1963 percentages.

Malaysia (West)
1958. Series D data were given for Malaysia and Singapore combined. *Yearbook* data in later (1960) gave 1958 data separately. The *Yearbook* data were retained except for the following divisions for which Malaysia's share in each category from 1960 series D data were used to derive 1958 figures: imports—00, 09, 21, 24, 25, 26, 27, 32, 41, 42, 43, 53, 57, 61, 63, 81, 82, 83, and 85; exports—00, 02, 06, 09, 21, 25, 32, 41, 43, 51, 52, 53, 54, 55, 56, 57, 58, 59, 61, 62, 63, 64, 66, 69, 81, 82, 83, 84, 85, 86, and 89.

Malta
1958. (a) Imports: divisions 24 and 26, based on 1963 percentages. (b) Exports: sections 3–8 based on 1959 percentages.

Nigeria
1958. (a) Exports: sections 1, 3, 5, and 8 based on 1960 percentages; section 1 based on 1954 percentages.

Panama
1958. (a) Imports: sections 2 and 4 and divisions 03, 06, 07, 08, and 09 based on 1963 percentages. (b) Exports: sections 2–8 and divisions 01, 02, 06, 07, and 08 based on 1963 percentages.

Paraguay
1958. Data classified to SITC revised from principal commodity.

Peru
1958. Data classified to SITC revised from principal commodity.

Philippines
1958. (a) Imports: section 4 based on 1963 percentages. (b) Exports: section 8 based on 1963 percentages.

Sri Lanka
1958. (a) Imports: section 4 based on 1963 percentages. (b) Exports: sections 5–8 based on 1963 percentages.

Singapore
1958. See Malaysia. The following sections were based on 1960 series D percentages: exports—00, 01, 08, 09, 21, 24, 25, 26, 27, 28, 32, 34, 35, 41, 43, 51, 52, 53, 54, 55, 56, 57, 58, 59, 61, 62, 63, 64, 66, 81, 82, 83, 85, 86; imports—00, 09, 01, 21, 24, 25, 26, 27, 28, 32, 34, 45, 41, 43, 52, 53, 56, 57, 61, 62, 63, 66, 81, 82, 83, 85.

Spain
1958. (a) Imports: divisions 00, 08, 09, 11, 29, 41, 43, 52, 57, 58, 59, 61, 62, 63, 81–85, and 89 based on 1963 percentages. (b) Exports: divisions 00, 01, 06, 08, 09, 21, 41, 43, 52, 54, 56, 57, 58, 59, 61, 62, 64, 73, 81, 82, 83, 85, and 86 based on 1963 percentages.

Switzerland
1958. (a) Exports: sections 3–8 and divisions 00, 03, 04, 05, 06, 08, 09, 11, 21, 23, 24, 25, 27, 28, and 29 derived by using SITC section totals given in 1958 *Yearbook* and allocations on basis of 1960 percentage composition. Remainder of divisions obtained from principal commodity list. (b) Imports: sections 3–8 and divisions 03, 08, 09, 12, 21, 23, 25, 28, and 29 derived by using SITC section totals given in 1958 *Yearbook* and allocating on basis of 1960 percentage composition. Remainder of divisions obtained from principal commodity list.

Thailand
1958. (a) Imports: original division 59 allocated to 57, 58, and 59 based on 1968 percentages; section 4 based on 1963 percentages. (b) Exports: original division 67 allocated to 66, 68, and 89 based on 1968 percentages; sections 3, 5, 7, and 8 based on 1963 percentages.

given and some 2-digit division breakdowns, but cross reference to the closest available year of the *Series D* clearly showed trade in particular categories. These omissions were partially remedied by using division (2-digit) shares for the closest available year and allocating the section totals. These adjustments are noted in table B.6.

Trade Accounting Systems

The analysis of trade structure in a cross-country framework raises issues concerning the measurement of trade flows that do not arise in a country specific framework. These issues arise due to the differences in the systems used to record the value of external transactions.

In general, there are two systems in use to record international transactions, the general and special trade systems, which use different definitions of the statistical boundary. Under the general trade system, any commodity that crosses the national frontier of the country is recorded. Under the special trade system, any commodity that crosses the customs boundary is recorded. Neither system records "direct transit trade," which refers to the movement of commodities across national frontiers solely for transport reasons. In order to understand how trade flows recorded under these two systems could affect our analysis, we shall need to consider each system in more detail.

In the general trade system exports consist of the following:

1. exports of national produce;
2. exports from customs bounded manufacturing plants;
3. nationalized exports;
4. exports from customs bonded warehouses and free areas.

In addition, some countries choose to further classify exports as

A. national exports—which consist of
1. exports of national produce and
2. exports from customs bonded manufacturing plants;
B. reexports—which consists of
3. nationalized exports and
4. exports from customs bonded warehouses and free areas.

National exports are considered to be those commodities that have had value added by the domestic economy. Thus national exports consist of not only goods produced solely domestically but also commodities that were imported but have undergone some transformation. Reexports consist of commodities that were imported and then exported in essentially the same physical condition. Imports under the general trade system consist of

1. imports entering directly for home consumption or use,

2. imports into customs bonded manufacturing plants, and

3. imports into customs bonded warehouses and free areas.

The exports from (and imports into) customs-bonded warehouses and free areas is what is commonly called entrepôt trade. Despite the passive meaning of the word entrepôt, this type of trade can represent an important economic activity in many countries. Thus warehousing, repacking, blending, and other simple processing of goods (not involving a transformation of the commodity) all contribute to the GDP of the domestic industry.

The primary difference between the general trade system and the special trade system is that in the special trade system entrepôt trade is excluded. Thus exports under the special trade system consist of

1. exports of national produce,

2. exports from customs-bonded manufacturing plants, and

3. nationalized exports,

which imports consist of

1. imports entered directly for home consumption or use,

2. imports into customs-bonded manufacturing plants, and

3. commodities withdrawn (inward) from customs-bonded warehouse and free areas.

This exclusion of entrepôt trade from the special trade system means that under identical conditions, recorded exports (imports) would be less than those under the general trade system. In terms of net exports this means that the special trade system biases downward the volume of net exports relative to the general trade system. The extent of this bias would appear

Table B.7
Trade-reporting systems

Special-special	General-general	National-general	National-special
Argentina	Afghanistan	Burma	Brazil
Austria	Australia	Cyprus	Honduras
Belgium-Luxembourg	Canada	India	
Brunei	Denmark	Ireland	
Chile	Dominican Republic	Jamaica	
Colombia	Ecuador	Libya	
Costa Rica	Finland	Malta	
Egypt	Ghana	Mauritius	
El Salvador	Hong Kong	New Zealand	
France	Japan	Nigeria	
Germany	Malaysia	Panama	
Greece	Mexico	Sri Lanka	
Iceland	Norway	Sierra Leone	
Indonesia	Philippines	Thailand	
Israel	Singapore	United Kingdom	
Italy	Sweden	United States	
Korea			
Liberia			
Netherlands			
Netherlands Antilles			
Paraguay			
Peru			
Portugal			
Spain			
Switzerland			
Turkey			
Yugoslavia			

to depend on the amount of value added in entrepôt trade. While the differences between the two systems as regards entrepôt is not expected to be of major importance, there is another problem. Some countries that record transactions under the general trade system report only national exports. As a result, computed net exports tend to be biased downward, since the country records all its imports, but only a fraction of its exports. Not only does this bias downward the measure of a particular country's net exports, but it also biases downward this country's net exports relative to those of the countries reporting on the special and "full" (national exports plus reexports) general system. For this reason, reexports were added to national exports where possible.

Table B.7 indicates the 1969 trade reporting systems. Twenty-seven countries reported special exports and special imports and thus, potentially, exclude value added in entrepôt activity. Two peculiar countries (Brazil and Honduras) reported special imports and national exports. This biases their trade down further than would otherwise be the case, since commodities that would have been recorded as nationalized exports have been excluded. For the 32 countries that report under the general trade system, half are seen to report national exports only. The decision to record under one system or the other does not seem to be related systematically to any national attribute such as income per capita.

Appendix C

Scatter Diagrams and Statistical Results

The GNP equations and the net export equations are discussed in more detail in this appendix. Each discussion is preceded by a list of the extreme observations, both absolute and relative to GNP or LABOR. These lists are used to identify countries that dominate the trade of each commodity aggregate and also to identify commodities on which countries are particularly dependent. Next the resources are selected that are most critical, in the sense of having Bayes beta values in table 6.7 in excess of .2. These beta values are reported in parentheses. These critical resources are called "robust" if the Bayes bounds in table 6.8 and the omitted observation bounds in table 6.2 do not include zero. Otherwise the critical resources are referred to as "fragile." Finally, in order to give a sense of the data that statistical analyses cannot provide, scatter diagrams are included comparing these data with selected resources. These graphs were selected from a larger set of possibilities and are probably as convincing a set of two-dimensional scatters as can be found. Very extreme observations are omitted from figures C.3, C.5, and C.8b. See text for details.

Aggregate 1: Petroleum (PETRO)

Major net importers		Major net exporters	
1958	1975	1958	1975
$ millions		$ millions	
−1,097 (US)	−23,858 (US)	195 (INDO)	7,286 (NIGR)
−932 (UK)	−20,239 (JAP)	64.2 (CLUM)	6,537 (LIBY)
−497 (FRA)	−10,706 (GER)	5.2 (PERU)	5,085 (INDO)
−407 (JAP)	−9,336 (FRA)	−2.7 (MAUR)	87 (CLUM)
−356 (GER)	−7,644 (UK)	−2.7 (LIBR)	48 (ECUA)
Percentage of GNP		Percentage of GNP	
−9.1 (SING)	−8.3 (MLTA)	2.2 (INDO)	53.0 (LIBY)
−5.8 (ICE)	−7.7 (JAMC)	2.0 (CLUM)	28.7 (NIGR)
−4.0 (MLTA)	−6.8 (LIBR)	.03 (PERU)	19.3 (INDO)
−3.4 (CYPR)	−6.6 (SRIL)	−0.9 (MEX)	2.8 (ECUA)
−3.1 (HOKO)	−6.5 (KORA)	−.12 (YUG)	.07 (CLUM)

Major determinants of net exports (beta values)

	Robust	Fragile
1958	OIL (1.7)	CAPITAL (−1.51), LABOR 1 (−.69), COAL (−.21)
1975	OIL (.63), CAPITAL (−.45)	LABOR 1 (−.22)

The sample of countries includes only three net exporters of petroleum in 1958 (Indonesia, Colombia, and Peru) and five net exporters in 1975 (Nigeria, Libya, Indonesia, Colombia, and Ecuador). The major importers were the developed countries: the United States, the United Kingdom, France, Japan, and Germany in 1958 and the United States, Japan, Germany, France, and the United Kingdom in 1975. Relative to GNP, three countries had extreme dependence on petroleum exports in 1975 but not in 1958. These are Indonesia, Nigeria, and Libya.

The major determinants of petroleum net exports were CAPITAL and OIL. It is not surprising to find oil production as a major determinant. This is clearly illustrated in figure C.1 and confirmed by the regression estimates and sensitivity analysis in chapter 6. The influence of CAPITAL is less in both years, and also fragile in 1975. The contribution of CAPITAL and LABOR 1 to comparative disadvantage points to the importance of petroleum as an intermediate input, the demand for which is created by CAPITAL and LABOR 1 availability.

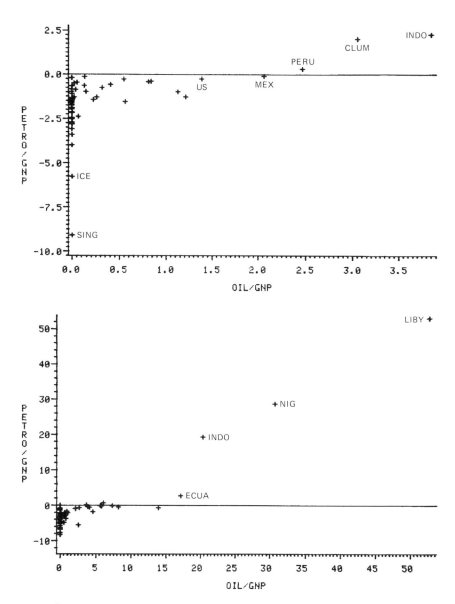

Figure C.1
Scatter diagram, PETRO net exports/GNP versus OIL/GNP: 1958 (top), 1975 (bottom).

Aggregate 2: Raw Materials (MAT)

Major net importers		Major net exporters	
1958	1975	1958	1975
$ millions		$ millions	
−576 (UK)	−10,248 (JAP)	1,028 (CAN)	4,676 (CAN)
−571 (FRA)	−2,978 (ITLY)	267 (CHLE)	3,578 (AUSL)
−439 (GER)	−2,945 (FRA)	165 (MALY)	1,119 (NETH)
−437 (US)	−2,2412 (GER)	114 (MEX)	693 (CHLE)
−417 (ITLY)	−1,884 (BLUX)	109 (PERU)	499 (US)
Percentage of GNP		Percentage of GNP	
−2.5 (AUST)	−11.6 (HOKO)	19.9 (LIBR)	43.7 (LIBR)
−2.3 (DEN)	−3.2 (BLUX)	11.0 (JAMC)	8.9 (PERU)
−2.0 (BLUX)	−2.3 (JAP)	7.9 (CYPR)	6.1 (CHLE)
−1.9 (IRE)	−2.0 (ITLY)	7.8 (MALY)	4.2 (AUSL)
−1.6 (NETH)	−1.7 (FIN)	6.6 (PERU)	4.1 (MALY)

Major determinants of net exports (beta values)

	Robust	Fragile
1958	LABOR 1 (−2.51), OIL (1.84), MIN (.72), LABOR 3 (.45), LABOR 2 (.44), LAND 4 (.44)	CAPITAL (−1.01)
1975	MIN (.66), COAL (.64), CAPITAL (−.55), LABOR 2 (−.53)	LABOR 1 (.36)

Canada was a very extreme exporter of raw materials in 1958, with $1 billion of net exports. The next largest exporter was Chile, with $267 million. In 1975 Canada was still the largest exporter with $4.6 billion, but Australia was close with $3.6 billion and The Netherlands had $1.1 billion. (This aggregate includes gas, natural and manufactured, which is The Netherland's large export item in this aggregate.) The big importers were the developed economies: the United Kingdom, France, Germany, the United States, and Italy in 1958 and Japan, Italy, France, Germany, and Belgium-Luxembourg in 1975. Japan in 1975 was an especially extreme importer, which is notable because it did not make the list in 1958. Exports as a share of GNP were large for Liberia in 1958 and extremely large in 1975. In terms of the trade dependence ratio, Hong Kong is notable, with substantial imports in 1975 but modest imports in 1958.

Raw materials exports are similar to the other natural resource product (petroleum) in the sense of having obvious sources of comparative advantage in the supply of natural resources (MINERALS, COAL, and OIL) and also in the sense of having major demand creating elements in CAPITAL and LABOR 1. (Note MAT includes natural gas exports and OIL includes natural gas production.) The association with MINERAL

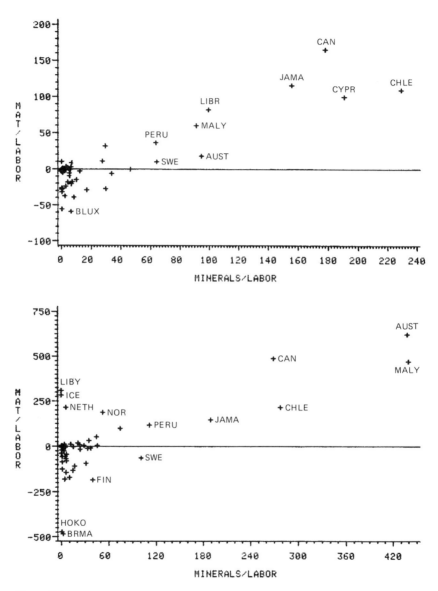

Figure C.2
Scatter diagram, MAT net exports/LABOR versus MINERALS/LABOR: 1958 (top), 1975 (bottom).

supply is illustrated in figure C.2. In 1958 the highly skilled work force (LABOR 1) created a comparative disadvantage in raw material net exports, but countries with an abundance of unskilled labor (LABOR 2 and LABOR 3) were forced to depend on earnings from raw material exports to pay for manufactured goods imports. This effect seems to have disappeared in 1975.

Aggregate 3: Forest Products (FOR)

Major net importers		Major net exporters	
1958	1975	1958	1975
$ millions		$ millions	
−946 (US)	−3,052 (JAP)	1,301 (CAN)	4,155 (CAN)
−868 (UK)	−2,913 (UK)	673 (SWE)	3,253 (SWE)
−370 (GER)	−1,637 (GER)	592 (FIN)	2,265 (FIN)
−181 (ITLY)	−974 (ITLY)	201 (AUST)	514 (AUST)
−141 (ARG)	−895 (FRA)	138 (NOR)	471 (MALY)
Percentage of GNP		Percentage of GNP	
−3.7 (ICE)	−2.8 (MLTA)	14.6 (FIN)	9.5 (FIN)
−3.4 (HOKO)	−2.6 (ICE)	6.0 (SWE)	5.7 (MALY)
−1.9 (JAMC)	−2.5 (CSTA)	3.8 (CAN)	5.3 (SWE)
−1.9 (CYPR)	−2.4 (JAMC)	3.8 (AUST)	3.0 (CAN)
−1.6 (SING)	−2.3 (EGPT)	3.6 (NOR)	2.4 (HOND)

Major determinants of net exports (beta values)		
	Robust	Fragile
1958	LAND 4 (.65), COAL (−.32)	LABOR 1 (−.98), CAPITAL (.66), LABOR 2 (.23)
1975	LAND 4 (.58)	OIL (.56), LABOR 2 (−.26), LABOR 3 (.24)

Canada, Sweden, and Finland were the major exporters of forest products in both years. The major importers were the developed countries. The United States, which was the largest importer in 1958, was replaced in 1975 by Japan, which was not even in the top five in 1958. Relative to GNP, Finland is very dependent on forest product exports, though less so in 1975 than in 1958.

LAND 4 is the only variable that has a consistent estimated effect on forest products regardless of the method of estimation, except for COAL in 1958, which reduced net exports of forest products, possibly because COAL was a source of comparative advantage in manufactures. The association between forest products and LAND 4 is illustrated in figure C.3. The Canadian data omitted in these figures are (21.5, 3.8) in 1958 and (5.2, 2.97) in 1975, where the second number is the ratio of net exports to GNP. These observations are off to the lower right of these figures and have the effect of making LAND 4 appear much less productive.

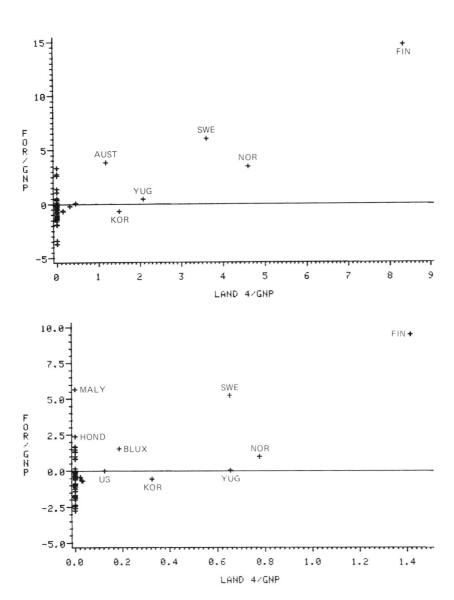

Figure C.3
Scatter diagram, FOR net exports/GNP versus LAND 4/GNP: 1958 (top), 1975 (bottom).

Aggregate 4: Tropical/Mediterranean Agricultural Products (TROP)

Major net importers		Major net exporters	
1958	1975	1958	1975
$ millions		$ millions	
−2,220 (US)	−4,987 (US)	879 (BRAZ)	2,416 (BRAZ)
−1,531 (UK)	−4,389 (GER)	509 (MALY)	1,072 (INDA)
−967 (GER)	−2,743 (JAP)	441 (INDO)	770 (CLUM)
−857 (FRA)	−2,573 (UK)	356 (CLUM)	746 (PLIP)
−376 (CAN)	−1,293 (CAN)	322 (INDA)	741 (ITLY)
Percentage of GNP		Percentage of GNP	
−6.0 (NETA)	−6.3 (MLTA)	24.0 (MALY)	35.4 (MAUR)
−5.4 (MLTA)	−4.5 (HOKO)	23.6 (MAUR)	19.7 (SRIL)
−4.7 (HOKO)	−2.3 (ICE)	21.6 (SRIL)	15.7 (CSTA)
−2.6 (ICE)	−1.6 (LIBY)	21.0 (LIBR)	12.9 (HOND)
−2.4 (NOR)	−1.5 (NOR)	19.0 (CSTA)	12.4 (ECUA)

Major determinants of net exports (beta value)

	Robust	Fragile
1958	LABOR 3 (.4), COAL (−.31) LAND 1 (.3)	LABOR 1 (−2.07), CAPITAL (1.05), LABOR 2 (.56)
1975	CAPITAL (−2.5), LAND 3 (.22)	LABOR 1 (−.56), OIL (.35), LAND 1 (.28), COAL (−.27)

Brazil was the major exporter of tropical/Mediterranean agricultural products, by a wide margin, in 1975. The United States was the major importer by a wide margin in 1958, but was closely trailed by Germany in 1975. Japan, which was not on the 1958 list, became the third-largest importer in 1975. Many of the developing countries are very dependent on exports of these products, less so in 1975 than in 1958.

Contrary to expectations, tropical/Mediterranean agricultural exports seem to be only weakly related to LAND 1 (see figure C.4a). In fact no resource has a robust effect appearing in both years. Figure C.4b suggests CAPITAL as a major source of comparative disadvantage. The CAPITAL effect does show up in 1975, but is hard to detect in 1958. The influence of LAND 1 seems clear in 1958, but if Brazil is omitted, the 1975 weighted least-squares estimate turns positive.

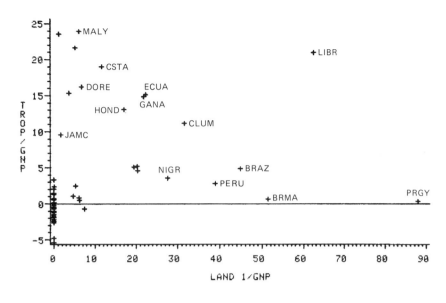

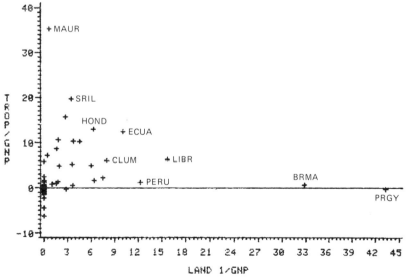

Figure C.4a
Scatter diagram, TROP net exports/GNP versus LAND 1/GNP: 1958 (top), 1975
(bottom).

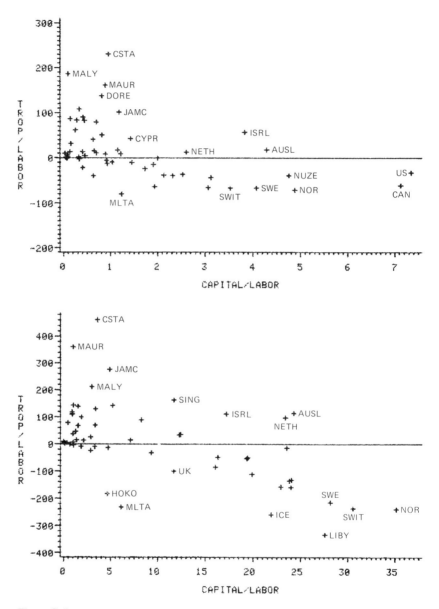

Figure C.4b
Scatter diagram, TROP net exports/LABOR versus CAPITAL/LABOR: 1958 (top), 1975 (bottom).

Aggregate 5: Animal Products (ANL)

Major net importers		Major net exporters	
1958	1975	1958	1975
$ millions		$ millions	
−1,622 (UK)	−3,750 (ITLY)	671 (DEN)	3,582 (NETH)
−611 (GER)	−2,769 (UK)	532 (NETH)	2,244 (DEN)
−606 (US)	−2,052 (GER)	389 (NUZE)	1,126 (IRE)
−292 (ITLY)	−1,924 (JAP)	380 (ARG)	1,120 (AUSL)
−97 (HOKO)	−1,625 (US)	293 (CAN)	1,091 (NUZE)
Percentage of GNP		Percentage of GNP	
−9.8 (HOKO)	−7.6 (HOKO)	24.7 (ICE)	17.6 (ICE)
−6.1 (MLTA)	−5.3 (MLTA)	13.5 (DEN)	14.3 (IRE)
−4.2 (NETA)	−3.5 (MAUR)	2.2 (NUZE)	9.0 (NUZE)
−3.0 (MAUR)	−3.0 (JAMC)	11.1 (IRE)	7.1 (DEN)
−2.9 (JAMC)	−2.5 (ITLY)	5.6 (NETH)	4.9 (NETH)

Major determinants of net exports (beta values)		
	Robust	Fragile
1958	LAND 3 (.28)	LABOR 1 (−2.0), CAP (1.47), LABOR 2 (.36), LABOR 3 (.35), COAL (−.35)
1975	LAND 3 (.27)	LABOR 1 (−.6), LABOR 3 (.39), LABOR 2 (−.27), OIL (.24)

Denmark and The Netherlands were the two major exporters of animal products. The major importers are the developed countries. Japan, which was not on the list in 1958, became the fourth-largest importer in 1975. Italian imports grew very rapidly over the period. Iceland is very dependent on exports of this category because it includes fish. Denmark's dependence fell substantially. On the import side, Hong Kong is very dependent on animal products.

Some association between animal products exports and LAND 3 is suggested by figure C.5. Paraguay, with data (61.1, 3.5) in 1958 and (30.1, 2.4) in 1975, is omitted from these figures. Because Paraguay is very abundant in LAND 3 but not very concentrated on ANL exports, the Paraguay data point casts doubt on the association.

LAND 3 has the only robust estimated effect on animal net exports. The Bayes beta values do select LABOR 1 as a major source of demand, but this conclusion is not robust to changes of the prior variance-covariance matrix.

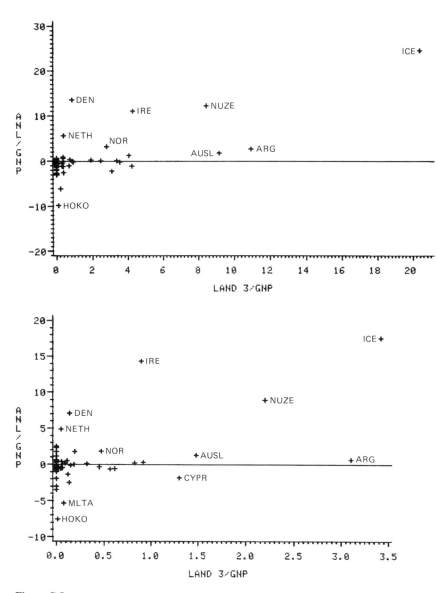

Figure C.5
Scatter diagram, ANL net exports/GNP versus LAND 3/GNP: 1958 (top), 1975
(bottom).

Aggregate 6: Cereals and Textile Fibers (CER)

Major net importers		Major net exporters	
1958	1975	1958	1975
$ millions		$ millions	
−1,665 (UK)	−6,287 (JAP)	2,484 (US)	18,096 (US)
−1,083 (GER)	−2,715 (GER)	736 (AUSL)	3,053 (AUSL)
−1,020 (JAP)	−2,550 (ITLY)	579 (CAN)	2,504 (CAN)
−573 (FRA)	−2,193 (UK)	516 (ARG)	1,483 (ARG)
−405 (ITLY)	−1,571 (SPAN)	308 (EGPT)	1,418 (BRAZ)
Percentage of GNP		Percentage of GNP	
−13.3 (HOKO)	−15.1 (SRIL)	10.7 (BRMA)	4.2 (MALY)
−9.2 (MAUR)	−9.8 (MLTA)	7.5 (EGPT)	3.9 (PERU)
−6.9 (SING)	−8.1 (HOKO)	6.9 (NUZE)	3.7 (THAI)
−5.6 (MLTA)	−8.0 (MAUR)	6.4 (THAI)	3.6 (AUSL)
−4.2 (SRIL)	−5.6 (CYPR)	5.9 (NIGR)	4.2 (ARG)

Major determinants of net exports (beta values)

	Robust	Fragile
1958	LABOR 1 (−2.4), LABOR 3 (.55), COAL (−.29), LAND 3 (.24)	CAPITAL (2.84)
1975	LAND 3 (.26)	LABOR 1 (.74), OIL (.72), LABOR 2 (−.55), CAPITAL (−.17), LABOR 3 (−.15)

The United States was by far the major exporter of cereals and textile fibers (including rice). Other developed countries were the major importers, especially Japan in 1975. Hong Kong in 1958 and Sri Lanka in 1975 were very dependent on imports of cereals (for example, rice). Burma had very large exports relative to GNP in 1958 but not 1975. Generally, the trade dependence ratios of the exporters declined between 1958 and 1975.

Figure C.6a suggests some association between CEREALS exports per worker and land per worker, though Paraguay and New Zealand are outliers. Figure C.6b hints at labor as the source of comparative advantage in CEREALS. The statistical analysis does identify LAND 3 as a clear contributor to comparative advantage in CEREALS. In 1958 LABOR 1 and COAL were sources of comparative disadvantage, possibly because of their positive effects on the production of manufactures and their consequent influence on the demand for CEREALS.

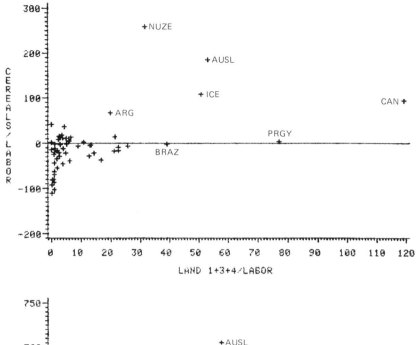

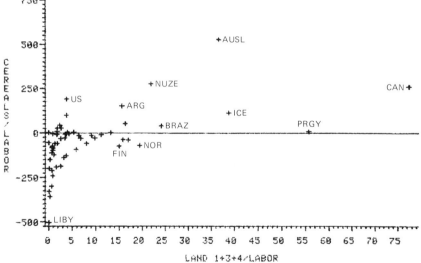

Figure C.6a
Scatter diagram, CEREALS net exports/LABOR versus LAND 1 + 3 + 4/LABOR: 1958 (top), 1975 (bottom).

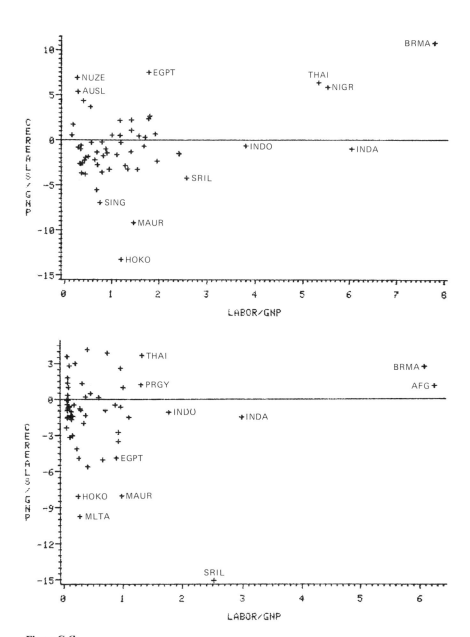

Figure C.6b
Scatter diagram, CEREALS net exports/GNP versus LABOR/GNP: 1958 (top), 1975
(bottom).

Aggregate 7: Labor Intensive Manufactures (LAB)

Major net importers		Major net exporters	
1958	1975	1958	1975
$ millions		$ millions	
−596 (CAN)	−6,188 (US)	562 (UK)	5,332 (ITLY)
−106 (AUSL)	−2,274 (GER)	444 (FRA)	2,464 (HOKO)
−99 (SWE)	−2,172 (CAN)	440 (JAP)	1,794 (KOR)
−89 (NETH)	−1,738 (NETH)	377 (US)	1,652 (JAP)
−73 (NIGR)	−1,076 (SWIT)	251 (GER)	836 (SPAN)
Percentage of GNP		Percentage of GNP	
−9.6 (NETA)	−4.3 (LIBY)	2.1 (HOKO)	32.4 (HOKO)
−5.4 (MAUR)	−3.8 (SING)	2.7 (SING)	11.0 (MLTA)
−4.4 (CYPR)	−3.7 (LIBR)	1.4 (JAP)	9.4 (KORA)
−3.9 (LIBR)	−3.5 (PANM)	.9 (BLUX)	3.5 (ITLY)
−3.3 (ICE)	−3.1 (MAUR)	.9 (UK)	2.0 (SRIL)

Major determinants of net exports (beta values)		
	Robust	Fragile
1958	LAND 4 (−.52), LABOR 3 (.51)	LABOR 1 (1.38), OIL (−.59), LABOR 2 (.32)
1975	LABOR 1 (−1.13), LABOR 2 (.93), LAND 4 (−.15)	OIL (−.24)

Aggregate 7, labor intensive manufactures, (clothing, footwear, and so on) has undergone a rather remarkable reshuffling of trade. The United States and Germany, which were the fourth and fifth exporters in 1958, became the fifth and fourth importers in 1975. France and the United Kingdom also were major exporters in 1958, but are gone from the list in 1975, replaced by Italy, Hong Kong, and Korea. Many of the developing economies and Italy became much more dependent relative to GNP on exports of these commodities.

Figure C.7 reveals a negative association between net exports per worker and capital per worker. Hong Kong is an extreme outlier in these graphs for both years, with much greater net exports per worker than any other country. Except for Hong Kong and the United States in 1958, one can see in these graphs a nonlinear relation similar to figure 1.9, with exporters having moderate levels of capital per worker and importers having either high or low capital per worker. This form of nonlinearity is studied in section 6.5.

The dramatic changes that are evident in the data on the five extreme countries are not so obvious in these figures, with the exception of the United States, which shifts to conform to the pattern of the other countries. Otherwise, there is slight tendency of the interval of values of capital

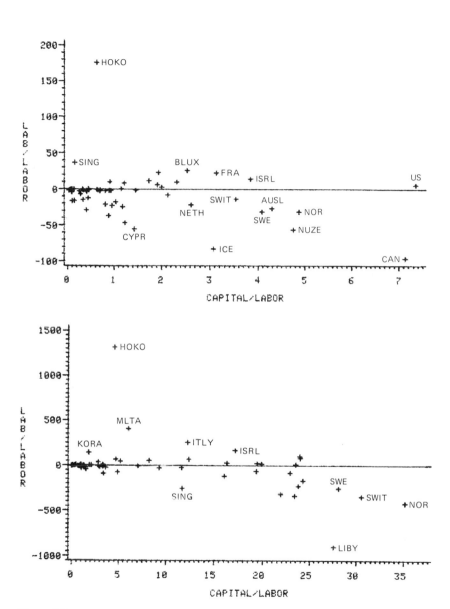

Figure C.7
Scatter diagram, LAB net exports/LABOR versus CAPITAL/LABOR: 1958 (top), 1975 (bottom).

per worker of the exporting countries to shift downward in the ranking of countries.

Abundance of LAND 4 is estimated to contribute to comparative disadvantage in LAB. Otherwise there is no variable with a consistent, robust effect. LABOR 2 clearly contributed to comparative advantage in 1975, but the effect was fragile in 1958, possibly because LABOR 3 played a more important role. LABOR 1 was a fragile source of comparative advantage in 1958 and a clear source of comparative disadvantage in 1975. This is the change in the estimates that seems mostly clearly to parallel the shift of production from the advanced developed economies to the middle tier of developing countries.

Two other incidental comments may be made. (1) The drop in the quality of fit as measured by the R^2 is substantial from 1958 to 1975 (table 6.1). The rearrangement of the trade that occurred between 1958 and 1975 has left the model hardly able to explain anything at all. (2) The United States is not an outlier in 1958 (table 6.3), even though it appears to be in figure C.7. Appearances built on two-dimensional scatters can be deceiving.

Aggregate 8: Capital Intensive Manufactures (CAP)

Major net importers		Major net exporters	
1958	1975	1958	1975
$ millions		$ millions	
−721 (CAN)	−1,801 (CAN)	1,308 (UK)	14,460 (JAP)
−247 (AUSL)	−1,636 (US)	1,056 (FRA)	6,787 (GER)
−228 (ARG)	−1,259 (NIGR)	1,023 (JAP)	3,721 (BLUX)
−207 (INDO)	−1,109 (BRAZ)	849 (US)	3,497 (ITLY)
−190 (DEN)	−888 (SING)	848 (BLUX)	2,257 (FRA)
Percentage of GNP		Percentage of GNP	
−10.1 (MAUR)	−16.5 (MLTA)	7.8 (BLUX)	6.3 (BLUX)
−9.5 (ICE)	−15.6 (SING)	3.2 (JAP)	3.2 (JAP)
−9.0 (LIBY)	−7.9 (LIBR)	2.7 (AUST)	2.3 (ITLY)
−7.4 (MLTA)	−7.4 (MAUR)	2.0 (UK)	1.9 (KORA)
−7.1 (NETA)	−6.7 (CYPR)	1.8 (FRA)	1.3 (GER)

Major determinants of net exports (beta values)

	Robust	Fragile
1958	LABOR 3 (−.53), LAND 4 (−.27)	LABOR 1 (1.94), CAPITAL (−1.24), LABOR 2 (.31)
1975	LABOR 1 (−1.8), LABOR 2 (.85), CAPTIAL (.78)	LABOR 3 (.37)

The major exporters of capital intensive manufactures (for example, iron and steel and textiles) were developed countries. Like labor intensive manufactures, there were some dramatic shifts in trade. The United States, which was the fourth-largest exporter in 1958, became the fourth-largest importer in 1975. Japan and Germany grew rapidly, but the United Kingdom, which was first on the list of exporters in 1958, fell off the list in 1975. Canada was the largest importer by far in 1958, though the United States was close in 1975. Relative to GNP, Belgium-Luxembourg is very dependent on exports and several of the developing countries are very dependent on imports.

Figure C.8a, which compares capital intensive net exports per man with capital per man, is rather similar to the figure for labor intensive net exports, with positive net exporters having moderate levels of capital per worker. This similarity extends even to the United States observation, which is an outlier in 1958 but not in 1975. A negative association between capital intensive exports and land is revealed by figure C.8b, which excludes Australia, Canada, and Libya. These three countries are very land abundant, with moderate levels of imports of capital intensive manufactures. These data points make the relation between net exports and land seem to curve back up at high levels of land abundance.

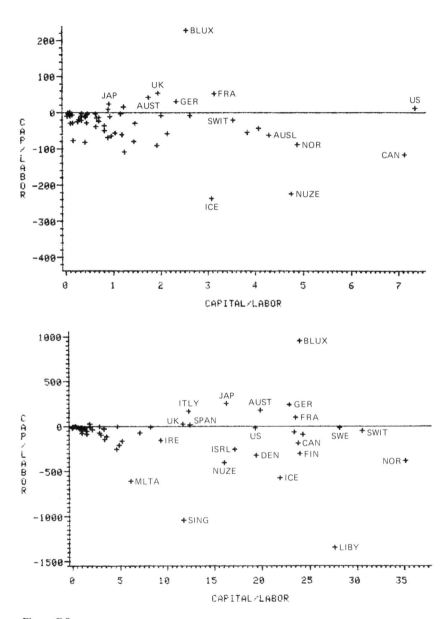

Figure C.8a
Scatter diagram, CAP net exports/LABOR versus CAPITAL/LABOR: 1958 (top), 1975
(bottom).

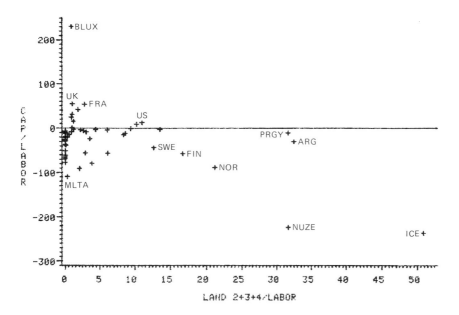

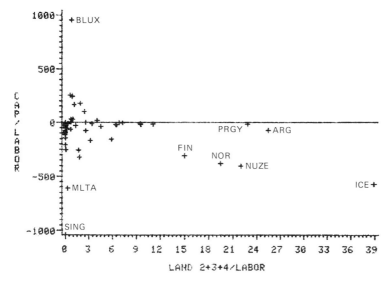

Figure C.8b
Scatter diagram, CAP net exports/LABOR versus LAND $2 + 3 + 4$/LABOR: 1958 (top), 1975 (bottom).

The statistical analysis identifies no robust contributor to comparative advantage in 1958, but LABOR 1 and LABOR 2 have fragile positive effects. This is much altered in 1975, since CAPITAL and LABOR 2 are clear sources of comparative advantage and LABOR 1 is a clear source of comparative disadvantage. This suggests a diminished role of knowledge capital as a source of comparative advantage in CAP and a shift toward physical capital and human capital.

Aggregate 9: Machinery (MACH)

Major net importers		Major net exporters	
1958	1975	1958	1975
$ millions		$ millions	
−1,397 (CAN)	−7,169 (CAN)	5,543 (US)	29,811 (GER)
−534 (INDA)	−3,684 (BRAZ)	3,352 (GER)	25,045 (JAP)
−533 (BRAZ)	−3,439 (AUSL)	3,324 (UK)	23,924 (US)
−507 (AUSL)	−2,645 (NIGR)	513 (FRA)	8,617 (UK)
−502 (MEX)	−1,963 (SPAN)	414 (SWIT)	6,839 (FRA)
Percentage of GNP		Percentage of GNP	
−21.1 (LIBY)	−17.5 (SING)	6.1 (GER)	8.0 (GER)
−13.8 (NETA)	−16.5 (LIBR)	5.6 (SWIT)	5.5 (JAP)
−13.1 (LIBR)	−13.0 (MLTA)	5.1 (UK)	5.5 (SWIT)
−12.1 (NOR)	−12.9 (ICE)	1.2 (US)	4.1 (UK)
−11.1 (ICE)	−12.0 (HOND)	1.1 (ITLY)	3.3 (ITLY)

Major determinants of net exports (beta values)

	Robust	Fragile
1958	COAL (.22), LAND 4 (−.21)	LABOR 1 (1.72), CAPITAL (−.53), LABOR 3 (−.36), LABOR 2 (−.34)
1975	CAPITAL (.49)	LABOR 1 (−.39), OIL (−.21)

The United States, Germany, and the United Kingdom were by a considerable margin the major exporters of machinery (for example, automobiles) in 1958. Japan replaced the United Kingdom in 1975, and the United States fell to third place. Canada was the major importer. India, which was the second-largest importer in 1958, fell off the extreme list in 1975. Relative to GNP, the exports of some of the developed countries are substantial, though not nearly so substantial as the imports of the developing countries.

There is little apparent association between machinery net exports per worker and capital per worker (figure C.9a), though a form of heteroscedasticity is evident, with the variability of net exports per man increasing as capital per man increases. MACHINERY exports seem to have been associated with coal production in 1958 but not in 1975 (figure C.9b).

The statistical analysis selects COAL in 1958 and CAPITAL in 1975 as robust sources of comparative advantage. There is also evidence of a shift from knowledge capital (LABOR 1) as a source of comparative advantage in 1958 to physical capital in 1975, though this is a fragile inference.

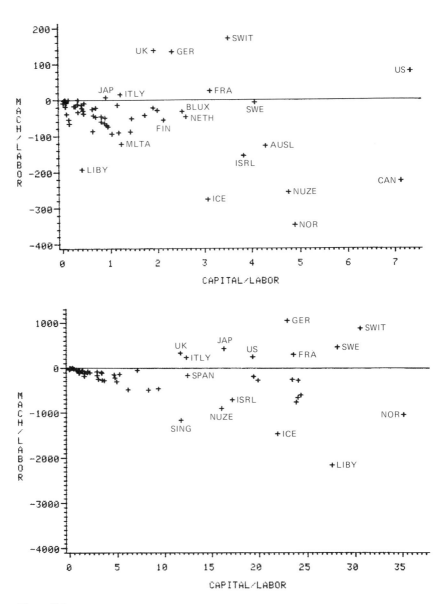

Figure C.9a
Scatter diagram, MACH net exports/LABOR versus CAPITAL/LABOR: 1958 (top),
1975 (bottom).

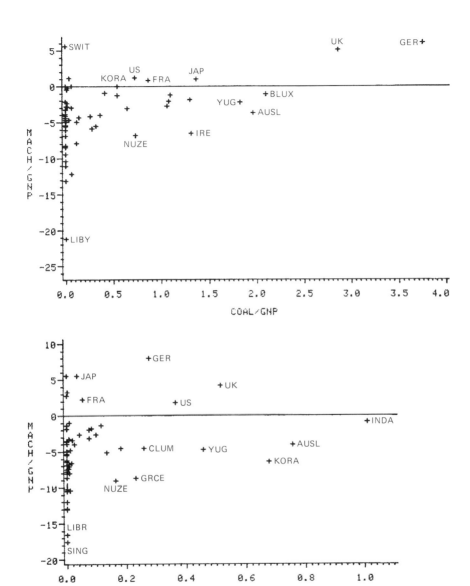

Figure C.9b
Scatter diagram, MACH net exports/GNP versus COAL/GNP: 1958 (top), 1975 (bottom).

Aggregate 10: Chemicals (CHEM)

Major net importers		Major net exporters	
1958	1975	1958	1975
$ millions		$ millions	
−137 (MEX)	−1,554 (BRAZ)	1,230 (US)	5,229 (GER)
−128 (INDA)	−1,003 (INDA)	668 (GER)	4,985 (US)
−122 (BRAZ)	−967 (SPAN)	401 (UK)	2,399 (NETH)
−106 (AUSL)	−783 (INDO)	203 (FRA)	1,825 (JAP)
−104 (SWE)	−721 (KORA)	132 (SWIT)	1,702 (UK)
Percentage of GNP		Percentage of GNP	
−7.3 (NETA)	−5.3 (ICE)	1.8 (SWIT)	10.8 (JAMC)
−5.1 (HOKO)	−5.0 (MLTA)	1.2 (GER)	3.3 (NETH)
−5.0 (MAUR)	−4.8 (CSTA)	1.0 (PRGY)	2.7 (SWIT)
−3.6 (LIBY)	−4.8 (MAUR)	.7 (NETH)	1.6 (BLUX)
−3.4 (CSTA)	−4.8 (SING)	.6 (CHLE)	1.4 (GER)

Major determinants of net exports (beta values)

	Robust	Fragile
1958	COAL (.58), LABOR 2 (−.49)	LABOR 1 (.86), CAPITAL (.36), OIL (−.29)
1975	LABOR 2 (−.7), CAPITAL (.35), LAND 3 (−.22)	LABOR 1 (.87), OIL (−.28), LAND 4 (−.13)

The United States was the major exporter of chemicals in 1958, but was surpassed by Germany in 1975. The major importers are a collection of the middle-tier developing countries. Relative to GNP, Jamaica is surprisingly dependent on chemical exports. In fact it is surprising to see Jamaica, Chile, and Paraguay exporting chemicals at all. The discussion in chapter 4 indicates that this is a defect of the aggregation scheme, since CHEMICALS include some items that are quite different in production than most of the commodities in the category. Jamaica exports aluminum oxide, which is a byproduct of its bauxite mines; Chile exports Chilean nitrate, which is also mined; and Paraguay exports the extract of the Quebracho tree, which is used in tanning.

Figure C.10a reveals no association between chemical exports and capital abundance. COAL (figure C.10b) seems to contribute positively in 1958 but negatively in 1975. No other figure indicates the determinants of chemical exports, which may mean that our model is incapable of explaining chemical trade; or it may mean that a multivariate explanation is required.

The multivariate analysis does not appear to suffer from an inability to explain chemical trade. The R^2 in table 6.1 and the Bayes beta values in table 6.7 are as high for this aggregate as for many of the others. LABOR

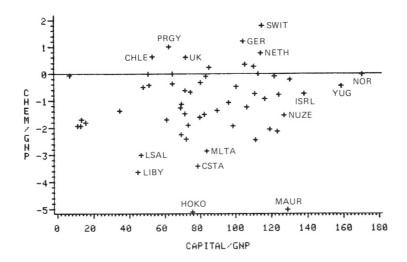

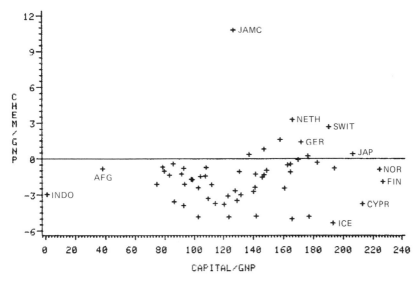

Figure C.10a
Scatter diagram, CHEM net exports/GNP versus CAPITAL/GNP: 1958 (top), 1975 (bottom).

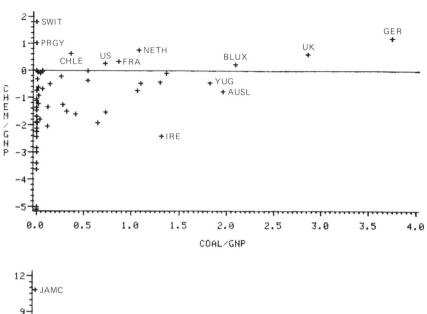

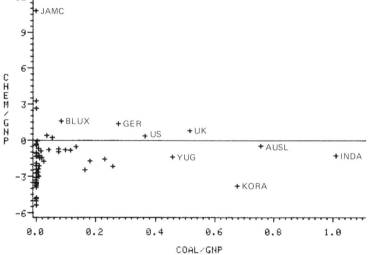

Figure C.10b
Scatter diagram, CHEM net exports/GNP versus COAL/GNP: 1958 (top), 1975
(bottom).

1 has the highest Bayes beta value in both years, though the estimate is fragile in 1958. LABOR 2 has a robust major negative effect on chemical exports. CAPITAL has a positive effect, which is, however, fragile in 1958. This coincides well with the evidence in chapter 3 that chemical production is the most skill intensive and the most capital intensive of all the manufacturing aggregates. COAL, which was suggested by the figures as an important determinant in 1958, is confirmed to have a robust positive effect.

Gross National Product (GNP)

Smallest		Largest	
1958	1975	1958	1975
$ billions		$ billions	
.14 (MAUR)	.27 (MAUR)	455.0 (US)	1,332.1 (US)
.14 (MLTA)	.42 (MLTA)	64.7 (UK)	450.6 (JAP)
.18 (LIBR)	.55 (PRGY)	58.3 (FRA)	372.8 (GER)
.20 (ICE)	.71 (LIBR)	55.1 (GER)	297.8 (FRA)
.27 (PRGY)	.71 (CYPR)	33.9 (CAN)	206.1 (UK)
Per capita GNP		Per capita GNP	
128 (BRMA)	159 (AFG)	6,644 (US)	21,086 (LIBY)
165 (INDA)	164 (BRMA)	5,469 (CAN)	17,078 (SWE)
180 (NIGR)	334 (INDA)	3,743 (NUZE)	16,039 (SWIT)
187 (THAI)	397 (SRIL)	3,499 (SWE)	15,627 (NOR)
263 (INDO)	559 (INDO)	3,455 (AUSL)	15,238 (BLUX)

Major determinants of net exports (beta values)

	Robust	Fragile
1958	CAPITAL (.85)	LABOR 1 (1.2), LABOR 2 (−.38), LABOR 3 (−.26)
1975	LABOR 1 (1.2), CAPITAL (.64), LABOR 2 (−.38), LABOR 3 (−.20)	

The model that serves as a working hypothesis for the study of the trade data expresses net exports as a linear function of the resource endowments. The same set of assumptions can be used also to express GNP as a linear function of the resource endowments with coefficients equal to the factor returns. If the GNP regressions exhibit important nonlinearities, as they might if factor price equalization is seriously violated, then it is more likely that nonlinearities will be evident in the trade regressions. If the estimated coefficients of the GNP regressions do not imply sensible marginal products, or if the proportion of the explained variance is low, then we may infer either that the functional form is inappropriate or that there are economically important omitted variables.

Per capita GNP is very well explained by capital per man as illustrated by figure C.11. The importance of CAPITAL is confirmed by the least-squares estimates, the Bayes beta values, and the Bayes bounds, though LABOR 1 is even more significant. LABOR 2 and LABOR 3 have negative effects that are robust in 1975. The data thereby seem to suggest that the marginal products of LABOR 2 and LABOR 3 are negative, but the consideration of nonlinearities in section 6.5 partially resolves this anomaly.

The finding that CAPITAL is an important determinant of GNP is,

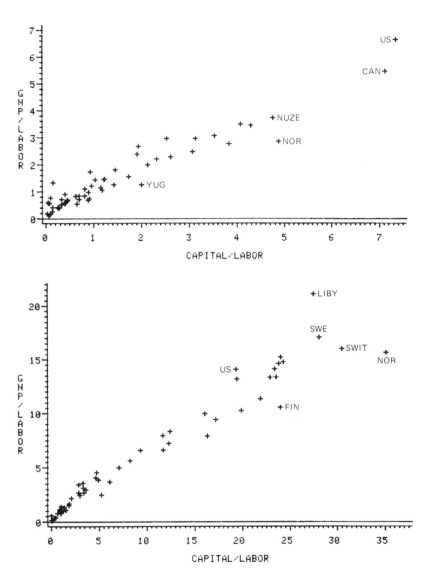

Figure C.11
Scatter diagram, GNP/LABOR versus CAPITAL/LABOR: 1958 (top), 1975 (bottom).

in retrospect, not surprising. The method by which the capital stock is measured is to accumulate past investment flows. These flows are saving rates times GNP. The savings rates do not vary enough to cause much variability in measured capital. Thus it is not altogether inaccurate to say that the capital stock is a constant (depending on the saving rate) times past GNP. The statistical significance of the capital variable as an explainer of GNP then becomes easy to understand; countries with large measured GNPs in the recent past are quite likely to have large measured GNPs currently, and are able to save more in total than countries with small GNPs. But that still leaves undecided why these countries had larger GNPs to begin with. This creates an econometric chicken-or-egg problem that might be resolved if data series were long enough to allow savings rates to have a more pronounced impact on measured capital stocks.

Appendix D

Trade Dependence and Resource Abundance Profiles

This appendix contains graphs that illustrate the composition of trade and the relative abundance of resources for each of the countries in each of the 2 years under study. Detailed discussions of these graphs may be found in section 4.3. Full descriptions of the 10 trade categories may be found in table 3.1. Descriptions of the 11 resource categories are given in section 4.2. The "resource" labeled SIZE in the resource abundance profiles refers to GNP.

In order to form comparable graphs for all countries, the trade data have been transformed according to the function sign $(T/Y) \times \ln(1 + 100|T/Y|)$, where T refers to the net export data and Y refers to GNP. The resource data have been transformed according to the function $(5x - 5)/(x + 5)$, where x is either the resource abundance ratio (the resource share divided by the GNP share) or the GNP ratio (the ratio of GNP to average GNP). Correspondences between the original numbers and the graphed numbers may be found in tables D.1 and D.2.

Table D.1
Correspondence between graphed numbers (z) and trade shares $(T/Y)^a$

z	.5	.7	1.0	1.1	1.5	2.0	3.0	4.0
$100|T/Y|$	.65	1.00	1.72	2.00	3.48	6.39	19.09	53.60

a $z = \ln(1 + 100|T/Y|)$.

Table D.2
Correspondence between graphed numbers (z) and resource ratios $(x)^a$

z	-1	$-.8$	$-.6$	$-.4$	$-.2$	0.0	0.5	1.0	2.0	3.0	4.0	5.0
x	0	.17	.36	.56	.77	1.0	1.7	2.5	5.3	10.0	25.0	∞

a. $z = (5x - 5)/(x + 5)$.

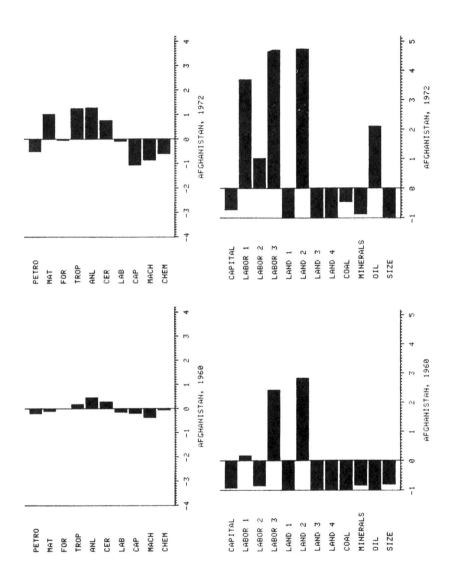

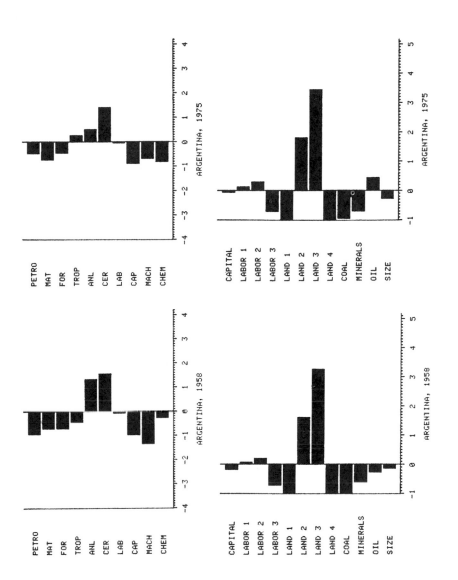

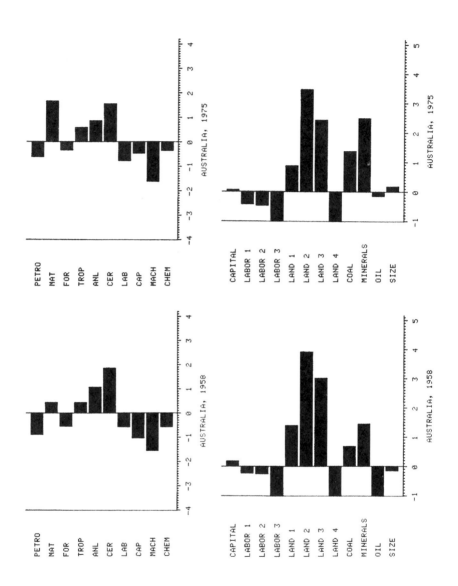

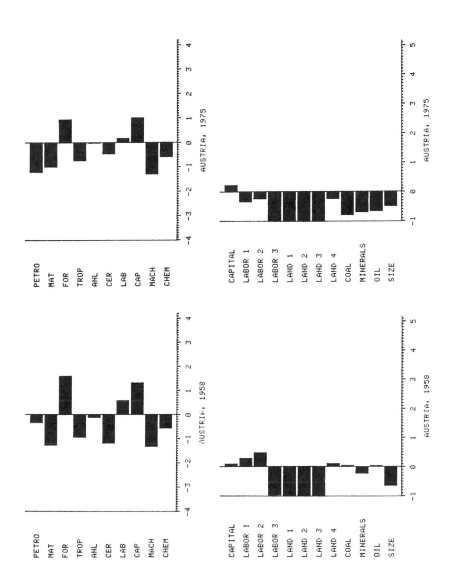

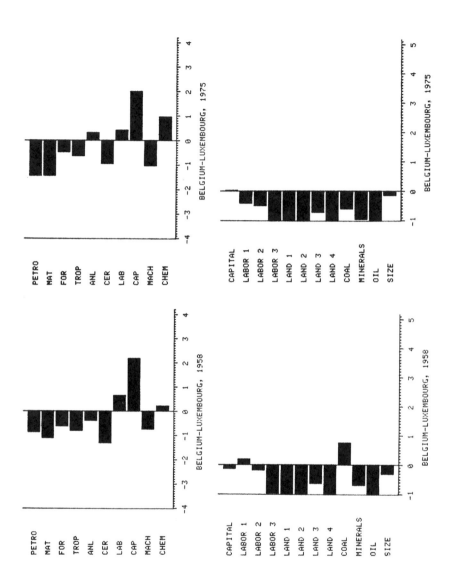

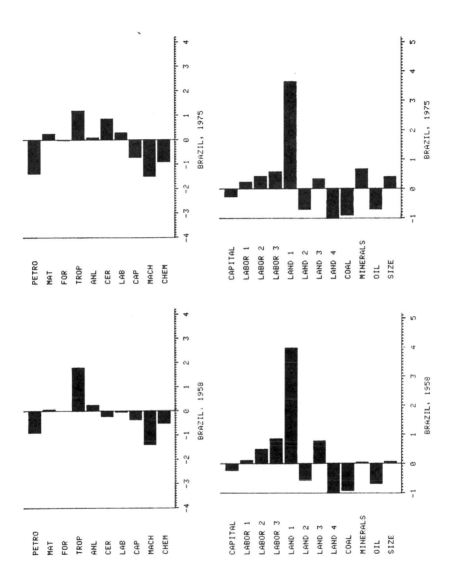

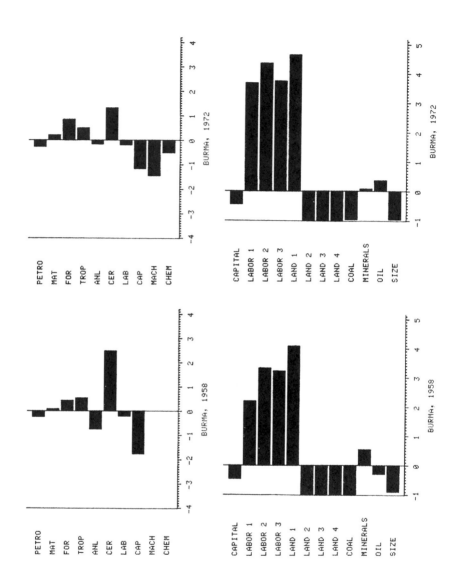

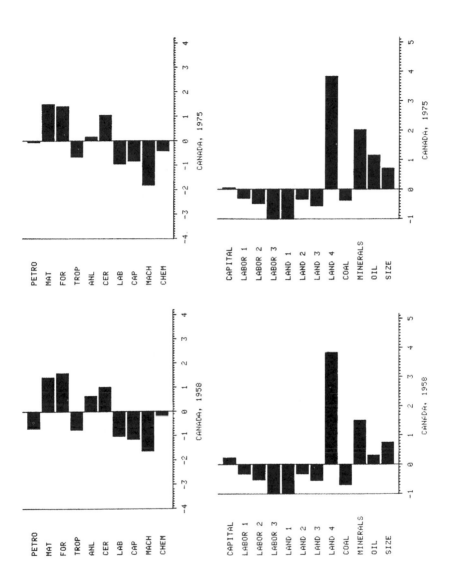

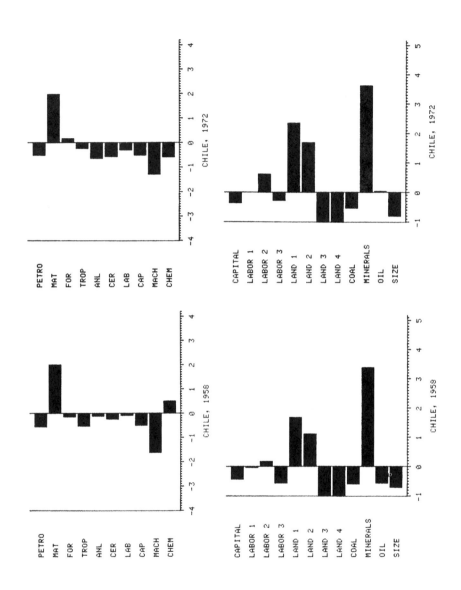

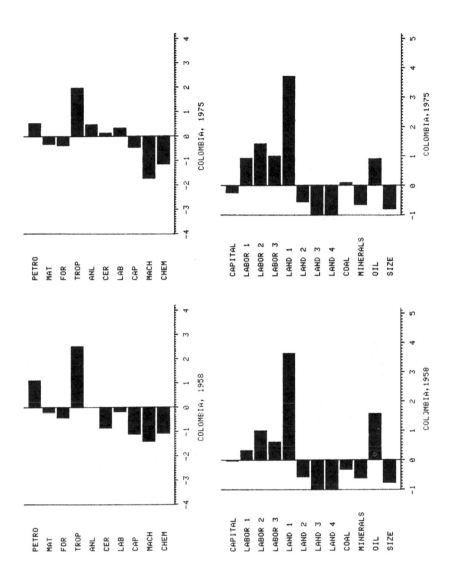

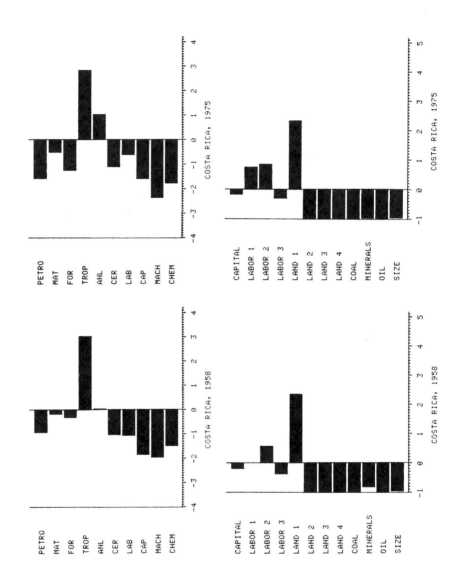

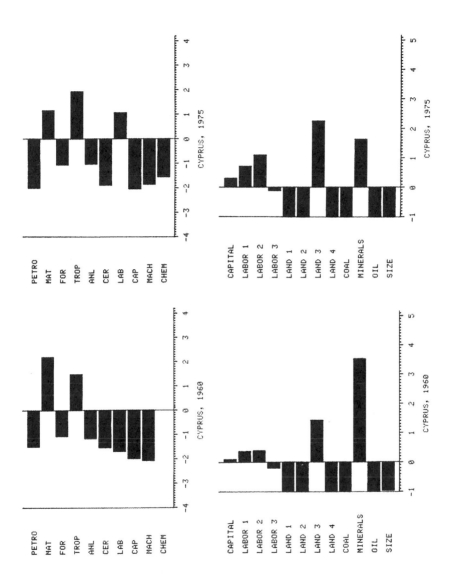

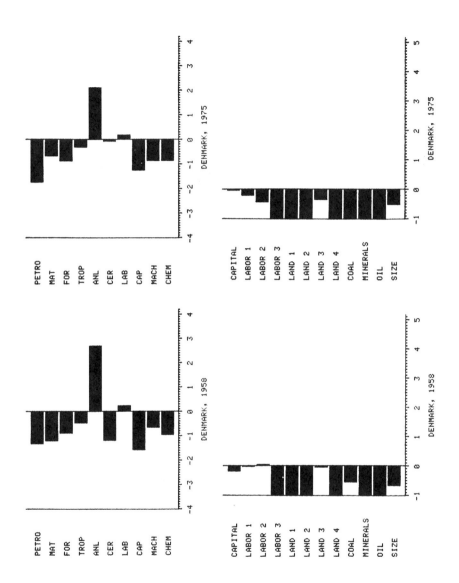

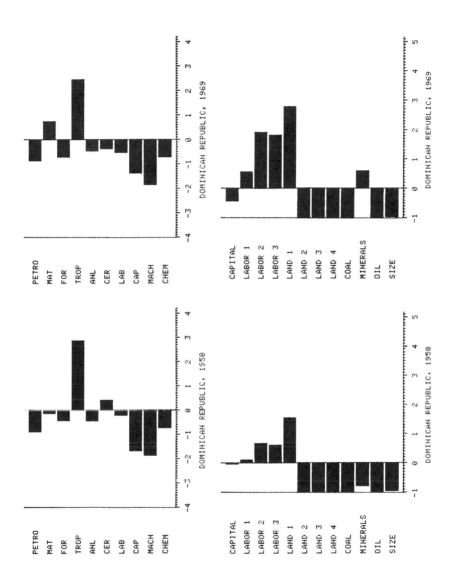

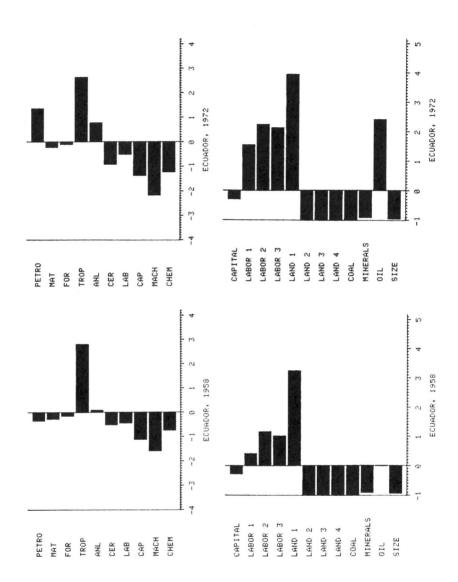

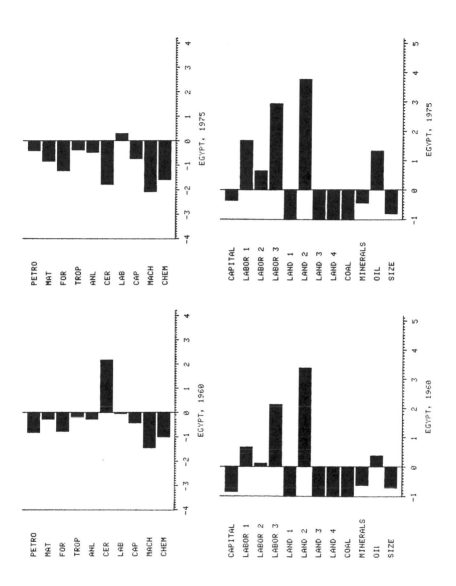

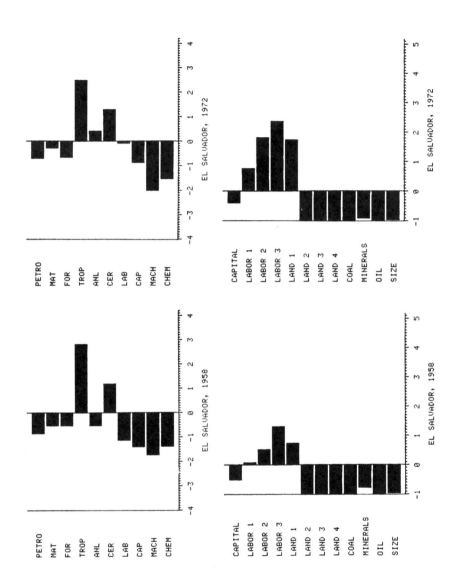

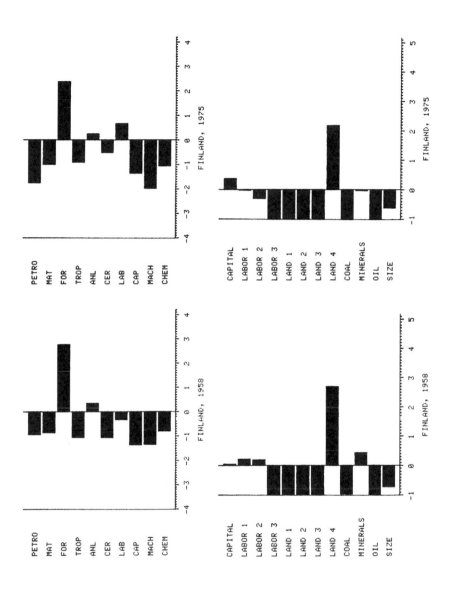

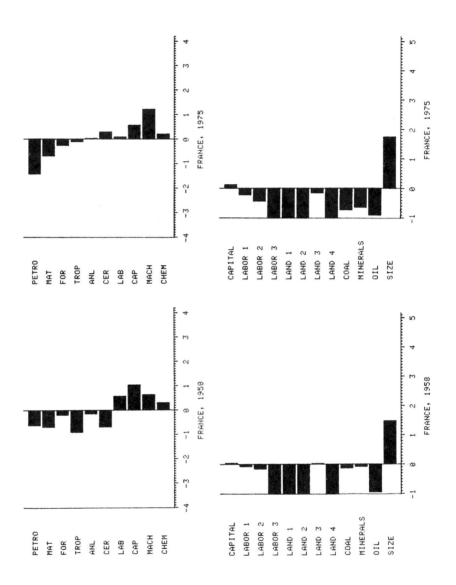

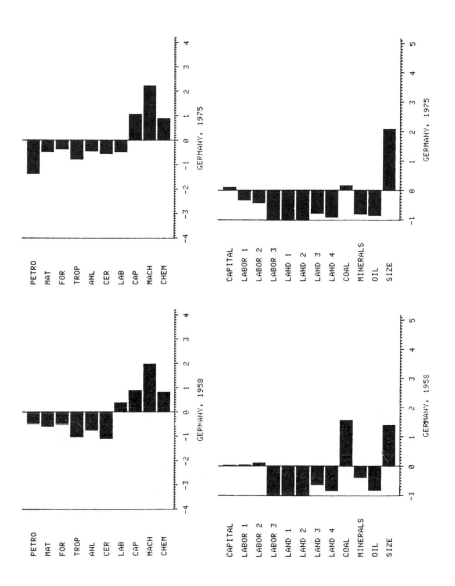

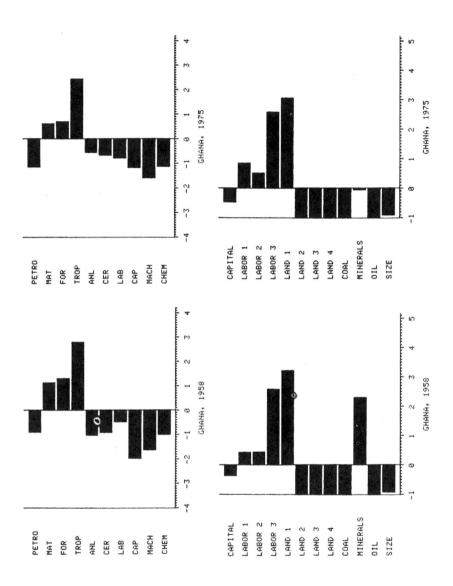

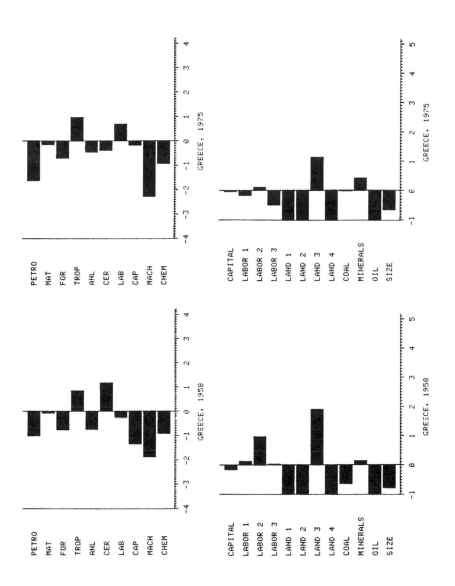

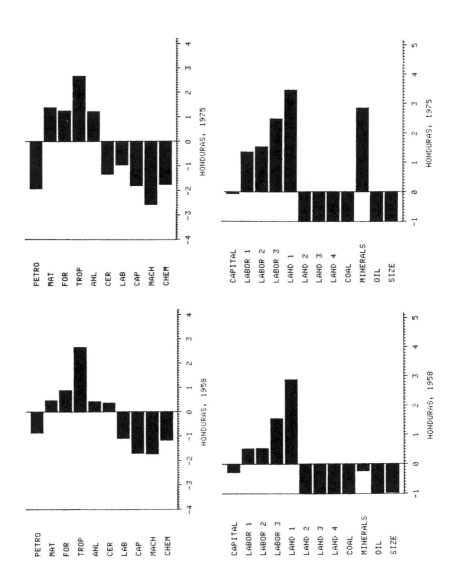

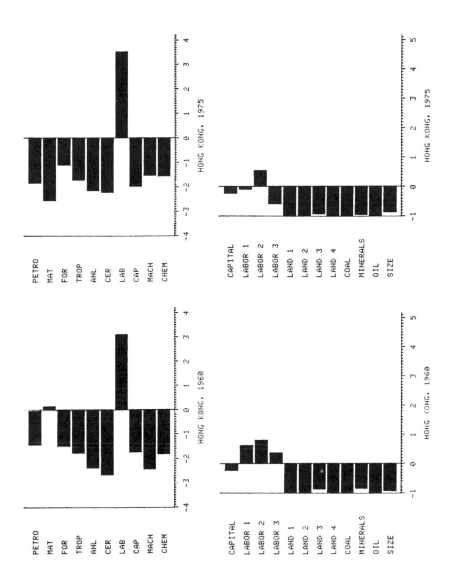

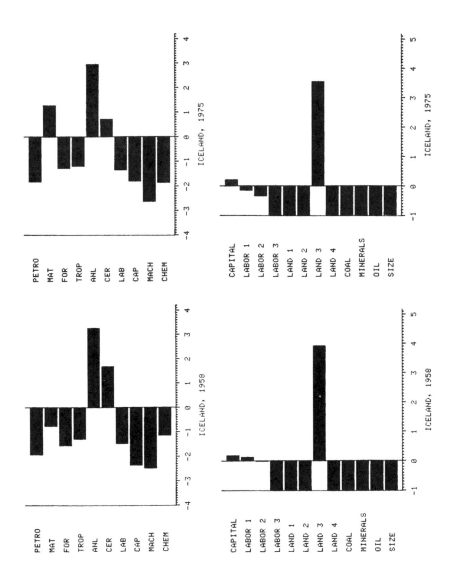

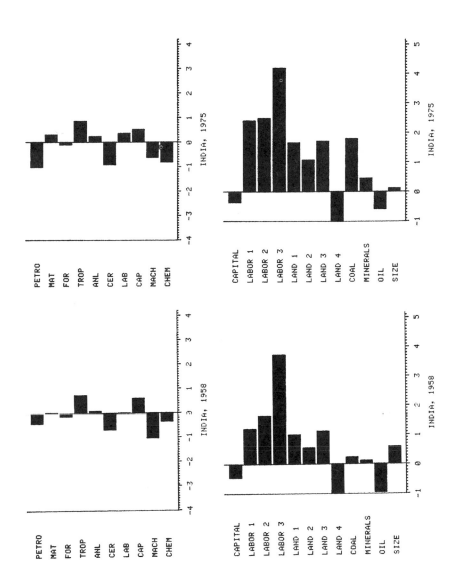

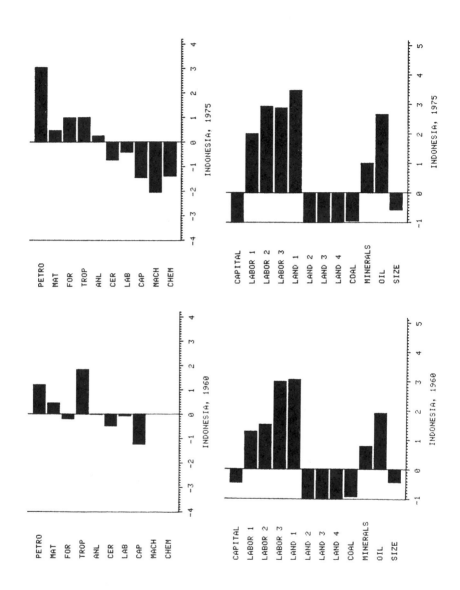

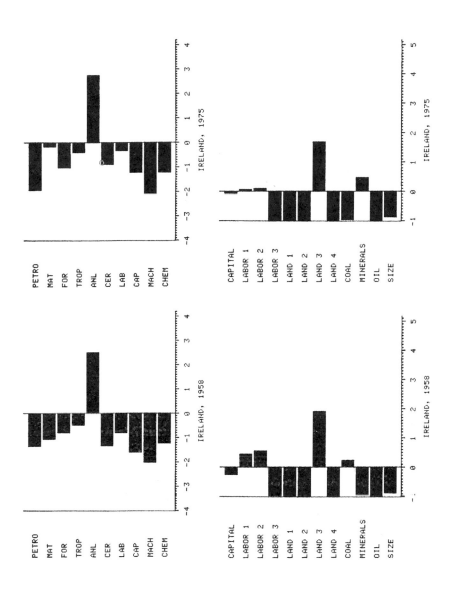

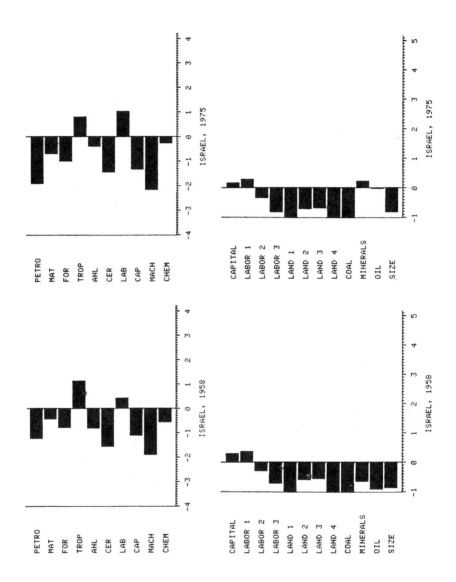

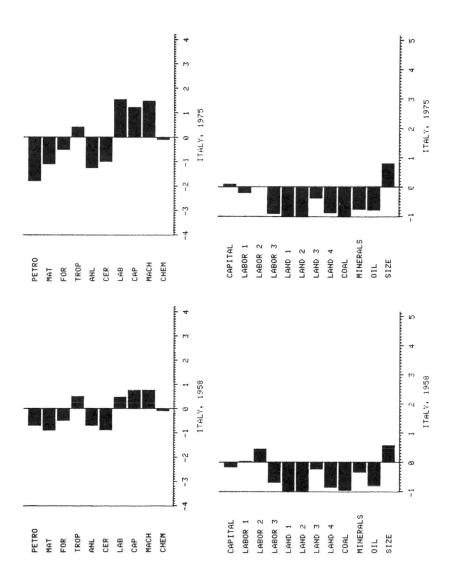

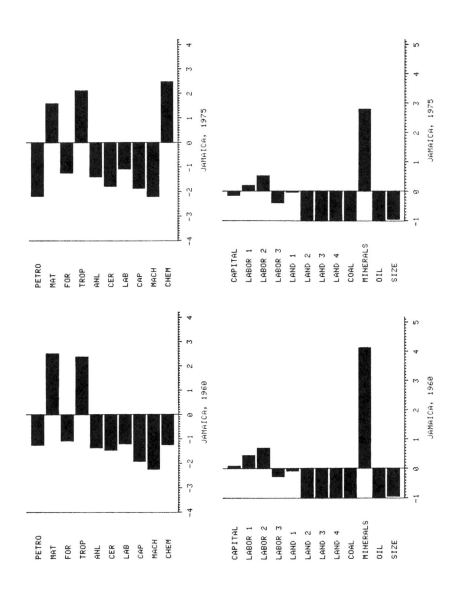

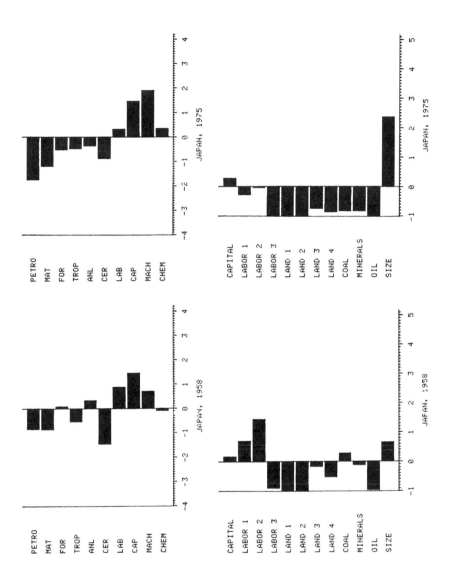

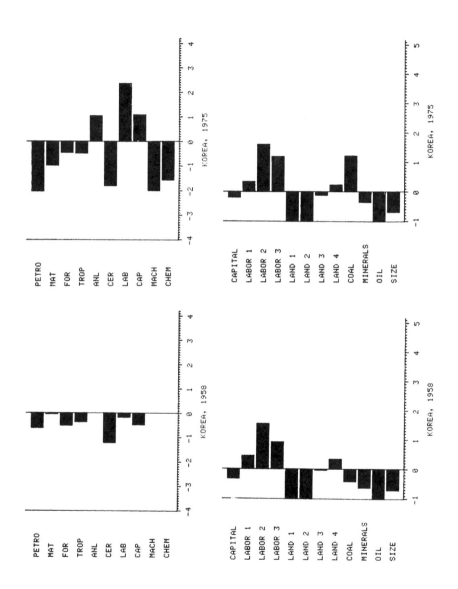

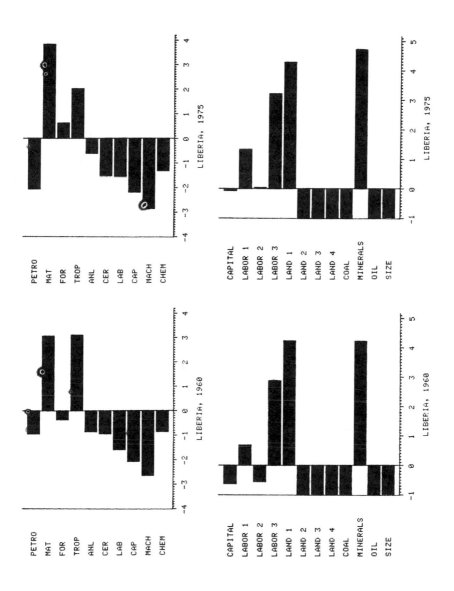

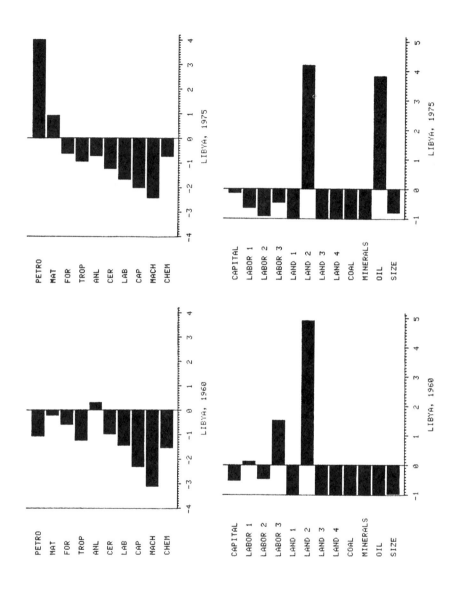

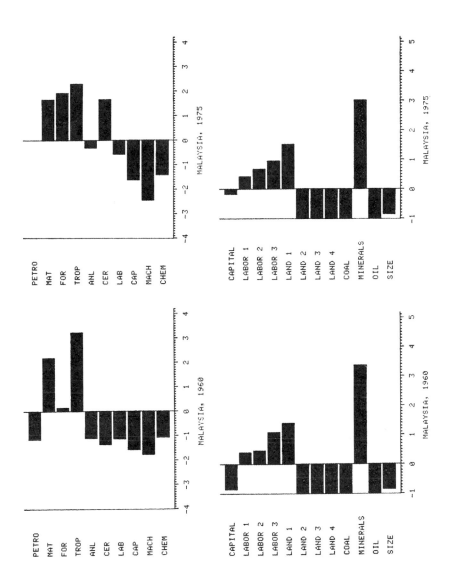

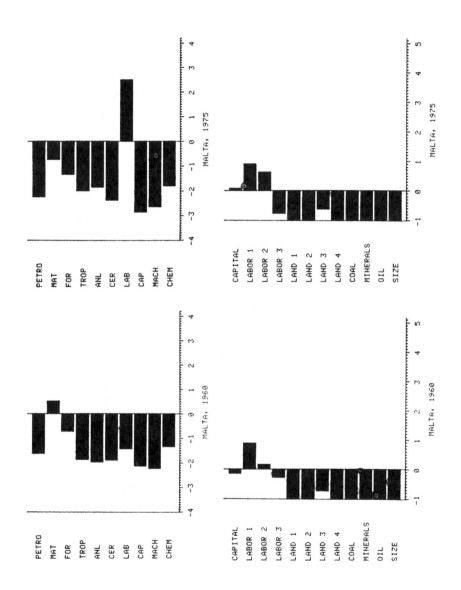

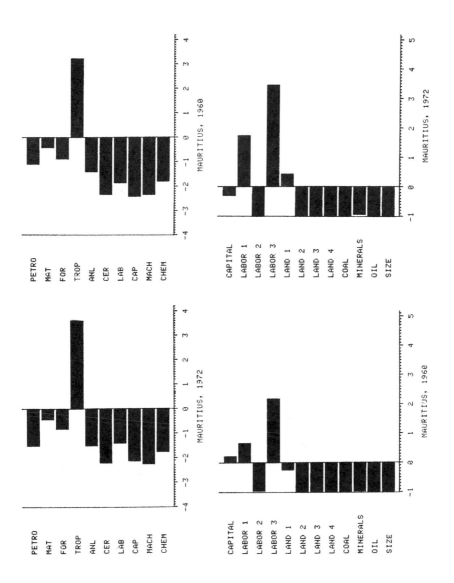

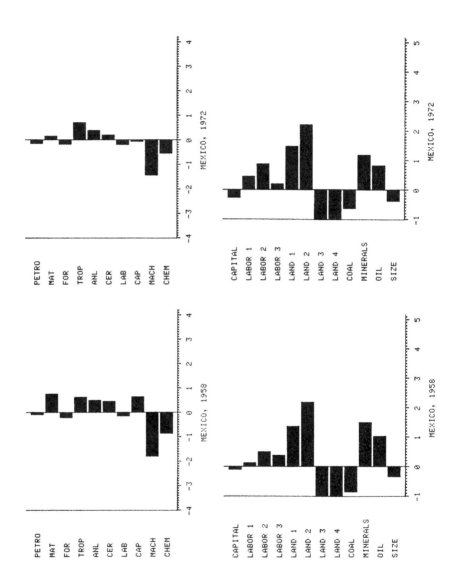

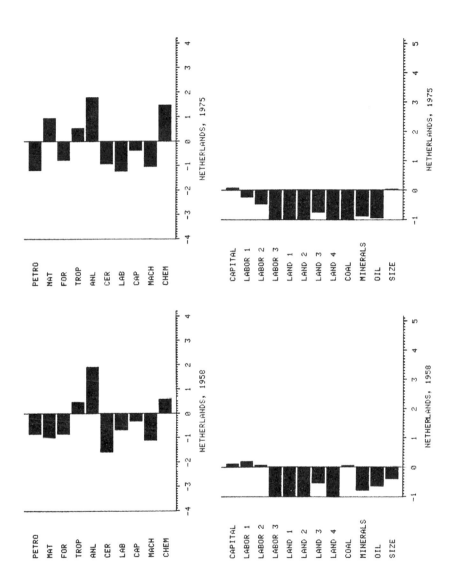

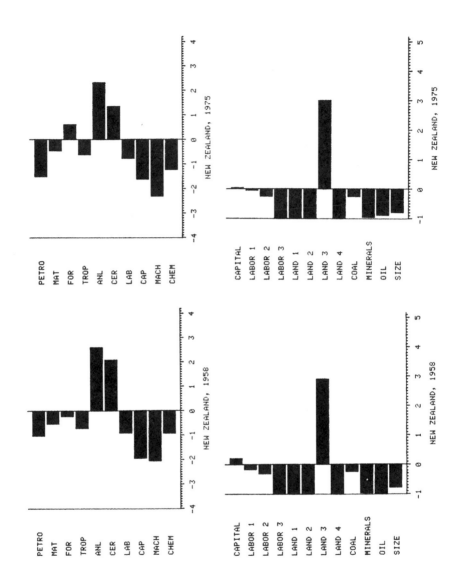

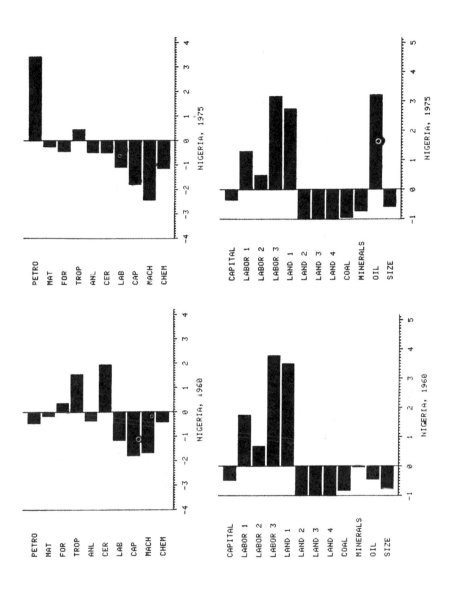

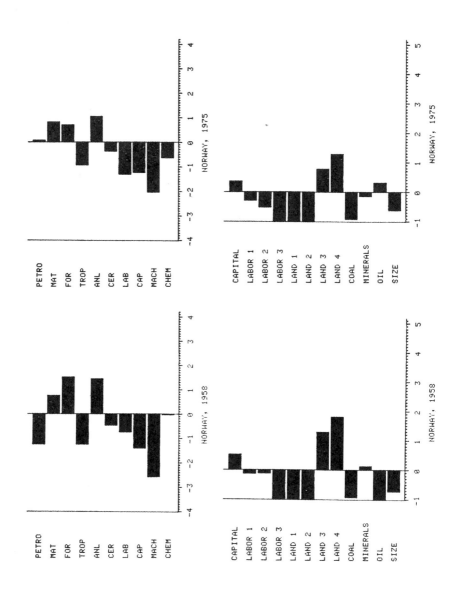

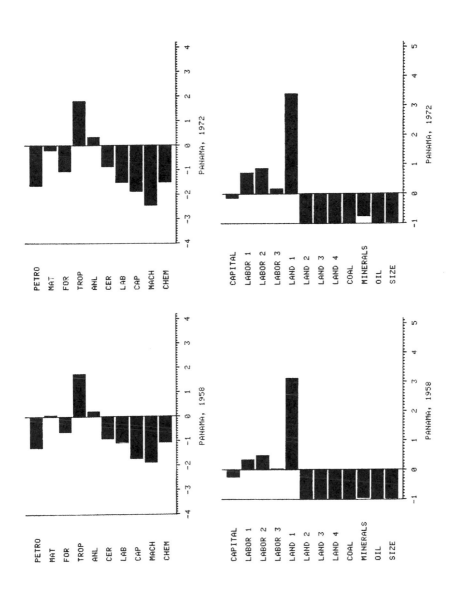

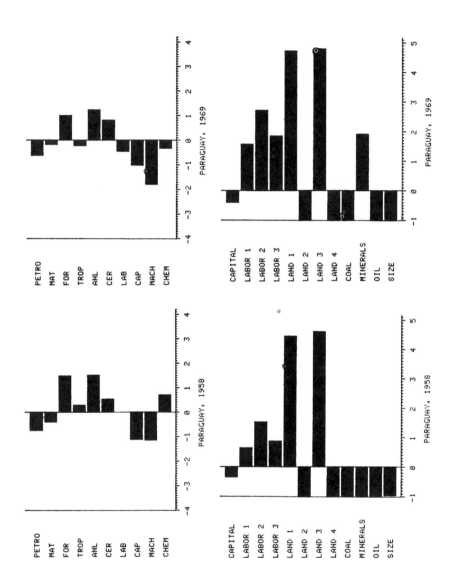

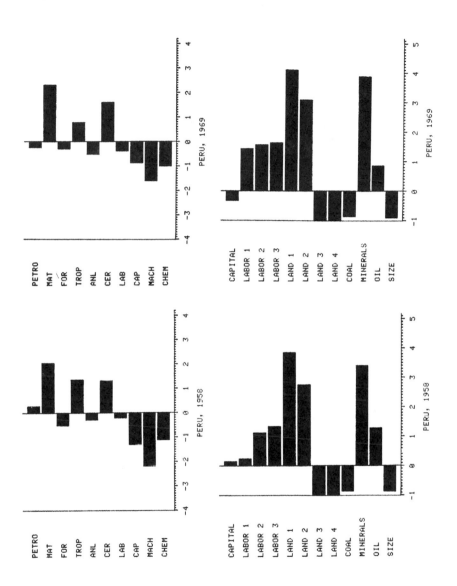

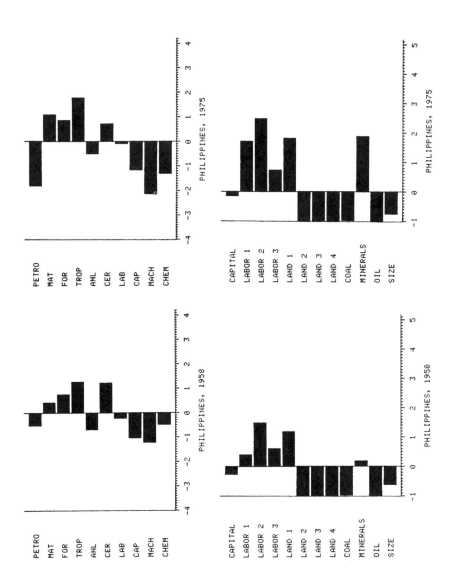

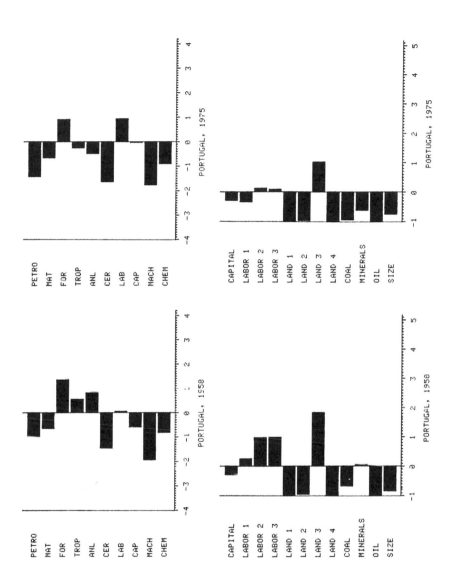

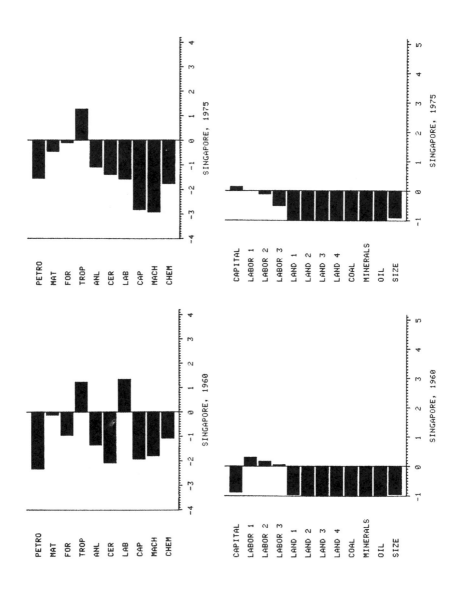

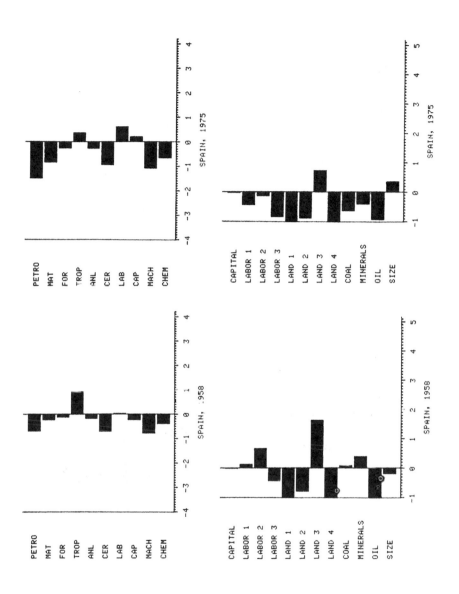

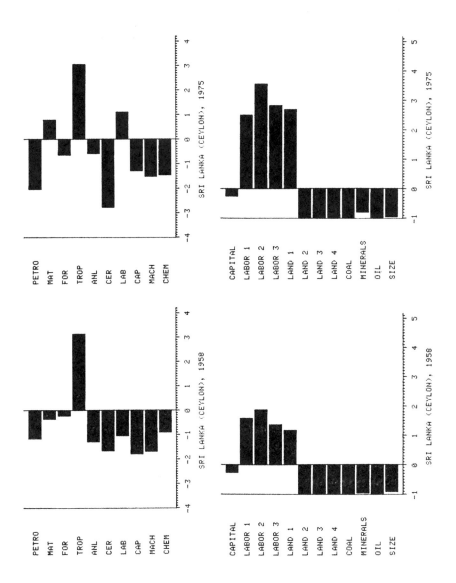

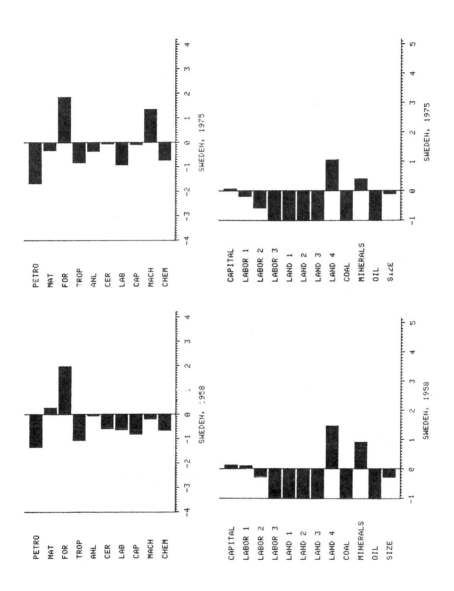

330

Appendix D

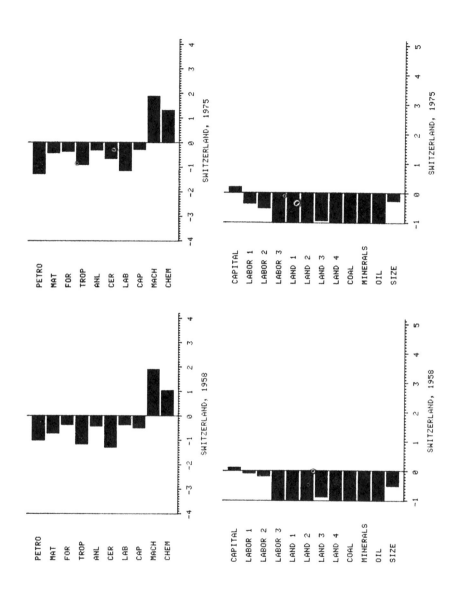

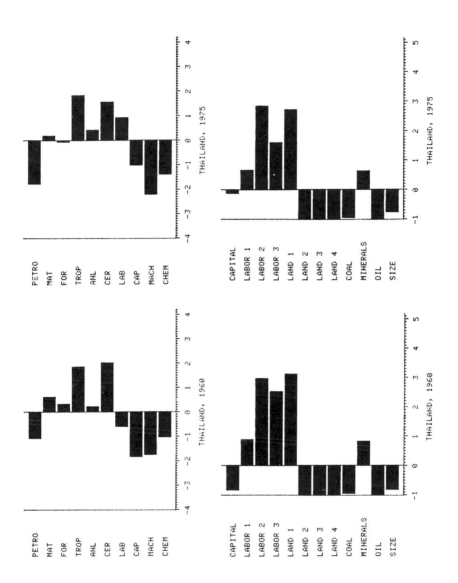

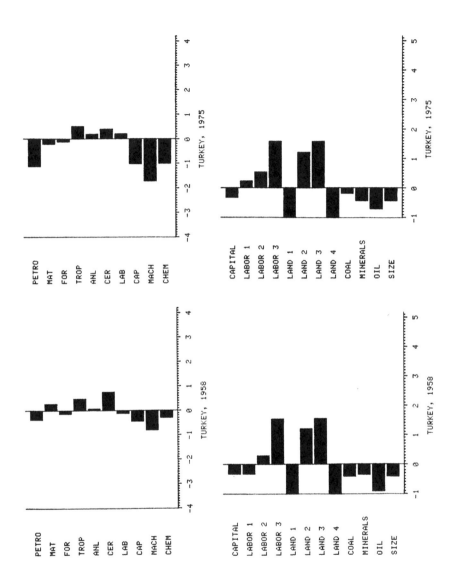

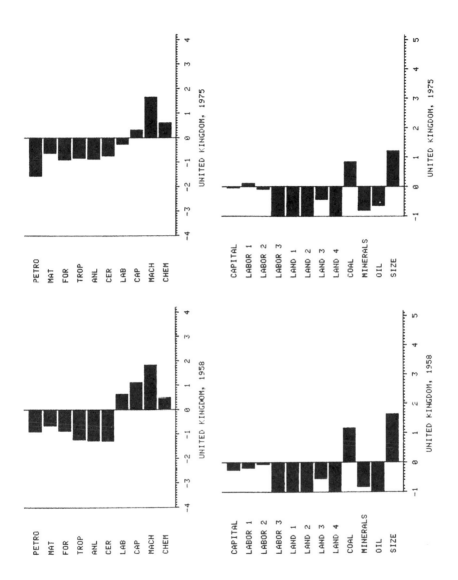

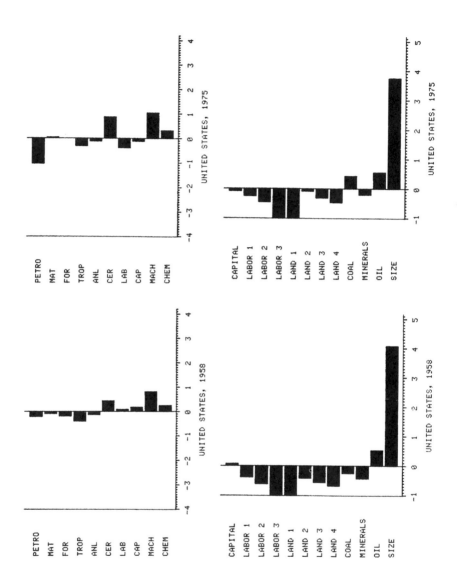

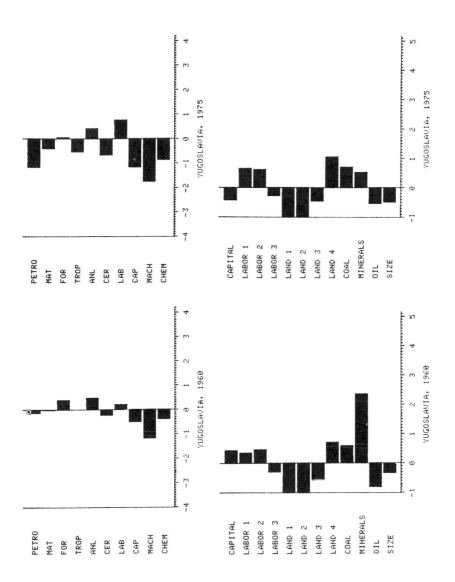

Notes

Chapter 1

1. In preparing this chapter I have been fortunate to have copies of many of the chapters to the *Handbook of International Economics*, published by North-Holland. I have drawn especially on the excellent general review by Jones and Neary (1982), Ethier's (1982c) discussion of dimensionality, Helpman's (1982) chapter on increasing returns, and Deardorff's (1982b) review of the empirical literature.

2. For theorems using autarky prices, consult Deardorff (1980), (1982a) and Ethier (1982c).

3. Trade need not be exactly balanced to have the Heckscher-Ohlin result. If B is the trade balance, then $B = p'X - p'C = p'X - sp'X_w$, and the consumption share becomes

$$s = (p'X - B)/p'X_w.$$

This consumption share can still be between the endowment shares, provided the trade imbalance is not too great, in which case the excess factor supply vector has the desired sign pattern. This condition, $L/L_w < s < K/K_w$, implies

$$1 - (K/K_w)/(Y/Y_w) < B/Y < 1 - (L/L_w)/(Y/Y_w),$$

where Y and Y_w are own and world GNP. If the trade balance goes outside of this interval, then both goods are exported ($B > 0$) or both are imported ($B < 0$).

4. If F is the production function for X_1, then the unit isoquant is $1 = F(a_{K1}, a_{L1})$. Minimizing cost subject to this constraint implies $w_K = \lambda F_K$ and $w_L = \lambda F_L$, where λ is the Lagrange multiplier. But along the unit isoquant $0 = F_K da_{K1} + F_L da_{L1} = \lambda^{-1}(w_K da_{K1} + w_L da_{L1})$.

5. Ethier (1982c) provides an excellent and thorough review of the problems of dimensionality, though often referring to autarky prices, which for empirical reasons I shall not use.

6. Defining a factor intensity reversal is a difficult matter in high dimensions. If the factor intensity matrix A is a continuous function of the vector of factor prices w, then in 2 dimensions there are no factor intensity reversals, provided A is nonsingular for all w. In higher dimensions, this is not enough. See Ethier (1982c) for references and discussion.

7. Ethier (1974) has shown that if A is strictly positive, each column of A^{-1} must have at least one negative and one positive element. A proof is simple: If δ is the vector with a 1 in the first element and 0's elsewhere, then the first column of A^{-1} is $z = A^{-1}\delta$, which can be rewritten $\delta = Az$. Since A is strictly positive, the only way for this equation to be satisfied is for z to have both positive and negative elements. By the same logic each row of A^{-1} must have at least one negative and one positive element.

8. The reader may verify that the derivative of GNP $= \sum_j p_j X_j$ with respect to the number of workers is the wage rate. GNP per worker is found by summing the three output functions. In the regions of complete specialization these are just the individual output functions. In the cones B and D, two functions need to be added, producing the straight line segments in figure 1.7. If $pf(k)$ stands for GNP per worker and pfL for GNP, then the derivative of GNP with respect to L is $pf - pkf'$, which implies that the wage rate can be found by extending a straight line tangent to $pf(k)$ until the line intersects the vertical axis. In the two cones B and D, f is linear in k, and the wage rate is correspondingly constant. (It should also be noted that Y/L is convex.)

9. With constant returns to scale we may write $F(L, M, K) = LF(1, M/L, K/L)$, and the marginal product of capital depends on only the ratios M/L, K/L. If M/L is fixed, constant marginal product of capital implies that K/L fixed.

10. Notice that a parameter of the function h_1 is w_K/p_1. This might lead you to question the Stolper-Samuelson result, since a change in p_1 seems to necessitate a change in F_1^*. It is left as

an exercise to verify that the Stolper-Samuelson result holds in the small country case (w_K fixed).

11. This discussion takes factor prices to be equalized, but factor price equalization is not assured, even for infinitesimally different countries, if there are nontraded goods. For examples of sufficient conditions for factor price equalization see Ethier (1972) and Woodland (1982, pp. 228–232).

12. Another way to get to the same result is to imagine firms that produce both X_1 and X_2, but that use all of the X_2 as intermediate inputs in the production of X_1. The final output of such a firm is $X_1 = F(K_1^*, L_1^*, G(K_1 - K_1^*, L_1 - L_1^*, X_{12})) - X_{12}$, where K_1 and L_1 are the total resources used by the firm. If the allocation of capital and labor K_1^*, L_1^* and intermediate product X_{12} are done optimally, output can be written as a function of K_1 and L_1: $X_1 = F^*(K_1, L_1)$. This completely internalizes the intermediate input, and since F^* can be shown to exhibit constant returns to scale, the model is unaltered by the existence of intermediate inputs.

13. Cost minimization implies $(dB)p(1 + p) + (dA_L)w = 0$. Thus differentiating (1.13) produces

(i) $[I - B(1 + \rho)]d(p) = [Bp, A_L][d(1 + \rho), d(w)]'$.

Define final output as X minus the time augmented intermediate inputs $F = [I - B(1 + \rho)]X$. Then using (1.14), we obtain

(ii) $[I - B(1 + \rho)]^{-1}F = [Bp, A_L]'^{-1}V$

Equation (i) is analogous to (1.5), from which we derive the Stolper-Samuelson result. Reciprocity follows from a comparison of (i) and (ii).

14. Ethier's (1979b) paper is basically a comment on Steedman and Metcalfe (1973, 1977), who conclude (1973, p. 50) that "the existence of heterogenous capital goods does lead to a breakdown of the logic of the HOS theory and hence to that of its major conclusions." Metcalfe and Steedman (1981) object to Ethier's (1979b) contrary conclusion, but Ethier's reply is unbending. The logic of the HOS theory is affected, since factor intensities depend on commodity prices, but the conclusions are unaffected. In particular, the cross-section data analysis reported in this book need not be overly concerned with the definition of capital.

Chapter 2

1. See Hilton (1981) for discussion of demand models that give some justification for using net exports as the dependent variables and interpreting the estimated coefficients as factor cost differences. Deardorff (1982b) also offers a model that explains autarky price differences in terms of factor intensities and a measure of relative factor abundance.

Chapter 3

1. The clustering results based on the regression estimates are discussed in a separate paper available on request.

Chapter 4

1. See the discussion in the chapter on Chile by T. Jeanneret in Balassa (1971).

Chapter 5

1. Estimates formed by omitting an observation can be easily computed. The least-squares estimate based on the whole data set, $\hat{\beta}$, and the estimate with observation i omitted, $\hat{\beta}_i$, are related by the formula $\hat{\beta} - \hat{\beta}_i = (X'X)^{-1} x_i e_i/(1 - h_i)$, where X is the matrix of explanatory variables with row i equal to x_i', e_i is the ith residual, and h_i is the ith diagonal element of $X(X'X)^{-1}X'$. The t-value attaching to a dummy variable that selects the ith observation is $t_i = e_i/s_i(1 - h_i)^{1/2}$, where s_i is the estimate of the residual variances if the ith observation is omitted. The usual estimate of the residual variance s^2 is related to s_i^2 by the formula $(n - k - 1)s_i^2 = (n - k)s^2 - e_i^2/(1 - h_i)$, where $n - k$ is the degrees of freedom of s^2.

The effect of deletions on t-values can also be a useful statistic. For example, the omission of the extreme observation from the data depicted in figure 5.1 has a dramatic effect on the t-value, but has an unclear effect on the estimate. The computation of the t-value is somewhat more troublesome, and the material that follows is based on the hope that t-sensitivity is revealed by estimate sensitivity.

2. Any three-step procedure, in which least-squares residuals are used to estimate a model of systematic heteroscedasticity and then the model is estimated with weighted regression, cannot adequately deal with a scatter such as figure 5.1 because the least-squares residuals would not suggest heteroscedasticity, and weighted least squares would be the same as ordinary least squares. The real error in this procedure is that inaccuracy in selecting the weights does not affect the standard errors in the weighted regression formula, and the standard errors are consequently underestimated. A full maximum likelihood solution with the inverse of the estimated information matrix as the covariance matrix can be expected to yield much larger standard errors of the coefficients in the case of a data set such as the one depicted in figure 5.1.

3. The seminal paper is by James and Stein (1961), who produce an estimator with smaller risk than least squares. Ridge regression proposed by Hoerl and Kennard (1970) is also based on quadratic constraints such as (3). Judge et al. (1980) have an extensive discussion.

4. This curve has been called the "ridge trace" by Hoerl and Kennard (1970) and the "curve decolletage" by Dickey (1975).

5. Wages and salaries per full-time equivalent worker, U.S. National Income and Products Accounts.

Chapter 6

1. The consumption shares are also recoverable if the model is enlarged to allow trade imbalances. If B indicates the trade surplus, then the consumption share is $(Y - B)/Y_w$, which replaces Y/Y_w in (6.1) and (6.2). Consequently, to (6.1) and (6.4) we must add the term $B(\beta_{iL}L_w + \beta_{iK}K_w)/Y_w = BQ_{iw}/Y_w$, which suggests regressing trade on endowments and the trade imbalance, with the coefficient on the trade imbalance interpreted as the output share Q_{iw}/Y_w. This is not further explored because the trade imbalance ought to be related to rates of return to capital at home and abroad, and consequently be itself a function of factor supplies. This causes econometric difficulties if all resources are not measured.

2. A Bayes estimator, corrected for measurement errors, can be written as $(X'X - D + H^*)^{-1}(X'Y + H^*b^*)$, where D is a diagonal matrix with error variances on the diagonal, Y and X are arrays of data, H^* is the prior precision matrix, and b^* is the prior mean vector. If $b^* = 0$, a sensitivity analysis of this formula with respect to changes in H^* can be interpreted as a sensitivity analysis with respect to $H^* - D$, and this Bayesian sensitivity analysis can be thought to include the possibility of some measurement error. In this book, however, b^* is not the zero vector.

Chapter 7

1. These shares were computed from data on domestic consumption (final demand less net exports) from the 1967 *Input-Output Structure of the U.S. Economy*, U.S. Department of Commerce, volume 1. A correspondence between the BEA categories and the SITC categories was formed from the correspondence between BEA and SIC of the U.S. Department of Commerce and from the correspondence between SIC and SITC in *U.S. Foreign Trade Statistics, Classifications and Cross Classifications*, 1968, U.S. Department of Commerce, Bureau of the Census.

Appendix B

1. A complete description of the full data set is available from Professor Bowen.

2. This corresponds to "gross domestic capital formation" as defined in the U.N. system of national accounts (SNA). See United Nations Statistical Office, *A System of National Accounts*, Studies in Methods, series F, no. 2, rev. 3 (New York: United Nations, 1968).

Bibliography

Anderson, James E., "Cross-Section Tests of the Heckscher-Ohlin Theorem: Comment," *American Economic Review*, December 1981, *71*, 1037–1039.

Arad, Ruth W., and Hirsch, Seev, "Determination of Trade Flows and Choice of Trade Partners: Reconciling the Heckscher-Ohlin and the Burenstam Linder Models of International Trade," *Weltwirtschaftliches Archiv*, 1981, *117*(2), 276–297.

Armington, Paul S., "A Theory of Demand for Products Distinguished by Place of Production," *IMF Staff Papers*, March 1969, *16*, 159–178.

Arrow, K. J., Chenery, H. B., Minhas, B. S., and Solow, R. M., "Capital-Labor Substitution and Economic Efficiency," *Review of Economics and Statistics*, August 1961, 225–250.

Balassa, Bela, "Trade Liberalization and 'Revealed' Comparative Advantage," *The Manchester School*, May 1965, *33*, 99–123.

Balassa, Bela, *Trade Liberalization among Industrial Countries*, New York: McGraw-Hill, 1967.

Balassa, Bela, "The Changing Pattern of Comparative Advantage in Manufactured Goods," *Review of Economics and Statistics*, May 1979, *61*, 259–266.

Balassa, Bela, and associates, *The Structure of Protection in Developing Countries*, New York: Pergamon Press, 1971.

Baldwin, Robert E., "Determinants of the Commodity Structure of U.S. Trade," *American Economic Review*, March 1971, *LXI*(1), 126–146.

Baldwin, Robert E., "Determinants of Trade and Foreign Investment: Further Evidence," *Review of Economics and Statistics*, February 1979, *61*, 40–48.

Banks, Arthur S., "Cross National Time Series: 1815–1973," *Inter-University Consortium for Political and Social Research*, Ann Arbor.

Belsley, D. A., Kuh, E., and Welsch, R. E., *Regression Diagnostics*, New York: Wiley, 1980.

Betancourt, Roger R., Clague, Christopher K., and Panagariya, Arvind, *Capital Utilization: A Theoretical and Empirical Analysis*, New York: Cambridge University Press, 1981.

Bhagwati, Jagdish N., "The Pure Theory of International Trade: A Survey," *Economic Journal*, March 1964, *74*, 1–84.

Bhagwati, J., ed., *International Trade: Selected Readings*, Cambridge, MA: M.I.T. Press, 1981.

Blattberg, R. C., and Gonedes, N. J., "A Comparison of the Stable and Student Distributions as Statistical Models for Stock Prices," *Journal of Business*, 1975, *47*, 244–280.

Bowen, Harry P., "A Multicountry Test of the Product Cycle Model," paper presented to the Econometric Society Annual Meetings, Washington, D.C., December 1981.

Bowen, Harry P., "Changes in the International Distribution of Resources and Their Impact on U.S. Comparative Advantage," *Review of Economics and Statistics*, August 1983, *65*, 402–414.

Bowen, Harry P., "On the Theoretical Interpretation of Indices of Trade Intensity and Revealed Comparative Advantage," *Weltwirschaftliches Archiv*, forthcoming.

Bowen, Harry P., Leamer, Edward, and Sveikauskus, L., "A Multicountry Multifactor Test of the Factor Abundance Theory," mimeo, 1982.

Braeutigan, Ronald R., "The Deregulation of Natural Gas," in L. W. Weiss and M. W. Klass, eds., *Case Studies in Regulation: Revaluation and Reform*, Boston: Little Brown, 1981.

Branson, William, "U.S. Comparative Advantage: Some Further Results," *Brookings Papers on Economic Activity*, 1971, *3*, 754–759.

Branson, William, and Junz, Helen B., "Trends in U.S. Trade and Comparative Advantage," *Brookings Papers on Economic Activity*, 1971, *2*, 285–345.

Branson, William, and Monoyios, Nikolaos, "Factor Inputs in U.S. Trade," *Journal of International Economics*, May 1977, *7*, 111–131.

Brecher, Richard A., "Minimum Wage Rates and the Pure Theory of International Trade," *Quarterly Journal of Economics*, February, 1974, 98–116.

Brecher, Richard A., and Choudhri, Ehsan U., "The Leontief Paradox, Continued," *Journal of Political Economy*, August 1982, *90*(4), 820–823.

Brock, W. A., and Magee, S. P., "The Economics of Special Interest Politics: The Case of the Tariff," *American Economic Review Papers and Proceedings*, May 1978, 246–250.

Burgess, David F., "Tariffs and Income Distribution: Some Empirical Evidence for the United States," *Journal of Political Economy*, February 1976, *84*(1), 17–45.

Burgess, David F., "Protection, Real Wages, and the Neoclassical Ambiguity with Inter-industry Flows," *Journal of Political Economy*, August 1980, *88*(4), 783–802.

Carruth, A. N. A., and Oswald, A. J., "The Determination of Union and Non-union Wage Rates," *European Economic Review*, June/July 1982, *16*, 285–302.

Caves, Richard E., and Jones, Ronald W., *World Trade and Payments*, 3rd ed., Boston: Little Brown, 1981.

Chacholiades, Miltiades, *International Trade Theory and Policy*, New York: McGraw-Hill, 1978.

Chang, Winston, "Some Theorems of Trade and General Equilibrium with Many Goods and Factors," *Econometrica*, May 1979, *47*(3), 709–726.

Chang, Winston, "Production Externalities, Variable Returns to Scale, and the Theory of Trade," *International Economic Review*, October 1981, *22*(3), 511–525.

Chang, Winston, Ethier, Wilfred, and Kemp, Murray, "The Theorems of International Trade with Joint Production," *Journal of International Economics*, August 1980, *10*, 377–394.

Chenery, H. B., "Patterns of Industrial Growth," *American Economic Review*, September 1960, *1*, 624–654.

Chenery, H. B., and Syrquin, M., *Patterns of Development, 1950–1970*, London: Oxford University Press, 1975.

Chenery, H. B., and Taylor, Lance, "Development Patterns: Among Countries and over Time," *Review of Economics and Statistics*, November 1968, *L*(4), 391–416.

Chipman, John S., "A Survey of the Theory of International Trade," *Econometrica*, July 1965, 477–519; October 1965, 685–760; January 1966, 18–76.

Chipman, John S., "External Economies of Scale and Competitive Equilibrium," *Quarterly Journal of Economics*, 1970, *84*, 347–385.

Chipman, John S., "Towards the Construction of an Optimal Aggregative Model of International Trade: West Germany, 1963–1975," *Annals of Economics and Social Measurement*, Winter/Spring 1977/1978, *6*(5), 535–554.

Corden, W. Max, "The Structure of a Tariff System and the Effective Protective Rate," *Journal of Political Economy*, June 1966, *74*(3), 221–237.

Dasgupta, P. S., and Heal, G. M., *Economic Theory and Exhaustible Resources*, Cambridge: Cambridge University Press, 1979.

Davies, Robert, "Product Differentiation and the Structure of United Kingdom Trade," *Bulletin of Economic Research*, May 1975, *27*, 27–41.

Deardorff, Alan V., "Weak Links in the Chain of Comparative Advantage," *Journal of International Economics*, May 1979, *9*(2), 197–209.

Deardorff, Alan V., "The General Validity of the Law of Comparative Advantage," *Journal of Political Economy*, October 1980, *88*(5), 941–957.

Deardorff, Alan V. (1982a), "The General Validity of the Heckscher-Ohlin Theorem," *American Economic Review*, September 1982, *72*, 683–694.

Deardorff, Alan V. (1982b), "Testing Trade Theories and Predicting Trade Flows," in R. W. Jones and P. B. Kenen, eds., *Handbook of International Economics*, Amsterdam: North-Holland, 1982.

Deardorff, Alan V., and Stern, Robert M., "A Disaggregated Model of World Production and Trade: An Estimate of the Impact of the Tokyo Round," *Journal of Policy Modeling*, 1981, *3*, 127–152.

deMelo, Jaime, and Robinson, Sherman, "Trade Policy and Resource Allocation in the Presence of Product Differentiation," *Review of Economics and Statistics*, May 1981, *63*, 169–177.

Dickey, James M., "Bayesian Alternatives to the *F*-test and Least-Squares Estimates in the Normal Linear Model," in S. E. Fienberg and A. Zellner, eds., *Bayesian Studies in Econometrics and Statistics*, Amsterdam: North-Holland, 1975.

Dixit, Avinash, and Norman, Victor, *Theory of International Trade*, Cambridge: Cambridge University Press, 1980.

Dornbusch, Rudiger, Fischer, S., and Samuelson, P. A., "Comparative Advantage, Trade, and Payments in a Ricardian Model with a Continuum of Goods," *American Economic Review*, December 1977, *67*(5), 823–839.

Dreze, J., "Quelques reflexions sereines sur l'adaptation de l'industrie belge au Marche Commun," *Comptes rendus des Travaux de la Société Royale d'Economie Politique de Belgique*, December 1960, *275*, 4–26.

Dreze, J., "Les exportations intra-C.E.E. en 1958 et la position belge," *Recherches Economiques de Louvain*, 1961, *8*, 717–738.

Ethier, Wilfred, "Nontraded Goods and the Heckscher-Ohlin Model," *International Economic Review*, February 1972, *13*(1), 132–147.

Ethier, Wilfred, "Some of the Theorems of International Trade with Many Goods and Factors," *Journal of International Economics*, 1974, *4*, 199–206.

Ethier, Wilfred (1979a), "Internationally Decreasing Costs and World Trade," *Journal of International Economics*, February 1979, *9*, 1–24.

Ethier, Wilfred (1979b), "The Theorems of International Trade in Time-Phased Economies," *Journal of International Economics*, May 1979, *9*(2), 225–238.

Ethier, Wilfred (1982a), "National and International Returns to Scale in the Modern Theory of International Trade," *American Economic Review*, June 1982, *72*, 389–405.

Ethier, Wilfred (1982b), "Decreasing Costs in International Trade and Frank Graham's Argument for Protection," *Econometrica*, 1982, *50*, 1243–1268.

Ethier, Wilfred (1982c), "Higher Dimensional Trade Theory," in R. W. Jones and P. B. Kenen, eds., *Handbook of International Economics*, Amsterdam: North-Holland, 1982.

Fareed, A. E., "Formal Schooling and the Human Capital Intensity of American Foreign Trade: A Cost Approach," *Economic Journal*, June 1972, *82*, 629–640.

Findlay, Ronald, "Relative Backwardness, Direct Foreign Investment, and the Transfer of Technology: A Simple Dynamic Model," *Quarterly Journal of Economics*, February 1978, *92*(1), 1–16.

Findlay, Ronald, "Economic Development and the Theory of International Trade," *American Economic Review*, May 1979, *69*(2), 186–190.

Finger, J. M., "A New View of the Product Cycle Theory," *Weltwirtschaftliches Archiv*, March 1975, *111*, 79–99.

Gilstein, C. Z., and Leamer, E. E. (1983a), "Robust Sets of Regression Estimates," *Econometrica*, March 1983, *51*, 321–333.

Gilstein, Z., and Leamer E. E. (1983b), "The Set of Weighted Regression Estimates," *Journal of the American Statistical Association*, December 1903, *78*, 942–948.

Graham, Frank D., "The Theory of International Values Reexamined," *Quarterly Journal of Economics*, November 1923, 54–86.

Grubel, Herbert G., "Intra-Industry Specialization and the Pattern of Trade," *Canadian Journal of Economics and Political Science*, August 1967, 374–388.

Grubel, Herbert G., "The Theory of Intra-industry Trade," in I. A. McDougall and R. Snape, eds., *Studies in International Economics*, Amsterdam: North-Holland, 1970.

Grubel, Herbert G., and Lloyd, Peter J., *Intra-Industry Trade: The Theory and Measurement of International Trade In Differentiated Products*, London: Macmillan, 1975.

Gruber, William H., and Vernon, Raymond, "The Technology Factor in a World Trade Matrix," in R. Vernon, ed., *The Technology Factor in International Trade*, New York: Columbia University Press, 1970, 233–272.

Gruber, William H., Mehta, Dileep, and Vernon, Raymond, "The R&D Factor in International Trade and International Investment of United States Industries," *Journal of Political Economy*, February 1967, *75*, 20–37.

Harkness, Jon, "Factor Abundance and Comparative Advantage," *American Economic Review*, December 1978, *68*, 784–800.

Harkness, Jon, and Kyle, John F., "Factors Influencing United States Comparative Advantage," *Journal of International Economics*, May, 1975, *V*, 153–165.

Harrod, Roy, "Factor Price Relations under Free Trade," *Economic Journal*, June 1958, 245–55.

Harvey, A. C., "Estimating Regression Models with Multiplicative Heteroscedasticity," *Econometrica*, 1976, *44*, 461–465.

Heckscher, Eli, "The Effect of Foreign Trade on the Distribution of Income," *Ekonomisk Tidskrift*, 497–512; reprinted as chapter 13 in A.E.A. *Readings in the Theory of International Trade*, Philadelphia: Blakiston, 1949, 272–300.

Heller, Peter S., "Factor Endowment Change and Comparative Advantage: The Case of Japan, 1956–1969," *Review of Economics and Statistics*, August 1976, *58*(1), 283–292.

Helpman, Elhanan, "International Trade in the Presence of Product Differentiation, Economies of Scale and Monopolistic Competition: A Chamberlin-Heckscher-Ohlin Approach," *Journal of International Economics*, September 1981, *11*(3), 305–340.

Helpman, Elhanan, "Increasing Returns, Imperfect Markets, and Trade Theory," in R. W. Jones and P. B. Kenen, eds., *Handbook of International Economics*, Amsterdam: North-Holland, 1982.

Helpman, Elhanan, and Razin, A., *A Theory of International Trade under Uncertainty*, New York: Academic Press, 1978.

Herberg, Horst, and Kemp, Murray C., "Some Implications of Variable Returns to Scale," *Canadian Journal of Economics*, August 1969, 403–415.

Herberg, Horst, and Kemp, Murray C., "In Defense of Some 'Paradoxes' of Trade Theory," September 1980, 70(4), 812–814.

Hilton, R. Spence, An Estimatable Model of the Commodity Version of Trade, unpublished Ph.D. dissertation, University of Wisconsin, Madison, 1981.

Hirsch, Seev, Location of Industry and International Competitiveness, Oxford: Clarendon Press, 1967.

Hirsch, Seev, "Trade and per Capita Income Differentials: An Empirical Test of Burenstam-Linder's Theory," draft manuscript, Tel Aviv University, September 1969.

Hirsch, Seev, "The Product Cycle Model of International Trade—A Multi-Country Cross-Section Analysis," Oxford Bulletin of Economics and Statistics, 1975, 37, 305–317.

Hoerl, A. E., and Kennard, R. W., "Ridge Regression: Biased Estimation for Nonorthogonal Problems," Technometrics, 1970, 12, 69–82.

Houthakker, H. S., "A International Comparison of Household Expenditure Patterns: Commemorating the Centenary of Engel's Law," Econometrica, October 1957, 25, 532–551.

Huber, P. J., "Robust Statistics: A Review," The Annals of Mathematical Statistics, 1972, 43, 1041–1067.

Huber, P. J., "Robust Regression: Asymptotics, Conjectures, and Monte Carlo," The Annals of Statistics, 1973, 1, 799–821.

Hufbauer, G. C., Synthetic Materials and the Theory of International Trade, appendix B, London, 1966.

Hufbauer, G. C., "The Impact of National Characteristics and Technology on the Commodity Composition of Trade in Manufactured Goods," in R. Vernon, ed., The Technology Factor in International Trade, New York: Columbia University Press, 1970, 145–231.

James, W., and Stein, C., "Estimation with Quadratic Loss," Proceedings of the Fourth Berkeley Symposium on Mathematical Statistics and Probability, Berkeley: University of California Press, 1961.

Johnson, Harry G., and Mieszkowski, Peter M., "The Effects of Unionization on the Distribution of Income: A General Equilibrium Approach," Quarterly Journal of Economics, November 1970, 84, 539–561.

Jones, Ronald W., "The Structure of Simple General Equilibrium Models," Journal of Political Economy, December 1965, 73, 551–572.

Jones, Ronald W., "Variable Returns to Scale in General Equilibrium Theory," International Economic Review, October 1968, 9(3), 261–272.

Jones, Ronald W., "A Three-Factor Model in Theory, Trade, and History," chapter 1 in J. Bhagwati, R. W. Jones, R. Mundell, and J. Vanek, eds., Trade, Balance of Payments, and Growth, Amsterdam: North-Holland, 1971.

Jones, Ronald W., "Trade with Non-Traded Goods: The Anatomy of Interconnected Markets," Economica, May 1974, 41, 121–138.

Jones, Ronald W., and Neary, P., "The Positive Theory of International Trade," in R. W. Jones and P. B. Kenen, eds., Handbook of International Economics, Amsterdam: North-Holland, 1982.

Jones, Ronald W., and Ruffin, R., "Trade Patterns with Capital Mobility," in M. Parkin and A. Nobay, eds., Current Economic Problems, New York: Cambridge University Press, 1975, 307–332.

Judge, G., Griffiths, W., Hill, R. C., Lee, T. C., The Theory and Practice of Econometrics, New York: Wiley, 1980.

Katrak, Homi, "Human Skills, R and D and Scale Economies in the Exports of the United Kingdom and the United States," *Oxford Economic Papers*, 1973, *25*(3), 337–360.

Keesing, Donald B., "Labor Skills and International Trade: Evaluating Many Trade Flows with a Single Measuring Device," *Review of Economics and Statistics*, August 1965, 287–294.

Keesing, Donald B., "Labor Skills and Comparative Advantage," *American Economic Review*, May 1966, *56*(2), 249–258.

Keesing, Donald B., "The Impact of Research and Development on United States Trade," *Journal of Political Economy*, February 1967, *75*, 38–49.

Keesing, Donald B., "Population and Industrial Development: Some Evidence from Trade Patterns," *American Economic Review*, June 1968, *LVIII*(3), 448–455.

Keesing, Donald B., and Sherk, D. R., "Population Density in Patterns of Trade and Development," *American Economic Review*, December 1971, *LXI*(5), 956–961.

Kemp, Murray C., "Heterogenous Capital Goods and Long-Run Stolper-Samuelson Theorems," *Australian Economic Papers*, 1973, *12*, 253–260.

Kemp, Murray C., "How to Eat a Cake of Unknown Size," in M. C. Kemp, ed., *Three Topics in the Theory of International Trade*, Amsterdam: North-Holland, 1976, 297–308.

Kemp, Murray C., and Inada, K., "International Capital Movements and the Theory of International Trade," *Quarterly Journal of Economics*, August 1969, *83*, 524–528.

Kemp, Murray C., and Jones, R. W., "Variable Labor Supply and the Theory of International Trade," *Journal of Political Economy*, February 1962, *70*, 30–36.

Kemp, Murray C., and Liviatan, Nissan, "Production and Trade Patterns under Uncertainty," *Economic Record*, 1973, *49*, 215–227.

Kendrick, John W., *Postwar Productivity Trends in the United States, 1948–1969*, New York: NBER, 1973.

Kendrick, John W., *The Formation and Stocks of Total Capital*, New York: NBER, 1976.

Klein, Roger W., "A Dynamic Theory of Comparative Advantage," *American Economic Review*, March 1973, *63*(1), 173–184.

Klepper, S. and Leamer, E. E., "Sets of Maximum Likelihood Estimates for Regressions with All Variables Measured with Error," *Econometrica*, January 1984, *1*, 163–183.

Komiya, Ryutaro, "Non-Traded Goods and the Pure Theory of International Trade," *International Economic Review*, June 1967, *8*, 132–152.

Köppen, G., *Grundriss der Klimakunde*, Berlin and Leipzig: W. de Gruyter, 1931.

Kravis, I. B., "'Availability' and Other Influences on the Commodity Composition of Trade," *Journal of Political Economy*, April 1956, 143–155.

Kravis, I. B., "The Current Case for Import Limitations," in *United States Economic Policy in an Interdependent World*, Washington: Commission on International Trade and Investment Policy, 1971.

Kravis, I. B., Heston, A., and Summers, P. (1978a), *International Comparison of Real Product and Purchasing Power*, Baltimore: Johns Hopkins University Press, 1978.

Kravis, I. B., Heston, A., and Summers, P. (1978b), "Real per Capita Income for More than One Hundred Countries," *Economic Journal*, June 1978, *88*, 350.

Kravis, I. B., Kenessey, Z., Heston, A., and Summers, R., *A System of International Comparison of Gross Product and Purchasing Power*, Baltimore: Johns Hopkins University Press, 1975.

Krueger, Anne O., "Factor Endowments and *per Capita* Income Differences Among Countries," *Economic Journal*, September 1968, *LXXVIII*, 641–659.

Krueger, Anne O., "The Political Economy of the Rent-Seeking Society," *The American Economic Review*, June 1974, *64*(3), 291–303.

Krugman, Paul R., "Increasing Returns, Monopolistic Competition and International Trade," *Journal of International Economics*, November 1979, *9*(4), 469–479.

Krugman, Paul R., "Scale Economies, Product Differentiation, and the Pattern of Trade," *American Economic Review*, December 1980, *70*, 950–959.

Krugman, Paul R., "Intraindustry Specialization and the Gains from Trade," *Journal of Political Economy*, November 1981, *89*(5), 959–973.

Kuznets, S., "Quantitative Aspects of the Economic Growth of Nations," parts IX and X: "Level and Structure of Foreign Trade," *Economic Development and Cultural Change*, October 1964, *13*(2), Part 2, and January 1967, *15*(1), Part 2.

Kuznets, S., *Economic Growth of Nations: Total Output and Production Structure*, Cambridge, MA: Harvard University Press, 1971.

Lary, H. B., *Imports of Manufactures from the Less Developed Countries*, New York: NBER, 1968, 36–37.

Leamer, Edward E., "The Commodity Composition of International Trade in Manufactures: An Empirical Analysis," *Oxford Economic Papers*, 1974, *26*(3), 350–374.

Leamer, Edward E., "A Result on the Sign of Restricted Least Squares Estimates," *Journal of Econometrics*, 1975, *3*, 387–390.

Leamer, Edward E., *Specification Searches*, New York: Wiley, 1978.

Leamer, Edward E., "The Leontief Paradox, Reconsidered," *Journal of Political Economy*, June 1980, *88*, 495–503.

Leamer, Edward E., "Sets of Estimates of Location," *Econometrica*, January 1981, *49*(1), 193–204.

Leamer, Edward E., "Sets of Posterior Means with Bounded Variance Priors," *Econometrica*, May 1982, *50*(3), 725–736.

Leamer, Edward E., "Global Sensitivity Analysis for Generalized Least Squares Estimates," *Journal of the American Statistical Association*, forthcoming, 1984.

Leamer, Edward E., and Bowen, H. P., "Cross Section Tests of the Heckscher-Ohlin Theorem: Comment," *American Economic Review*, December 1981, 1040–1043.

Leamer, Edward E., and G. Chamberlain, "Matrix Weighted Averages and Posterior Bounds," *Journal of the Royal Statistical Society B*, 1976, *38*, 73–84.

Leamer, Edward E., and H. B. Leonard, "Reporting the Fragility of Regression Estimates," *The Review of Economics and Statistics*, May 1983, *LXV*, 306–317.

Leamer, Edward E., and Stern, Robert M., *Quantitative International Economics*, Chicago: Aldine, 1970.

Leontief, W. W., "Domestic Production and Foreign Trade: The American Capital Position Re-examined," *Proceedings of the American Philosophical Society*, September 1953, 332–349.

Leontief, W. W., "Factor Proportions and the Structure of American Trade," *Review of Economics and Statistics*, November 1956, 386–407.

Lerner, Abba P., "Factor Prices and International Trade," *Economica*, February 1952, *19*(73), 1–15.

Linder, Staffan Burenstam, *An Essay on Trade and Transformation*, New York: Wiley, 1961.

Linnemann, H., *An Econometric Study of International Trade Flows*, Amsterdam: North-Holland, 1966.

Lipsey, R. E., and Weiss, M. Y., "The Structure of Ocean Transport Charges," *Explorations in Economic Research*, 1974, *V*, 162–193.

Lowinger, Thomas C., "The Technology Factor and the Export Performance of U.S. Manufacturing Industries," *Economic Inquiry*, June 1975, *13*, 221–236.

Magee, Stephen P., "Factor Market Distortions, Production, Distribution and the Pure Theory of International Trade," *Quarterly Journal of Economics*, November 1971, 623–643.

Magee, Stephen P., "Three Simple Tests of the Stolper-Samuelson Theorem," in P. Oppenheimer, *Issues in International Economics*, London: Routledge and Kegan Paul, 1980, 138–153.

Manoilesco, Mihail, *The Theory of Protection and International Trade*, Philadelphia: Porcupine Press, 1931.

Markusen, James R., "Trade and the Gains from Trade with Imperfect Competition," *Journal of International Economics*, November 1981, *11*(4), 531–551.

Markusen, James R., and Melvin, J. R., "Trade, Factor Prices and Gains from Trade with Increasing Returns to Scale," *Canadian Journal of Economics*, 1981, *14*, 450–469.

Marris, Robin, *The Economics of Capital Utilization*, Cambridge: Cambridge University Press, 1964.

Mayer, W., "Short-Run and Long-Run Equilibrium for a Small Open Economy," *Journal of Political Economy*, 1974, 955–967.

Melvin, James R., "Production and Trade with Two Factors and Three Goods," *American Economic Review*, 1968, *58*, 1249–1268.

Melvin, James R., "Increasing Returns to Scale as a Determinant of Trade," *Canadian Journal of Economics*, August 1969, *3*, 389–402.

Metcalfe, J. S., and Steedman, I., "On the Transformation of Theorems," *Journal of International Economics*, May 1981, *11*, 267–271; with reply by W. Ethier, 273–277.

Mussa, M., "Tariffs and the Distribution of Income: The Importance of Factor Specificity, Substitutability, and Intensity in the Short and Long Run," *Journal of Political Economy*, 1974, 1191–1203.

Neary, J. Peter, "Dynamic Stability and the Theory of Factor-Market Distortions," *American Economic Review*, September 1978, *68*(4), 671–682, reprinted as Chapter 14 in Bhagwati (1981).

Ohlin, B., *Interregional and International Trade*, rev. ed., Cambridge, MA: Harvard University Press, 1967.

Oniki, H., and Uzawa, Hirofumi, "Patterns of Trade and Investment in a Dynamic Model of International Trade," *Review of Economic Studies*, January 1965, *32*(89), 15–38.

Panagariya, Arvind, "Variable Returns to Scale in General Equilibrium Theory Once Again," *Journal of International Economics*, November 1980, 499–526.

Panagariya, Arvind, "Variable Returns to Scale and Patterns of Specialization," *American Economic Review*, 1981, *71*, 221–230.

Posner, M. V., "International Trade and Technical Change," *Oxford Economic Papers*, October 1961, 323–341.

Preeg, *Traders and Diplomats*, Washington: Brookings Institution, 1970.

Roskamp, K. W., "Factor Proportions and Foreign Trade: The Case of West Germany," *Weltwirtschaftliches Archiv*, 1963, 319–326.

Roskamp, K. W., and McMeekin, G. C., "Factor Proportions, Human Capital and Foreign Trade: The Case of West Germany Reconsidered," *Quarterly Journal of Economics*, February 1968, 152–160.

Ruffin, Roy J., "Growth and the Long-Run Theory of International Capital Movements," *American Economic Review*, December 1979, *69*(5), 832–842.

Ruffin, Roy J., "International Factor Movements," in R. W. Jones and P. B. Kenen, eds., *Handbook of International Economics*, Amsterdam: North-Holland, 1982.

Rybczynski, T. M., "Factor Endowments and Relative Commodity Prices," *Economica*, November 1955, *22*, 336–341.

Samuelson, Paul A., "International Trade and the Equalization of Factor Prices," *Economic Journal*, June 1948, *58*(230), 163–184.

Samuelson, Paul A., "International Factor-Price Equalization Once Again," *Economic Journal*, June 1949, *59*(234), 181–197.

Samuelson, Paul A., "Prices of Factors and Goods in General Equilibrium," *Review of Economic Studies*, 1953/1954, *21*, 888–908.

Samuelson, Paul A., "Trade Pattern Reversals in Time-Phased Ricardian Systems and Intertemporal Efficiency," *Journal of International Economics*, 1975, *5*, 309–364.

Steedman, I., and Metcalfe, J. S., "The Non-Substitution Theorem and International Trade Theory," *Australian Economic Papers*, 1973, *12*, 267–269.

Steedman, I., and Metcalfe, J. S., "Reswitching, Primary Inputs, and the Heckscher-Ohlin-Samuelson Theory of Trade," *Journal of International Economics*, 1977, *7*, 201–209.

Stern, Robert M., "Testing Trade Theories," in P. B. Kenen, ed., *International Trade and Finance: Frontiers for Research*, New York: Cambridge University Press, 1975.

Stern, Robert M., "Some Evidence on the Factor Content of West Germany's Foreign Trade," *Journal of Political Economy*, February 1976, *84*, 131–141.

Stern, Robert M., and Maskus, Keith E., "Determinants of the Structure of U.S. Foreign Trade, 1958–76," *Journal of International Economics*, May 1981, *11*, 207–224.

Stolper, W. F., and Samuelson, P. A., "Protection and Real Wages," *Review of Economic Studies*, 1941, *9*, 58–73.

Summers, R., Kravis, I. B., and Heston, A., "International Comparison of Real Product and Its Composition: 1950–1977," *The Review of Income and Wealth*, March 1980 *26*(1), 19–66.

Tatemota, M., and Ichimura, S., "Factor Proportions and Foreign Trade. The Case of Japan," *Review of Economics and Statistics*, 1959, *41*, 442–446.

Travis, W. P., *The Theory of Trade and Protection*, Cambridge, MA: Harvard University Press, 1964.

Trewartha, G. T., *An Introduction to Weather and Climate*, New York: McGraw-Hill, 1943.

United Nations, *Classification of Commodities by Industrial Origin: Relationship of Standard International Trade Classification to the International Standard Industrial Classification*, New York: United Nations, 1966.

United Nations, Statistical Office, *The Growth of World Industry: 1938–1961*, New York, 1963.

U.S. Department of Agriculture, *Farm Real Estate Market Developments*, Washington, D.C.: U.S. Government Printing Office, issues dated 1962ff.

Vanek, Jaroslav, *The Natural Resource Content of United States Foreign Trade, 1870–1955*, Cambridge: M.I.T. Press, 1963.

Vanek, Jaroslav, "The Factor Proportions Theory: The N-Factor Case," *Kyklos*, October 1968, *21*(4), 749–756.

Vernon, Raymond, "International Investment and International Trade in the Product Cycle," *Quarterly Journal of Economics*, May 1966, *80*, 190–207.

Vernon, Raymond, "The Product Cycle Hypothesis in a New International Environment," *Oxford Bulletin of Economics and Statistics*, November 1979, *41*, 255–267.

Weiser, Lawrence A., "Changing Factor Requirements of United States Foreign Trade," *Review of Economics and Statistics*, August 1968, 356–360.

Wells, Louis T., Jr., "Test of a Product Cycle Model of International Trade: U.S. Exports of Consumer Durables," *Quarterly Journal of Economics*, February 1969, *82*, 152–162.

Williams, James R., "The Resource Content in International Trade," *Canadian Journal of Economics*, February 1970, *3*, 111–122.

Wilson, Charles, "On the General Structure of Ricardian Models with a Continuum of Goods: Applications to Growth, Tariff Theory, and Technical Change," *Econometrica*, November 1980, *48*, 1675–1702.

Woodland, A. D., *International Trade and Resource Allocation*, Amsterdam: North-Holland, 1982.

Index